TRADITIONAL SLOVAK FOLKTALES

Folklores and Folk Cultures of Eastern Europe

SERIES EDITOR:
Linda J. Ivantis
Department of Slavic Languages
Pennsylvania State University

Ukrainian Minstrels
And the Blind Shall Sing
Natalie Kononenko

An Anthology of Russian Folk Epics
*Translated with an Introduction and Commentary
by James Bailey and Tatyana Ivanova*

Traditional Slovak Folktales
*Collected by Pavol Dobšinský
Edited and Translated by David L. Cooper*

TRADITIONAL SLOVAK FOLKTALES

Collected by Pavol Dobšinský

Edited and Translated by
David L. Cooper

M.E.Sharpe
Armonk, New York
London, England

Library of Congress Cataloging-in-Publication Data

Traditional Slovak folktales / David L. Cooper, editor/translator; Pavol Dobšinský, collector.
    p. cm.—(Folklores and folk cultures of Eastern Europe)
    Includes bibliographical references.
    ISBN 0-7656-0718-2 (alk. paper)
    1. Slovaks—Folklore. 2. Tales—Slovakia. I. Cooper, David L. , 1970–. II. Dobšinský, Pavol,
1828–1885. III. Series.
GR 154.4.T73 2001
398.2′094373—dc21

1002305102

∞

BM (c)   10   9   8   7   6   5   4   3   2   1

622216

To my friends, colleagues, and former students in Slovakia.

Contents

Acknowledgments

I never would have undertaken an edition of Dobšinský's Slovak folktales, and certainly never would have completed this book, without the suggestion, guidance, support, and hard work of many other people. The germ of this book goes back to my days as a Peace Corps English instructor in a *gymnazium* in Trnava, Slovakia. I was fortunate to be given a desk in the general faculty room, that is, among intelligent and communicative people, many of whom did not speak English. These fine teaching colleagues became my demanding and persistent Slovak-language teachers, out of the unavoidable need and, more importantly, the mutual desire to communicate. As my language skills grew, so did their expectations. More than once I was told that if I really wanted to learn good Slovak and develop a better understanding of Slovak culture, I should read Dobšinský's tales. I found them much too difficult at the time, but I knew that one day I would return to them.

In an excellent course on the world folktale by Professor Stephen Belcher at Pennsylvania State University I did return to Dobšinský's tales, and found them more than intriguing. At the same time I was approached by Professor Linda Ivanits, who informed me of M.E. Sharpe's series, *Folklores and Folk Cultures* and asked if I knew of anything in Slovak that would be appropriate. Of course, I did. In retrospect, I doubt whether Professor Ivanits had in mind a young graduate student such as I was at the time undertaking such a large project, but at least she did not reject the idea and has provided support and criticism as needed throughout the past four years.

I owe my greatest debt of gratitude to Dr. Marta Botiková, who answered an email to the Department of Ethnography of Comenius University in Bratislava requesting help with a translation of Dobšinský—an email that must have seemed then as "out of the blue" as the shot from the hussar's gun that the bear describes to the mosquito in Tale 11. She likely had as little idea as the bear of what she was getting herself into. Over the past four years she has patiently, expertly, and diligently answered all of my hundreds of questions on Dobšinský's language and the folk realia and beliefs behind it, from the most naive inquiries to the frustratingly difficult. Moreover, she gave me her office to work in during my summer in Bratislava, introduced me to numerous colleagues, and facilitated my work in countless ways. This book would not have been possible without her expert assistance.

A grant from PepsiCo and the Harriman Institute at Columbia University allowed me to spend the summer of 1998 in Bratislava, where I was treated as a welcome guest of the Department of Ethnography of Comenius University. Dr. Hana Hlôšková of the Ethnology Institute of the Slovak Academy of Sciences provided me with a beginning bibliography, all the books I requested while there, and valuable comments on the introduction and history of the tales' collection which I managed to write that summer. More recently, she was instrumental in helping to secure an important copyright permission. Dr. Viera Gašparíková, also of the Slovak Academy of Sciences, gave generously of her painstaking work in classifying Slovak tales—all the cataloging in this volume was provided by her—and commented on my introduction and tale history. Just as importantly, her excellent published work on Slovak tales always answered the questions I was asking. Dr. Ján Michálek of the Department of Ethnography gave helpful criticism on my introduction, and Dr. Braňo Hochel of the Department of English read and commented on several tale translations. To all these people and institutions go my heartfelt thanks.

My translations would have been much the poorer without the assistance of Klement Šimončič, former lecturer in Slovak at Columbia University, in the book's final stages. He saved me dozens of errors and, by checking several translations word-by-word, helped me in revising the translations of *all* of the tales. His excellent ear for American colloquial English saved the characters from speaking like dictionaries—if the characters swear, curse, and call each other names believably, credit goes to Mr. Šimončič. Professor Bradley F. Abrams of Columbia's Department of History provided helpful comments on my sketch outline of Slovak history in the nineteenth century, and Professor Peter Kussi of Columbia's Slavic Department commented on several tale translations.

Special thanks to Ján and Peter Pauliny for granting permission to translate from their father's edition of Dobšinský's tales, including commentaries, and to the Matica Slovenská for permission to reproduce the photograph of Dobšinský, the original of which can be found in the photo collection of the Archive of Literature and Art at the Matica Slovenská in Martin, Slovakia. Thanks also to Ester Plicková for permission to reproduce the illustration from her book, *Maľované salaše*, on the cover, and to the Rare Book and Manuscript Library of Butler Library, Columbia University, for permission to reproduce the illustration from their copy located in the Graphic Arts Collection. It has been a pleasure working with M.E. Sharpe, and I would like to thank Patricia Kolb, Elizabeth Granda, Irina Belenky, Ana Erlić, and Leslie English, and Paula Cook for their support, their efficiency, their patience, and their excellent work.

Finally, for essential contributions that I cannot begin to describe, my deepest gratitude to Valeria Sobol.

Pronunciation Guide

Slovak words, with all their accents and diacritical marks, can be off-putting to the English speaker, but when the marks are understood, most words can be easily pronounced.

Slovak vowels (a, e, i, o, u) are similar in quality to Spanish vowels (English "ah," "eh," "ee," "oh," "oo"), but are pronounced so short as to sound clipped to an English speaker. Slovak *y* is a variant of *i*, and *ä* is pronounced like *e*. The vowels are long, like English vowels, when accented (á, é, í, ó, ú, ý). The circumflexed o, *ô*, is a diphthong pronounced like the *uo* in the English "duo," but with more stress on the *o* than the *u*.

Slovak *č* is like the English ch, *š* like sh, and *ž* like the z in "azure."

Slovak *ď*, *ť*, *ň*, and *ľ* are palatal and are similar to the d, t, n, and l in the English "duty," "tune," "new," and "lute." They are pronounced this way also before the vowels *e* and *i*, though they are not marked.

Slovak *ch* is like the German ch in "Bach," the *j* like the English *y*; all other consonants are similar to English.

The stress on Slovak words always falls on the first syllable.

Glossary

bača	the chief shepherd, hired by the owners' collective of a sheep farm (salaš), usually located at high elevation near the grazing territory. The bača was responsible for the production of milk products and the state of the entire herd. See valach and Demitra.
borovička	brandy made from juniper berries.
Brezeň	an old Slavic name for March.
Demitra	or Demeter. The calendar saint for October 26. The cult of saint Demeter came to Slovakia with the valach colonization. This day was the major holiday for bačas and valachs. They would wear their finest clothing, and after squaring their accounts with the sheep owners (after the sheep had been pastured all summer) they would share a feast.
fujara	a large wooden shepherd's fife similar in form to a bassoon, common in central Slovakia.
groš	a groš is a small coin. The charachter of the Grošking is small like a groš but very powerful.
halušky	small potato dumplings, usually served with fermented sheep cheese (bryndza) in the traditional dish, *bryndzové halušky*.
Laktibrada	a malicious, dwarf-like character with four fingers on each hand, associated with rocky, mountainous regions. He is often introduced by the phrase "a span of a man with a beard to his elbow." The prince in the story "Sitno" is also known as Laktibrada although he has no connection to this character.
Lipeň	an old Slavic name for June.
Loktibrada	see Laktibrada.

Lomidrevo "Breakwood," a heroic character with supernatural strength, which he demonstrates by tearing large trees out by the roots. Also known as Valibuk, that is, "Rollbeech." Dobšinský left both of this hero's names in the story's title so that the tale would reflect the way the hero is known in different areas of Slovakia and not just one region. See also his companions, Valivrch and Miesiželezo.

Miesiželezo "Mixiron," a character with supernatural strength, which he demonstrates by mixing iron in his hands. A companion of Lomidrevo.

Mitra see Demitra.

Parom (sometimes uncapitalized) see Perún.

Perún Slavic god of thunder and lightning, who probably occupied a similar place in the Slavic pantheon to Thor among the Germans and Zeus among the Greeks. Most of our knowledge of Perún comes from the eastern Slavs. Among the Slovaks his name appears most commonly in curses, e.g., "May Parom strike you!"

Popolvár (sometimes Popelvár or Popelčík) "Ashboy," a lazy boy known for sitting on the stove all day and thus, likely, associated with ash. He becomes a heroic character in stories like "Popolvár, the Greatest in the World."

Rujeň an old Slavic name for October.

Sečeň an old Slavic name for January.

Sitno a mountain in central Slovakia, near Banská Štiavnica, frequently associated with legends of hidden treasure or of knights, sleeping and waiting to come forth and rescue the land.

slivovica plum brandy

valach originally an ethnic term for a group of fourteen-century migrant shepherds from Romania (Wallachia) and the southeast who were pushed out by Turkish occupation of their homeland and who settled in the mountainous regions of what is now Slovakia. The term lost its ethnic character as the migrants mixed with the local population. Today it refers to one who practices the characteristic trade of these migrants, tending sheep in mountain meadows at high elevation. See bača and Demitra.

valaška   a small axe with a long handle used for support in walking, defense, and as a cutting tool. Originally associated with the valach trade in central Slovakia, it later became associated with highwaymen in Robin Hood–like legends (Jánošík legends) and took on symbolic importance. Now a requisite prop for folk-dance groups.

Valivrch   "Rollpeak," a character with supernatural strength, which he demonstrates by rolling mountains around. Companion to Lomidrevo.

Introduction

The world of traditional Slovak folktales is a marvelous world, full of derring-do heroes and terrible, twelve-headed dragons, clever maidens and lucky fools, tales that will give you a shiver, and tales that will have you laughing so hard, your bladder may burst (see "Bladder-Blatherskite and His Friends"). It's a world that will be familiar to readers who know the tales of the Grimm brothers and the Russian tales of Afanas'ev, but strangely so—for the heroes and villains have new names and act, if sometimes only slightly, differently. In short, it's a new world to the English-speaking reader, a parallel universe with its own population, geography, and language. This world was embodied in its classic form in collections of tales compiled, edited, and published by Pavol Dobšinský between 1858 and 1883. Few have been translated since then, and yet these Slovak tales deserve a place alongside the major collections of world folklore, for they are tales of the highest quality.

The population of the world of Slovak tales is as diverse as any. Some of its heroes are larger than life, such as Lomidrevo, a.k.a. Valibuk, whose names could be rendered Breakwood and Rollbeech (characters' names and other Slovak terms are explained in the Glossary). Like all epic heroes, Lomidrevo is born under unusual circumstances, demonstrates his unusual potential early, and visits the underworld in the course of his adventures, emerging triumphantly. But while the adventures may be familiar from other heroic tales, in the final combination, Lomidrevo is a Slovak hero. Heroes may also be smaller than life, like Johnny Pea (Janko Hraško), or the person everyone least expects to be heroic, like Popolvár, the youngest brother who sits on the stove all day and is ignored. Of course, when we translate his name—Ashboy—we realize that we are in familiar territory, for he is the male counterpart to *Cinder*-ella. Popolvár is perhaps more popular than his female counterpart in Slovakia, but Popeluša (Cinderella) nonetheless has her place in Slovakia as elsewhere. In fact, Dobšinský published three tales based on what is recognized as the Cinderella plot. We have selected one, "The People-Eaters," in which the young

heroine remains nameless. This tale combines the Cinderella motif with a series of events that our readers will recognize from "Hansel and Gretel," a combination that is often found in the Central European region. Aside from these
traditional fairy-tale heroes, there are also the heroes of other types of tales,
like Kubo, the fool who, by luck or by chance or even through plays on words,
turns his mistakes to his own advantage (see "Kubo's Adventures" as well as
"The Wooden Cow"). There is also the murderous Mataj, whose tremendous
sins are overcome only by a more incredible penance.

Of course, heroes need helpers. Where would Cinderella be without her
fairy godmother? Maruška, in the story "Salt over Gold," depends on the help
of a wise old woman, one of the closest figures to a fairy godmother in these
tales. A much more common helper in Slovak tales is the grey-headed old
man, in whom Dobšinský, a Lutheran minister, saw the mythological picture
of the primeval Slavic God. But they are not the only helpers, for animals can
be helpers, too, as well as fish and ants. Perhaps the most important animal
helper in Slovak tales is the fairy horse, for which Slovak has a single word,
tátoš, borrowed from the Hungarians, who, after all, swept into the Danube
River basin centuries ago on horseback. The heroes often receive magic objects from their helpers, including golden wands, magic rings, and sabers.

Heroes are necessary because there are villains. Evil stepmothers dot the
landscape of Slovak tales just as in other fairy-tale worlds, as do supernatural characters from folk superstition, including witches and warlocks, dwarves
and dragons, and even the devil himself. Unlike the red devils of Germanic
tradition, the Slovak devil is black and hairy, with pointed ears, horns, a
cow's tail, and horse's hooves (see "The Man Who Never Sinned"). While
the devil causes humans harm, he often appears dull-witted and all-too-hu-
man in these tales (see "The Old Maid and the Devil" and "The Gypsy Duped
the Devil"). But he can also appear as a dangerous foe, overcome only by the
help of God ("The Tinkers and the Evil One"). Dragons have one, three, six,
nine, twelve, or even twenty-four heads and are often the sons or helpers of
witches. They travel on winged fairy horses and demand maidens as sacri-
fices or keep them captive in the underworld. Another character from the
underworld is Laktibrada (Elbowbeard), the dwarf, "a span of a man with a
beard to his elbow." Normally cruel and lying, he can be made to help if one
discovers his weakness—his beard (see "Lomidrevo or Valibuk").

The Tale Tradition

In order to familiarize the reader with the landscape of the world of Slovak tales, we need briefly to consider the question, what is a folktale?
Folklorists and other interested parties have long battled over the question
of the "folk" whose property the tales are and the nature of the "oral tradi-

tion"—the manner in which the tales circulate. In Europe, and sometimes more broadly, a certain body of tales circulated among the largely illiterate population for centuries. This primarily oral tradition, however, was not isolated from the written literature of the time but, symbiotically, both drew upon it and contributed to it. These tales were the entertainment of all, from kings and queens, often themselves illiterate, to the lowliest peasant. As literacy advanced, literature began to distance itself from this body of tales. Well-intentioned church clerics condemned many tales as superstitious humbug and, later, the enlightened intelligentsia could freely look down upon these "popular" tales. Thus it was possible, on the eve of the nineteenth century, for a few romantic souls, searching for new artistic values and national cultural resources, to rediscover the "folk" and their tales, for the circulation of these tales, both orally and in popular chapbooks, had definitely moved to the lowest classes of the population.

Folktales are traditional both in the sense of belonging to a relatively stable body of tales that are in circulation—the tale tradition—and in the sense that these tales are told in communities where traditional community organization and work habits provide occasion for the telling of tales and thus the need for the tales. The tale narrator learns his tales from previous tellers and polishes his own tales within a community that is familiar with the tales and knows what it likes to hear. The latitude given to individual creativity and expression varies within these boundaries.

Who were the folktale narrators and when did they tell their stories? Research on the European tale tradition as it existed from the mid-nineteenth century through the middle of the twentieth century suggests that storytelling communities included migrant working communities of craftsmen, soldiers, sailors, lumbermen, herdsmen, and those of similar occupations; village communities during communal work and winter evenings; and involuntary communities in hospitals and jails.[1] What all of these communities have in common is long periods of communal idleness or quiet activity, which provide a need for entertainment and thus an occasion for storytelling. Stories might be told in turn, with everyone required to participate, or a gifted narrator might be invited along to shorten a long hour. Wandering craftsmen might trade an evening's entertainment for a place to sleep and a meal. In the nineteenth century, journeymen from the Slovak part of the Austro-Hungarian empire traveled far and wide within the empire and beyond. In the course of their wanderings, they would meet other craftsmen and hear their tales—one manner in which the stories circulated. We know, for example, that Slovak potters and tinkers were popular storytellers in Transylvanian villages.[2] Thus, the heroes of "The Tinkers and the Evil One" were probably carrying home new stories along with their hard-earned wealth.

One Slovak narrator from whom a later generation of folklorists collected tales, Jozef Rusnák-Bronda, can serve us as an example of a gifted story-teller. Born in 1864 in the upper Hron River valley, he learned the trade of carpenter from his brother-in-law and traveled around northern Slovakia (then Upper Hungary) for his trade. From 1895 until 1900 he worked in a foundry in the United States and then returned to his home to continue in the woodcutter's trade. Unable to continue working due to an injury, he never-theless continued to go to the mountains with the woodcutters, where he performed various duties, including cooking and guarding the hut. Later, when even this work became too strenuous for him, the woodcutters helped him with his duties in order that he stay with them and tell his stories, which he told during the evenings and when there was bad weather. He would tell stories of accidents and jokes as well as demonological stories and the longer wondertales. Often he would receive an extra portion of liquor for his tales. In the village he would occasionally be invited to women's spinning parties to tell tales, but he would change his tales when children were present.[3]

These last details might surprise the reader who assumes that folktales are for children. In fact, these tales were adult entertainment, though the preju-dice that they are for children is an old and storied one, reflected in figures like "Mother Goose." Storytellers were, in fact, more frequently men, though women could and did become excellent narrators. Even the Grimm brothers titled their famous collection of tales *Domestic and Children's Tales* (Kinder-und Hausmärchen). From all the evidence that we have it seems apparent that those who collected the material that later was compiled and used in creating these classic Slovak folktales shared this prejudice as well, and prob-ably collected largely in domestic spheres. Readers who are interested in the details of the collecting and editing of these tales should read the appendix "Tale Collection in Nineteenth-Century Slovakia and the Origin of Tradi-tional Slovak Folktales." In brief, many tales were recorded in the early 1840s by students of Lutheran secondary schools and were put together in large manuscript volumes by the students. When Dobšinský published his tales—first with Augustín Horislav Škultéty, *Slovak Tales* (Slovenské povesti), 1858–61, and later alone, *Slovak Folktales* (Prostonárodnie slovenské povesti), 1881–83—he drew largely upon these early manuscripts. But he also used the collections of others who, like himself, had continued to collect tales, including Škultéty and the well-known Czech writer Božena Němcová, who collected tales during her travels in Slovakia. Dobšinský, like the other Slo-vak folktale publishers from his generation, would compare various versions of a tale from different narrators and collections and would base his pub-lished version on one or two of them, drawing upon the others for additional motifs or interesting words and phrasings in an attempt to produce the most

The writer Ján Botto and Pavol Dobšinský while Dobšinský was living in Drienčany. Photograph collection of the Archive of Literature and Art, Matica Slovenská, Martin, Slovakia.

complete and "well-preserved" versions of the tales. Such methods make contemporary folklorists wince, but they were common in that day. The tales were considered to be treasures of the ancient, national past, and Dobšinský attempted to preserve the style and archaisms in the language. Fortunately, Dobšinský knew the folk narrative technique quite well—he was able to describe aspects of it very accurately in his theoretical writings—and captured something essential of the nature of the tales in his published versions.

Tale Genres

Of course the essential nature of the tales varies for different types of tales, and the reader should be aware of the boundaries between them in order to better orient himself in the world of Slovak tales.[4] The most common tales in Dobšinský's collections are fairy tales proper, or, as some folklorists prefer, wondertales, since fairies actually appear rarely in this type of tale. It is unlikely that these tales were the most widespread in the oral tradition when these tales were collected—humorous tales probably reigned supreme then as they do today. The longer and more complex wondertale requires special conditions for its telling, including an audience that is open to its fantastic content. However, the early collectors focused on the wondertale because of its obvious esthetic qualities as well as their belief that this type of tale preserved the ancient mythology and beliefs of the Slovak nation. The first collection published by Dobšinský and Škultéty consisted almost exclusively of wondertales, and, in total, nearly two-thirds of the tales Dobšinský published were of this type. In our selection, wondertales make up just under one-half of the tales.

Wondertales take place in an unspecified place and time and follow a hero as he overcomes various obstacles. The hero comes into contact with supernatural beings who serve either as helpers or as villains to be overcome, sometimes with the help of magic objects. The stories often begin with the hero leaving home and end happily, often in a wedding. The characteristic charm of these tales may be a result of the fact that the natural and supernatural exist side by side, undifferentiated. No hero ever gasps over a miracle in a wondertale, for the fantastic is as common as the everyday. In fact, they expect and rely on the supernatural, like the two parting brothers in "The Enchanted Forest," who drive their knives into a tree and expect to see either blood or water when they pull them out, which will indicate to them the fate of the other.

Many have seen in the wondertale the victory of good over bad and beauty over ugliness, and thus have been tempted to ascribe a certain morality to the wondertale. While the wondertale does prefer sharp oppositions and while good characters do often triumph over bad, especially in tales involving an evil stepmother, one cannot speak of the moral character of the tales *in general*. As the Slovak writer Štefan Krčmery observed about Slovak tales, villains like dragons and witches are often quite human and potentially sympathetic characters—the dragons even keep bees and play cards. Moreover, the dragons keep their word, while the maidens lie and deceive to get away from them.[5] Defeated dragons can even become helpers (see "Vintalko"). But listeners and readers identify with the heroes and not their obstacles, no matter how sympathetic they may be. The wondertale requires that the hero emerge victorious. Sometimes the hero's siblings fail for no apparent reason, so that the hero—usually the youngest sibling—has to save them, and sometimes the hero has to lie or mistreat someone to accomplish his goals. When Radúz sends his wife away in favor of Ľudmíla the reader does not blanch, for the logic of the tale requires that the lovers from the start of the tale be reunited. In general, then, it is better to say that wondertale heroes always triumph, much to the delight of the audience, and leave judgments about their morality aside.

Also characteristic of the wondertale is a certain abstraction of style, including the predominance of certain cardinal numbers: three, seven, and multiples of three. Scenes and actions are often repeated three times. The language tends toward the formulaic, with commonplaces of phrasing and description, most markedly in the tales' openings and closings. The Slovak equivalent of "Once upon a time" is "Kde bolo, tam bolo, raz bol . . ." (Where there was, there there was, once there was . . .). A common closing formula is "And they bought a cow, and on the cow a bell; that's all there is to tell" (a kúpili si kravu a na tú kravu zvonec a tej rozprávke koniec).

Novelistic tales are in some ways closely related to wondertales, but insofar as the fantastic element is almost entirely removed, they can also stand as the antipode to the wondertale. The time and place remains undefined for these tales, but the setting—Slovak towns and villages—reflects the everyday life of the common person. Like wondertales, novelistic tales delight in contrasts, although here the pauper is more frequently contrasted with the judge and merchant than with the king. Some elements of the fantastic can still be found in adventure tales, but the hero overcomes the obstacles most often by his own wit and imagination, rather than through the help of supernatural beings and objects ("Klinko and Kompit King"). Other tales do away entirely with the fantastic element and place the hero entirely on his or her own resources ("A Woman's Wit" and "Right"). The language of novelistic tales is less formulaic in general, including a less frequent use of opening and closing formulae, and relatively simple. There is often an element of humor. Dobšinský published this type of tale only in his later collection, and the reader will find a half-dozen or so of these tales in this selection.

Humorous tales are closely related to novelistic tales, but emphasize typical situations and characters and the humor that arises from them. This is the home of heroes like Kubo and the foolish woman who destroys everything, but nonetheless wins riches. Humorous tales are and were widespread and common in Slovakia, and are well represented in the manuscript collections of the students. But Dobšinský and Škultéty, in their publication, ignored humorous tales. The early collectors of folktales had serious political and cultural goals that folktales were supposed to help fulfill, including providing a basis on which a literature and a nation could be built, and thus had little interest in frivolous and sometimes obscene tales. Only much later did Dobšinský come to appreciate the humorous tale, of which he included a few examples in his later publication.

Another class of tales that includes an element of humor based on the typicality of characters is *animal tales*. Animals or animated objects ("Bladder-Blatherskite and His Friends") here take center stage, and humans appear only as supporting characters. Animals speak and act like humans and may represent particular types. The plot of these tales tends to the simple accumulation of motifs and events, but the style is worth noting: there is frequent poetic use of names (again, see "Bladder-Blatherskite") and dialogue predominates, often itself taking poetic form ("The Kids"). This type of tale is relatively rare, but well represented in Dobšinský's collection.

Legendary tales represent a halfway point between folktales and legends. Like other folktales and unlike most historical and local legends, legendary tales usually take place in an unspecified setting, although there is a tendency to give the tale some time setting in the opening ("When the Lord Jesus was a boy . . ."). However, unlike in most other folktales, the supernatural does not easily blend in with the everyday in legendary tales. Rather, as the legend, the legendary tale celebrates the meeting of the everyday with the supernatural. Here a miracle is truly a miracle. Legendary tales often have biblical characters for their heroes, and the language of the tales is itself often biblical. These tales were quite popular and reflect the influence of the Catholic Church on the popular imagination. The fool becomes a saint ("Stovey the Fool") and the sinner is saved ("Mataj").

Demonological stories also represent a kind of midpoint between tales and legends, although certainly of a different sort. Rather than the influence of the church, we see here the remnants of ancient animistic beliefs as they have survived in popular beliefs. The main figures in these tales are witches, warlocks, devils, water and wood sprites, brownies (house spirits), and ghosts of various types, or the people who meet up with them. These characters also appear in wondertales, but are often stripped of their pertinent individual features as they play the role of the villain. In demonological stories they reach their true proportions. These tales are often given localized settings (see "The Tinkers and the Evil One"), and the supernatural is often met with fear and trembling, though, as we have already noted, the devil *can* play the fool.

Since we have mentioned historical and local legends, we should note that they are just one of a whole series of types of prose folklore that are not represented in this selection of traditional Slovak folktales, including jokes, riddles, proverbs, memorates, oral personal narratives, and so on. Riddles were actually included by Dobšinský and Škultéty in their first collection, to fill space between the tales, and Dobšinský collected a variety of other types of folklore, including proverbs and descriptions of games, dances, holidays, and festivals, which he published separately. Other genres (memorates and oral personal narratives) have only been collected and studied more recently, by other generations of folklorists.

How does the fairy-tale world reflect the real world of Slovakia? As we have already suggested, novelistic tales can provide an accurate picture of social relations and the everyday realities of village and city life. Demonological stories and legendary tales provide a picture of communal beliefs, both sanctioned and unsanctioned. But even the more stylistically determined wondertales reflect local social reality, though the researcher must be careful in drawing conclusions, for the social reality is here subordinate to the requirements of the story. Sometimes major social rituals are reflected in the tales, as in the burial rites in "Beautiful Ibronka." The material culture of Slovakia also works its way in: no bačas or valachs are heroes of wondertales (though they often are in other types of tales), but wondertale heroes like Lomidrevo *do* often carry their characteristic tool—the valaška. Most of all, local reality creeps into the details of language. Everyone will recognize "The Spinner of Gold" as the tale of "Rumpelstiltskin," but the Slovak villain has another name. Even more telling, the other girls look at the youngest with envy, but assume that they, too, will "get under a bonnet" if their lazy sister does. The other girls believe that they will marry as well: in traditional folk dress, married women wore bonnets. Local reality here is the only guide to the meaning of what is told.

When these folktales were being collected, they were considered national treasures, just as they are today. Then, the collectors believed that the wondertales held the key to the ancient past of the Slovak nation, both its history and its beliefs. Dobšinský believed the wondertale reflected the historical events of the ancient past only symbolically, but was keen to decipher the beliefs of the Slovaks' ancestors from these tales. Today folklorists are far more careful in interpreting the wondertale, because of the way the story form shapes the material drawn from social reality. Now these stories are considered national treasures both for the way they embody traditional societal values and, more importantly, for their esthetic qualities, particularly the language of the tales. In most cases, Dobšinský bears final responsibility for this language, and not the folk narrators.

Dobšinský published these tales at a time when the Slovak literary language was still being formed, and the tales certainly influenced the final form the standard language took. In fact, his entire generation of writers clearly benefited from their participation in the collecting of tales as students, both in the poetics they practiced and in the very natural Slovak language they employed. Dobšinský hoped to provide reading material for all, not just the highly educated, in order to inculcate the habit of reading in the nation. Thus he published the tales following the forms of the written norm and left only a few humorous tales completely in dialect. But he did not overcorrect—he left numerous dialectal terms and archaisms in all the tales in order to give a better sense of place and character. The result is a rich and subtle Slovak drawn from the language of the people and their environment.

Translations and Sources

The oldest translations of these traditional Slovak tales into English that I could find are translations of those tales that Karel Jaromir Erben included in his collection of one hundred Slavic tales, which was to provide the basis for a study of Slavic mythology (to correspond to Jacob Grimm's study of German mythology). Erben included about a half-dozen Slovak tales, which he took from the published editions of Ján Francisci (see the appendix for more on this collection) and Škultéty–Dobšinský. In 1890, A.H. Wratislaw published *Sixty Folk-Tales from Slavonic Sources* (Boston: Houghton), a translation of selections from Erben's volume that included four Slovak tales (designated "Hungarian-Slovenish Stories"). "The Golden Spinster" and "Are You Angry?" are from Škultéty–Dobšinský. Wratislaw was hampered by a lack of specific knowledge of the Slovak idiom, and his style strikes one as far too literary for the folktale.

W.W. Strickland's volume, *Panslavonic Folk-lore in Four Books* (New York: B. Westerman Co., 1930), a translation of Erben's entire volume along with essays in solar mythological interpretation of the tales, ultimately suffers from the same faults, although I must admit that he saved me one error of my own. Tales from Škultéty–Dobšinský include "Bird-Brother," "The Golden (Darling) Peahen," "The Golden Spinneress," "Are You Angry?" and "We Three Brothers."

Parker Fillmore published two volumes of Czechoslovak tales: *Czecho-slovak Fairy Tales* (New York: Harcourt, 1919) and *The Shoemaker's Apron: Czechoslovak Folk and Fairy Tales* (1920). I was unable to examine the first volume, but in the introduction to the second volume, he clearly defines the role he has played: "My work has been that of retelling rather than translating since in most cases I have put myself in the place of a storyteller who knows several forms of the same story, equally authentic, and from them all fashions a version of his own." He wants to raise the stories "from the realm of crude folklore to the realm of art."[6] Of the tales in that volume, only "Clever Manka," which is recognizable as adapted from "A Woman's Wit," is definitely from Dobšinský—he may have taken "Batcha and the Dragon" from Němcová's collection of Slovak tales. The fact that he takes the word *bača* (see the Glossary) for the first name of the shepherd already demonstrates his method and level of understanding, and makes one question his esthetic judgment of the tales as well.

The first and only work to include a significant number of Dobšinský's and Škultéty's tales, *The Enchanted Castle and Other Tales and Legends* (Brno, Czechoslovakia: Artia, 1967), is properly described as "adapted by Ann Macleod," for the thirty tales it contains are, like those of Fillmore, not translated in any proper sense. A much more recent volume, *Rose Ann* (Bratislava, Czechoslovakia: Mladé Letá, 1988), is well translated by Heather Trebatická, but contains only four tales and was translated from a Slovak text *adapted for children* from Dobšinský's collections. It is a nicely illustrated children's book and deserves a wider audience than it has probably found. However, it is not representative of Dobšinský's and Škultéty's work, which was aimed at a much broader, adult reading public.

This translation, then, makes available in English for the first time the work of Pavol Dobšinský, so well known in Slovakia, in a representative selection. It has been prepared from the edition of Eugen Pauliny, which includes all Dobšinský's tales published with Škultéty as *Slovak Tales* (Slovenské povesti), 1858–61, as well as those from his later collection, *Slovak Folk Tales* (Prostonárodnie slovenské povesti), 1881–83. Of the 153 tales, fifty have been chosen that represent all the major tale genres in Dobšinský's collections in a proportion close to that of his later, more balanced publication.

Notes

1. See the work of the Hungarian folklorist Linda Dégh, *Folktales and Society: Storytelling in a Hungarian Peasant Community*.
2. Ibid., p. 72.

3. See Mária Kosová, "Rozprávkár Jozef Rusnák-Bronda," pp. 13–19.

4. For what follows I have relied mostly upon Viera Gašparíková, "Pohádka," and articles on the various genres in the *Encyklopédia ľudeovej kultúry slovenska*.

5. Štefan Krčmery, "O poesii našich povestí," pp. 809–10. See also Max Lüthi, *The European Folktale: Form and Nature,* pp. 30, 70–75, 81–93.

6. Parker Fillmore, *The Shoemaker's Apron: Czechoslovak Folk and Fairy Tales*, pp. v–vi. See Ján Stefánik, *Bibliografia vydaní slovenských ľudových rozprávok slovenských zberateľov a Slovenských pohádek a povesti B. Němcovej* (1845–1974), for an incomplete but useful bibliography of Slovak tales that includes translations into other languages.

TRADITIONAL SLOVAK FOLKTALES

❧ 1 ❧

The Enchanted Forest

*I*n a small house there lived a poor widow with her two sons, and these were so alike, it was as if one had fallen out of the other's eye. Their own mother could hardly tell them apart. The brothers were perfectly alike in everything and their mother wouldn't have given them up for the whole wide world. So, year after year passed by and all was well for them.

But as the fine lads grew up and saw others going out into the world, they began to be drawn away from home, and they told their mother that they wanted to take a look at the world. But this was not to her liking: "Ah," she said, "don't you like it at home, that you want to go out into the world? Who knows what might happen to you there? You just sit at home and don't leave me all alone!" But all her entreaties were of no use; they would never allow what they had once taken into their heads to be knocked out. The poor mother cried day and night and doused every corner in her tears.

"Ah, mother dear," her sons comforted her, "don't weep and worry so much about us. After all, we're not the first to go into the world, and in three years you will have us back here. Whatever you will need until then we will provide ahead of time." Then they began right away to gather rye, flour, other edibles, lard, and wood so that there was enough of everything for three years. When their mother saw this, her heart was lightened a bit and she also began to get one thing and another ready for their trip.

Everything was ready, except they lacked a good piece of roasted meat. "My children," she said, "could you run and shoot something? It would bother me to let you go without meat." They walked and wandered through the forest from morning to noon, from noon to evening, but they didn't even come upon a single track. So, they prepared to return home. Just then two wolves ran in from opposite sides and began to scuffle. The brothers were inclined, though unwilling, to shoot at them. "If we both don't aim well," said one, "an infuriated wolf might set upon us. Let's try throwing them each a piece of bacon with bread instead." When they threw it, the wolves stopped scuffling and followed the brothers quietly, like dogs, until they had good and well led them home. They shut the wolves up in the stable and themselves went into the room.

"Well, what did you shoot?" asked their mother.

"We didn't shoot anything," they said, "but we led two wolves home and shut them in the stable."

"Alas, woe is me," their mother cried, "that's it for my cow! Go, run and save it!" They all ran to the stable. The cow was standing just fine in her place and the wolves silently in the corner. On their muzzles were large locks. They couldn't have marveled more at that.

The next day they again left to hunt, but again they didn't shoot anything. However, on the way back they caught sight of two bears tearing at each other. They threw them each a piece of bacon with bread: the bears stopped tearing at each other and followed the brothers all the way home, where they shut them in the stable. Their mother, when she heard about the bears, again took fright. But when they went for a look, everything was peaceful. The bears, too, had locks on their muzzles.

The third day they readily killed nothing, but simply quieted two lions that had been clawing at each other and led them home. "I see that nothing will come of your meat!" said their mother. As there was nothing else to do, they packed everything into their pouches, took leave of their mother, and took the animals with them.

Three days and three nights the brothers strode side by side until they came to a crossroads. A linden tree stood there. "My brother," said the older one, "we are at a pass. We shall have to part here. You take that road, and I'll turn down the other. But you know what? When one or the other of us returns this way, so that he will know how it is going with the other, let's carve our names into this linden and drive our knives into it. Whoever returns first, let him pull out the knife from his brother's name, and if blood comes out, he will know that his brother is alive, but if water flows, he is certainly dead."[1] The younger brother agreed and they immediately carved their names and drove their knives into the tree. Then they divided the animals, shook hands, and each went his own way.

For a long time the older brother walked here and there through thickly wooded mountains and beautiful fields, until he came to a town that was completely draped in black cloth. He entered an inn and asked the innkeeper, "What good tidings have you?"

"Huh, nothing at all good, but plenty of bad," responded the innkeeper. "Here in town we have but one well from which we all drink, but we pay dearly for the water, for a dragon with twelve heads lives in a lair outside of town and every day we must give him one maiden to devour, for if we did not, he would allow no one to approach the well and we would all perish from thirst. From each and every house the citizens have already given their daughters, and now it is the turn of the king's daughter. For that reason the king has commanded the town be draped in black cloth, but he also proclaimed that to the one they found to kill the dragon he would give his daughter to wife and half of his kingdom, and after the king's death he would receive the entire kingdom."

No sooner had our fine lad heard that than he had a taste for proud son-in-law-hood and said that he would like to kill the dragon, if only he would be able. The innkeeper ran straight to the king and told him that he had such and such a guest with three animals who is willing to kill that serpent; that he's dressed simply, it's true, but nonetheless must be powerful if he could tame such wild animals. The king was delighted by the news. He immediately sent him nice clothing and ordered him not to delay in coming. Our fine lad dressed himself and went to the palace along with his animals. There, everyone was thankful and the king promised him that if he could put an end to the dragon, his daughter would certainly be his. But the lad requested that they give each of his animals two rams apiece and prepare a sharp saber for him.

It had just begun to lighten when the king's daughter sat in the coach. The coach began to move and the fine lad strode along behind it with his animals and a sharp saber in his hand. When they were not far from the lair, he told the coachman to stop. The king's daughter stepped out of the coach and mounted a horse. "Now," he said, "just hold on tightly and flash by the front of the lair to decoy the dragon out. The coach will remain here."

The king's daughter flew by the opening like a shot. The dragon caught scent of it and stuck out a head. But instead of a beautiful maiden, a sharp saber flashed in his eyes. The fine lad was not idle: off came the dragon's head. The dragon became enraged at that and stuck out three more heads from which terrible flames lashed.[2] With that, the animals jumped forward and began to pluck at the beast from every side while the dear lad hacked and cut with all his might, and four heads were soon off.

But to what end? The dragon at once thrust out eight more heads and lashed out with terrible flames. Exhausted, the fine lad could barely hold on to his saber, even the wolf and bear could take it no longer and merely jumped about on the sides. But then the lion ran up and jumped on the dragon's back and with his powerful paws tore all eight heads including the necks from the dragon's repulsive body. The dragon collapsed and the heads continued to wriggle about on the ground for some time.

The lad took out his knife, cut out the tongues of the dragon, placed them in his pouch, and ran to the king's freed daughter. In her great joy, she couldn't thank him enough and embraced him and kissed him. Then she took her ring, broke it in two, and gave him half. Exhausted, he lay his head in her lap and napped. The animals, too, lay down and fell asleep.

When that scoundrel the coachman saw that everyone was asleep, he grabbed the saber and lopped off the dear lad's head. He made the princess swear seven times that she would not betray him. Then he took the dragon's heads as a sign that he had killed the beast and flew with the princess to the king.

When the animals awoke they saw their murdered master. They howled and roared terribly from their great sorrow. Then the lion commanded the wolf, "Run quickly along this path, you'll meet up with a snake carrying an herb in his mouth to revive his brother who was crushed under a wagon. Ask for half of the herb from him, and if he doesn't want to give you it willingly, take it by force!" The wolf at once hied his way, but he met up with some carters' wagons. When the people saw him, they grabbed some stakes and in fright he rushed back.

"Well, you're a fool," said the lion. "You run, bear, and bring the herb!" The bear ran off and also ran into the wagons, but when the carters saw the bear, they hid themselves in their wagons like mice in a hole before a cat. The bear came to the snake and asked for half of the herb. But the niggard was evasive and tried to release poison into the bear's body. The bear was annoyed and trapped the doggone snake with his paw and forcefully tore away half of the herb. Then he flew like lightning to the lion, who immediately rubbed the neck of his master with the herb and attached his head, but poorly, for his face was turned to his back.

When the bear saw the master walking badly and stumbling and willy-nilly falling to the ground, he tore off his head, rubbed it with the herb, and set it on right this time, and it attached immediately. The fine lad came to himself, jumped to his feet and sighed. "Umm!" he said, "did I ever sleep well." As though nothing had happened, he took his animals and went wherever his eyes led.

One month later he again came to that town and saw it was now draped in red cloth. He settled at the same inn as before and asked what was new there. "Good news," the innkeeper responded. "Our daughters have nothing more to be afraid of, for the king's coachman killed the dragon. Why, just now he's collecting his dowry and tomorrow is his wedding to the king's daughter."

When the lad had heard that, he became lost in thought. It irked him that the coachman had driven him out of such happiness. But suddenly he jumped up and said to the innkeeper, "Let's bet that I will eat at that wedding!" The innkeeper didn't believe it, so they bet.

The fine lad requested a basket: he wrote a letter into which he wound his half of the ring, put the letter in the basket, put the basket in the bear's mouth, and sent him to the palace. The bear came to the courtyard, whereupon all the dogs and hounds began to bark at him, but he just continued softly on. Only when most of them began to badger him did he set the basket down and chase off the barkers, then returned for the basket and entered into the very room where the nobility were feasting. The bear simply walked up to the king's daughter and gave her the basket from his mouth. As soon as the coachman saw the bear, he began to sit less comfortably, as if three pillows had disappeared from beneath him.

The princess read the letter, stood up from the table, loaded the best morsels into the basket, even added a full glass of wine into which she dropped both halves of the ring, and the bear carried it all off to his master.

The innkeeper lost his bet, and the fine lad enjoyed what the king's daughter had sent. When he had eaten his fill, he took the glass and drank it in one gulp, upon which he saw the ring at the bottom, for the two halves had grown nicely together. That was a sign to the lad that luck was on his side today.

He immediately left for the palace with his animals and stepped directly into the room where they were feasting. When the king's daughter saw him, she jumped up in joy to meet him and embraced him in front of everyone. The king and his guests stared in wonder at what was going on, and the scoundrel of a coachman shook like an aspen leaf. All the pillows disappeared from beneath him. The princess had to explain everything, and the fine lad showed the dragon's tongues in evidence.

They made quick justice for the embittered coachman: they gave him to the animals to be torn to bits. The king was thrilled and gave his daughter to her true liberator. Our fine lad became the king's son-in-law, received half of the kingdom, and lived so well that he could not have wished for better.

One morning as a boy was dressing him, he looked out the window: on one side he saw beautiful, green forests, on the other, however, there was a sad forest, yellowed as in the autumn. This seemed quite strange to him, for the most beautiful spring had just arrived.

"Why is it," he asked, "that all the forests all around are in such pretty bloom and just that one is so yellowed?"

"Sir," replied the boy, "that is the enchanted forest. Many people have died there, for whosoever visits it never returns." He just listened and didn't say anything, but the forest irked him.

So far, so good. Once he told his wife that he was going on a hunt, took his animals, and left. Hardly had he left the garden, when—whence it came, thence it came—out jumped a fox in front of him. He took after it along with his animals, but they couldn't chase it down and didn't approach close enough to shoot.

So it went for quite some time: the fox would stop for a moment and then immediately run off ahead, all in order to entice them further and further.

The king's son-in-law quickly lost his patience, became irked, and cursed, something he had never done before. And the fox was waiting for just that, for she had no power over the innocent. She suddenly vanished from his sight and he found himself in a thicket. Around him it was as dark as midnight. He began to feel anxious and would have been glad to get free. But he only became entangled deeper and deeper, for the forest was deceiving him.

He stopped beneath an oak, and since he was hungry, he built a fire and began to cook some bacon. Thereupon he heard a call from above him: "I'm cold, I'm cold!" He looked around and saw a stooped old woman sitting in the tree.

"If you're cold, come warm up," he said from below, whereupon it became silent.

Again after a moment she announced, "I'm cold, I'm cold!"

"I'm telling you, if you're cold, come warm up." Again it was quiet.

For the third time she announced, "I'm cold, I'm cold!" and irked at her, he called out, "Come warm yourself, or be quiet!"

"Well, I would come down, but I'm afraid of your animals. Here's a stick. Strike them with it and then I'll come down." He struck the animals and the crone came down, ran off to the side and from somewhere or other brought a frog impaled on a twig and began to rotate it above the fire. As she turned the frog, she began to badger him: "You are cooking bacon, I am baking a frog: the bacon is for me and the frog for you." And with that, grease from the frog dripped on the bacon and she immediately drew it across his mouth.

When she had repeated this a few times, he became angry and sicced his animals on her. But they didn't move from their places, for they had turned to stone from the wand. He turned to them, but then the crone struck him with the wand and he at once turned to stone, too. Then she took him and hauled him off to a lair where she had already done in numerous people.

In the king's palace they waited and waited for the young king, but a day passed, and another, and he simply didn't return. Everyone was sad and thought nothing else but that he must have gotten lost in the enchanted forest and perished there.

The younger brother was returning home and passed by the crossroads. "How," he asked, "is it going for my brother?" He pulled out the knife and with that, from one end out trickled blood, from the other water. "Well," he thought, "that's not good. He's both dead and alive. I have to go search for him."

And he left at once on the road that his brother had chosen. He walked and walked, with his animals, too. He walked through thickly wooded mountains and beautiful fields until he came to the palace where his brother had been married. The king's daughter just happened to be standing in the courtyard and when she saw him, she ran to meet him, overjoyed. "Oh," she said, "where have you been? How hard it has been waiting for you!" She recognized him as her husband for, as we know, they were as alike as one. He made excuses as best he could, for he immediately realized that he was with his brother's wife.

When night came and they went to lie down, the younger brother drove his sword into the bed between himself and his brother's wife. She had no idea what to think, that her husband had in that time become so estranged from her, and she cried the whole night through.

He arose late in the morning, for he was quite worn out. When the boy was dressing him, he too saw the sad, yellowed forest and asked, "Why is it that the forests all around are in such pretty bloom and just that one is so yellowed?"

The boy rolled his eyes. "But I've already told you," he said. "Don't you remember?"

"I don't remember that you told me of it," replied the younger brother.

And the boy told him that it is such and such an enchanted forest, and whosoever visits it never returns. He had heard enough. He immediately thought that his brother must have misstepped there somewhere.

He, too, left on a hunt, and everything happened to him with the fox as it had with his brother, except the younger brother didn't curse. He came to that oak, built a fire, and began to fry some bacon. The animals stood to the side and licked their brothers who had turned to stone. "I'm cold!" announced the crone from the oak.

"If you're cold, come warm up," he called from below.

"Well, I would come down, but I'm afraid of your animals. Here's a stick. Strike them and then I'll come down."

The fine lad turned around and next to his animals he saw those that had been turned to stone. It immediately occurred to him: "Wait," he thought, "I'll deceive you." He didn't strike his animals, but the ground.

The crone came down and brought a frog impaled on a twig and began to rotate it. "You are cooking bacon, I am baking a frog: the bacon is for me and the frog for you," she badgered the fine lad, and with that, grease from the frog dripped on his bacon and she immediately drew it across his mouth. The lad was irked and boxed her ears. The crone jumped at him and throttled and throttled him, but he called his animals and they came after her. In fear, the crone began to beg him not to let her be torn to pieces.

"Revive these animals," he said, "then I'll let you go!"

She removed her boots and gave them to him to put on, so that he could climb up the tree where he would find a golden wand to strike the animals with. He did everything just so, and when he struck the animals with the golden wand, they at once revived. "You seize her as well," he called again, "and scratch her to death, until she tells where she hid my brother." The crone couldn't stand the pain and gave him a salve and told him to go this way and that to the lair and to rub his brother's neck with it. His brother immediately revived and they both returned to the animals.

But just listen to what happened next. Without being sicced at all, the animals all went after the crone. Her bonnet flew off into the fire and crackled horribly; they tore her to shreds. When it was all over for the crone, it began to lighten at once all around, and the entire forest delightfully turned green.

And then what happened after that! The first animals who had been turned to stone turned into armed knights and cut the animals who hadn't turned to stone into small pieces and put them in a small pile. Hardly had they made the pile when three similar knights rose from the cut meat. With that, they all kissed each other like brothers and forgave each other their wrongs.

Our brothers looked on in wonder and barely believed their own eyes. Then one of the six said, "Don't be amazed, benefactors of ours, but listen to what we have to tell you! We are six brothers from a king's clan, but our parents allowed our relations to remain undefined so that we were always quarreling over who would be king. For that reason, one member of the family cursed us that we should fight among ourselves like wolves, bears, and lions until two innocent brothers calmed us and we did each other a good turn. And now you know everything that happened and how it happened and had to happen. But we shall give you all our riches and under your care we would like to finish our lives."

They all returned to the king's palace. There husband was distinguished from non-husband, brother from brother, and a banquet was held one hundred times larger than before.

Shortly thereafter the brothers brought their mother as well. The older brother remained king there, and the younger brother left with the six for their country, where they thankfully handed the crown over to him and, having made their peace, lived together tranquilly and happily.

Notes

1. According to other versions, he says, "Let's drive our valaškas into this linden tree. Whoever returns first and sees blood flowing from his brother's mark . . . ," etc.

2. Some versions add that, while this brother was leaving the crossroads he was about to shoot two doves, but they begged him to leave them be, saying that they would be of service to him. Now these doves flew to him and chased the flames away from his face with their wings.

❦ 2 ❦

Two Rascals

Once over on the oak mountain there lived a rascal who only wanted to make his way by light work and nothing else. So he scared up a full sack of pine cones and went to traffic with them in the world. He came to a certain inn and there awaited some kind of luck.

Another such rascal lived with the charcoal makers on the other mountain. And he, when he could, liked to put something over on a fella. He poured fine ashes into a bag to sell as flour. Then he went forth into the world to seek his fortune and came to the same inn where the first rascal had established himself.

"Godspeed!" this fellow said when he stepped inside.

"Godspeed," said the first. "Where are you headed?"

"To sell some flour. Well, and you?"

"I'm selling walnuts."

At night, while the flour-monger was sleeping, the cone-monger jumped to his feet and thought to himself, "I'll take his sack instead of mine; why, he won't know." And he took the sack of ashes onto his shoulder and lit out for home.

The second awoke and said, "Wherever did that other fellow get to? He took my ashes instead of his walnuts. Well, that's good. Just hump it home, before he returns." With that he threw the darn sack with the cones on his back and hied it home. "Woman, bring a tub," he shouted from the road. "I'm bringing you walnuts."

"But where did you scrape them up?" asked his wife. "Aren't you ashamed of yourself, duping people?" and she brought a tub into which he poured, in great hope . . . pine cones.

"Woman, bring a tub!" the second fellow also called when he was arriving at home. "I'm bringing you flour." His wife laid out the tub and with great joy was already thinking of what wonderful halušky she would strain out. But out poured ashes.

Those two wiseacres then set out to find each other, and they met again at that inn. "Eh, brother," one said, "you're quite a wise guy!"

"Eh, well, you're a wise guy yourself!" said the second. "But since we wags have duped each other, let's go earn our bread as partners." And so they went, until they came to a little house that stood on a big meadow. There they found an old hag.

"Godspeed you, granny!"

"And you, my children. Where are you headed?"

"To seek work. Won't you take us on?"

"Why, I'd even take the both of you."

"And we would gladly go, even the both of us. And what will you give us to do?"

"One of you will pasture my heifer and the other will clean her shed."

And so, early the next morning the cone-monger went to pasture a skinny heifer and the flour-monger to sweep out the run-down shed and carry out the manure. When he stepped into the shed he saw less than two wheelbarrows full of manure. But when he opened the door and let the sun in and began to rake it and carry it out, more and more kept appearing, and the more he drudged, the more he saw before him.

The cone-monger, in the morning before the sun was hot, started beating the cow and still she just barely put one leg in front of the other. But when the sun began to get hot and the heifer warmed up, she lifted her head, perked up her ears, and became frisky, and went leaping over rocks and in the underbrush. The fellow had already lain down in the grass and begun to nap, since she wouldn't even move from her place, he said. But then he was scared when he saw the cow jumping about. He called her and lured her—Here Bessy, here!—and chased her, but she just leapt higher and further, so that he could hardly run after her. After midday it seemed to him that she would escape into the world and he was already afraid of the old crone. But when the sun began to set, even the cow began to weaken, and when it set, she became so weak that she just heaved from side to side. With great effort he drove her into the yard. There the flour-monger met him with a wheelbarrow of manure.

"Brother, did you wear yourself out with that wheelbarrow?"

"Hardly! I'm taking one load out now and this morning I took out another, what kind of work is that? And did you run ragged behind that toothless bossy?"

"Hardly! I slept all day and she didn't even move from me."

The next day the fellow who had cleaned the shed yesterday said, "Brother, let me go with the cow today. Let me see the fields and warm myself in the sun."

"Fine, pal, go if you want. But I warn you ahead of time, take a stool with you, for you won't have anything to sit on and standing will make you weary.

And take a pipe with a long stem to entertain yourself." So they gleefully exchanged work: the flour-monger went to pasture the cow and the cone-monger stayed behind to put the shed in order.

The flour-monger could hardly lead the cow out of the shed in the morning. But by the time he prepared his pipe, cut the tobacco and tied the stool to his back, the sun was beating down. He went out with the cow behind the barn, and she began to move more spiritedly. When they came to the mountain, the sun began to bake: the darn heifer set to leaping, now in the bushes, now in the meadow, uphill and down. He tried to follow her uphill, but his pipe wouldn't allow him, for he had prepared one that reached to the ground. He tried to follow her into the undergrowth, but his stool became entangled in the bushes and he himself hardly got free. Meanwhile, he had lost sight of the heifer and he nearly turned grey in fright. But in the dark of the evening, the cow herself headed home, and toward the end he even had to beat her with a stick, just to keep her moving.

When he arrived at the shed he saw the cone-monger, who had been carting and carting since morning, and more and more kept appearing, and he was angry at himself and at the other, that it was also hard work. "Eh, buddy," he said, "you're a dirty dog!"

"Eh, why you're a dirty dog too!" And they said no more, but simply laughed at each other.

The third day they asked the old hag for their pay, saying they wanted to work no more, that they couldn't, for they had to try more of the world.

"Well, then, how shall I pay you, my children?" asked the old hag.

"Just with money, granny, just money."

"Go off over there to that hole and fill your sack to the brim with ducats!"

The cone-monger jumped in and the flour-monger stayed above to pull him and the ducats out. The fellow inside filled a sack halfway with ducats, but then he thought of something and bent himself in two and scrunched into the sack.

"Pull up the ducats!" he called to the one above.

The fellow above pulled with all his might until he had pulled out the sack, then he threw it all on his shoulder and lit out, running and running so that they couldn't have caught him with a hundred horses. When he had exhausted himself, he threw off the sack, took shelter in the bushes and went to sleep.

Then the sack opened and out jumped a man like an oak. He looked around to see if anyone was there, and when he saw the other sleeping, he tossed the sack with the ducats on his back and lit out to the forest off to the side.

At dusk the flour-monger rascal awoke in the bushes. Where the devil was the sack? The area was vacant to the right and to the left. "It was that bum carried it off for certain," he told himself. "Just you wait, little birdie, why, you'll perch on my glue; after all, you can't have gotten far." And he began to walk through the bushes and whinny like a horse.

And the doggone cone-monger was indeed hidden in the thicket, for he was afraid simply to take the road home, lest the flour-monger catch up to him. No sooner had he heard the whinny than he thought, "Hey, it would be good to go home on a horse!" He came out of the bush and began to lure the horse, "Here horsey, here!"

"Aha, there you are, you smart aleck!" said the flour-monger, standing in his road.

"Well, it's you, you joker! I thought it was some kind of horse."

"That's just what I wanted. Come on, let's go together." So they went on together to the cone-monger's wife, saying they would live there, for the flour-monger said he didn't have any kin. They lived together about two days. Then the flour-monger disappeared at night with the money and went straight home to his wife.

"Woman, here, take this ducat and run to the priest. Tell him I died and to use it to bury me today. But pour these ducats into my coffin so no one will steal them. But don't close my grave except with boards, and I'll come back in three days. And if anyone asks for me for any reason, tell them I'm already buried."

Everything was done as he had told her. They buried the said joker by just laying him in the grave, without even nailing shut the coffin or burying it, for his wife wanted to visit him and mourn, since he died so unexpectedly.

The cone-monger knew well and good that the flour-monger had a wife and thought for certain he'd find him there, but wondered what kind of trick he had again thought up. He came to the wife of the dead man and said, "Where's my good brother, good sister?"

"Where else? My lord, I've lived to my widow's bread. The poor fellow died on me. The Lord God grant him the joy of resurrection! He simply took ill and died."

"So," he said, "and no old sack remained after him?"

"Nothing remained. Everything that I had went with him to the grave."

"Well then, at least lead me to his grave, so I can weep for the pour soul as well since we once worked as partners."

But the good sister didn't want to lead him or have anything to do with him other than to get rid of him. With that he took off himself for the cemetery and began to low like a bull. The other fellow in the grave was just counting those coins, but when he heard the bull, he stopped counting and called out, "Hey, Bessy, hey!"

The bull on two legs heard that and simply lowed right up to the new grave and began to dig with his feet and pour dirt into the hole. The buried one was afraid and tried to frighten it off as best he could. Finally, the bull couldn't restrain himself from laughter anymore and called out, "Are you there, buddy?"

"I'm here."

"Eh, you're a dirty dog!"

"Why, you're a dirty dog too!"

They said no more, but divvied up the money and each went his own way.

❦ 3 ❦

The Wizard

$\mathcal{S}$omewhere, at some time, there lived a wizard, and that wizard had one big book that he always read from when someone came to him for advice. Once a neighbor came into his house and asked him if he didn't know how to help somehow with his cows, for they had stopped giving milk on him. "I'll help you with that," said the wizard, and taking the book in hand, he read in it and finally said, "Neighbor, you've got a couple of devils, Jufo and Galgína, in your barn; that is why your cows have no milk. But no matter. Just you fire up your stove with wood that you haven't cut but have only found, and I'll get rid of those devils. Then you'll be able to milk your cows, and even fill three buckets."

The neighbor gathered wood, fired up the stove, and in the meantime the wizard reached under the floor-beams and chased and drove the devils. In a while he came into the shanty all covered in manure and dirty like a swine, carrying a bag tied up in his hands. "Well, neighbor," he told him, "don't worry about a thing. Jufo and Balgína are in this bag. I caught them, but with trouble enough. They won't harm you anymore." And with that he tossed the bag into the stove that was hissing and popping so that it was a wonder it didn't fly apart. But they say that the neighbor still didn't milk his cows with three buckets; the milk only returned when he began to feed them clover.

That same wizard knew how to disenchant money and treasure from underworld spirits and obtain them. Once, on Maundy Thursday he lured the farmers from the third village out on Hradok mountain, saying he would bestow enough upon them to last for their children's children.

The farmers arrived at night, as he had told them to, in two carts. But these had to stay far off from Hradok when they unloaded the empty trunks from the wagons so that nothing would stand in the way of the disenchantment. The wizard himself, however, went up on Hradok, mumbled something there, and jingled something as if he were speaking with the spirits. After a long while he came to the farmers and told them to take the trunks full of treasure, but to open them and check them only at home, otherwise they might find something other than treasure in them.

The farmers did so and left after giving the wizard good reward for his labor. The old master raced ahead to where they would have to pass and hid himself there up in an oak tree.

Mountain roads can be bad and bumpy, especially at night when it's as dark as in a ram's horn. That rocky road was no different. Just as they were passing the oak in which the wizard sat silently, the cart was struck from beneath by a large stone so that a heavy trunk broke open and stones galore poured out.

The farmers, when they saw what had happened and what was up, began to moan, scratch behind their ears and grumble: "Eh, he betrayed us, if only we could catch him here somewhere!"

He began to whinny just like a horse, jumped out of the oak and vanished in the dark. They would have run after him, but how in the dark?

Another time it got into his head that an evil spirit was tormenting him. So he went to his neighbor, Ďuro, and invited him home, saying he could no longer defend himself alone against that evil spirit. The wizard's wife had just finished putting some malt and a black jug of brandy on the bench behind the table, and those two entertained themselves well with it until eleven. Near midnight the wizard said to his neighbor, "Ďuro, we have to go already!"

"Where to?" he asked.

"To the cemetery," answered the wizard.

"I swear to God, I'll not go to the cemetery no matter who offers me no matter what in the world. But anyway, since you were so friendly to me all evening at your place, I'll go for old pops Brncík to ask him to go with us. Then I won't be afraid of anything." Ďuro went there and came right back with old Brncík.

The cemetery was outside the village beyond the big ditch. So they set out that way. The wizard went ahead, reeling all the way on one leg, and the two behind him on all fours. When they arrived, the wizard ordered those two to stand there outside the wall, but said that he would go into the cemetery.

When he was already in the cemetery, he stopped over a grave and began to quarrel with some witch: "You bother me! You torment me! You rotten whorish so-and-so!" Those two waiting outside the wall also heard a smack, as if he had slapped her.

"Ack, pops," said Ďuro, whose broad-brimmed hat began to rise on his head, "I won't stay here. I'm going home."

"Don't be afraid, fool, grab hold of me!" said old pops Brncík, shoring up Ďuro's bravery. "I have a hard old club in my hands!"

Meanwhile the wizard came out of the cemetery, reeled home again on one leg and those two followed him to the very threshold of his hut, where they remained with him until daytime.

The next morning, when those two had gone home and dreams had overcome the wizard, his wife looked in the jug of brandy, and the jug was empty! Well, she thought, he had reason to quarrel with witches!

❦ 4 ❦

Stovey the Fool

In a village there once lived a man, a fool as one has to be. He had never been further than "two miles behind the stove," and that's why they called him Stovey. Poor Stovey was the butt of everyone's jokes, they would dust the corners with him, plow him and harrow him, but he never even hurt a fly.

Once, mind you, he went to church and heard the priest preaching, "Whosoever goes by the thorny road will reach heaven." When our dear fool arrived home, he told his wife, "My dear, I'm going to heaven!"

"Well then, go, fool, you jackass of the Lord Jesus you. At least I won't have to take care of you and worry about you," said his wife, and she baked him a black ashcake for his journey, stuck it in his bag, and led him out the door.

Stovey, recalling the words of the priest, didn't go the way everyone else went, but went off the beaten path, through thorns, rocks, and ditches. People laughed at him, but he paid no attention. His thoughts were all on heaven. He roamed about a long time, tore his clothes to shreds, and was battered; well, he was on the point of perishing, but still hadn't found heaven.

Famished and thirsting, he made his way to the door of a monastery. The doorkeeper found him there, barely breathing, and led him inside. They gave him food and drink and told him that if he knew how to stoke a stove, it would go well for him with them. But when the fool saw the beautiful room and how the monks did nothing but pray, eat, drink, and walk in the garden, he thought nothing other than that this was paradise, that he himself was already in heaven. And indeed, whenever the masters ate, he too received a full bowl; as long as he had lived, he had never smelled such food, and he had never been so well off. No one teased him and he consumed his food in peace wherever he pleased.

Once he slipped with his food into a great hallway where an old wooden crucifix hung on the wall. Stovey sat down before it, looked at it for a long time until he said, quite sorrowfully, "Poor thing, my but you're thin! Why don't they take care of you here in heaven as they ought? Come and eat with me!"

With that he pushed his bowl closer to the cross and laid his spoon beside it to give the Lord Jesus, as the guest, preference. And Christ leaned down from the cross and ate with him. After that Stovey always went with his bowl to the image of the Passion and didn't touch his food until he had offered it to the Lord Jesus. No one knew of this. The monks went to the church to pray and then each set to his work and no one even glanced at the old wooden cross and the fool in front of it.

Once the doorkeeper was looking for Stovey for something and found him sitting in the great hallway under the old cross. And on the cross he saw Christ in a halo of light and heard him say to the fool, "Today you shall dine at my table!"

And the doorkeeper ran to the abbot and told what he had seen and heard. The monks, as if horrified, all ran into the hall, took the fool among them and led him into the most beautiful room, where they questioned him about everything. When Stovey told them everything honestly, they realized that here was a man dear to God and that God wanted to call him home. They prepared him for his death, and the dear fool passed peacefully away that very day.

The Spinner of Gold

*F*ar away, way off there beyond the red sea, there once lived a young gentleman. When he had already come of age and reason, he considered that it wouldn't be a bad idea to take a look around the world and seek out some good housekeeper and proper wife. Well, behold! He did as he had determined. He set out into the world, but it didn't go so well for him, for he couldn't find a woman like he wished.

Finally, he inadvertently entered the room of a widow who had three girls, all marriageable. The two older girls—indeed, I've forgotten their names—worked like wasps, and the youngest, who was called Hana, worked like a leaden bird. When the young gentleman came to their house midway through a spinning party, he wondered at the fact that Hana could nap by the stove while the other spinners raced.[1] And he said to their mother, "Tell me, old mother, why don't you tie that one to the distaff? After all, she's already a fit maiden, and she could shorten a long hour by the work."

"Ah, youngster," the mother answered, "my heart would certainly allow her to spin, and I myself would even turn for her, but what's the use? After all, she's such a spinner that by morning, all by her lonesome she would spin not only all our fiber but also all the straw on the roof into golden threads. Why, she would even begin to work on my grey hair. So I have to leave her in peace."

"If that's the case," the overjoyed suitor said, "and if it is God's will, you could give her to me to wife. You see that I have a decent estate: heaps of flax, hemp, hair, and tow; she could spin to her heart's content."

The old woman didn't think such words over very long, but awoke Hanka from her nap. They brought the suitor an oil-dyed shirt from the trunk, washed it with periwinkle, and took care of the betrothal wreath that very evening. The other girls at the spinning party envied Hanka her luck a bit, but in the end satisfied themselves with the fact that they too would get under a bonnet[2] if "lazy hand," as they called Hana, had gotten a husband.

The next day our young son-in-law had his horses hitched up, and when they were hitched, sat the tearful bride beside himself in the nice carriage, shook hands with his mother-in-law, called out to his bride's sisters, "Good health to you here!"—and they left the village at a gallop.³

So far, so good. But dear Hanka sat tearful and sad by the young son-in-law as if the hens had eaten her bread. He tried enough to start conversation, but Hanka held her tongue like a fish. "Are you pining?" he asked. "Don't worry! You'll have no occasion to nap at my place. I'll give you whatsoever your soul desires. And you will have enough flax, hemp, hair, and tow for the entire winter. I've even scraped up some apples for spittle."⁴ But our Hanka only became sadder the farther they went.

Thus they arrived that evening at the gentleman's mansion, got out of the carriage, and, after dinner, they led the future gentlewoman into a gigantic room, which was stocked from top to bottom with fiber. "Well," he said, "here's your distaff, spindle, and bob, and red apples and a few peas for spittle—now spin! If you spin everything into golden thread by morning, we'll be wed immediately. But if not, I'll put an end to you without further ado." With that the gentleman exited and left our spinner to spin.

When Hanka was left alone, she didn't sit by the spindle, for she couldn't even spin a thread, but instead began to sadly say, "Lord, my Lord, why, I'm going to shame myself like a dog. Why didn't my mother teach me to work and spin like my sisters? I could have been resting at home in peace now, and this way, sinful being, I have to die in vain."

While she was scolding herself that way, suddenly the wall opened and in front of the startled Hanka stood a tiny man with a red cap on his head, an apron belted at the waist, and pushing a golden wheelbarrow in front of him. "Why are your eyes all cried out?" he asked Hana. "What happened to you?"

"How could a sinful soul like me not cry?" she said. "Just consider: he ordered me to spin all this fiber into golden threads by morning, and if I don't do it, he'll put an end to me with no further ado. Lord, my Lord, what shall I ever do abandoned in this foreign land!"

"If that's all," said the little man, "don't worry about a thing! I'll teach you lickety-split to spin golden threads. But only if you promise me that in one year I'll find you in this very place. At that point, if you do not guess my honorable name, you will be my wife and I will cart you away on this wheelbarrow. But if you guess it, I will leave you in peace. But I tell you, if you want to hide from me somewhere on that day at the end of the year, even if you're flying beneath the bare heavens, I'll find you and wring your neck. Well, do we have a deal?"

Hana, to be sure, did not like the idea very much, but what was the poor girl to do? In the end she thought, "I should die one way or the other; here goes, I agree!"

The little man, when he had heard that, ran around her three times with the golden wheelbarrow, sat down at the spindle, and saying:

> "This way, Hanička, so and so!
> This way, Hanička, so and so!
> This way, Hanička, so and so!"

taught her to spin golden threads until she knew how. With that he left the way he had come, and the wall closed all by itself behind him.

Our maiden, thenceforth a genuine spinner of gold, sat at the spindle and, watching how the fiber disappeared and golden threads accumulated, spun and spun, and by morning she had not only spun everything, but had even slept her fill.

In the morning, as soon as the gentleman awoke, he dressed himself and went to see the spinner of gold. When he entered the room he was nearly blinded by the glitter and refused to believe his own eyes, that it was all gold. But when he was convinced, he began to embrace the spinner of gold, and they were wed immediately.

Thus they lived in the fear of God, and if before our gentleman had loved Hanička for the golden yarn, now he loved her even more for the beautiful son she bore him in the meantime.

But to what end? There are no songs without end—and the joy of our couple couldn't last forever either. Day by day passed—until in the end, like the slap of a palm, the year came round. With that our Hanka became sadder from moment to moment, her eyes red as roast, and she just dragged from room to room like one reeling. And after all, it's no picnic to have to lose a good husband and a success of a son at one stroke! The dutiful husband as yet knew nothing and tried to cheer his wife as best he could, but she would not be cheered. When she thought that for such a man-sized husband she would get such a disgusting little pipsqueak, she did well not to climb the walls in distress.

In the end she somehow found the strength to tell her husband everything that had happened to her on that first night. He turned white as a wall from fright and had it proclaimed throughout the countryside, that whoever had known such and such a pipsqueak somewhere and let his true name be known would be given a piece of gold as big as his head.

"Eh, wouldn't that be worth a toast, so much gold?" whispered one neighbor to another, and they scattered in all directions, looked in every corner, and went so far as to check even the mouse-holes. They looked and looked as if for a needle, but couldn't uncover a thing indeed. No one had seen or known the pipsqueak, and not a single living soul could guess his name.

Thus passed the final day, without a bit of news about the little man, and our Hanka, with the boy in her arms, wrung her hands over her husband as well. The poor husband, who himself was nearly in tears, in order that he not have to witness the suffering of his wife, took his musket on his shoulder, put his best hounds on a leash, and went hunting.

During the hunt, somewhere about tea time, lightning began to flash criss-cross from all sides, the rain poured down so heavily that one wouldn't have even chased a dog out into it, and in that storm all our gentleman's servants wandered off and got lost so that he was left all alone with but a single servant in that unfamiliar forest and as wet as a mouse.

But where to take shelter against this overwhelming thunderstorm, where to dry off, where to kneel the night through? The poor fellows looked around, the servant and the gentleman, on all sides to see if they couldn't catch sight of at least a shepherd's or ox-tender's shelter. But nothing was to be seen. Finally, their eyes nearly failing, they spotted puffs of smoke coming out of a hole as if from a lime-kiln. "Go, son," the gentleman said to his servant, "and find out where that smoke is coming from. There must be people there. Ask them if they wouldn't shelter us for the night." The servant went and in no more time than it takes for a rooster to lay an egg, he returned with the news that, on his soul, there wasn't a door or a shelter or any people there.

"Aye, you're just a bungler," said the gentleman, gritting his teeth. "I'll go myself, and as a punishment you can get wet and freeze." Well and good. The gentleman started off, but indeed, he couldn't unearth a thing either, it just kept smudging from that place in the crag. In the end, vexed, he said "Even if there be devils carrying devils, I have to find out where so much smoke is coming from!"

He approached the hole itself, knelt, and looked inside. When he looked, he saw somewhere beneath the earth how food was frying and a stone table was set for two. Around that table ran some little man in a red cap with a gold wheelbarrow in front of him, and with each time around the table he sang:

> "I gave the man a spinner of gold,
> who will try to guess my name this night.
> If she guesses my name, I don't want her,
> If she fails to guess, I'll take her.
> My name is Martinko Klyngáš."[5]

And he ran again around the table like a fool and called out:

> "I'm making nine dishes for dinner,
> I'll lay her in silken sheets.
> If she guesses . . . etc."

The gentleman needed no more; he ran off as quickly as his legs would carry him to his servant, and, since it had let up a bit, with a bit of luck they found a path along which they hurried homeward.

He found his wife at home worried to death, wretched, and all cried out, for she thought that she wouldn't even be able to bid farewell to her husband, since he hadn't come for so long. "Don't worry, my dear, about a thing," were the first words of the gentleman when he entered the room. "I know what you need: his name is Martinko Klyngáš."

And with that he told her everything nicely and fittingly, where he had gone and what had happened. Hanka nearly fell over from joy, embraced her husband and covered him with kisses, and, overjoyed, went to the room where she had been spinning the first night to spin a few more golden threads.

About midnight the wall opened and the little man with the red cap came, as it was the end of the year, and running around her with the gold wheelbarrow, shouted at the top of his lungs:

"If you guess my name, I don't want you,
 If you fail to guess, I'll take you.
 Guess, just guess."

"I'll try to guess," said Hanka. "Your name is Martinko Klyngáš." No sooner had she said it than the little pipsqueak grabbed the wheelbarrow, threw his cap to the ground, and left the way he'd come, the wall closing behind him. Hanička breathed a sigh of relief.

Ever since that day she has spun no gold, but she didn't need to, for they were rich enough. They loved each other and the boy grew by leaps and bounds. And they bought a cow, and on the cow a bell, that's all there is to tell.

Notes

1. They would race in this manner: Two girls sit together and when the first is winding a thread on a bobbin, she says, "I'm rolling the barrel." The second, her competitor, asks, "Where are you rolling it?" The first again, "To Keľ 's." (Thus naming the first house in the village from the lower end.) The second answers again, "And I'm rolling to Lepiš's." (Thus naming the first house from the upper end of the village.) With the second thread, the first names the second house from the lower end, and the second names the second house from the upper end of the village, and thus by threads they pass through the entire village, not leaving out a single house. The one that traverses the entire village first wins the race.—Janko Kmeti note.

2. Traditionally, married women wore bonnets; thus, to get under a bonnet meant to get married.—Trans.

3. Another version of the tale's opening goes like this: A widow had a daughter who wouldn't learn to spin, so she led her to a spring, where she ground her fingers with stones. The girl cried from pain, and her crying was heard by a gentleman who was passing in a coach. He asked the mother why she was grinding the girl's fingers. The mother answered that the girl spun everything she touched into gold, and she wanted her to spin less. The gentleman took the girl, etc.—from the Michalovič version.

4. When spinning by hand, the spinner moistens her fingers with saliva.—Trans.

5. In some versions, Kynkaš Martinko.

❧ 6 ❧

The Gypsy Duped the Devil

The devil came to a woman and demanded something to eat, saying it was lucky he hadn't gone hooves up from hunger. She gave him an egg. But when he had swallowed it, she scared him saying the egg had been charmed, so he should prepare to lie down and have a son. The terrified devil ran up to the Gypsy in the field where he was pasturing the hogs. He begged him to help him out.

"Eh, I'll gladly help you out," said the Gypsy, "just lie flat on your back."

The devil did so and the Gypsy smacked him across the stomach with his stick so that he immediately doubled up from the blow and couldn't even say yow, his throat was so tight. But with the smack a frightened rabbit jumped out of a nearby bush and ran across the field for the forest. The Gypsy pointed him out to the devil: "See there, there goes your boy; you no longer have to fear that he will come back to you."

"Well, you're a man!" the devil praised him, and the Gypsy replied, "Indeed, I am a man! Wouldn't you like to try yourself against me?"

"And why not!"

"Well," said our moor, "which of us will press milk from those rocks?"

The devil grabbed some flint and when he pressed it, it all crumbled in his hands. But the Gypsy placed a piece of bread sopped in milk between two rocks on the sly and pressed milk from them. The devil was alarmed by him and slipped away, not stopping until he came to his mother. And his mother said to him, "Why are you so startled?"

"It's like this," said the devil, telling what had happened to him with the Gypsy.

"Eh, that's no good," said the devil's mother. "That Gypsy might light into you at any given time. You'll have to dispose of him. Go back to him and contend with him! If he perseveres, give him a sackful of money. If not, do him in."

Well and good. The devil ran to the Gypsy and said, "Gypsy, come contend with me again! I'll give you a sackful of money if you persevere. If not, I'll do you in."

"Well then, fine, if that's how you want it," said the Gypsy. First they set about determining who could carry off the most plums. The devil gathered them in a basket and the Gypsy began to turn over entire trees from their roots and gather them in a pile.

"What are you doing?" asked the devil in wonder. And the Gypsy said, "Why should I traipse about with each petty little plum? This way I'll take it all up at once, including you and the tree you're dallying on, and carry it home." The devil was frightened that he would lose his entire garden and, what's more, it might not go well for him personally. "Well," he said, "let's leave this be and try our hands at something else."

Next they set about determining who could carry off the most wood. The devil began to fell the forest, and indeed, it began to disappear beneath his axe. The Gypsy took a long rope and began to tie up the entire forest from oak to oak.

"What tricks are you up to again?" asked the devil.

"Nothing," answered the Gypsy, "but I don't want to place each log on my shoulder one by one, so I'll tie up the whole forest, tear it out and carry it off with the roots." The devil was frightened that he would lose the entire forest, so they let that be as well.

The third test was who could carry off the most water. The devil collected all the waterskins in the world, it seemed, and filled them with water so that not a drop would spill. The Gypsy collected boards and beams and made to block the entire stream.

"What are you blocking?" asked the devil.

"What am I blocking?" answered the Gypsy. "I'll stop all the water and carry it away at once." The devil was frightened that he would lose all the water.

"Leave it be," he said, "and take this sackful of money instead. Here you go!"

The Gypsy took the sackful of money and he didn't have to contend with the devil anymore, for the latter had snuck off in an easier direction!

❦ 7 ❦

Radúz and Ľudmíla

Once there was a king. The king had three sons and one daughter. "Eh, wife," he said one day to the queen, "we're a few too many. We should do something, or nothing will come of us. You know what? Let's send one of our sons into the world. Let him seek work and make his way as best he can."

"Well," said the queen, "I like the idea as well. Perhaps it would be best if we sent Radúz."

"Quite right," answered the king. "I was also thinking of him. So, send him on his way! Maybe he'll get on in the world somehow." And off they sent him.

Radúz took leave of his parents and went over hill and dale for many days until he finally came to a dense forest where there was a house. He thought: "I'll announce myself here. Maybe they'll take me into service." Three people lived in that house: a witch, her husband the warlock, and one pretty girl named Ľudmíla.

"God grant you fortune, good people!" Radúz said in obeisance as he stepped into the room.

"And to you," answered the witch. "What brings you here?"

"I've come to seek work. Won't you take me on?"

"Oh, son," said the witch, "everyone would like his bread, but few know how to earn it. What kind of work do you know?"

"Well, whatever you give me. I'll just work to the best of my abilities. I'll certainly make an effort."

The witch had little desire to take him on, but the warlock persuaded her, and in the end she agreed. Radúz rested up from the journey through the night. In the morning when he awoke, he went to the witch.

"What kind of work will you give me today, my hostess?" The witch measured him from tip to toe and led him to a certain window.

"Look out that window," she said. "What do you see there?"

"What do I see? I see a glade in the forest."

"Well, here, take this wooden hoe. You'll go to that glade, dig it up and plant trees, but in such a way that they grow, blossom, and bear fruit by morning. In the morning you'll bring me the ripe fruit. And now away with you!"

Radúz worried his head when he came to the glade: "What should I do? Why, who has heard of such a thing, such work with a wooden hoe and in such a short time!" He began to dig, but had hardly struck three times when the hoe broke. He saw that nothing would come of the work, so he threw aside the handle and sat down beneath a beech tree and, vexed, idled away the time there.

Meanwhile the witch had boiled up some frogs and ordered Ľudmíla to take them to the servant for his lunch. Ľudmíla knew what was up, and so she picked a moment when the witch went out of the room and took a wand that was on the table, taking careful note of how the wand had been lying.[1] She also thought, "How will that poor boy eat frogs? I'll take my lunch with me and give it to him."

So she left to see Radúz and found him sitting vexed under that beech. "Eh," she said, "don't worry! It's true, the lady sent you boiled frogs for lunch, but I tossed them out on the ground thinking it wouldn't be proper for you to eat them. Instead I brought you my lunch. Never fear about the work," she continued. "Behold this wand! I'll strike the ground here with it and everything will grow and blossom and bear fruit by morning, as the lady ordered." Then Radúz didn't know how to thank Ľudmíla enough.

Ľudmíla struck the ground with the wand, and fruit-bearing trees immediately were planted, grew, blossomed, and bore fruit. Radúz cheered up immediately and ate what Ľudmíla had brought him. He spoke with her and would have continued conversing until evening, but she had to hurry home.

In the morning Radúz brought the fruit and gave it to the witch. She hadn't thought that he would complete the task and just shook her head. "Well, and what kind of work will you give me today?" said Radúz after a bit. The witch led him to another window and asked him what he saw there. "What do I see? Just a rocky knoll overgrown with thorns."

"Well then, take the hoe from behind the door and go there! Clear it for me and plant vines, and in the morning bring grapes."

Radúz went and began to clear the knoll. He had hardly given one good blow with the wooden hoe when it flew into three pieces. "What'll you do, sinful man?" he thought to himself. He threw the handle aside and sat down on the rocks, vexed, for he couldn't even imagine completing the work by morning. So he sat pensively for a long time and waited to see what would happen.

At home the witch cooked him a pot of snakes and near lunchtime said, "Ľudmíla, get ready and take this food to the servant." Ľudmíla obeyed and straight-away took with her both the wand and her own lunch.

Radúz was already impatient for her to arrive, and his heart rejoiced when he saw her coming from far off. "It's good," he said, "that you came. See, I've been sitting here vexed since morning. The work is beyond me and my hoe broke. If you don't help me, things will go badly for me."

"Don't worry so much," said Ľudmíla. "It's true, the lady sent you boiled snakes, but I tossed them out on the ground and brought you my lunch. I also brought the wand. We'll make the vineyard here and tomorrow you'll bring grapes." She gave him his lunch and struck the ground with the wand. Immediately everything was planted, grew, blossomed, and bore grapes. They enjoyed each other's company a bit longer, then Ľudmíla took the pot and the wand and went home.

In the morning Radúz came with grapes. The witch couldn't believe her eyes. He asked for new work. She led him straight to the third window and told him to look what he saw. "What do I see? Just some large boulders."

"Well, by morning you have to grind me flour from them and bake bread. If you don't do it, it will go badly for you!"[2]

Radúz became somewhat afraid that she had threatened him so. But what could he do? So he went about his work. But the fruit and the grapes were spinning in the witch's head.

"Father," she said to the warlock, "it doesn't seem right. Our girl must be in alliance with the servant, otherwise he'd never manage it by himself. I have to nose it out and then I'll pay them both back. I'll go with the lunch myself."

"Eh!" said the warlock, "what are you saying? Ľudmíla is a good girl. We've tested her loyalty countless times. There's no doubt about her. Leave it be. What good is it to spy on them?"

"Well then, father, you'll see. It still irks me."

"Irksome or not," said the warlock, "that's enough! You'll not sin on me that way." And the witch fell silent.

Meanwhile she cooked up some lizards and sent Ľudmíla off with lunch. To be sure, Ľudmíla had caught wind of the old folks' conspiracy and of what the warlock had grumbled. And that's why she stole the wand carefully from the table, hid it under her apron, and left with the pot as if she didn't know a thing.

Radúz was just chipping away at the rocks—but no flour or bread was to be seen. He waited anxiously for Ľudmíla and finally spotted her hurrying his way. "I was supposed to bring you boiled lizards," she said from afar, "but it bothered me that they were sending you such a disgusting lunch, so I brought mine instead." And she gave it to him very willingly. "The lady already suspects that I am helping you, but the old man turned her thoughts to better things. She nearly brought you lunch herself, God forbid! She would have figured out right away what we are doing, and that would have been the end of both you and me."

"Ah, dear soul, I see what a help you are to me," said Radúz. "Only how shall I ever repay you?" They would have gladly bantered on for a long time, but Ľudmíla reminded him that they had to think of his work. So she struck the boulders with the wand and a mill immediately appeared and the millstone ground. Flour poured out in a trough, the bread rose, and the stove burned. Then Ľudmíla got ready and hurried home.

In the morning Radúz brought bread and the witch nearly exploded from rage. But she said nothing, except: "I see that you've managed everything I ordered. Now you can rest up from your work."

Evening came. The old woman discussed something with the old man and ordered Radúz to fill the kettle with water. When he had brought the water, she set the old man by the kettle to boil the water and to awaken her when it boiled. But Ľudmíla brought the old man some powerful wine and he fell asleep from it. Then she came to Radúz and told him, "You see how things stand: they'll cook you in that kettle if they find you still here in the morning. But I'll set you free and go with you if you swear to me that you'll never forget me."

Radúz gladly swore to that, for he wouldn't have given her up for the whole world anyway. Then Ľudmíla spat on one log on the fire, took the magic wand with her, and they hurried away.[3]

The warlock awoke not much later. "Servant," he said, "are you still sleeping?"

"I'm not," answered the spittle, "but I'm still stretching."

After a while the warlock again spoke: "Servant, get up! Give me my boots!"

"Right away, right away!" answered the spittle. "Just wait a bit until I lace up my own boots!"

With that the witch awoke: "Ľudmíla, get up! Give me my petticoat and skirt!"

"Right away, right away!" answered the spittle. "Just let me get myself up!"

"Why is it," asked the witch, "that you are taking so long to get dressed?"

"Straight-away," answered the spittle.

The witch lost patience and raised her head and she saw only an empty bed. "What the devil, father, why on my soul, they're not here! You see their empty beds? They ran off!"

"Parom's bolt strike them!" answered the warlock. Then they got up and the witch just grumbled, "That's your faithful little Ľudmíla for you. She behaved nicely for you. Just go ahead and believe the girl the next time, you old stiff!" The old man was chastened. "And now fly after them at once, so you catch them right away and lead them back here." The old man up and flew off.

With that Ľudmíla said to Radúz, "My, if my left cheek isn't burning! Look back, my dear. What do you see behind us?"

"Nothing," he said, "except one black cloud flying behind us."

"Well, that's the old man on a black fairy horse," said Ľudmíla. "Stop here, we have to do something!" And she struck the wand on the ground, which turned into a plowed field. She turned herself into a bunch of wheat and stood him there to reap the wheat and answer wisely when the old man came. Then the old man tore up on the black cloud with a storm and hail, nearly crushing all the wheat.

"Ah, old man," the reaper said to him, "if you don't crush all the wheat I still may have some profit from it."

"Why, I'll leave it for you," answered the old man and he flew down. "But tell me if you didn't see two young people run this way?"

"Oh, as long as I've been reaping here not a soul has passed this way. But when they were sowing this wheat they say two such passed through here."

The warlock shook his head, lost himself in the cloud and went home. Radúz and Ľudmíla went on right away.

"What have you accomplished, master," said the witch to the old man, "that you are returning so soon?" And he replied, "Who knows where they went. I didn't see a soul, just a reaper and some wheat."

"Well, what do you think? That was them. Ah, to be deceived so! Couldn't you have at least brought a head of that wheat home? Get after them."

The old man flew off, chastened.

"My," said Ľudmíla, "if my left cheek isn't burning! Look back, Radúz, look what's happening behind us."

"Nothing," he said, "except one grey cloud is flying behind us."

"Well, that's the old man on a grey fairy horse. But never fear, just answer wisely!" Then she struck her hat with the wand and it became a little church. She turned herself into a fly and made a bunch of other flies around her. She made Radúz into the hermit of that little church to preach to the flies there.

With that the grey cloud flew up with snow and such a freeze that the roof just cracked. The warlock dismounted from the fairy horse and went to the hermit in the little church. "Haven't you seen two wayfarers here?" he asked. "One girl and one lad?"

"What would have brought them here?" answered the hermit. "I've just been preaching to these flies as long as I've been here. Only one time, back when they were building this church, two such passed this way. But you shouldn't let in so much cold," he said, "or all my audience will freeze."

"Well, never fear, I'll come back. I've just wasted my energy so far." And with that he flew away.

The old woman was waiting for him in the yard, and when she saw him coming alone, she shouted at him right away, "You ninny, you're not bringing anyone again! Where did you leave them?"

"Where should I leave them if I didn't see them? Nothing but a little church was there and a hermit was preaching to the flies in it. And I let in so much cold that everything nearly froze at once."

"Why you fool, that was them. Couldn't you have at least brought back a shingle? Just you wait, I'll get them!" With that she up and flew off.

"My," Ľudmíla said again, "if my left cheek isn't burning! Look back, Radúz, and see if someone isn't chasing us."

"Indeed, a red cloud is catching up to us."

"That's the old witch on a red fairy horse. Up to now it's been easy enough, but now you'll have to be brave to deceive her. Look, I'll turn myself into a golden duck and swim about on this sea. You submerge yourself in the water so she won't burn you, and when she chases me, leap up to her horse and grab him by the halter and then have no fear!"

With that the old woman rode up with such flames that everything around burned up. She dismounted from the fairy horse by the sea and began to chase the duck. But it kept enticing her further and further, until it had lured her far away from the horse. Then Radúz leapt out of the sea and grabbed the horse by the halter. The duck flew up to him quickly and turned into a maiden. They mounted the fairy horse and flew away over the sea.

When the witch saw that she began to curse terribly. She cursed Radúz so that he would forget Ľudmíla the moment he was kissed by someone the first time. And she called out to Ľudmíla, "You, my girl, you shan't live with that scoundrel for seven years."

The witch had to complete the entire trip back on foot. She lost all her powers and her husband laughed at her, that she had let herself be so deceived.

Only now did Radúz and Ľudmíla really fly on that fairy horse, until they arrived at the town where Radúz's parents lived. "What's new here?" he asked one townsman they met in the town.

"Well, what else?" the townsman answered. "Our king and his sons and daughter died, and only the old queen remains. And all she does is cry constantly for a son who is somewhere out in the world. That's why we have nothing but quarrels and intrigues over who will be king."

"They died?" said Radúz. "Well, that's no good indeed." Then he left the townsman and called Ľudmíla aside. "You know what we'll do? You stay here by this well, for I can't take you before my mother as you are, in torn clothes. Hide in that thick-spreading tree and wait for me to return. Meanwhile I'll go in and when they recognize me and make me king I'll come with nice clothes for you."

Ľudmíla agreed and Radúz went into the castle. His mother recognized him immediately and ran to him with outspread arms, hugged him joyfully and tried to kiss him, but he wouldn't let her. The others also recognized him, proclaimed him king, prepared a great feast, and celebrated happily.

Radúz, worn out from the trip, lay down before the others to rest, and when he was sleeping his mother came and kissed both his cheeks. From then on he forgot completely about his Ľudmíla. He even married another later on.

The abandoned Ľudmíla lamented a long time, wondering what to do now. She had nowhere to go, poor thing, so she stood herself in the yard of a farmer not far from the castle and grew into a beautiful poplar. The poplar was an ornament for the entire countryside, let alone the yard, and only bothered the king himself. It irked him that he couldn't see far out of his window. Finally he lost patience and ordered it felled. The farmer begged him not to have the nice tree cut down, but even begging was of no use and the king had the poplar felled.

Not long after that a beautiful pear tree sprouted up right below the castle, and it bore golden pears. When they gathered them in the evening, by morning it was again heavy with fruit. The king had them gathered every day and the tree was very dear to him. But the queen was constantly angry with it. "If only that pear tree would die as soon as possible," said the queen. "That tree vexes me so."

The king begged and persuaded her to leave it be, since it was so pretty. But the queen insisted so much that the king had it felled according to her will.

By then the seven years was coming to an end. So Ľudmíla turned into a golden duck and swam back and forth under the royal window, quacking. The king finally caught sight of it and it occurred to him that he had seen such a duck somewhere before. So he ordered it caught. But there wasn't a single person who could catch that duck. Then he had fishermen and birders summoned from all over the land, but even they couldn't catch it. This bothered the king more and more every day.

"If that's how it is, that no one can do my will," he said one day, "I'll try my own luck." And he set out for the lake and after the duck. The duck led him hither and thither for a long time and he followed right along. Finally he caught her. No sooner did he have her in hand than the golden duck turned into beautiful Ľudmíla and said, "You certainly rewarded me poorly for my faithfulness! But I'll forgive you, for it could not have been otherwise."

The delighted Radúz took his Ľudmíla to the castle and led her straight to the old queen. "Here's the one," he said, "who saved my life so many times. She will be my wife and no other." He let the other wife go right away and took Ľudmíla. They held twice as big a wedding and lived together happily—and they're still living today, if they haven't died.[4]

Notes

1. According to other versions, it was a fife; when she piped on it, everything happened as it was supposed to.
2. According to other versions, his third task consisted in emptying a lake of water with a net, plowing the ground that remained, sowing wheat, and baking bread from it by morning. Ľudmíla threw a small stone into the lake and it immediately dried up, was plowed, grew, etc.
3. According to other writers, they turned into doves and flew away.
4. The end of the tale can also be that Ľudmíla got into the king's castle as a seamstress and before Radúz's eyes turned three magic wands into doves that spoke to him: "Radúz, Radúz, you've forgotten your Ľudmíla." He remembered her then, sent away his first wife, and took Ľudmíla.
Or: Radúz long refused to marry, and finally had it proclaimed that he would marry the one who embroidered him the prettiest flower. Ľudmíla embroidered the prettiest flower and so won him.
Or: She remained hidden in that tree by the well for seven years. Then the king's oxen were going that way to pasture in the mountains, but they couldn't pass the tree because Ľudmíla chanted at them:

> "Oxen, oxen, don't forget your strength
> Like your master his Ľudmíla true."

That happened twice. The third time Radúz himself came. Ľudmíla came down out of the tree and he recognized her, had a beautiful dress brought to her, and so she returned to the castle with him.
Another title of the tale is "Janko and Ivanka."

❧ 8 ❧

The Golden Horseshoe, the Golden Feather, and the Golden Hair

There was a peasant who had twelve sons, but they never called the youngest one "brother." The twelve of them all left once to enter service, and they came to a certain king. "Your Glorious Majesty, would you take us into service?"

"Why not?" said the king. "Just serve honestly!"

They served there for one year. And when the year had passed, the king asked them, "Well, what have you earned?"

"Your Glorious Majesty! Just give us each a single ox!"

"Good," said the king. "There is the herd. Choose the ones you like!"

The servants went to the herd, chose twelve nice oxen, and so returned home.

"Run and call father out!" they said to the youngest. Father came out in the yard and saw twelve nice oxen.

"Well," he said, "you behaved honestly, I like that."

After a while, all twelve of them again left to enter service. They came to the same king. "Your Glorious Majesty, won't you take us into service again?"

"Why not?" said the king. "Just serve honestly!"

They served for another year. And when the year had passed, the king asked them, "Well, what have you earned?"

"Your Glorious Majesty! Give us each a single cow!"

"Good," said the king. "There is the herd. Choose the ones you like!"

The servants went to the herd, chose twelve nice cows, and arrived home again.

"Run and call father out!" they said to the youngest. Father came out in the yard and saw twelve nice cows.

"Well," he said, "again you behaved well, I like that."

Now they had twelve oxen and twelve cows, but they wanted still more. Again all twelve left to enter service and stopped at that king's out of familiarity. "Your Glorious Majesty! We would still like to serve you!"

"I don't mind," said the king. "Just serve me honestly again!"

Again they served a year. When the year had passed, the king asked, "Well, what shall I give you now?"

"Your Glorious Majesty! Just give us each a single horse!"

"Good," said the king. "There's the herd. Choose the ones you like!"

The servants went to the herd and eleven of them chose the finest horses, but the twelfth one, the youngest, just walked about among the horses. He was afraid to take a large one for fear it would brush him off and afraid to take a wild one for fear it would carry him off.

He left the herd without a horse. As he was walking along, a pony was grazing in a pool and that pony told him, "Janko, take me, I'll be of great assistance. And when we come to the king, they will give you the nicest saddle, but don't take it. Just ask for the one that has lain in the loft for seven years . . ."

So it was.

The king needled him, asking if he would really take it, but he wanted no other. So the king had it cleaned and oiled for him.

As they rode out over the town, his brothers were already a five-mile piece ahead. The fairy horse asked, "Janko, how shall we go, like the sun or like the wind?"

"Just so, my pony, so that neither you nor I shall be injured."

The pony shook itself once and Janko became copper and the pony copper, and they arrived at the inn sooner than his brothers. The brothers arrived, and Janko was sitting at the table. "Have the evil ones brought you already?" they shouted at him.

"Who, me? I just make my way slowly along the path, but you, who knows along what crow's paths."

And they replied, "Silence, you fool! You should have gone with us. You would have seen a prince who was all copper, and even his steed was copper." Janko hushed up and said not a word more.

When they left that inn, his brothers were far off from him. The pony asked him, "Janko, how shall we go, like the sun or like the wind?"

"Just so, my pony, so that neither you nor I shall be injured."

The pony shook itself and Janko became silver and the pony silver. They ran ahead of his brothers and stopped at the inn. The brothers arrived, and Janko was sitting at the table. "Maybe the evil ones brought you again?" they attacked him.

"Who, me? I just make my way slowly along the path, but you, who knows along what crow's paths."

And they replied, "Silence, you fool! You should have gone with us. You would have seen a prince who was all silver, even his steed was silver." Janko hushed up and said not a word more.

The eleven set out and ran ahead. Janko could barely put one leg in front of the other. Beyond the inn the pony asked, "Janko, how shall we go, like the sun or like the wind?"

"Just so, my pony, so that neither you nor I shall be injured." The pony shook itself: Janko became gold and the pony gold. Janko was home sooner than his brothers. His brothers arrived and Janko was sitting by the stove. "Look at him," they marveled, "why, he's here again! What devil carried you home sooner?"

"Who, me? I just make my way slowly along the path, but you, who knows along what crow's paths."

And they replied, "Silence, you fool! You should have gone with us. You would have seen a prince who was all gold, even his steed was gold." Janko hushed up, afraid to utter a word. Father wasn't home just then, and when he came, he praised the older ones for their fine horses, but Janko got an earful for his mangy nag.

The next day they told their father, "Father, we have served enough. Now we shall marry. We are all of the same father, so find us maidens of the same mother." The oldest saddled his horse, father mounted and went to find those brides.

As he was going along, he saw an old granny plowing with six steeds. He asked her if she didn't know of a mother with twelve girls. And she told him to go on, that he would find them in such and such a house. And it was her, the old crone, who had twelve girls. She cracked her whip over the heads of the steeds and was straight-away home.

When father arrived at that house, they were very glad to see him, and he requested to see the maidens. With that the witch ran to the stable, took the whip from behind the door and as she struck each horse in turn, there were twelve maidens right away.

"Out, you nags," shouted the old woman, "some suitors have come for you." And they went one after the other into the room from the eldest to the youngest. Father liked the girls and they immediately settled on when they should come for the wedding. On the appointed day, the twelve sons saddled their horses and went for their brides.

When they arrived at the wedding house, the fairy horse told Janko, "They are going to try to seat you in the middle. Don't sit even on the edge, but make the excuse that as you're the youngest brother you have to watch out for the horses. And when I stomp, come out! They'll offer you the first goblet to drink. Take that goblet and pour it out beneath the table. Its contents will become a glass. Hide that glass quickly in your pouch!"

Janko went into the room and did just so. He had the glass in his pouch.

The fairy horse stomped and Janko went out. The fairy horse told Janko, "They'll offer you soup, but the first spoonful you take, pour it out under the table. It will become a brush. Take the brush and hide it in your pouch!"

Janko went into the room and did everything so. Now he had the brush in his pouch, too. The fairy horse stomped and Janko went out. The fairy horse told Janko, "They will place a roast before you on the table, but throw the first piece under the table along with the fork! It will become a comb. The old granny will gather something is up and will move to give you the fork, but you hurry and take that comb and hide it in your pouch! Then eat assured!"

Janko went into the room and did everything just so. He had the comb in his pocket and then he ate his fill. After they had eaten, they lay down to sleep, each in his own bed, and each maiden in hers. In a while, the old witch lay down too.

The fairy horse stomped and Janko came out. The fairy horse told Janko, "Place your brothers where the maidens are sleeping and the maidens where your brothers are lying. Make no mistake about it, then lie down yourself!"

No sooner had he moved them and changed his own place than the witch came with a sword straight to the beds. She twisted their hair about her hand and lopped off the heads of all twelve maidens—she thought they were the lads. Overjoyed that she had twelve souls, she went to sleep.

The fairy horse stomped and Janko came out. The fairy horse told Janko, "Awaken your brothers and have them saddle their horses and ride on ahead. You stay behind to shut the door." The brothers arose, saddled their horses and flew ahead. Janko stayed behind to shut the door. He shut the door and the fairy horse spoke up, "Janko, mount up, and don't stop me no matter what you see along the way!"

He mounted and when they were flying by the window he called out, "Granny, granny, old granny who killed her maidens, we thank you for the supper!" The witch was startled out of her dreams and ran to the maidens, but the maidens were dead! It's a wonder she didn't explode in rage! She sat on her shovel and set out to chase them down. But they were far off.

"You wait," grumbled the old granny, "why, I'll stop you!" And she threw a golden horseshoe.

"Eh, pony," Janko called out, "there's a *golden horseshoe* on the road. Should I pick it up?"

And the fairy horse answered him, "If you pick it up, things will go badly, if you don't, they'll go worse!" Janko jumped down and picked up the horseshoe, but while he was fooling around with the horseshoe, the witch caught up to them.

"Things are bad, Janko," called out the fairy horse. "Cast the comb on the ground!" Janko dropped the comb, which turned into a thickly wooded mountain. While the witch was clawing her way over the mountain, they ran off quite a way again.

"You wait! Why, I'll get you!" and she threw a *golden feather*.

"Eh, pony," Janko called out, "there's a golden feather on the road. Can I pick it up?"

And the fairy horse told him, "If you pick it up, things will go badly, but if you don't, they'll go worse!" Janko jumped down and picked up the feather. With that the hag again caught up to them so that the pony's tail was burned, since flames burned in her gorge.

"Things are bad, Janko," called out the fairy horse. "Cast the brush on the ground!" Janko parted with the brush, which turned into a sharp thornbush. While the hag clawed her way through the thorns, they ran off quite a way again.

"You wait! You'll not escape me!" and she threw a *golden hair*.

"Eh, pony," Janko called out, "there's a golden hair on the road! Can I pick it up?"

"If you pick it up, things will go badly, but if you don't, they'll go worse!" Janko picked up the golden hair, and while he was fooling around, the witch was on their heels and grabbing for the horse's tail.

"Things are bad, Janko," called out the fairy horse. "Throw the glass!" Janko threw the glass, which turned into a great sea. She couldn't chase them over the sea and had to return in shame, while they arrived home happily. Now Janko had peace from his brothers, for they were glad he had saved them from death. They didn't call him names anymore and he was "little brother" to everyone. But Janko was sad that they hadn't called him brother before. So he left his father and brothers, saddled up the fairy horse, and went to seek work.

After they had been traveling a long time, a town appeared before them.[1] "Janko," the fairy horse spoke up, "do you see that town? A king lives there, and you should ask to enter service there. When they take you, behave honestly! Don't cause any problems for the gentleman, and if you lack anything, just tell me and I will be of assistance!"

When they were entering the town, the fairy horse shook himself. He became thin straight away and all covered in tow as if he hadn't been combed in twelve years. Janko approached the king: "Your Glorious Majesty, won't you take me into service?"

"And why not?" said the king. "I just happen to lack one servant."

They gave him twelve horses to care for, and the thirteenth, the fairy horse, stood in the corner. The other servants who were there burned a pound of candles every week;[2] but Janko took nothing, and his horses were still the finest. The king wondered greatly at this and cursed the other servants for burning a lot of light though their horses were still worse. This vexed the servants.

"Just wait," one said, "we have to find out, what sort of ruse does he have?"

And that very evening they espied through a crevice that a golden horseshoe shone by the horses. That was all they needed. Right away the next morning they went with a complaint. "Your Glorious Majesty! We know now why he doesn't burn candles. Why, he has a golden horseshoe that makes light for him." When the king heard this, he had Janko summoned immediately.

"You," he said, "what kind of horseshoe do you have? Bring it here at once or I'll have you done in without further ado." Janko went to the stable, threw his arms around the fairy horse and broke into sobs.

The fairy horse asked, "Janko, why are you crying? What's wrong with you?"

"Ah, my pony, why shouldn't I cry when the master told me that if I don't give him the horseshoe, he'll have me done in without further ado."

And the fairy horse answered, "I told you if you picked it up things would go badly; but if you hadn't picked it up, things would have been worse. Don't cry, Janko. Give it to him!"

Janko brought the horseshoe, thinking he would be left alone. But the king asked him, "Where did you get that horseshoe?"

"In such and such a place, I found it on the road!"

The king stared, then looked back and forth from his servant to the horseshoe, and said in the end, "Look, I don't care where in the world you found it, but listen well to what I tell you. If you don't obtain the horse for me from which this horseshoe came, I'll have you done in. But if you bring it, you'll receive a lot of money."

He returned to the stable and, crying, said, "Ah, my pony, after all he told me that if I don't obtain the horse that the horseshoe is from, he'll have me done in. But if I bring it, I'll receive a lot of money."

"Well, don't worry so, what will be will be," answered the fairy horse. "Just fodder me honestly, for tomorrow we set out."

It had just begun to lighten and they were under way. They flew over hill, over dale, until they came to the hag's house, and by then it was already night.[3] The fairy horse stopped and said, "Here we are, Janko, and we've come just in time. Our old crone is asleep now and has that horse in the barn. Go in quietly, pull out the keys slowly from under the pillow, throw the sword that is lying by her side somewhere into a corner, open the barn, and lead the horse here! Just be careful and come back quickly!"

Janko did everything to a T. He pulled the keys out from under the pillow, threw the sword into a corner, opened the barn, and a flash of light from the golden horse stopped him. He untied it and led it to the fairy horse.

"Mount up," said the fairy horse. "And hold on to the horse firmly!"

Janko mounted the fairy horse, and when they were flying by the window he called out, "Granny, granny, old granny who killed her maidens, we are leading off the golden horse!" The hag jumped up and tried to grab the sword, but it was gone. By the time she had searched the corners for it, they had flown over three hills. Only when they were already by the sea did the witch see them, and she called out, "Janko, will you come see me again, will you?"

"I will, I will, but take more care of your keys!"

The witch lost her power by the sea and had to return in shame, while they led the golden horse home.

The king was quite pleased with the horse and had it placed in a separate, opulent barn. He praised Janko, but he didn't want to recall the fact that he had promised him money. Janko was vexed that he had been gotten rid of so easily and went to address the king, but his fairy horse said, "Just leave him be and be patient!"

As before, Janko took care of twelve horses, and the thirteenth, the fairy horse, stood in the corner. And the other servants spied on him, because even now he took no candles, and his horses were still the finest.

The king wondered greatly at this and cursed the other servants. "What kind of work is this?" he said. "He no longer has the golden horseshoe and your horses are still worse, yet you burn so much of my light?"

"Your Glorious Majesty! What need has he of candles when he has a golden feather!"

When the king heard this, he had Janko summoned immediately. "I hear," he said, "that you have a golden feather. Bring it to me at once, or I shall do you in without further ado."

Janko went to the stable and threw his arms around the fairy horse and broke into sobs. The fairy horse asked him, "Why are you crying again? What's wrong with you?"

"Ah, my pony, why shouldn't I cry when the master told me that if I don't give him the golden feather, he'll have me done in without further ado."

And the fairy horse answered, "I told you if you picked it up things would go badly; but if you hadn't picked it up, things would have been worse. Don't cry, Janko. Give it to him!"

Janko brought the golden feather. The king stared, then looked back and forth from his servant to the feather. "Look," he finally spoke, "you brought me the golden horse, but you must also obtain the duck from which this feather fell for me. If you do so, you'll get half my kingdom. But if not, I'll have you done in."

He returned to the stable and, crying, began to say, "Ah, my pony, after all, he told me again that if I don't get the duck from which that feather fell, he'll have me done in. But if I get it, I'll get half the kingdom."

"Well, don't worry so. What will be will be! Just fodder me honestly, for tomorrow we set out!"

It had just begun to lighten and they were already under way. They flew over hill, over dale, until they came to the hag's house, and by then it was already night.

"Here we are, Janko," said the fairy horse, "and we've come just in time. Our old crone is asleep again and the duck is sitting on twelve eggs in the other room in a golden cage, and every day she lays another. Go in silently, but be careful not to awaken the old crone, for now she has the keys around her waist! Pull them out slowly, break the sword laying by her side and scatter it in the yard, open the door to the room and bring the duck along with everything! Just go quietly and come back quickly!"

Janko did everything to a T. He pulled the keys from her waist slowly, broke the sword and scattered it in the yard, opened the door to the room, grabbed the cage with the duck, and brought it to the fairy horse.

"Mount up," said the fairy horse, "and hold on to the cage firmly!" Janko mounted the fairy horse and when they were flying by the window, he called out, "Granny, granny, old granny who killed her maidens, we are carrying off your golden duck!" The hag jumped up and tried to grab the sword, but it was gone. By the time she had gathered the pieces in the yard, run to the smith and had it welded and soldered, they had flown over five hills. Only when they were already by the sea did the witch see them. "Janko, will you come see me again, will you?"

"I will, I will, but take more care of your keys!"

The witch lost her power by the sea and had to return in shame, while they carried the golden duck home.

The king was very pleased by the golden duck and hung it in its cage over his bed. He praised Janko, patted his back, but that he had promised him half his kingdom, that he had forgotten already. Janko was even more vexed that he just made him promises and didn't fulfill them. He wanted to go straight before the king, but his fairy horse restrained him: "Just leave him be and be patient."

As before, he took care of twelve horses, and the thirteenth, the fairy horse, stood in the corner. He took no candles even now, and still his horses were the finest. And the other servants kept an eye on him. The king wondered greatly at this and cursed the other servants, "What kind of work is this?" he said. "He no longer has the golden horseshoe nor the golden feather and your horses are still worse, and I can hardly keep you in enough light!"

"Your Glorious Majesty! What need has he of candles when he has a golden hair!"

When the king heard this, he had Janko summoned immediately. "You," he said, "what kind of golden hair do you have again? Bring it here at once or I shall have you quartered."

Janko went to the stable and threw his arms around the fairy horse and broke into sobs. The fairy horse asked him, "Janko, why, you're crying away again. What's wrong with you?"

"Ah, my pony, why shouldn't I cry when the master told me that if I don't give him the golden hair, he'll quarter me?"

And the fairy horse answered, "I told you if you picked it up things would go badly; but if you hadn't picked it up, things would have been worse. Don't cry, Janko. Give it to him!"

Janko brought the golden hair. The king stared, then looked back and forth from his servant to the hair, and said finally, "Look, you've already brought me the golden horse, and I already have the golden duck, but you must also obtain the one who lost this hair for me. If you manage it, I'll give you my whole kingdom. But if not, I'll have you done in."

He returned to the stable and, crying, began to say, "Ah, my pony, after all he told me again that if I don't get the one who lost that hair, he'll have me done in. But if I get it, he'll give me the whole kingdom."

"Well, don't worry so. What will be will be! Just fodder me honestly, for tomorrow we set out!"

It had just begun to lighten and they were under way again. They flew over hill, over dale, until they came to the hag's house, and it was so dark you could cut it with a knife.

"Here we are, Janko," said the fairy horse, "and we've come just in time. Our old crone is asleep again and has the maiden in the third room behind glass. Enter quietly, but it's no joke to get the keys this time, for now she's holding them in her teeth, and if she awakens, it would be our ruin. As slowly as you can, pull the keys from between her teeth, break the sword in pieces, and throw it out the window. Then open the door to the third room, and worry not, the golden maiden will gladly go with you. But I tell you, don't dare kiss her or it would go badly for us. Just go quietly and return quickly!"

Janko did everything to a T: he pulled the keys out from between her teeth quietly, broke the sword and threw it out the window, and went to open the third room. With that the golden maiden sparkled in his eyes like the sun and smiled at him sweetly. He ran straight up to her and all but kissed her immediately, but he recalled the fairy horse's words after all. So he just took her by the right hand and led her to the fairy horse.

"You're a man, Janko," said the fairy horse. "And now mount up, both of you!"

The golden maiden and Janko both mounted, and when they were flying by the window he called out, "Granny, granny, old granny. We are carrying off your golden maiden."

The hag jumped up and tried to grab her sword, but it was gone. By the time she had gathered the pieces in the street, run to the smith and had it welded and soldered, they had flown over seven hills. Only when they were already by the sea did the witch see them. "Janko, will you come see me again, will you?" she shouted after them.

And he answered back, "I shan't, granny. As far as I'm concerned you can live in peace." When the witch heard that he wouldn't return to her, she cursed them horribly and turned to pitch out of rage.

The fairy horse and Janko and the golden maiden flew happily home. Then the king didn't know for great joy whether he was sitting or standing, and wanted the maiden to marry him immediately. But indeed, in the end she was not willing and said she would only marry the one who liberated her. The king pleaded and threatened, but all in vain. She didn't even want to see him.

Then, in anger and rage he got the worst idea: to execute Janko. For it seemed to him that when the other met his ruin, she would love him. And he immediately let Janko know that he must die at such and such a time, but he would leave it up to him to choose the manner of death he wanted.

When he heard the bad tidings, he nearly fell over. He cried and lamented, poor thing, like a baby, and called out unceasingly, "Why, I deserve it, I deserve it!"

And his fairy horse spoke up from the corner, "Janko, why, you're crying again! What's wrong with you?"

"Ah, my pony, what's wrong with me? The king gave me word that I have to die at such and such a time, but I have to choose my own death."

"That's no joke," said the fairy horse, "but wait, we'll find a way out of it. Request that they boil a large cauldron of milk and that they boil you in it. But beg them to lead me to you; tell them you want to say farewell to me."

The next day the king had Janko summoned. "Well," he said, "have you come up with something already?"

And Janko answered, "If that's how it is, that I must die, then boil me in a cauldron of milk."

The milk was boiling in the cauldron and Janko stood sadly beside it. "Oh," he said, "I ask but one thing of you, bring my pony here so I can take my final leave of him."

"Bring it to him," said the king, and the fairy horse came.

When the milk was boiling at its peak, Janko was supposed to jump into it. But the fairy horse drew all the heat from the cauldron into itself with one breath. The lad jumped in and turned completely golden.

When the king saw this, he too had the desire to pretty himself so. He ordered Janko to get out quickly. Janko jumped out and the king jumped in. With that the fairy horse blew all the heat back into the cauldron with one breath. The king passed out immediately and boiled away completely.

The pretty stolen one married Janko, who was made king in place of the one boiled to pieces. Ever since, he has had it good, and his fairy horse too, at his side.

Notes

1. Some add: They came to a meadow where the fairy horse stopped and told Janko to go to such and such a place, to a king's to enter service, saying that he would remain there, but would come to visit him every day, just so he would save him some hearty food.

2. Others indicate that they were his brothers.

3. Others tell that they arrived while it was still evening. The old crone seemed to welcome them nicely: "Welcome, Janko!" she said. But she thought to herself, "You wait, tomorrow you'll stop being Janko, since you're here!" She gave them food and drink, but he didn't drink anything. After dinner he said he was going to look after his horse and that's when the fairy horse gave him advice about what to do when the old woman fell asleep.

❦ 9 ❦

Brother Birdie

Somewhere in a little cottage in the desolate forest there lived two children with their witch-stepmother, like two birdies with a cat. Their father came home from wood-cutting only occasionally, but even then the poor orphans didn't dare to complain how their mother beat them and starved them, for they thought: It's been bad until now, but afterward it would be even worse!

And so they kept quiet and suffered. Their stepmother ran the house for herself alone, for her own gullet, as best she could, until she had run everything nicely into the ground. Once when her hungry husband was to come home from work, there wasn't a thing in either the bin or the trunk. She began to tug her bonnet to the right and then to the left on her head, trying to think what to cook for her husband. Then she had an unfortunate idea! Just as the boy ran inside with some wood chips, passing his sister, she shut the door behind him and with a long knife, swoosh! cut off the dear boy's head! Then she butchered him, cut him up, put him in the pot, and cooked a sour soup from him.

When father came home, his dinner was already waiting on the table. He dug into it like a man, without noticing anything amiss. Why, he would have eaten even what the old devil himself placed before him, he was so hungry. The girl just looked on sadly from the corner at her unfortunate father; but she dared not say what she knew. She just gathered up the little bones one by one as they fell beneath the table, and when she had gathered them all, the poor child snuck out and buried them along the road beneath a green dog-rose.

In the morning at dawn a pretty little bird was chirping on the already-blooming dog-rose, chirping so shrilly, as if its heart were being cut open:

> "Mommy put me to the knife, Daddy ate me whole.
> And my sissy, that poor missy,
> gathered up the bones and then
> 'neath the dog-rose buried them:

Up sprouted a birdie,
a wretched little birdie.
Tweet-tweet, tweet-tweet!"

Some peddlers were just passing that way and stopped to hear the pretty
bird. It touched them so much that upon leaving they placed their finest silk
kerchief on the dog-rose, on the grave of the unfortunate orphan, for the
song.

Soon after them some hatters came by, and the birdie just hopped about
the green dog-rose and sang:

"Mommy put me to the knife, Daddy ate me whole.
And my sissy, that poor missy,
gathered up the bones and then
'neath the dog-rose buried them:
Up sprouted a birdie,
a wretched little birdie.
Tweet-tweet, tweet-tweet!"

The master hatters stood stock still—they couldn't even move until the
song was over. Then they took out the nicest hat: "Eh," one said, "since you
sang so nicely for us, we shall give you something in exchange!" and hooked
it on a thorn.

In a moment the birdie began again:

"Mommy put me to the knife, Daddy ate me whole.
And my sissy, that poor missy,
gathered up the bones and then
'neath the dog-rose buried them:
Up sprouted a birdie,
a wretched little birdie.
Tweet-tweet, tweet-tweet!"

Some stonecutters who were passing by couldn't get enough of that shrill
song. "Eh," one of them said, "since you sang so nicely for us, we'll have to
give you a nice stone on that green grave!" And just as they said, so they did:
they rolled the largest stone up under the dog-rose.

During the night—God only knows how—the pretty birdie carried all the
gifts to the top of father's roof, and early in the morning it began to sing:

"Mommy put me to the knife, Daddy ate me whole.
And my sissy, that poor missy,

gathered up the bones and then
'neath the dog-rose buried them:
Up sprouted a birdie,
a wretched little birdie.
Tweet-tweet, tweet-tweet!"

Sister ran out after the dear voice, asking who or what it was. She looked about on all sides, but she didn't figure anything out until a pretty silk kerchief fell down into her hands.

Right behind her came father, marveling. A brand-new hat fell on his head.

"What in God's name is going on?" said stepmother, running out in joy that something would remain for her too. Hardly had she stepped out from under the roof when—crash came the stone down on her head!

With that the birdie stopped singing and flew off, flew way off to the end of the world! Whoever wants to know more about him, let them go there.

10

Lomidrevo or Valibuk

Once there was a woman, old, it's true, but healthy and lively. She gave birth, in her ninetieth year, to a son. Following his birth, his mother and father couldn't marvel enough at their extraordinarily large and strong child. The neighbors and other acquaintances all came for a look, and in the end, when word had got around, people even from other countries came to look the boy over, for no one could recall that any woman anywhere had given birth to such a child.

In the meantime the question had arisen, how were they to name him? They sought advice here and there, but to no avail, until finally a woman said, "That child is unusually large, so give him an unusual name as well."

"Quite right, granny," said the father. "We will call him Lomidrevo." And so they did.

"Mother dear, oh mother, you know what?" said the father sometime later. "If the Lord God will keep us, you should nurse that boy for seven years, and just maybe something worthwhile will become of him."[1]

"Well then, yes," said the woman, "if that's what you want, so be it." And so it was.

The mother nursed the boy and the boy grew stronger day by day. The parents didn't know where to hide in their amazement when they saw him, in his third year, tearing fir trees as thick as a leg from the ground. In his seventh year he had already taken to oaks. His mother wanted to stop nursing him, but her dear little boy asked her to nurse him for just seven more years. The mother wasn't pleased, but promised him anyway.

After fourteen years he had such terrible strength that he pulled the largest oaks and beech trees from the ground like the thinnest hemp and carried them home on his shoulder, eight and nine at a time.

"Hey mama, mama!" he addressed his mother once. "You've nursed me well, but I'm still afraid that I might harm myself someday, tearing up oaks. If only you would nurse me three more winters!"

"If you think so," said his mother to him, "why, then I'll do that for you."

In his seventeenth year, Lomidrevo could no longer remain at home. He had no work and wanted to try the world. In the end he said to his parents, "Listen, father dear and mother dear! You know well that 'he who on the stove does dwell has nothing much of worth to tell.' I, too, would like to learn how people get on in the world. I'm setting out into the world. Worry not, for I shall not forget you, but will care for you in your old age."

His parents agreed, for they did not want to oppose his will in anything. "Just go with God," said his father, "be good and never harm anyone!"

Lomidrevo took leave of his parents and set out into the world. He went and went until he came upon a man who was toppling mountains and carrying them from one place to another. That man immediately rolled a mountain into Lomidrevo's way so that he could not pass. "Take that mountain out of my way," Lomidrevo told him.

"I've never done that for anyone," answered Valivrch,[2] "but I'll move it for you if you're stronger than me."

"Well, then, come and wrestle!" said Lomidrevo.

They grasped each other and Lomidrevo dashed Valivrch to the ground like a cask. But they in no way became angered, and instead became friends. Valivrch carried that mountain out of the way and they continued on together.

They went and went for some time until they came upon a man who was always, and even then, mixing iron in his hands and didn't want to get out of their way. "Give way!" Lomidrevo said to him.

"I will not give way to the likes of you," said Miesiželezo curtly, "unless one of you happens to be stronger than me."

"Come and wrestle!" said Lomidrevo.

They grasped each other so that their bones cracked! Lomidrevo shook Miesiželezo so much that an hour passed before he could get up. Then they set out and traveled on together. They met up with some carters who were carting iron and who had become stuck in the clay in a steep hollow so that they couldn't even move. The carters were just moaning over their carts, wondering what they would do now. "What's the problem?" Lomidrevo asked them.

"Ay, the Deuce take a fit," answered one of them. "We're carting iron and we're stuck in the clay. We've hitched up all our eight-and-thirty horses but we cannot even budge from the place. Why, it's unheard of. We'd appreciate your help, if you're men."

"Well, well," answered Lomidrevo, "that might happen, too, if you give us as much iron as one of us can carry." The carters agreed to that. "Take as much as you can carry," said one, "even all three of you, but just help us out of the clay, for we will have to dig out."

"Well, just unhitch your animals!" said Lomidrevo. And with that he took a cart by the shaft and with his little finger pulled it out to the top like nothing. And in the same way the second and the third and all of them.

"Well lawd a'mighty, what's this?" said the owners, and looked at Lomidrevo with their mouths ajar. But the work, in a wink, was done.

"Now, give us what you have promised us," said Lomidrevo. "And you, Valivrch, show what you know." Valivrch took the iron from all of those carts on his shoulders and still shouted that it was little and wanted to take the carts and horses and people and everything. But Lomidrevo stopped him. "Let it be," he said. "Let's stick with the iron."

Then Miesiželezo spoke up, "Fellows, you know what? I'll mix us three flails from that iron and let's go threshing."

"Really? That would be fine," said Lomidrevo, and he sat next to Valivrch on a log. They watched Miesiželezo. And he just rolled and rolled it, like dough, and glued and fastened those flails. In a moment, they were done. Those three flails weighed two hundred ninety hundredweight.

With that they set out and came to a certain gentleman's place. He had large ricks of wheat but couldn't find threshers anywhere. They asked him, then, if he wouldn't give them those ricks to thresh. "If there were at least a hundred of you," answered the gentleman, "I'd think nothing of it and would let you start on those ricks. But I won't let the three of you ruin my ricks."

"Well, sir! Why should you talk so?" said Lomidrevo. "If we don't thresh them all by tomorrow evening, do with us as you will. Even if our necks are at stake, we'll comply, just give us work!"

"Well, and what part do you want for your threshing?" the gentleman asked.

"Who knows?" answered Valivrch. "We've never threshed for a share before, but if you give us what we can carry for our labor, we will agree."

The gentleman gladly agreed to that, for he thought they couldn't carry even fifteen kilograms. With that the dear boys, though the dawn had hardly broken, took their flails and began to thresh, not a single sheaf, but a whole stack, so that in a short time they had beaten an entire stack to powder. Then stack after stack, so that the dust rose like smoke from a charcoal pile! "Fellows!" said Valivrch, "we have no shovels, so let's blow away the chaff!" And in a wink the stubble was carried far and wide, and grain, pure as gold, remained on the ground. The gentleman was angry that they had blown away his straw, but Valivrch told him, "What do you have to regret? You won't have to cart it out onto the fields, it'd hardly be useful. The straw is worth nothing, but the wheat . . . just get your bins ready!"

"They're long ready," said the gentleman, "but you have no sacks for your part."

"Well, you could lend us some. We'll honestly return them."

"I have no sacks to lend."

"Well, then," he said, "we'll just carry the grain to your silo."

"Why yes, just carry it there."

So they poured all the grain into the silo, secured all the doors and windows well, and when everything was ready—Valivrch grasped the silo, took it on his shoulder, and off they went. The gentleman's eyes bugged out at what was happening now. And he was terribly vexed but could say nothing, for he had promised them that what they could carry was theirs. He thought, what should he do now? He had a mean wild bull in his barn. He ordered that it be let out after them, thinking that it would run them through. Meanwhile those fellows strode along their way as if safe and delighted. But Lomidrevo knew that it couldn't be had for nothing. When they had gone a piece he said to Miesiželezo, "Why, look back there, brother, do you see anything?"

"Why, yes, I see something. They've let a wild bull out after us," he said. "Let's run!"

"Well, go on and run if that pleases you," said Lomidrevo. "I'll wait for it here." Those two lit out ahead, and Lomidrevo awaited the bull all by his lonesome. When it ran up to him and simply came at him with its horns, Lomidrevo grabbed it by the horns, twisted its neck and hurled it to the ground, and that was all for it. He took the bull on his shoulders, caught up with the other two, placed it on the silo for Valivrch, and on they went.

The gentleman watched from the top of his manor what was happening, and when he saw Lomidrevo kill the bull, he immediately ordered a wild boar set after them that immediately tore apart whomever it met up with. Lomidrevo ordered Miesiželezo to look back again, to see if anything was behind them. "How could I not see," he said, "a wild boar running after us, his mouth just foaming in rage."

"Well, go on. I'll wait for it here."

With that the boar caught up and set at Lomidrevo, trying to cut him with his tusks. But Lomidrevo caught him and tore him straight in two. He then set out after the other fellows and placed the boar on the silo for Valivrch. They went on in that way.

The gentleman became enraged and ordered his wagon hitched. He mounted the wagon along with his servants and charged after them until the smoke flew, saying he would take it all from them. When they saw what was happening, Lomidrevo said, "Well, dear brothers, I don't want to harm them. But you just go on, I know what I'll do."

In the meantime they had entered the forest. Well, Lomidrevo quickly tore up the largest oaks and blocked the way quite handily with them, so that the gentlemen and his servants could follow them no more. So they finally had peace. They carried part of their profits to Lomidrevo's parents, another to Miesiželezo's, and the remainder to Valivrch's.

"But boys," Lomidrevo now said, "we shan't profit more this way. We must continue further into the world. You, Miesiželezo, make me a single valaška from those flails, one like the world has not yet seen."[3]

As soon as the valaška was ready, Lomidrevo wanted to test if it was strong enough, so he threw it into the air, and where it was to fall, he placed his back. The valaška fell down and immediately broke in two upon his back. "We'll get nowhere that way," he said. "You have to mix it even stronger." Miesiželezo set to it and mixed it even stronger. Now, when he threw it, it no longer broke on Lomidrevo's back. "Now then," he said, "let's go!"

They went and went and went for a long time, until they came once to a town. The whole thing was draped in black cloth. They entered an inn, ordered a cask of wine from the basement overturned, and drank: drank a lot of that good little wine, until at last they asked what tidings they had there.

"Eh, would that there were better tidings," answered the innkeeper. "Our whole town is in great mourning, but our king is aggrieved the most. In recent days his three daughters have vanished. They went to a certain place every day to bathe, and God only knows where they wandered from there. Certain people say that they saw with their own eyes how three dragons ran up and carried them off. But no one knows where they are now. They only say that those dragons dragged all three of them into the same hole and let themselves down under the earth with them. Our king doesn't know what to do from grief, but promises that to the one who finds and rescues his three daughters he will give any of them to wife."

"If that is all," said Lomidrevo, "help is on the way. Away with you to the king and announce the three of us, that we will attempt the rescue of his three daughters if he will stand by his word." The innkeeper immediately ran off as fast as his legs would carry him to the king.

"Most gracious king," he said, "I have brought you joyous tidings, just listen!"

"Eh, what kind of good tidings could you have brought me in my grief?"

"Behold! Three wayfarers have just come to my inn asking what are the tidings here and why are we draped in black cloth. I told them everything, and, well, one of them told me that if that is all, help is on the way and that they are prepared to rescue your daughters if only you will stand by your word and give each of them a daughter to wife."

The king was very encouraged by this and ordered the three foreigners brought before him right away. Our three boys stood boldly before the king and had to tell him once again how everything had happened. "So, your majesty," said Lomidrevo in the end, "that's a job for us. Just have twelve oxen, twelve kilos of porridge, and twelve loaves of bread, and with that hemp and flax for a rope prepared for us—and then rely on us and God, we'll get it done."

"I'll give you whatever you want," said the king. And by the next day, everything was prepared. With that the three of them set out into the forests and came to the meadow where it was said the king's daughters had vanished. There they found a little house ready as if for them and took up quarters in it right away.

"We'll be fine here," said Lomidrevo. "And when two of us go to find that lair, the third will stay behind and prepare the food and wind the rope." The very next day Valivrch remained behind while Miesiželezo and Lomidrevo went into the forest to seek the lair. Valivrch went straight-away to work: he collected firewood, built a fire, hung the cauldron with water over the fire, poured the porridge in, even butchered one of the oxen and threw it in the cauldron to cook. In the meantime he wove and wove the rope and watched so that it wouldn't boil over. Once the porridge was done he entered the shelter to set it aside. With that something called to him down the chimney, "And what are you doing in my house?"

Valivrch looked up and saw a Laktibrada: a span of a man with a beard to his elbow. He took a bit of a fright at first, but answered him boldly, "I'm cooking porridge."

"Eh, you're cooking it, you are, but you shan't eat it."

"Eh, why neither shall you, but Lomidrevo will with his friends!" he said and tried to set the porridge aside. But Laktibrada started in again, "You're cooking the porridge, you are, but you shan't eat it."

"And neither shall you, but Lomidrevo shall, with his friends," said Valivrch, and he set the porridge aside. But Laktibrada again said, "You're cooking the porridge, you are, and you've cooked it already?"

"Yes I have, why?"

"I shall eat it hot off of your bare belly." And with that Laktibrada came down the chimney, pinned dear Valivrch to the ground, dumped the scalding porridge out on his belly and ate it up. Then off he went and disappeared back up the chimney.

Valivrch, with his scalded belly, arose with great difficulty, and what was the poor fellow to do? In order not to be shamed before his friends he again brought water, poured the porridge in, chopped up the meat and somehow cooked it and then scarcely could wait for his friends. They didn't come home until evening and straight-away asked, "Well, have you cooked for us?"

"Eh, I cooked, I did. You can just set it aside."

"Well, and you?"

"I'm ill, I shan't eat."

They set it aside and tested it—and the porridge was undercooked and the meat raw. "Eh, why didn't you cook it more fully for us?" asked Lomidrevo. "And didn't you even wind the rope?"

"You see that I am ill," moaned Valivrch, but he didn't say what the problem was.

"Well, we have all just wasted the day today, for we didn't find the lair either. But tomorrow Miesiželezo will better do a man's work around here and we will go search."

Lomidrevo and Valivrch searched every corner and every mountainside the next day, but found nothing. Miesiželezo was cooking and cooking the porridge and winding and winding the rope. Once the porridge was done he went to stir it and set it aside. With that Laktibrada began from within the chimney, "You're cooking the porridge, you are, but you shan't eat it."

"Neither shall you, but my friends shall," answered Miesiželezo. But in a moment Laktibrada said again, "You're cooking the porridge, you are, but you shan't eat it."

"Eh, neither shall you, but Lomidrevo and his friends shall." And for the third time, when Miesiželezo set the cauldron aside, Laktibrada said, "You're cooking the porridge, you are, and you've cooked it already?"

"Yes I have, why?"

"I shall eat it hot off your bare belly!" And Laktibrada let himself in. He pinned dear Miesiželezo to the ground, dumped the porridge on his belly, gulped it all up, and disappeared again.

"Well, may Old Harry eat your soul, there where you are," thought Miesiželezo and got up as best he could and again gathered wood and water and stood and cooked as well as he could. In the evening his hungry friends returned home and sat down to eat. But the porridge was undercooked and the meat raw. "Well, how is it you didn't cook it better?" asked Lomidrevo. "And didn't you even wind the rope?"

"Ah, I would have," said Miesiželezo, excusing himself, "but today I've not been myself and I've been all thumbs."

"Well, forget it," answered Lomidrevo, "for we didn't find the lair either. Tomorrow you two will go into the forest and I shall remain home."

On the third day those two left for the forest with food, for they were afraid that they would come home to a bare kitchen. Lomidrevo gathered wood and water in a moment, butchered the ox and set the porridge to cook, and by the time the porridge was boiling he had wound a rope three thousand yards long. He went to set aside the porridge, and with that Laktibrada called out from within the chimney, "Hah, what are you doing in my house? Cooking that porridge?"

"Indeed, I'm cooking, so you know, and it is just done. Come in, what do you want with it?"

Laktibrada let himself down the chimney thinking he would also eat off this one's belly. But Lomidrevo caught dear Laktibrada firmly by the beard; he had an inkling, even yesterday, that something new was going on here, so he had prepared a beech beam and had split it a bit. He hauled Laktibrada over to that beam and trapped his beard and fingers in the split and then began to beat him with a cudgel. Laktibrada began to beg as prettily as he could that he let him go, saying he wouldn't set upon him again. But Lomidrevo just beat him further and called on him to give up his beard, that then he would let him go, for he well knew that all his strength was in that beard. Laktibrada refused a long time and just begged him, saying he would show him the lair they sought. But Lomidrevo simply grew angry and said, "Well, then, if you won't go nicely, you'll have to go the hard way. We'll see if you sooner tire of taking it or I of beating."

In the end, when he saw that there was no other way, Laktibrada gave up his beard and Lomidrevo, when he saw that, pulled it out and hid it in his pocket, then let Laktibrada out, and told him, "You see, you madman! If you had done right off what I told you to there would have been no beating."

Laktibrada, when he saw he was free, kicked up his heels and lit out of there, so that it just smoked behind him, straight to the middle of that meadow, where he lifted a stone and disappeared. But Lomidrevo well noted where Laktbrada had lit out to, and when he saw him disappear in the middle of the meadow, he needed no more.

Late that evening the other two fellows returned home from their search. They delayed intentionally, so that they wouldn't have to eat raw porridge.

"Well, have you found our lair?" said Lomidrevo, welcoming them.

"We found naught," they answered. "And have you cooked the porridge?"

"I cooked it, come eat!"

"But cook, let it cook a bit more and cool down," said Miesiželezo, wanting to irritate him.

"Why don't you just try it," he said, "and see how it is."

They tried it, but it was cold. They immediately figured what was up and it irked them that they had scalded bellies and Lomidrevo didn't. They said nothing, but looked at one another as if something was understood. And when Lomidrevo began to tell them how he had caught Laktibrada in the beam and showed them the beard, and said they needn't take a step more, that the opening to hell was here in the middle of the meadow, they became even angrier at him, but even then they didn't let on.

First thing in the morning they went to the center of the meadow, rolled away the stone, and the opening appeared. Now the question arose as to which of them would enter. Miesiželezo showed the strongest desire. He tied himself to the rope and they let him down into the depths. They hadn't even lowered him a good twenty yards when he began to cry for help and jerk at the rope, so that they would pull him out. They did so. "Well, brother, what's there?"

"Humph, what's there . . . darkness like at midnight, and from all sides frogs began to jump on me and snakes to hiss, so that I feared they would eat me up."

"Well, if that's all you're good for," said Valivrch, "then I'll go." And he straight-away entered. But hardly had they let him down a hundred yards when he was jerking the rope like mad, so that it nearly broke. So they pulled him out.

"Ay," he said when he came out, "why, mere frogs and snakes are nothing! But a stench and flames started to beat at me, so that I became afraid I would suffocate."

"Now I know that neither of you is worth a dog!" said Lomidrevo. "Let me down now. But I tell you this, not a step from the opening! You'll be on guard here, and don't pull the rope out until I shake it firmly three times." Then he took his valaška, tied himself to the rope, and flew down, down, for the longest time, until he finally reached that underground world.

Now that he was down there, he didn't know which way to go, for it was terribly dark. But suddenly something called out from behind him, "Give me my beard!"

"Aha," he said, "it's you, my little bird! Why, I'll give it to you if you first lead me to the oldest princess." Laktibrada rejoiced that he would get his beard, and gladly led him through that hell. It was dark and empty. But then a small light glimmered far off in the distance.

"So then," Laktibrada told him, "go toward that light. You'll find the oldest one there; now give me my beard!"

"I won't give it to you yet; you have to await me here. I'll tell you then what you have to do." Laktibrada waited there and Lomidrevo went toward the light. For a long time it was awfully small, until at last he saw a copper castle ahead that just shined far and wide and shook on a magpie leg so that there was no way in. But Lomidrevo stomped his foot once, and the castle stood still. The oldest of the king's daughters was inside, embroidering. When Lomidrevo walked in she took a terrible fright, seeing a person.

"Dear fellow," she said, "what brings *you* here? Why, there's never been hide nor hair of anything here."

"Well, I've come to set you free."

"Ah, how could you set me free? Why, I have a husband who is a dragon with six heads, and when he catches you here he'll likely breathe flames on you, cook you, and eat you up."

"Eh, the deuce he'll eat, for I have a valaška."

"Well, if that's how it is, if you want to test your mettle, take this glass of wine,[4] drink it, and you'll immediately be stronger. And hide behind the door, for you're lucky my husband isn't here. He went off that way three miles to see to his bees."

And with that the six-hundredweight cudgel, which the dragon threw home ahead of himself when he left the bees, crashed down in the courtyard. Lomidrevo went out into the yard, grabbed the cudgel, and hurled it back nine miles. The dragon understood right off that there must be some man at the house, and returned for it, upset that he would have to carry it home on his shoulders. He came home enraged, with flames rolling out of his maw, sniffed every corner, and roared, "Phooey, woman, it stinks of human flesh. Bring it here, let me eat it."

"Ah, what would bring a person here? Why, you know that there's never been a person here, and there never will be."

"You don't say . . . just bring him here, wherever he is, for if you don't, perhaps I'll eat you!" With that Lomidrevo jumped out from behind the door and stood boldly before him.

"Here I am," he said, "what do you want with me?"

"Hm," said the dragon, beginning to rethink things when he saw Lomidrevo before him with his valaška. "Was it you who threw my cudgel back?"

"Aye, it was, and I've come to test my mettle against you."

"Well, if that's how it is, we shall see. But first let us eat something, then we'll go wrestle on my threshing floor. Woman, give us some grub."

The princess arose and brought leaden bread and a wooden knife and laid them on the table. The dragon took it and offered it to Lomidrevo to cut. "I don't need your bread," said Lomidrevo, "but if you're hungry, eat and strengthen yourself!" The dragon broke of the leaden bread and ate it in a flash.

"Well, are you ready?" asked Lomidrevo.

"Ready!" answered the dragon. "Let's go to my threshing floor." They went to the threshing floor, which was covered in a layer of lead instead of clay. "Grab me and drive me as far as you can into the lead," said the dragon.

Lomidrevo didn't wait to be asked twice, but grabbed the dragon and dashed him into the lead up to his waist. The dragon jumped out of the lead and dashed Lomidrevo in over his waist. Lomidrevo bounded lightly out and hurled the dragon back so that only his six heads were sticking out of the lead. Then he grabbed his valaška, lopped off those heads and cut them to shreds.

The princess couldn't thank him enough for freeing her from that dragon. She begged him to just run with her out of that hell, saying they would be well off at her father's. "No," said Lomidrevo, "I also have to set your sisters free. Only then can we return to your father's; but first I must lead you off to a safe place. Just take what you have or can take from the castle."

She begged and begged him not to go further, saying that her sisters were in the power of even worse dragons and that he would perish there. But he would not be moved. So she took a copper wand from over the door, struck the castle with it, and it immediately changed into a copper apple along with all the wealth within it. Lomidrevo placed it in his pocket and set out for the opening. With that Laktabrada said from behind them, "Give me my beard!"

And Lomidrevo replied, "Ask for nothing, you, and lead us to the opening; why, there's time enough for that."

Laktibrada led them well and good to the opening. Lomidrevo tied the princess to the rope and tugged it three times, and they pulled her up.

Now Laktibrada had to lead him to the middle princess. They traveled long in the dark until again a small light glimmered in the distance. "Well, that's where the second one lives," said Laktibrada. "Go, you can see now."

"And you're not going?"

"I'm afraid. And please give me my beard, so it won't disappear on me there."

"Don't blather on at me so! Just be handy when I need you again."

The way grew lighter for Lomidrevo until he came before a silver castle turning on magpie claws so that it was impossible to enter. Lomidrevo stomped his foot twice, and immediately the castle stood still and the gate opened. He entered. There, by the window, sat the second sister, embroidering. As soon as she saw a person, she jumped up and ran to meet him. "Whatever," she asked, "brings you here, dear fellow? Go back, for you shall not leave here alive!"

"Just be calm, little princess!" said Lomidrevo. "I bring you greetings from your father and your older sister, whom I have already set free and sent to the world above. And, God willing, you too shall no longer tarry here."

When she heard that the first dragon was killed and her sister free, her face immediately brightened. She led Lomidrevo into the room and gave him a glass of wine to drink, saying he would be stronger for that. But she also warned him to be more on his guard from her husband, for he is a dragon with nine heads and he is just lucky he was not at home because of his bees, which he had gone off nine miles to see to.

With that a nine-hundredweight cudgel banged in the courtyard, and one could no longer go in or out. "Well," said the princess, "my husband is on the move and will be right here. Watch that he doesn't cook you and eat you up."

"That's not so tough," said Lomidrevo, and he went out. He picked up the cudgel, twirled it around, and threw it back twelve miles. The dragon observed that the cudgel had returned, stomped so that the earth trembled, picked up the cudgel, placed it on his shoulders, and grumbled the whole way that he had to carry it on his shoulders. He came home quite enraged, so that, instead of steam, flames rumbled from his maw. He sniffed every corner and growled, "Phooey, it stinks of human flesh! Woman, where is he?"

"Don't be silly," she said, making excuses. "What would bring a person here? Why, not even a sparrow flies here from that world!"

"Phooey, it stinks of human flesh!" he roared for the second time. "Out with him, wherever he is!"

"Here I am," said Lomidrevo, jumping out from behind the door, "what do you want with me?" And he looked quickly into his eyes.

"Oh, you really are here, well, well," said the dragon thoughtfully when he saw Lomidrevo with his valaška. "Are you the one who threw my cudgel back?"

"It was me," answered Lomidrevo. "If you don't believe, let's test our mettle."

"Why not," said the dragon, "but wait, let's eat. Woman, bring us some of my food."

The princess set iron bread and a leaden knife on the table. "Cut it," said the dragon, "and strengthen yourself, for you'll have a time with me."

"I'm strong enough and don't need to be stronger. But if you need it, eat up!"

The dragon bit into his bread so that the ground caught fire from the sparks falling from his teeth. But Lomidrevo was tiring of waiting, "Haven't you finished eating?" he asked.

"Finished," he answered. "Come out where there's more space and we'll test who's stronger." They went out on the threshing ground, which was covered in iron instead of clay. "You grab me first," said the dragon, "for if I grab you first, I imagine you won't have any more time to have a go at me."

"Eh, if that's what you dare, just for that I won't take you. Here I am, grab me first. My life is in your hands." With that the dragon took Lomidrevo by the waist and hurled him into the threshing floor up to his armpits. Lomidrevo jumped out so powerfully that he tore up nearly half of the threshing floor with him. The dragon's heart fell.

"Well, perhaps that is enough," he said. "We can leave it in peace."

"Peace?" said Lomidrevo. "Really, peace? I have to show you how they drive stakes in the woods. And he grabbed the dragon and drove him into the ground so that only his heads remained. "Well, well, come on out!" taunted Lomidrevo. But the dragon couldn't move. So he took his valaška and shattered all the dragon's heads to dust with a blow.

The freed princess didn't know what to do for joy. Lomidrevo just told her to get ready, that they would pull her out. So she took a silver wand from over the door, struck the castle with it, and it immediately turned into a silver apple with everything in it. Lomidrevo put that, too, into his pocket. Laktibrada was waiting there, ready, and led them to the opening, where they pulled the princess out.

And those fellows up top had already squabbled over whose the first princess would be. And now, when they had two, they divided up and wanted to leave everything there. Only when the princesses begged them, saying that, dear Lord, their third sister was still there and that they couldn't return to their father without her, did they decide to stay.

The obedient Laktibrada had led Lomidrevo to the third castle in the meantime. From a distance he showed him its glitter and would go no further, but just pestered again, "Give me what's not yours, Lomidrevo!"

"Shush!" he said, "why, you'll get it." With that he went straight to the castle. He had never seen such beauty and splendor. Everything glittered with gold! But how to get in? The castle shook on a magpie leg and never stopped. Lomidrevo stomped his foot three times and immediately the castle stood stock still and the gates flew open. He entered. The princess had seen him through the window where she was embroidering and ran to meet him.

"Ah," she said, "what are you thinking, dear fellow! Why have you come here? Run as fast as you can, run! My husband, a dragon with twelve heads, has just gone off twelve miles to his bees. If he catches you here, that'll be all for you. And it's time for him to return home."

"Little princess, don't worry," said Lomidrevo. "I'm not afraid of your husband." Then he told her of her two older sisters. With that her heart rejoiced for the first time since she'd been there, but she also began to fear for Lomidrevo, for her husband was very powerful. She sat him right down beside her and brought him a glass of wine, to gird himself, saying he would immediately be three times stronger. He had hardly drunk it when the ground shook and the windows trembled, for the dragon had just left his bees and thrown his twelve-hundredweight cudgel into the courtyard, so he wouldn't have to carry it. Lomidrevo leapt outside and twirled it over his head and threw it back twice as far. The dragon began to swear that he'd show the one who carried out such schemes. But he went back for the cudgel, placed it on his shoulders, and hurried home, enraged. He arrived with hackles raised and grinding teeth and flames pouring out his maw. He caught wind of Lomidrevo from a distance and roared, "Phooey, it stinks of human flesh!" as soon as he arrived.

"Who would dare to come here?" the princess soothed him. "Why, they would be afraid of you!"

"Don't interfere with me, just out with him, wherever he is!" roared the dragon.

"Here I am!" said Lomidrevo, standing before him with his valaška.

"Here you are," said the dragon, "and aren't you afraid of me?"

"Why should I be afraid of you? I can throw the cudgel better than you."

"Well then, if that was you, you're a man! Give me your hand, so I can welcome you properly." They shook hands; blood ran from Lomidrevo's fingers, but the bones in the dragon's fingers were grinding. The dragon whistled in pain and stopped him with flames. "Eh," he said, "no one has heard of such a man. But let's dine, then we shall see what we're made of. For it would be quite a disgrace if your single head were to rule over my twelve." And the dragon just boiled like a cauldron from anger.

The princess brought steel bread and an iron knife and the dragon offered it to Lomidrevo. "I don't need to steel myself," answered Lomidrevo. "My mother for seventeen years steeled me for all the ages and I've strengthened myself enough in the world. But by your fingers I know you haven't seen enough, so just steel yourself up!"

After dinner they went to wrestle on the steel threshing floor. "Hey there, ho," the dragon began to storm, "do I have to fight with such a fly? It will be a shame and eternal disgrace to me if I trifle with you. But just breathe out your soul to whomever you chose. And you, Harpy, don't play (Harpy was his horse with twelve wings on which he rode about), and you, bird, don't sing until I rid the world of him."

With that he grabbed Lomidrevo and hurled him into the steel up to his waist. Lomidrevo became angered at that, jumped out, embraced the dragon so that his bones cracked and threw him into the steel like a stone into water. Three heads shook into senselessness right away. Meanwhile he grabbed his valaška and heads shattered into dust or fell like poppy pods before him. He then caught his breath after such a battle and went for the princess.

She wasted no time getting ready. She took the golden wand from over the door, struck the castle with it, and it turned straight-away into a golden apple. She gave it, along with the wand, to Lomidrevo, telling him to return it to her only when she gives him her hand for it. Then they left. The golden apple lit the way, and so Lomidrevo had already forgotten Laktibrada. But just as they arrived at the opening they heard from behind them, "Give me my beard!"

"Here you have it, and don't bother me anymore!" said Lomidrevo, and threw it to him. And Laktibrada then ran off so that all the devils together couldn't catch him.

Now Lomidrevo tied the princess to the rope and tugged it, and those above pulled her up. But then he thought of something: "Wait," he said, "they could betray me!"

When the rope fell down, instead of tying himself to it he tied on a gigantic rock and let them pull that up while he stood off to the side. Those two pulled that stone up over halfway, and then cut the rope. The stone fell back into hell and made such a thundering that everything with legs ran to the other end of hell.

Lomidrevo walked and wandered aimlessly through that empty hell, until finally he happened upon living souls. Those were young knochta birds[5] that a snake was about to eat out of their nest. Lomidrevo threw off the snake with his valaška and chopped off its head.[6] But with that the old knochta bird flew back and wanted to gobble up Lomidrevo, saying it had not yet tried human flesh and therefore could not let him go. But the young chicks begged for his life, saying that he had saved theirs. When the old bird heard that, he immediately let him go and asked what he would take for saving the young ones' lives.

"Nothing," he said, "just carry me out of here to the other world!"

"It will be as you wish, but first go: you will find rams grazing by the stream there. Kill me one hundred of them and load them into barrels, then fill just as many barrels with water, then we'll go out. When flames pour from my mouth during the flight, throw one ram into my mouth each time and pour in the water. If you don't do it even one single time you will fall down and splatter like pitch."

Lomidrevo went right off to slaughter the rams, and when he had slaughtered one hundred, he loaded them into barrels. Then he loaded as many barrels of water on the bird and out they flew. Flames constantly flew from the bird's mouth, but there were rams and water aplenty to put them out. But at the very top such a flame burst forth from his mouth as none before, and Lomidrevo had no more meat. He quickly grabbed his knife from his belt and cut a piece of flesh from under his knee and threw it to the bird. Thus he arrived at the top. The knochta bird said, "Eh, tell me, what was that sweet meat that you threw to me at the end?"

"That was meat from my thigh."

"Well, if I had known that human flesh is so good after all I never would have let you go. But we shall fix that as well, now!"

And he coughed it back up into its place, where it grew together right away.

Lomidrevo went straight to the royal town. Now it was all draped in red cloth. He went to the innkeeper and asked, "What's the good word here?"

"We're men!" answered the innkeeper. "The king's three missing daughters have been found. Now the two oldest are getting married to the two who freed them and the youngest has many suitors, and is nearly engaged to one of them. But she doesn't want to be wed until all three have the same kind of dresses as they wore in the other world. That's why we're seeking a tailor to sew those dresses, and then the town will have a great wedding.

Lomidrevo let it be known about town that he was a journeyman tailor and that he would sew those dresses. Suddenly he had ten master tailors for every finger, and each one wanted to take him in for work, for much money was promised for those dresses. But Lomidrevo sought out the poorest of the masters and began to work for him. He asked for a separate shack, saying he would sew the dresses by morning. "You'll sew aught," thought the tailor, "with nothing to sew it from!" and he watched through the keyhole to see what would happen in that shack. Lomidrevo took a piece of cloth from his pocket and cut it into little pieces. When it was cut he called the tailor in: "Well, the devil himself couldn't sew that together by morning!" he said, and went to bed.

When all in the house was sleeping, Lomidrevo pulled the copper, silver, and golden apples from his pocket, struck them with the wand, and each became a castle. He took from them what was necessary and slept soundly until morning.

They came from the king in the morning, asking if the dresses were ready. "Ready," he said, "but let them send the fee for them."

They brought a bushel of ducats straight-away for him to take out the dresses. "I won't take them out," he said, "until the princesses themselves come for them!" And he gave the ducats to the master, saying he didn't need them for himself.

In a moment the oldest princess came running for her dress, and Lomidrevo slapped her, asking if he had sewn a dress for such a monster. The princess left, and the master jumped at him: "What are you thinking?" he said. "They'll kill us both!"

But Lomidrevo calmed him, telling him to fear nothing, and sent the dress after the princess. In a bit the second one came for hers. He welcomed her in the same fashion, saying he doesn't sew dresses for such monsters. The master wanted to chase him out of the house, for he again feared for his life, but Lomidrevo showed the silver dress, sent it after the princess, and calm returned. Now the youngest came and Lomidrevo kissed her. The master flew at him to push him away, but the princess recognized him and embraced him. She immediately put on the golden dress and they went straight to the wedding.

After the wedding, all was explained. The king wanted to cut off those two daughters and punish them, but Lomidrevo wouldn't allow it, saying those two fellows deserved them. In the end he took the three apples out of his pocket and made a golden castle from the golden apple right before everyone's eyes. The silver one he threw a mile from the town and it turned into a silver castle there. The copper one he threw two miles and a copper castle stood there. The three divided up the castles and each went with his princess to his own, and Lomidrevo was king over them all.

Notes

1. Concerning this nursing I feel I must add that in the Muránská valley and elsewhere in the Gemer region, as concerns the people of Hronec, that is, the strong, original residents of the mountainous regions around the Hron River, beneath Kraľová hoľa (one of the peaks in the Low Tatra mountains), the supposition still remains that mothers there nurse even grown boys. They say to spoiled boys when they ask for

something sweet, "Well, you really don't want to suckle like a Hronec boy, do you?" And then the tale is told how once in Jelšava in the market a Hronec boy was sitting on a cart with a whip in his hand. His mother, who had gone somewhere away from the cart, came up to him. "Mama," he said, "give me suck, I'm starving." Whereupon his mother climbed up to him on the cart and gave him suck. Even today there are examples of mothers who nurse their children until the third year. And they say of a strong boy, in order to indicate his strength, "His mother suckled him three years."

2. In some versions Valivrch is called *Kopivrch* (Digpeak), in others also *Skalilamaj* (Breakrock), who mills stones into dust in his hands; in others still *Studniar* (Weller), who is able to dig good wells. Miesiželezo is also known as *Zelezimej* (Ironmix) and also as *Húžvär* (Lasher), who twists the largest birches and trees into lashes. Lomidrevo is also known as *Valibuk* and *Valihora* (Rollbeech and Rollmountain).

3. We must observe here that others narrate this differently. They tell that Lomidrevo sought out a smith who had once lived on the high cliff, and he forged the valaška for him.

4. Others tell that he received a golden ring that gave him the strength of three hundred men when turned on his finger.

5. Knochta bird is also pronounced *knofta bird* and always means the hugest bird in the world.

6. Others tell that rain and hail were falling on these young giant birds when the old bird was not there. And when a mere drop fell on them, they immediately perished. Still others tell of a burning wind that blew on them and from which they were dying. Lomidrevo covered them with his coat and thus saved them from these disasters.

11

The Bear and the Mosquito

A bear and a mosquito met up. The bear said, "You, mosquito . . . you sit on every creature and suck your fill. Tell me, what kind of blood is the sweetest?"

The mosquito told him, "Why, human blood is the sweetest."

Well and good. The bear set out for that human blood. He met a boy:

"Stop! Are you a person?"

"Not yet, but I will be!" the boy said, jumping proudly, as though he wanted to grow up immediately into a whole person.

"Well, just keep jumping," mumbled the bear. "What's 'not yet but will be' is no good for me."

The bear went on and met a beggar:

"Stop! Are you a person?"

"I was once!" coughed the beggar and shrank so as not to be seen.

"Well, just keep shrinking," mumbled the bear, "what was is even less good for me."

Going on and on, the bear met a hussar on a horse:

"Stop! Who are you?"

"A person with a head!" thundered the hussar and he spurred his horse.

But the bear was on his heels and gaining and gaining. The hussar spun around and lit into him with his sword, cut him to the quick so that the blood gushed from him. The bear didn't take it lightly and showed the hussar his heels. The hussar, who wasn't idle, snatched a carbine from his shoulder and shot after him.

The bear met up again with the mosquito:

"You, mosquito . . . you may be right that human blood is the sweetest. But it is also the most unruly!"

"Oh, why?" laughed the mosquito.

"Well, because people don't joke. I'd just started after him when he shot out his tongue at me, but such a large one that it hit me a good reach away, and so sharp that it reached my bones. So I'd already left him there then, but he turned around and spit after me, and like a shot from the blue it splattered into my side so that I nearly perished from the pain; it still itches under my skin.

The clever mosquito shook with laughter at the blundering bear nearly to the point of exploding. But that, they say, cannot be, for he has no fat, though he sucks the blood of every creature.

12

The Little Deer

Once there was a poor forest ranger who already had his second wife. From the first wife two children remained, one little girl and one little boy; they were named Evička and Janík. These poor souls endured a lot with their evil stepmother; she never gave them a kind word, her eye never warmed to them, she just harassed them unceasingly, wore them down and thrashed them every godforsaken day. In those times people barely eked out a living, and it looked especially bad for rangers, who were the poorest, so that at times they didn't have even a morsel of bread in the house for as much as three days. One morning the ranger asked, "Woman! What will we give our children to eat?"

"Why should you ask me?" she replied. "Go to the forest, perhaps you'll find something or other there." So he left for the forest, walked and hunted right up till twilight, but could shoot nothing more than a single bird.

"Here you are," he told his wife, "cook us this bird!" The bird was cooked, and whatever bit each of them lapped up, that had to serve.

The next day the ranger again spoke up, "My lord, my lord, what ever are we going to eat?"

And his wife responded curtly, "Well, lord or no lord, why should you be lording my ears? Instead go and get something!"

He again left for the forest and somehow or other he lucked into shooting a rabbit. Elated, he carried it to his wife for her to bake it for dinner and said he would try his luck again; and with that he returned to the forest. The stepmother cleaned the rabbit and was ready to set it on the pan, but first she went for some water. With that the cat slunk in, grabbed our rabbit and devoured it. When she returned with the water and didn't see the rabbit, she nearly died both from fright and rage. In fear of the scene her husband would create, she grabbed a knife, cut off her breast and threw it on the pan. Her husband returned home that evening and she served him dinner. As he ate, he shook his head: "I have never," he said, "eaten such a roast. Woman, aren't you going to eat with me?"

"Oh, I don't feel like it. I've been worthless all day today," the stepmother excused herself. And so he ate it all himself.

On the third day it had hardly begun to grow light when the ranger already began, "Oh woman, woman, what are we going to eat?" And she quickly asked him whether yesterday's dinner had been good. "It sure was," he assured her. Then she revealed to him what dinner had been.

"And now," she said, "do you know what, hubby? We'll butcher those ugly children of yours!"

The devil proposes and a demon carries it out. "I agree," the ranger responded, "but first let's swear seven times that we will never turn on each other." They swore seven times and then decided that they would do away with the boy first, followed by the girl. While the adults were discussing that, Janík was snoring on the stove, but Evička awoke for a moment and overheard everything. The poor soul, her whole body shook like an aspen leaf, but she didn't even blink.

When they rose in the morning, the wicked stepmother called out, "Children, get on with you to the forest to collect dry twigs. We are going to bake a roast!" Evička and Janík set out. As they were gathering twigs, the sister told her brother, "Do you know, Janík, what we are gathering these twigs for?"

"For a roast, of course!"

"Yes, for a roast! For your roast!" And she then told him how their father and stepmother had agreed that they would butcher them one after the other. "But don't you worry!" she said. "When we arrive home, I'll ask our stepmother to comb my hair for a while. You come into the room and grab my ribbon. I'll run out after you and then we'll run away together."

They carried the twigs into the yard and their stepmother praised them for hurrying. Then Evička asked her stepmother to comb her hair a bit. "Right away," she said, "right away. Just run and put water on in the big pot!"

Evička put the water on, ran to the loft where she had two pieces of wild fruit laid aside, took them, and returned to her stepmother. A knife, sharp as a razor, glittered on the table. Her stepmother undid her braid, laid the ribbon aside, and began to comb her hair. With that Janík ran up, grabbed the ribbon and out the door he went! Evička dashed after him and called out, "Give me my ribbon! Give me my ribbon!"

After a bit their stepmother went out into the yard, because she didn't hear them talking. And then she saw them leaving and that they were already near the forest. She perceived what was going on, became extremely enraged, and shouted after them wrathfully, "May you turn into whatever beast whose track you drink from!"

The brother and sister ran away over hill and dale, wherever their eyes led them. But the sun was beating down and Janík began to suffer from thirst.

They came to a bear track filled with rainwater. "Evička, sissy, ah, I would so like a drink!"

"Oh, don't you drink it on me! Don't! Why, it is a bear's track. You would become a bear. Have this piece of wild fruit instead and perhaps your thirst will pass." Janík gnawed at the fruit and his thirst disappeared.

They went and went for another good piece. Then they came upon a wolf track and Janík suffered from an even greater thirst. "Evička, sister, ah, I would really like a drink. I'll drink from this puddle!"

"Oh, don't you drink it on me! Don't! Why, it is a wolf's track. You would become a wolf. Have this piece of wild fruit instead and perhaps your thirst will pass." Janík gnawed at the piece of fruit and felt somewhat better.

They went and went again, but the further they trod, the more the sun beat down and Janík was on the verge of fainting. "Sissy Evička, give me more, give me another fruit!"

"Oh, my dearest brother, I have no more. Just wait a bit longer, there will be a well nearby." They came to a deer track. "Sissy Evička, I can't go on. I have to drink."

"Oh, don't you drink it on me! Don't! Why, it is a deer's track. You would become a deer." But no sooner did she turn around than he leaned over to the puddle and immediately turned into a deer.

When she saw him like that, she wrung her hands and began to cry, "Oh lord, my lord, my poor brother. What shall I do with you now? Oh, the dogs will come and tear you to pieces! The hunters will come and shoot you!" And the sad deer just strode along at her right side.

They hadn't gone ten steps and there stood a beautiful little well, like the clearest glass. The girl drank as much as she wanted, whereupon a golden star immediately began to glitter on her forehead and her hair turned golden. They went on from the well and came to a little clearing in which stood a haystack. "Ah, brother, little deer," she said, " we are going to live here. Our stepmother won't find us here!" They dug a hole in the haystack and hid there at night from the wind and rain. When the sun came out, Evička sat on the haystack and combed her hair, her so golden hair, crying, "Oh, if only my mother knew that I'm shaking on this haystack and combing my so golden hair! But my mother is embroidering linen in the great beyond!" The deer went to graze while she lived on berries and roots.

Thus it remained for a long time.

A young king often went to that very forest to hunt. Once when she was sitting out and combing her hair, the hunted deer ran up with a dog on his heels. The deer swooshed into the haystack and the dog, when it caught sight of the girl, wagged its tail and ran back to its master.

Its master threw it a piece of roasted meat. The dog grabbed it in its mouth and went straight to the dear girl, dropped the meat in her lap and ran back to its master. It did this a second time as well, and the master wondered where it was dragging the meat. He threw it another piece, and when it ran off that way again, the young king took off after it and came well and good to Evička.

"Well! What are you doing here?" he asked her. And Evička told him everything and how it had gone for them. "And won't you come with me?" the prince responded.

"No, believe me, for you would just have the deer shot on me."

"Don't worry," he said, "I won't have him shot. Just come. You'll be well off with me." At those fine words, she consented to go with the prince. They sat in the coach and were taken to the castle.

There Evička found everything that she needed. They even took good care of her brother, the little deer. She had her pick of dresses, each one nicer than the last, and she simply blossomed in them. At the same time they taught her everything that a queen needs to know, and when she had grown, the young king took her as his wife. But first he had to swear to her that he would never allow the deer to be harmed.

So far, so good. An old granny lived in the king's castle and she was quite vexed when the king was married that way, for she had thought he would choose her girl. The king had to go off to war, and he instructed the old granny to take good care of the queen, for in a short while she would enter labor. A lovely boy was born, and a golden star shone on his forehead. But the queen was very weakened from the delivery. She asked for some water, but the old granny told her, "The Danube is flowing just under the window. Lean out and drink!"

"Oh, my lord, how should I lean out, when I am so worn!"

"To each his own," grumbled the old woman. "You won't lean out and I won't give you any water!" The queen couldn't continue with that thirst, so she leaned out the window, and when she was bent over like that, the old granny pushed her into the water and immediately laid her own daughter in her place on the bed. She couldn't see her way to do in the boy with the golden star; it was enough for her that she could substitute her girl.

The queen didn't drown, but simply turned into a golden duck and swam with the other ducks on the Danube. But the poor little boy, when he no longer heard his mother, began to cry and howl and could not be soothed. Just then the deer ran into the room and rocked its horns as a sign for them to lay the child on them so it could rock him. The old granny didn't know what else to do with him, so she laid him on the horns. "Go," she said, "and both of you break your necks!"

The deer took off down the bank of the Danube, and when it saw some ducks swimming, it stopped and called out to them:

"Little duckies, little pearls,
have you seen this child's mother?"

"We have, we have, in the wide garden,"
answered the ducks.

And with that the golden duck flew to the bank, changed into the beautiful lady, took the child, and told him, "My darling son, my golden one, be bathed, be nursed, and be changed!"—and everything happened just so. Then she hugged him and kissed the child again and laid him on the deer's horns. She then turned again into a golden duck and flew off to the Danube. And so it went for a long time: the deer carried the child to the Danube every day, and the child was good, as beautiful as a rose.

Finally the king wrote from the war for them to expect him at such and such a time at home. The old granny ordered the girl to lie in the bed and become sick; and when the king comes, to request meat only from that deer.

Happily, the king returned home and was overjoyed with the beautiful child. But he couldn't wonder enough over the one lying in the bed, and strangest of all, he didn't see the golden star on her forehead or the golden hair. The old granny immediately knew how to dance around that, and said that the illness would certainly not kill anyone and that the golden star and golden hair had passed from the queen to the child.

And the one in the bed began to call out, "Oh, I would so like some deer meat. Let me have that little deer butchered!"

"Huh," answered the king, "why, I had to swear to you that no one could ever harm that deer. How is it that now, you yourself order him butchered?" She made no reply but simply called louder, "Oh, I would so like some deer meat. Let me have that little deer butchered right now!"

In the end the king agreed and straight off began to whet his knife and heat the water to butcher and cook it. Just then the child awoke and began to cry and howl. With that cry, the deer ran in and began to rock its horns. The old granny tried and tried to soothe him, but he didn't want to be quiet and the deer continued to wave its horns. It struck the king as strange—what was that deer doing? And the old granny told him that it wanted to rock the child on its horns. So the king ordered the child placed on his horns. But no sooner did it have him on its horns than the deer ran out the door. In fear lest some harm befall the child, the king took off as well. The deer went straight down along the bank, and as soon as it saw the ducks, it stopped and called out to them:

"Little duckies, little pearls,
have you seen this child's mother?"
"We have, we have, in the wide garden."

She flew at once out of the Danube, changed into the beautiful lady, took the child in her arms, and told him, "My darling son, my golden one, be bathed, be nursed, and be changed!" And everything happened just so. Then she again began to hug and kiss him, "Ah," she said, "whatever is your father doing; oh, if he only knew what they did to me; if he knew how that old hag pushed me into the Danube!"

With that the king leapt out from behind a bush and threw his arms around her neck. At that moment she turned into a golden duck and then lord knows what other kinds of beasts. But the king held on tight and said, "I won't let you go, I won't until you turn into what you were before." He had hardly said that when his beautiful, golden-haired wife embraced him and instead of a deer, a dashing young man rocked the child in his arms.

Elated, they all returned to the castle, and the king led the queen with the child and his brother-in-law into a separate room so that no one else knew of it. It seemed to the old granny that the deer and the child had somewhere met their ruin and she was glad.

The next day the king ordered a great feast prepared and had many nobles summoned. The old granny just swelled with pride when she saw her girl sitting at the head of the table by the king. When the eating and drinking reached its peak, the king stood and announced: "My dear gentlemen! I have a question to lay before you. Tell me, what does one deserve who tried to do in two innocents and to ruin the happiness of a third?"

The old granny quickly answered, "He deserves nothing else than to be placed, along with his entire band, into a barrel run through with nails and set to roll down a hill."

Just then the side doors opened and in walked the queen with her child in her arms and the dashing young man, and the king told of everything that had happened. The old granny and her girl were immediately led off, and as she herself had judged, so were they dealt with.

The king seated the queen to his right and the dashing Janík to the other side, and then everyone rejoiced indeed, and they are still rejoicing, if they haven't died.

13

Kubo's Adventures

He sure was a fine fellow, our Kubo, once upon some time! Whole summers would pass for him on the ridges, tending sheep, and he didn't even take a peek down into the village; he didn't even know what's what, whose is what, or where's what in the village. In the fall, when they were supposed to come and transfer the sheepfold to the growing plot to fertilize it, his father told him to fold the sheep in the plot that they had not far from the village, bordering on the forest.

Kubo gathered the sheep from the ridge into the field and built a fold in the plot, so that the plot would produce twice the rye as the neighbor's. Then his father came to the fold, but he simply wrung his hands: "Gosh, Kubo, what have you done?"

"Gosh what? I built you a fold to fertilize your ground!"

"You'll fertilize the neighbor's for sure, but not mine!"

"Oh, zounds, is that right?"

"That's how it is. Our fields won't get dressed that way."

"But I could've sworn it was ours. Anyway, father, it's nothing. There's a way out of everything, and we'll fix this!" He called the shepherd boy to help, and they both grabbed the earth as if it was some tablecloth, one by one end, the other by the other, and tossed it with all the manure on their own plot. So the plot was dressed. His father went home in peace and Kubo went to the shepherd's hut.

Suddenly he looked back at the plot . . . and did he ever see something! Hemp had sprung up on it in the meantime, and such hemp as reached to the heavens. Kubo fastened on an idea and lit out for heaven for all he was worth. He clawed his way there up that hemp, for he was no milksop, all the way up-up-up to heaven, thinking he would herd sheep there on Abraham's meadow. Alas! But they didn't let him tend the sheep and he didn't know how to do anything else. He would have had a fine time with everything there, he said, but he was terribly bored without that bit of work. And he also began to wonder what was new down here with his fold and his sheep. Well, that made him want to get back down here all the sooner.

Up was a cinch, but down was a pinch. There had been a storm meanwhile on the earth that knocked down his hemp. To jump? It was too high. Wings? They weren't growing on him. He set out to look for rope-makers in heaven to wind him a rope to climb down on. But there were no rope-makers there. There wasn't even anything to wind for a rope if he himself had decided to take up the trade. He returned to heaven's gates and scratched behind his ears, wondering what to do there. With that he spotted a full barrel of bran behind the doors. He soon wound himself a cord from it that reached the whole way, but it was too thin. He was afraid, lest it break at the very top and lest he bite the dust below and bite the dust perhaps for all time. He twisted it double and boldly made his way down it. He climbed neatly down to the very end of the cord, but was still quite far from the ground. Here goes, nonetheless! He closed his eyes so as not to see how far he was flying and jumped. He flew like an angel and fell like the devil . . . and planted himself in the ground!

How to get out? He ran home for a hoe and dug himself out. And my! did he ever breathe a sigh of relief, like one who has thrown a hundredweight off his shoulders!

Later, at home, there was no other work to do except to take care of the doggone fuel for winter. He started off, you know, for that high maple wood to chop wood and took his axe, the one with the gigantic handle. He didn't even think about what might be sitting in that handle. He laid it on his shoulders and went. With that some starlings began chirping behind his ears. He looked back, but didn't see a thing. They just kept chirping behind his very ears.

"Lord almighty, where *are* those starlings, in my head or in that handle? They have to be here somewhere!" Should he bang his head against a rock somewhere first? That would hurt, after all! So he took the axe and banged with the handle against a rock. So many starlings dropped out of the handle, it was as if all the starlings from the whole village had taken to that handle for winter.

Now what to do with them? He didn't have any pockets, but they wouldn't all fit in a single pocket anyway. Luckily he had a long, thin rope with him. He had soon attached them to it, and so that it wouldn't be in his way, he wound it around himself and jumped for joy at how well he had arranged it. But at that moment, the dear starlings unfolded their wings, picked up the man and carried him high, high up in the air. Dear Kubo flew with them all the way until he was somewhere over the Black Sea.

There, when people spotted him, they ran down to the banks and shouted: "A sorcerer, a sorcerer flying! Knock him down, tie him up!" He heard them, but thought they were calling, "Down! Untie!" And the starlings were quickly approaching the bank, and well, he thought, it was time to untie himself. He untied the cord and got rid of his wings—but too soon. He kerplunked into the wide sea far from the bank. Well, a fish was swimming there at the surface of the water, and he crashed into it, so that it immediately kicked the bucket and turned belly-up. Kubo the Champion sat on it like on a horse. But what then? They attached twelve pairs of oxen to a chain, but the chain broke and they didn't manage to drag Kubo and the fish onto the bank. Finally, after some time, an armless man ran up to the bank. He plucked up the fish and Kubo like a feather and showed them to the audience till they knew them like the back of his hands. Their jaws simply dropped at that, and they had such big mouths that the armless man simply stuck it all into the last one's muzzle. That fellow then paid for his porridge, because in order that they take it out, he had to fill the naked man's pockets with money, which he then shared with the armless one. A blind beggar also got a bit out of them. The blind one then led our Kubo home from those distant countries.

When he was home, he drove to the mill to grind some rye for bread. He stopped in front of the mill, and because the ground was soft, he stuck his whip into the ground, thinking it would stand better there than at the head of the cart behind the wattle barrier, so that he wouldn't lose it. The whip certainly wasn't lost in the time he unloaded the cart, but just guess what had happened!

The handle had grown in the meantime into a large aspen tree and the whip end shook up at the very tip where it was set. No matter! Kubo had long hair: he grabbed a tuft and yanked himself up into the air, broke off the tip of the aspen with the whip, just enough to serve as a handle. He whipped his horses and was home at once.

Later on he became very ill. The women hunted up all the medicines, but really, not all the women in the world could have helped him. At night he dreamed that, no matter about his illness, he should simply get up and catch fish and crayfish in the old jar and eat them to his heart's content. That was on the very eve of St. John the Baptist's Day.[1] The next day, John's Day, he got up, then, and went with the old jar to the brook. But the whole brook was frozen like glass! He knocked on the ice with the jar, thinking to break an air hole. But the jar flew into pieces. He became quite angry, grabbed his own head from his shoulders and knocked it on the ice. He immediately had an air hole.

But what should he catch things in? He went home for another jar. Along his way, he heard people threshing in a barn. "Eh, what a waste—it's St. John's and they're threshing!"

He went in, and a young farmer was really threshing along with three roosters. Kubo told him, "Have you lost your mind, hiring such threshers! Can't you see that every grain they thresh they peck up and swallow—you loon, you!"

"You're the loon," the farmer said, "walking around the world without a head!"

At that moment our Kubo recalled that he was indeed without a head. He remembered only that he had last left it there, on the brook. He returned for it. His head was there on the ice, but what good was it when in the meantime crows had flown up and pecked out all his brains—if he'd ever had any!

But they say he then gathered up all his brains into his head, so that it wouldn't be empty!

Note

1. St. John's Day—June 24, the summer solstice. A number of folk rituals and beliefs are associated with this date. Hidden treasures are said to reveal themselves in the meadows and forests, and the day is considered advantageous for gathering medicinal herbs.—Trans.

14

Mataj

Once there was a rich miller who had seven millstones under his control. He was known far and wide, for people said of him that he measured his ducats and thalers with a tollhouse scale. The miller also had a beautiful, fair wife whose equal was not to be found. But all of that didn't comfort the miller very much for this reason: he couldn't produce an heir.

Every three years he went on a long trip to procure new millstones, and he always made his rounds successfully. When the time came, he headed off again. He loaded as many millstones on the wagon as he thought his six horses could manage. Slowly, he returned home. About halfway there he had to pass over a steep knoll. The day before, plenty of rain had pounded the earth. And indeed, no sooner did he set forth up the hill than all four wheels were caught in the mud to their very tops. He whipped the horses, but the wagon didn't move.

"This will be a real job," he said, jumping down. He heeyahed and heeyahed and began to lay about with his whip. And six powerful horses set to it again, but the wagon didn't move a span further and only sank deeper in the mud. "Let them rest a while, then they'll pull it out quicker," thought the miller.

The horses rested, then set to it again with all their strength, but in vain. The wagon remained stuck in the mud. The miller whipped the horses until all of his patience had left him. "Maybe a devil is holding you in the mud!" he said.

"Ah, yes, you should know I am here!" answered the devil from under the wagon. "But what will you give me if I pull you out?"

"What would you like?" asked the miller.

"I don't want money, I've got that like chaff," said the devil curtly. "But give me what you don't know about at home."

As a good manager, the miller considered that he knew about everything at home, so he promised to give him what he didn't know about. "Good," said the devil, "but give it to me in writing!" The miller consented even to that. So the cunning devil let blood from the miller's little finger and the miller had to sign his name in that blood. When the devil had the letter in hand, he grabbed the wagon by its shaft and pulled it out like a little feather. "In twenty-four years I'll come for what's mine!" the devil called to the miller and disappeared like a mist.

The miller mounted the wagon again and let the horses go at their own pace. But the closer he came to home, the more he thought and pondered, what could it be that he didn't know about at home? He racked his wits in vain, for he could come up with nothing, till he came well and good to the mill. His overjoyed wife ran to meet him, hugged and kissed her long-absent husband, and he, in the sweet embrace of his dear wife, forgot about the devil, the promise and the signature. But as soon as he crossed the threshold, he saw a cradle beside the bed and in the cradle a delightful little boy. Then, as if the sharpest knife had cut into his heart, he became numb with fright and as white as a wall. Only now he remembered that he had left his wife in a family way. He began to cry, and his wife and neighbors cried with him, for they believed he was crying in great joy over his long-awaited son. After a bit, the neighbors dried their eyes and his wife stopped crying. But days, months, and even years passed, and in the miller's eyes the tears did not dry up.

The miller was constantly sad and somber, he didn't have a nice word for anyone, not even his own wife, and he didn't even look at the beautiful boy. His poor wife often entreated him in every way, begged him just to tell her what had happened to him. But he always turned away and didn't say a word, as if he had turned to stone.

The little boy grew from year to year and became a keen and strapping lad. He went to various schools and everywhere, among all the boys, he was always first. They loved him everywhere and couldn't praise him enough, that he was such a disciplined and wise lad. But the older he became and the more people praised him, the sadder his father became, till he looked like some kind of shade. When his son saw him thus, more than once he begged him with clasped hands, "Oh, my dear father, why, why are you angry with me? Tell me, tell me in what way have I displeased you?" At such times the tears poured from the father's eyes, but that was the extent of his answer. He would just turn away and resume moping and grieving like before.

Soon the twenty-fourth year came around. It was as if a three-hundred-weight millstone lay over the miller's heart and a great fear ruled him. At night he couldn't get a wink of sleep and in the daytime it always seemed to him that the devil was coming with his signature. He couldn't take it any longer, and called his wife and son and told them from beginning to end what misfortune had befallen him back then and how he had unknowingly signed his son over to a devil. The mother nearly fainted in fright and began to cry inconsolably. But the son wasn't the least bit frightened, not even so much as a poppy seed.

"Don't you worry, father dear," he said, "and you, mother, don't cry! I'll set out with the help of God, and perhaps he will grant me the good fortune of discovering hell and wresting the signature from the devil's hand! I certainly didn't attend those schools for nothing?"

His frightened mother replied, "God forbid that you should run of your own volition into the devil's claws. I won't allow you a step away from me!"

"But mother," answered the son, "it's all the same to me to die this way or that. But perhaps, God willing, I can extract myself from hell. Don't hold me back even for a moment!" And in truth he did not allow himself to be restrained, but hugged his father, hugged his mother, and went on his way to find hell.

He walked and walked wherever his eyes led him and didn't look around much at hill and dale until he came to an enormous forest. He roamed hither and thither in that forest for a long time, until he came to a clearing. In the middle of the clearing was a house from the bottom up made only of human heads. It was missing only one head at the peak of the roof. Before the door stood a gigantic, dreadful man, as hairy as a bear and with a giant cudgel in his hand. The dear pupil stiffened when he saw the house and the man, but strode closer and bowed nicely: "The Lord God speed you!"

"It's good that you've come! A hundred peals of thunder tear your soul!" roared the colossus. "I'm missing exactly one head to top off my roof, and that head will be yours. Cross yourself and then death's your portion! For, you should know, I am Mataj, and whoever has fallen into my hands has given up his soul!"

"Oh, no, not that," begged the pupil. "It would be a tasty profit for you if you killed me, but I'd rather you showed me the way to hell."

"Where? To hell?" asked the astounded robber. "Perhaps you would like to go to hell? But what for?"

"This and that," the pupil told him. "My father signed me over to the devil, so I am going to see if I can't get that signature back."

"That's different," Mataj admitted. "So, I shall give you your life, but you must accomplish something for me along with your own task. Find out, there in hell, what my bed is like and ask how I can free myself from it. Swear that you will do it for me and that on the way back you will report to me."

The pupil was glad and thankfully took that oath. Mataj then showed another side of himself. He bid the youth come inside, gave him enough food and drink for a good appetite and even gave him something to fill his pockets. "Oh, and take this little saber," he said, "just in case. It may come in handy sometime. And have a pleasant journey!"

Our young man took the saber and when he had gone a piece, Mataj called out after him once more, "And don't forget about my bed! And come back this way!"

He traveled a long way, over hill and dale, until he finally met an ancient beggar. And he was an angel. "God grant you a good day, grandfather!" said the pupil, bowing.

"God grant it also to you!" the old man thanked him. "Where is the Lord God leading you, my son, where?"

"I'm going to hell for a promissory note that my father gave for me," the pupil answered. "But I've been wandering hither and thither for a long time and I can't find hell anywhere. Couldn't you point me in the right direction, grandfather?"

"I shall, my son, I shall thankfully. After all, I've been waiting here just for you. Just go right along this path. You'll come to a rock sticking half out of the ground. Beside that rock is the entrance to hell itself. On the right side of the rock a spring wells up and over the spring you will see three briar switches. This aspergillum[1] is for you, draw water for it from the well. Then break off those three briar switches and beat with each of them anywhere around the rock. The ground will open up to you. Hold on tightly to the aspergillum and switches! When you go inside, the ground will close behind you again. When you are in hell itself, all kinds of things will be going on around you, but don't even look around so you won't be taken with fright and the devils won't catch you. When they direct their attention to you, just sprinkle them with that holy water, sprinkle and ask for that promissory note! Never fear, they will give it to you. They can't take that sprinkling for very long. When you perform your task, come back the same way to the opening of hell and strike it once with each switch. It will open immediately and you will come out safely. God be with you, my son, and do as I've told you."

The pupil thanked the old man and went forth on his way. He came to the rock. Lo and behold! On the right there was a well and over it three switches. He drew water for the aspergillum, broke off the switches, struck the ground, and hell opened right away. He stepped inside, and all about was fear and horror! In one place pitch and lead were melting over a great bonfire and in another devils were throwing bad people into that hot pitch. In a third, they were tearing flesh and torturing with red-hot tongs. And on all sides were the shouts, cries, and gnashing of teeth of those most wretched souls. The pupil didn't look around at any of this, but just walked on.

When the devils saw him walking along, they crowded around him immediately from all sides, asking him what he wanted there and telling him to go away instantly! But the pupil began to sprinkle them and beat them force-fully, repeating ceaselessly, "Give me what's mine, give me what's mine!"

The devils writhed in pain like snakes and screeched terribly, "What have we done to you? Why are you beating us?"

"I will beat you," he said, "and will not stop until you return to me the letter that my father signed on me." And he just sprinkled and beat away at them. So they again cried out, "I don't have it! Me either! Nor I! Ow-ow-ow!" And so each of them in his turn. But he paid it no heed and just sprinkled and beat away: "Give me what's mine, give me what's mine!"

When the devils could no longer stand the pain, they began to shout out, "It must be that crooked Lucifer who has the letter! Ask him for it! Ask him!" The pupil turned to the crooked one and began to sprinkle and beat him. But the crooked one paid no heed to the sprinkling and beating and barked back again and again, "I won't give it up! I won't!" And truly, he in no way wanted to give it up, until the pupil began to sprinkle and beat the others in good order. So they all began to screech at the crooked one, "We'll put you in Mataj's bed if you don't want to give up that letter."

The crooked one, though he was the biggest one in hell, when he heard that they wanted to throw him in Mataj's bed, was stricken with horror and immedi-ately rid himself of the letter. The pupil caught it and hid it nicely under his arm.

In all that hullabaloo he had forgotten about his promise to Mataj, but luckily the devils themselves had reminded him about the bed. He decided that now was the best time, while the iron was hot, and he began to beat and sprinkle the devils all the more. The devils shouted and shouted, "Why are you still doing that? Why do you still beat us so?"

"I shall continue to beat you until you show me Mataj's bed."

"Eh, what is it to you?" bellowed the crooked one. "You've got what you came for. Now go!"

"Just wait, you'll show it to me soon enough!" said the pupil and again sprinkled and beat with all his might.

"It's not here! It's not here! Go on further!" shrieked the devils.

He went and went until he came to another gate. It was made of melting iron and burned one at a distance of five yards. "Open up!" he said to the devil. "Whoever wants in, let him open it himself," said the devil. The pupil spattered holy water between his eyes and the devil howled from the cruel pain and leapt a hundred yards into the air. When he came down, he dug the keys out of the ashes and opened the gate. The pupil entered: everything all around blazed with fire, but nothing was burnt up. Only devils were frying and whining until it sent shivers up one's spine. But wherever the pupil stepped, the flames were extinguished.

"Is Mataj's bed here?" he asked.

"No!" shrieked the devils. "One gate farther!"

So he went and went until he came to the third gate, which was woven from flaming snakes. The snakes hissed away, shot out their tongues, and flames blazed from their mouths. "Open up!" he said to the devil. "Whoever wants in, let him open it himself," said the devil. The pupil spattered him between his eyes. Suddenly he leapt three hundred yards upward, and when he came down, he dug the keys out of the ashes and opened the gate. The pupil stepped boldly inside and asked, "Is Mataj's bed here?"

So they showed it to him immediately, right next to the gate. One of its corners still stuck out. Mataj had only to kill one more person and the whole thing would slip inside. The pupil nearly fell off his feet, the bed struck him as so terrible. Something played across it like fire nor water, but it was neither fire nor water. He drew the saber that Mataj had given him in case of incident, and it flickered once in the atmosphere above the bed and only the hilt remained in his hand.[2]

"Oh Mataj, Mataj! It certainly will be nasty for you to lie here!" sighed the pupil, who then asked how Mataj could free himself from that bed.

"We won't tell you that," said the devils, putting up a front.

"You won't tell?" cried the pupil, and he began to sprinkle and beat them.

"Ow, we'll tell you, we'll tell. Just leave us be," shrieked the devils.

"So, how can he free himself?"

"So, he can free himself!" began one devil against his will, and every word caught in his gizzard. "He can free himself if . . . if . . . but must you know?" The student threatened him with the aspergillum, and the devil barked on, "if, on that high cliff from whence he watched for people, he digs a hole with his bare fingers and plants there the cudgel he killed the people with. Then, from that well from which he drank most often, he must carry water in his mouth, on his bare knees and bare elbows, up on that cliff and water the cudgel. If the cudgel takes and bears fruit, then Mataj will be free. Otherwise it cannot be."

The pupil needed to hear no more. He looked no more at the devils, but started back. He passed the third and second gates, and when he came to the first gate, he struck once with each switch. The gate opened right away and he happily arrived in the wide world.

The old man was waiting by the well, and hardly had he seen the arrival of the pupil than he called out with kind words, "Well, my son, how did it go?" "Oh, well, grandfather, well. I have my father's signature here. I also completed the job Mataj requested. Here, let me give you this aspergillum and the three switches, and thank you so much for the good help." "Don't thank me," said the old man, "but thank God, for you should know, He Himself sent me here to help you. Well, return home joyfully, now with the Lord God."

Hardly had he finished saying that, when he disappeared from before the pupil's very eyes. The pupil fell on his knees and sighed with a heart full of thanks to God for wresting him from eternal ruin! Then he started back along the same path by which he'd come.

He was still a long shot off from Mataj's home when Mataj began to call out to him, "Well, how does it stand? Did you accomplish your task and mine?" "I did, I did!" replied the pupil, and when he came closer he began to tell him. "Behold, here is my father's signature and I even saw your bed, but I certainly don't begrudge you it. Something quivers on it like fire or water, but it is neither fire nor water. See! Your saber only flickered once above the bed, and just the hilt remains! For the life of me I don't know where the saber vanished to."

Fear seized Matej. He became as white as a wall, the cudgel fell from his hand, his arms dropped and, for what must have been the first time in his life, he sighed: "Oh, God . . . God!"

Tears poured from him and he was silent for a considerable time. Then he turned to the pupil and asked him, "And did you find out how I could free myself from that bed?" "In this way," the pupil began to explain to him, "on the cliff from which you used to watch for people, you must dig a hole with your bare fingers and there plant your cudgel, with which you killed people. Then, from the well from which you used to drink most often, you must carry water in your mouth and on your bare hands and bare knees to water the cudgel. If it takes and bears fruit, then you are free from that bed, but if not, then you are lost for all eternity."

Mataj listened to this attentively, and when the pupil ceased speaking, he thanked him very much for fulfilling his oath. "And now," he said, "come with me for a bit!" He led him along a path until they reached the very peak of that high and moss-covered cliff. And Mataj spoke: "This is the cliff. Here I have to plant my cudgel. But I would like to know, what awaits you?"

The pupil answered him, "I dedicate myself to God alone—I will be a priest."

"Well, if that's how it is," said Mataj, "let it be so! If the Lord God grants it and my cudgel takes, then I'll know that after I die I will go to heaven. And you promise me that you'll come to cheer me sometime and, if necessary, also hear my confession." The pupil promised, and with that they parted.

Mataj immediately dropped to his knees: "Oh, God, help me!" He sighed deeply and began to dig into the rock with his fingers.

What joy there was when the pupil returned home, when his father and mother welcomed their son! They couldn't hug and kiss him enough. But he didn't delay very long at home. He went at once to finish school and became a priest. As a priest he soon enough became famous for his wisdom and piety, and so reached the rank of bishop.

His parents had long since returned to dust in their graves, and the bishop himself was as grey as a dove and his youth only twinkled before his eyes like an ancient dream. Once he started off, as it is a bishop's custom to do, to visit the churches in his diocese. He traveled, of course, by coach. But somehow they veered from the path and became lost in a forest. Suddenly, he was brought to a halt by the delightful smell of apples.

"Go," he told a servant, "find those fragrant apples and bring me a few of them!"

The servant jumped down and in a moment came to a spreading apple tree hung with beautiful red apples. When he reached to pick one, he heard a call, "Don't pick 'em! You didn't plant 'em!" But he didn't see anyone. In fear the servant ran back and told the bishop what he had heard. The bishop sent another servant for the apples. As he stretched out his arm he also heard, "Don't pick 'em! You didn't plant 'em!" But he was bolder. He picked an apple, though with no small degree of difficulty. But then blood began to run down his arm from the apple. He cast the apple on the ground and looked all around. Off to the side he saw a person with a long grey beard, with legs only to the knees and arms to the elbows, and he was covered with moss. The servant, astonished, flew like one who is already lost to the coach and "this way and that" told what had happened.

Only now did the bishop understand. He came down from the coach and went alone to see Mataj. Mataj raised his head from the moss and the bishop asked him, "Well, Mataj, are you still alive?"

"Oh, I'm alive, I'm alive," he whispered. "You probably remember what you promised me. Oh, hear my confession, hear it!"

He brought his stubs together and began to lay out his sins: "I killed my brother!" With that an apple immediately fell, changed into a dove, and the dove flew to heaven. So he confessed about his sister and others from the family and everyone he had ever killed. And with each an apple fell and a dove flew away. And Mataj's soul was lightened each time as though a hundredweight had been lifted from it.

All the apples had already fallen, except at the very tip the two largest still hung. Mataj stopped giving names and just looked and looked at the top of the tree. It seemed to the bishop that he was perhaps thinking and wanted to remember, so he gave him a moment. But when Mataj still didn't speak, the bishop asked him, "Well, whom else did you kill?"

"Oh, I cannot say, I cannot go on."

"If you don't say," protested the bishop, "it has all been for nought, for until you confess your very last sin, the Lord God will not have mercy on you."

"Oh, God have mercy on me!" Mataj forced out: "One is my father and the other my mother!"

Those two apples also fell and from them two doves flew to heaven. The bishop absolved Mataj and he passed away that very moment. The bishop blessed him once more and as he said "amen," the corpse also changed into a dove and it flew to heaven after the rest of them.

When he had finished his work, the bishop happily returned home. But as he stepped into his room, he fell from his feet and gave up his spirit to the Lord God as well.

Notes

1. A liturgical instrument for sprinkling holy water.
2. Some versions describe Mataj's bed in this way: It stood on four red snakes, whose heads stuck out above the bed and who jealously would have stung the one lying there in the breast. It was woven of flaming snakes whose fangs stuck out and would have pierced him. In place of a board there were razors that would cut into his body, but never would have cut it through. At the head was a worm to drink of his brain, and along the sides were two devils with pitchforks who were to poke at him endlessly.

15

Dalajláma

*I*n a run-down hovel alone as a thumb there lived a bonny laddie. His parents had died one after the other in the course of a week and he had no family on either his father's or his mother's side. So he lived for a time like some kind of hermit and kept himself as best he knew how, just barely scraping by. But he was unable to endure all by himself for long, for the longer it went, the stranger and more boring it became for him, and his guts were in knots from impatience. In the end, the loneliness completely vexed him and he thought, "Why should I suffer here so? There's no one here to cook or clean for me. It would be better to go into the world!"

The next day he took up his little club and went, the poor thing, wherever his two eyes led him. Along the way he met no one to guide him this way or that, so he himself didn't know how he ended up in a huge forest. There he took no more than a few steps and could no longer see either a road or a path ahead of him. Just dark, dense forest on all sides.

"Here goes," he thought, "whatever will be, will be," and he set out through the forest. He meandered about for a long time, but couldn't even find a little clearing and completely wore himself out.

Just as he was about to sit down to rest a bit, someone snatched him from behind by the shoulders. He spun around and saw a terrible giant before him—a sorcerer.

"How dare you come here to my forest?" he roared at him in a terrifying voice.

The lad began to make excuses in fear, saying he had no kin and that's why he had set out into the world, but that he had become lost in this forest.

"Well, don't fear a thing," said the sorcerer, "I'll show you the way. Just come with me." And some way or other he led him to a little hut where the sorcerer himself lived. Then he fed him and gave him drink to his heart's content, and then asked him if he knew how to read. Our fine lad had learned to read a bit while his parents were alive, but as if something had whispered it to him, he told the sorcerer that he couldn't. That pleased the sorcerer.

"All the better," he said, "if you don't know how," and he immediately began to persuade him to remain as his servant. "It will go well for you here," he said. "You'll have food and drink and no other work than to dust the books that you see and maintain the cottage while I'm not home. But you may not even peek at any book or the other room."

Our lad didn't think very long before agreeing to such light chores.

Well and good. He remained at the cottage for a time and the old sorcerer roamed about the world and sometimes didn't come home for over a week. And the dear lad dusted the books and kept the cottage in order. But like sometimes at home, it also became boring for him here, for the work took no more than an hour and then he just lay around. Then a desire to know what really could be in those books began to grow on him.

He looked in one, and there it was written, "Eh, Janko! If only you'd look into the next one!" He opened the next and there was written, "Eh, Janko! If only you'd look into the other room!" The bright lad opened the door and saw a stream of gold. He dipped in his finger and it became golden at once. But so that the sorcerer wouldn't find out, he wrapped it in a piece of cloth. The sorcerer returned a moment later and noticed that the servant had his finger wrapped.

"What's wrong with your finger?" he asked.

"Oh, nothing. I just cut myself a bit," answered the servant. But the sorcerer jumped up and tore off the piece of cloth, and gold flashed in his eyes. Then, like a devil had gotten into him, he began to shriek at the servant, "You no-good, rotten so and so! What the devil got into you? Is that how you're going to obey my orders?" And he cursed and swore that way for a good two hours, until the earth was heavy. But it all just rumbled over and he didn't do a thing to the servant. He just warned him not to dare do it again, or it would really go badly for him.

The sorcerer again roamed the world and the servant dusted the books and kept the cottage in order. But now he had no peace: the books constantly vexed him. He finally could endure it no longer and opened the book again. There it was written, "Eh, Janko! If only you'd look into the third book!" He took the third book and read there, "Janko! If only you'd go into the third room!"

He ran straight to the third room, and when he opened the door he saw a bunch of people, some dead and some alive, but none of them could move; and a grey horse stood there in the corner. It bounded up to the lad and said to him, "Janko! Take the ointment from the shelf and rub these people's necks with it!"

He took the ointment and when he rubbed each of their necks in order, the dead came to life and the others began to stir. Then everyone thanked him for freeing them from their enchantment and ran out overjoyed. Then the grey spoke up again, "Now go and wet your hair in the golden stream and choose the nicest clothes! But wrap yourself in this coat of mouse fur over them and put the lamb-skin cap on your head. You'll also find a fife and a wand there. Hide them, and also take the comb, flint, and sharpening steel with you. Then spit in the middle of the room where you lived and lock the door well! I'll wait for you in the yard."

The lad did everything just so, and went out into the yard to the grey. "Mount up!" called the grey. "And if the sorcerer catches up to us, first throw the comb, then the flint, and finally the sharpening steel." The lad sat on the grey and they flew off like a shot from the blue.

Just as they left, the sorcerer rumbled home. He banged his fist on the door and shouted, "Open up!" But the door didn't open, and the spittle in the middle of the room called out, "Right away!" And he shouted a second and a third time, and the spittle answered each time, "Right away, right away!" The sorcerer's patience was shot and he kicked the door in. He saw no one, but the doors to the second and third rooms were ajar. He immediately figured out what was up and up, and took off after them!

He would have certainly caught up to them quite soon, but the lad threw the comb and said, "Mountain, mountain, make me one like that comb!" And it was so. A nice green meadow before them and behind them a mountain as thick with trees as that comb. But the sorcerer was like a razor and cut his way through the trees as though he were sweeping a path.

The lad looked back once, and the sorcerer was still a long way off. He looked back again, and he was right behind them. He looked back a third time and he was already grabbing his horse. The lad threw the flint and again said, "Mountain, mountain, make me one like that flint!" And right away it was so. Before them was a nice meadow, behind them a mountain like a flint; and the sorcerer cut his way through again with razors.

The lad looked back once, and the sorcerer was still a long way off. He looked back again, and he was right behind them. He looked back a third time and he was already grabbing his horse. He finally threw the sharpening steel and just called out again, "Mountain, mountain, make me one like that steel!"

And right away it was so. Before them was a nice meadow, behind them a mountain like steel. And the sorcerer just cut his way even through that steel. The lad looked back once, and the sorcerer was still a long way off. He looked back again, and he was right behind them. He looked back a third time and he was already grabbing his horse.

He had nothing more to throw and the sorcerer stretched out his long arm to seize him. But luckily they had flown to a sea and the sorcerer's power reached no further. And he dissolved into a mound of pitch out of rage that he couldn't catch them.

When they were flying over the sea, they came to a town. The grey stopped there and told the lad, "A king lives in this town, and you'll enter service with him. But first I have to tell you something. I was once a king, but that sorcerer enchanted me and turned me into a grey horse and held me there for many years. But you can free me from the enchantment if you say nothing more for seven years than the word 'dalajláma.' Only when they don't know who you are will you be able to speak with them."

Well and good. The lad promised him that and became stove-boy for the king. The king was very powerful and rich and had three lovely daughters. Their names were: the eldest, Loveflower; the second, Nightbeauty; and the youngest, Fineta, and she was the prettiest among them.

Our lad served as the stove-boy and they liked him, because he was obedient and hard-working. But whenever they asked him something, he never replied with anything except "dalajláma." That's why they named him nothing other than Dalajláma. He always walked about wrapped in that coat with his cap pulled down on his head clear to his neck.

One Sunday they all went to church. No one stayed at home except the youngest, Fineta, because she was sick, and the stove-boy. And they told Fineta to keep an eye on the garden, for they had very pretty flowers there and didn't want the hens digging them up somehow.

No sooner had they left than the grey called out, "Janko! Throw off the coat and cap and mount up!"

The golden-haired, well-dressed lad mounted, and with that our grey went straight to the garden to where the nicest flowers were and broke them and mixed them all up. The sick one was looking out the window just then and saw everything that happened in the garden. But she said nothing and just marveled and marveled, for she liked the lad very much. When everything was mulched, the grey flew out of the garden like a shot and told the lad to bundle himself up as before.

When they returned from church they saw all the flowers broken and mixed up! They entered the room and asked the sick one who had done that to the garden? But dear Fineta kept it all secret and told them that she didn't know.

The next Sunday everyone went to church again, leaving only Fineta and the stove-boy at home. And the grey again said to him, "Janko! Throw off the coat and cap and mount up!"

The golden-haired, beautifully dressed lad mounted, and our grey again went straight to the garden! He ran about and jumped over all the rows. With that the entire garden was twice as beautiful as before. And Fineta observed it all from the window.

When they returned from church, they couldn't look enough at the beautiful flowers and marveled at what had happened to the garden. The last

Sunday, they said, and when we went to church this morning, how torn up it was. And now, how pretty it is, even prettier than before! Fineta kept everything secret this time as well, and the stove-boy, as if he knew nothing, stood wrapped up in his coat and cap.

From that time on our Fineta, not that she should have gotten up, but day by day she grew worse and wouldn't take food from anyone except the stove-boy, for she well knew who it had been in the garden on the grey. Once when he brought her lunch she asked him if he really couldn't say anything but "dalajláma"? And he told her that he could, but that he wasn't allowed to yet. When she heard that, Fineta was better straight-away and got up and was completely cheered. But the poor grey welcomed the lad very sadly: "Janko! Janko! What have you done? For those words that you spoke you'll have to remain mute for five years more than the seven. And if you dare to let any word besides the one I told you pass your lips during that time, things will go badly for me, and for you as well!"

The lad was very aggrieved. But anyway, it had to be that way, and his entire vocabulary was again "dalajláma."

The three maidens were old enough and fit to be wed. The king, their father, one day bought them three golden apples and three red handkerchiefs, one for each of them. And then he had it proclaimed that any rich and handsome lads should gather at his place at such and such a time, that his daughters would choose their husbands from among them. With that news, hoards of dashing young men converged on the castle, one outfitted more beautifully than the next. The king led his daughters to them and told them to wrap the golden apples into the red handkerchiefs and to throw them to whomever they would please. First Loveflower was to throw, then Nightbeauty, and then Fineta.

Loveflower and Nightbeauty soon spotted their lads and threw them the apples, one after the other. Then it was Fineta's turn; but she just stood and stood and didn't want to throw it to a single one. The king became annoyed at that and finally told her that if she wouldn't throw it to any of them, then he would have the crippled beggars called for her, and even the stove-boy.

They came and the king ordered her to throw. He had hardly finished saying that when the stove-boy held the handkerchief with the golden apple in his hand. The annoyed king didn't say a word at that, but just turned to the two proud sons-in-law and led them along with the other gentlemen into a chamber where he had a great feast prepared. He had Fineta and the stove-boy led to a run-down shack and wouldn't hear of her again, since he had given her such nice gentlemen to choose from and she had made such a laughingstock of him. Loveflower and Nightbeauty lived with their husbands in opulent, beautiful rooms, while Fineta and the stove-boy lived in the run-down shack.

Once his brothers-in-law went out on a hunt. And the grey called out, "Janko! Your brothers-in-law went to hunt. Don't sit at home, but go along to the forest! Take the fife, and when you're in the forest, pipe on it! But put on hunting clothes so your brothers-in-law don't recognize you!"

The other two walked hither and thither all over and couldn't even shoot a little birdie. But when Janko piped on his fife, twelve beautiful does ran up to him straight-away. He caught six of them and let the other six go free. With that his brothers-in-law arrived and begged him to give the does to them. He did as they wished, and those proud fellows led the does to the king. The king, delighted that they had brought him live animals, had the animals penned up right away and praised his sons-in-law greatly. Dalajláma, as if he knew nothing about it, went to his little house.

Some time later those two again left for a hunt, and the grey sent Dalajláma after them. They couldn't shoot a thing this time either; but as soon as he piped on his fife, twelve beautiful roe-bucks ran up to him. He caught six and let the other six go free. The other two were just passing that way again. They persuaded him to give the bucks to them.

"I'll give them to you," he said. "Why shouldn't I? But not for nothing."

And they asked him what he wished from them. "Nothing," said Dalajláma, "except to put a stamp on your foreheads!"

The brothers-in-law agreed to that and he pasted a stamp on both. The king was again very happy with those roe-bucks and placed them straight into the menagerie, bragging before all what dashing sons-in-law he had. Dalajláma was silent in his little home.

Once on a holiday he dressed in his nice clothes, threw off his cap, and took his wife's dress on which her name was embroidered in golden letters in his arms and fell thus into bed. Then the two older sisters of Fineta came on a visit and asked her who it was in the bed. She told them it was a certain gentleman.

"Well," they said, "and he has your dress?"

"Ah, you know, it was on the table so he took it."

Then they asked after her husband, where he was. And she told them she didn't know where he'd gone. Then they started to shame her: "Well, you're the one who chose him for a husband! Why, ours have already caught a menagerie full of animals, and yours hasn't done a thing."

Fineta shrugged her shoulders, saying she had what she'd chosen.

Not long after that, war broke out and the king, since he was too old himself, sent his two sons-in-law with the great army. As they were leaving, the grey spoke up, "Janko! Put on your nice clothes and take that wand: we're going to war. The wand you'll have in place of a sword and you'll slash about yourself with it!"

The golden-haired, beautifully dressed lad mounted the grey and they flew to the war. There things were going badly. The enemy's army was overpowering the king's and the proud sons-in-law were about to show their heels. With that, Dalajláma rode up and straight among the enemy. He flailed about to the left and to the right, and whomever he reached with his wand, that was all for him in an instant. Men fell like sheaves, and whoever remained untouched by the wand took to his heels. The proud sons-in-law marveled at what was happening, and when it was all over, they thanked him greatly and invited him to go with them before the king. He replied that he couldn't go just then, but that in a year he would certainly come. He turned about on his grey, and when the others arrived, Dalajláma had already been home a while.

A year later he got himself up nicely again, mounted the grey and flew to the king's castle. There they all but carried him about on their arms, and the old king especially was very thankful. He ordered a great repast prepared and everyone was happy.

While they were talking, the king began to brag of the beautiful animals that his dashing sons-in-law had brought him. "Dashing indeed," replied Dalajláma, "and what pretty stamps they have on their foreheads!"

With that he pulled aside their hair and told how they had gotten the stamps. It's a wonder they didn't burn up in shame, and they stood as if thunderstruck. Then Dalajláma asked after the king's children, if he didn't have more than those two daughters. After much questioning, the king admitted that he had a third daughter as well, but that he didn't want even to see her. Then Dalajláma began to request that she be summoned as well.

The king didn't like the idea, but after much begging he agreed and in a moment Fineta arrived. Dalajláma stood before her, took her by the hand and led her before the king: "Come along," he said, "your father doesn't believe that you are my wife!" Then it dawned on everyone and in wonder they didn't know whether to question him or to thank him.

Then the door opened: a tall, well-dressed man stepped into the chamber with a crown on his head. It was the grey, whose time of enchantment had just ended and who had turned into a king, as he had been before. At that moment the forest turned into beautiful countryside, and in place of the hut stood a lovely palace.

The disenchanted king thanked his liberator in front of everyone. He invited Dalajláma and Fineta to his country and had him declared king in place of himself, saying he would live peacefully at his side. But the father-in-law of those two proud sons-in-law, as punishment for lying to him, sent them to live in the hut, and before his death he entrusted the entire kingdom to his youngest son-in-law.

❦ 16 ❦

We Three Brothers

Once there was a farmer who had three sons. But the poor fellow was so poor, that he didn't have anything to look after himself with, let alone to raise three sons. But the boys were already grown enough. Once he said to the eldest, "Ďuro, you hear me?"

"Yeah, papa!"

"You should go off somewhere to find work!"

"Why then I'll go, if you don't need me at home." He took his pouch on his shoulder and off he went. He went along and went along through desolate forests and along the ore-mining roads, until he was met by a lame fellow.

"Where are you going, lad?"

"I am going to look for work. You wouldn't take me in?"

"Why, yes, I would take you, just come along! You'll do nothing at my place but cook and stir three souls in a cauldron, all the while calling out ceaselessly: 'We three brothers!'"

"Well," he said, "I'll agree even to that."

The cripple led him, led that youngster even further through those desolate forests, until he had led him to an old castle. There he led him into a room and showed him a cauldron under which a fire was burning even then.

"Here you have your work," said the cripple. "If you work for me as I've ordered to the end of the year, you can take as much gold as you'd like. You work, and I'll go about my business, and in a year I'll return."

The cripple left, and not even all the devils knew where he went! The dear lad fanned the flames under the cauldron and stirred those three souls in it, ceaselessly calling out until the end of the year: "We three brothers!" The cripple came after one year had passed and saw that everything was in order. He told him, "Take as much gold and silver as you want and go home!"

So he stuffed his pouch full as could be and hurried home. When he was still far off, he called out to his father, "We three brothers!"

"Eh, three you are, three, and all healthy since you are already coming home," answered his father, for it seemed to him that he was asking about whether his brothers were healthy too. But perhaps his dear son had forgotten everything in that year standing before the cauldron, for he repeated "We three brothers!" ceaselessly, no matter what they asked him there. His father rejoiced only when his son dumped the ducats from his pouch out on the table. He said to the second son, "You hear me, Andro?"

"I hear. What do you want then?"

"You could also go off somewhere and find work!"

"Well then, I'll go." He took his pouch and off he went. He, too, went along and went along through desolate forests, along the ore roads, until he met up with the cripple.

"Come along with me, lad!"

"Perhaps I'll go if you give me work."

"Yeah, I'll give you work. You only have to cook and stir three souls in a cauldron and call out constantly: 'For a sack full of pepper!' If you serve me honestly for a year, I'll give you as much gold and silver as necessary to thank you."

The cripple led him to the castle, showed him the cauldron, and our lad undertook to cook those three souls, and he cooked and stirred them in that cauldron to the end of the year, all the while calling out: "For a sack full of pepper!" After the year was over, the cripple gave him a pouch full as it could be of gold and silver.

He was still a long way off from home when his father called out to him, "Are you coming with good news?"

And he responded, "For a sack full of pepper!"

And his father answered, "Well, what good would so much do you; why, two handfuls ought to be enough for you!"

But the dear son could say nothing but what he repeated ceaselessly, "For a sack full of pepper!" True, when he dumped the gold on the table, everything was fine again. His father became greedy and said to the third one, "You hear me, Jano?"

"I do. What?"

"You go enter work there as well."

"Well then, I'll go." He took his pouch and went. He, too, went along and went along through desolate forests, along ore roads, until he too stopped at that cripple's. He cooked and stirred the three souls in the cauldron and called out all the while: "We'll be well off even there!"

When a year had passed, he took gold and silver and when he was coming home, he called out from afar, "We'll be well off even there!"

"Eh, maybe we will if you, too, are carrying so much gold!"

He brought a pile of it, it's true, but just kept harping "We'll be well off even there!" endlessly, which he had learned that year at the cripple's.

Well and good. "We three brothers" set out (for the people never called them anything else after that) with all of that money for the fair, intending to buy the entire fair. They caught up to a peddler along the way and went with him. The cripple soon caught up to them as well and went with them. That evening they arrived at the halfway point in a meadow and spent the night there. During the night the cripple killed the peddler, took all the money, and escaped. The next morning other people were going to the fair and saw the murdered peddler. They tied up the brothers straight-away and led them to the town before the magistrate, saying that no one else could have done it but they. Then the magistrate asked, "Who killed the peddler?"

"We three brothers!" the oldest called out.

"And why did you kill him?"

"For a sack full of pepper!" shouted the middle one.

"Well then, we'll have you all hanged!"

"We'll be well off even there!" added the youngest.

"Well, if so, then let it be!" said the magistrate and had them led off to the gallows.

The cripple-devil was standing there (for, if you want to know, it was the devil) waiting for them to lose their three souls. When they pulled them up on the platform they caught sight of him and pointed at him.

"We three brothers!" the first called out.

"We know that it was you who killed him," answered the people. "But why did you kill him?"

"For a sack full of pepper!" the second shouted.

"Just so, and for that you'll hang!"

"We'll be well off even there!" the third finished, and crack! That was all for them. The devil grabbed the three souls and took them to the cauldron to stir.

❦ 17 ❦

Lady Kitty

A rich gentleman had three sons. The two elder ones thought themselves wise and made the third out to be quite dumb. Their father, poor man, was already old. So he thought that it would be good if he would divide things among his sons right away so that when his eyes closed for good, sin would not arise among them. That very day he called all three and told them what he was thinking. "You," he said, "will get this, you that, and you the other. That way it won't be unfair for anyone."

But the two elder ones didn't like that distribution. Wise as they were, they would have preferred to get it all for themselves and leave just the cake-hole for the youngest. So they began to play their tricks and try every which way to make a deal with their father. But he spotted the chicanery right off and outwitted the wiseacres.

"Well," he said, "if you don't like my distribution, then everything will remain as it is and you will go out into the world. The one who shows himself in the finest clothing after a year will get it all."

Well and good. All three of them set out into the world at the same time. When they had come a good way, they came to a crossroads. Those two broke off here and traveled the nice, even roads. The youngest got the worst: all rocks and thorns; it seemed no one had come this way in years.

The oldest came to a town where a king lived and entered into his service. The middle one stopped at a manor house and hired himself out there. The poor youngest one beat his way along that bad road a long time, until he finally came to a wide meadow, and he spotted a black cat in the meadow. "Aha," he thought, "people can't be far off if there's a cat here."

With that the cat ran up to him and began to fidget around him, then ran off a few steps, but stopped again and looked back as if calling him after her. He didn't think much of it, but set out after her until she led him well and good to a castle. The cat ran inside and our lad after her. In the entrance way it was as quiet as a grave. From the entrance to the chamber, from the first chamber to the second, from the second to the third, so he passed through the entire castle and saw not a soul anywhere. In the end he came to a room where he found a table set for just one. All kinds of food sat on the table along with a glass of wine. He sat down and ate his fill like a beech, and sipped from the wine with pleasure. After dinner the door opened and the black cat ran into the room, jumped up on the table, and said, "Welcome to my place, welcome!"

It was strange for the lad when he heard the cat speak, but she immediately spoke again, "Don't worry even a mite, I well know what happened at your place and what you seek. I am the Lady of this castle, and you'll be well off here. You can eat and drink your fill every day at this table, and I'll also let you choose the most beautiful clothing. But you must obey me uprightly to the end of the year. Look, I'll come to wake you every morning before the sun rises. You'll take this wooden knife and go with it into the forest. There you'll cut off a single twig and bring it here. Then you'll beat me with that twig until I begin to claw at the door handle. That's how it should be day after day, and that is all the work you'll have to do."

"But my dear Lady Kitty, with what bad conscience could I beat you? Why, you've never done me any harm," spoke up the lad.

"As you wish," she cut him off. "If you don't want to, you don't have to, but otherwise you'll get no beautiful clothing."

And so, like it or no, he had to give in to what Lady Kitty ordered. It had hardly begun to lighten when she came to awaken him. He jumped out of bed, took the wooden knife, went to the forest and cut a twig. He returned home and then began to strike the cat. She began bounding all about the room and meowing at the top of her lungs, until he took pity and couldn't lift his arm. But she called out to him, "Have you already forgotten what I ordered you? Beat away! Beat!"

So willy-nilly, he had to begin again. But hardly had he struck with the twig three times when she jumped on the door-handle and with that, it was enough. But the next morning it was the same, and so it went every godforsaken day.

Once Lady Kitty told him, "Well, your brothers are already going home!"

"Really?" the lad marveled, for the year had passed very quickly for him.

"And now," she said, "go this way and that to the middle basement. There are golden clothes hanging there. Take them and be on your way! But do it like this! Put on the golden clothes underneath and yours on top. Go home that way, and show yourself in the golden clothes only after a bit!"

He took the golden clothes, thanked Lady Kitty nicely for her kindness, and left for home. At the crossroads he met up with his brothers who were resting there, and they were in their opulent clothes. When they saw him, there was no end to their laughter, and he had an earful of their pretty names! He said not a word to this, and so they arrived home. Father was pleased at the opulent clothing on those two, but the youngest received quite a large pouch and heard, "Get out of my sight! I don't even want to see you."

Our lad left the room, threw off the ragged cloak, went out in the court-yard and began to parade back and forth like a gentleman in the golden clothes. Father looked out the window and saw him in those beautiful clothes! He couldn't believe his own eyes, and when he had looked closely, he turned to those two and said, "Behold, behold what kind of clothes your brother has. They must certainly be gold."

Those two nearly fainted in wonder and became very ashamed, for those were the finest clothes among them all.

The youngest son had shown himself the finest and so everything should have fallen to him. But then father announced anew, "That isn't enough. You must go out in the world again, and the one who leads the finest horse home after a year will get everything."

They set out into the world again, each his own way. Lady Kitty was waiting again in that meadow and led the lad to the castle. Everything was the same as before; he even found dinner sitting prepared on that table. After dinner Lady Kitty ran in, jumped up on the table, and said, "Welcome to my place, welcome!"

One word led to another, and she promised him the finest horse if only he would serve her so uprightly again. Our lad went to the forest before the sun rose, cut those twigs with the wooden knife, and when he returned, struck the poor kitty until she clawed at the door-handle. So it went every godforsaken day.

After another year Lady Kitty said to him, "Well, your brothers are going home again and are leading horses!" He marveled that it had been a year already, for it seemed to him that he had just come a moment ago.

"Go," she said, "to the stable. There you'll see many horses. But you just take the pony in the corner. Don't worry that it's thin! Just pat him and you'll see what kind of horse you have!"

He took that thin pony, thanked Lady Kitty nicely, and set out for home. The little horse could barely put one foot in front of the other, but when he patted it, it suddenly turned into a golden-maned fairy horse and they flew like the wind. When they were already near the crossroads, it turned again into a bony nag and just crawled along. The brothers were grazing their brave steeds at the crossroads, and when they spotted him sitting on that pony, again there was no end to their laughter.

When they arrived home, their father was pleased with the horses of the two eldest, but welcomed the youngest poorly. All three led their horses to the stable and went to dine. After dinner the youngest left the room, put on his golden clothing, led the pony out of the stable, sat on it and patted it. With that the golden-maned fairy horse gave a stomp and flew around the courtyard at a gallop. Father looked out the window and saw his son on the fairy horse. He immediately called the other two, "Lo and behold what kind of horse your brother rides."

They both marveled and became vexed, but to no end, for they, too, had to praise it. "It's pretty, true, that horse, pretty, but one of ours is worth ten of that sort."

"Well," answered father, "we'll see about that straight-away. Go, saddle up your horses, and you'll all jump the gate."

When they were mounted up, the oldest gathered speed and tried to jump the gate, but then his horse's leg broke. The middle one gathered speed, but his horse broke its neck. Then the youngest spurred his fairy horse: they swished over the gate like a bird and then back into the courtyard. It's a wonder his brothers didn't burn up in shame, for now it was clear which was the finest horse and who should get everything.

But it still wasn't enough for father. "You'll have to go into the world once again," he said, "and to the one who leads home the finest bride after a year I will give everything."

They went again, each his own way. Lady Kitty again was just waiting in that meadow and led the lad to the castle. Then she welcomed him as before and said, "I well know even now what your father sent you out of the house for. Just do as you have done before, and I'll do right by you. After a year you'll have a bride that you'll not be ashamed of."

The lad returned, returned again to the forest before sunrise, cut twigs there with the wooden knife and whipped the poor thing. And so it went again every godforsaken day.

When the third year was ending, Lady Kitty again came before sunrise to awaken him. "Get up," she said, "your brothers are already going home and leading wives. It is high time you too got your bride. Today you shall no longer beat me, but will do this: take this wooden axe and go into the forest. There you will cut a cord of wood and bring it to the courtyard, but while you are at it, cut as many briars as you can carry, too, and when you have it all ready, come tell me!"

When he had stacked that cord of wood and brought those briars, he went to announce it. "That's good," said Lady Kitty. "And now take this sword and cut me in three pieces. Lay those pieces on top of that cord and light it from below! When it's all burning, all kinds of monsters will jump out of the embers and set upon you, but you just strike each of them with a briar and the ground will swallow them up. Finally a toad will slip out and will have keys in its mouth. Beat it with briars until it releases the keys. With that it will vanish, and you go open such and such a room. Now, take the sword quickly and do as I have ordered."

The lad's hands began to shake. "Alas," he said, "how could I do that to you?"

And she shouted at him, "Cut me up, cut me up, otherwise you'll have no bride!"

What could he do? He grabbed the sword and cut her in three pieces, brought the wood, placed her on top of the cord and lit it from below. The cord burnt to ash, and then all kinds of monsters began to jump out of the embers. But he beat them with briars and each was swallowed up right away. Finally a terrible toad slipped out with keys in its mouth, and he didn't stop whipping it until it dropped the keys. The toad vanished and he went with the keys in his hand to open the room. When he opened it, he saw a beautiful, fair maiden, and she called out to him, "Ah, thank you, thank you for liberating me!"

Then she told him what had happened to her. Her father was king, and she was left alone after his death. Then a witch came to ask for her hand for her son, whom she didn't wish to marry, so the witch turned her into a cat. But now she had nothing to fear, for the toad with the keys that vanished, that was the witch. And so, she said, if she was pleasing to him, to take her as his bride.

As you might imagine, the lad was glad and agreed thankfully. With that, joyous people began to descend on the castle from all sides, and everyone thanked him for their liberation from a difficult enchantment. That very day the wedding began, and after the wedding they had four horses hitched to an opulent coach and they flew to the lad's father.

The older brothers also led their brides home, but when this one showed her face, the other two wanted to hide. The elated father embraced his son and his fair bride. "My son," he said, "you've shown yourself the finest three times. I shall give you all my belongings."

But he refused nicely. "Thank the Lord, I have enough of everything," he said. "And what you have bequeathed to me, I will thankfully hand over to my brothers. Let them live in peace here. We will live by ourselves, and you, dear father, we are taking with us."

❦ 18 ❦

Bladder-Blatherskite and His Friends

ladder-Blatherskite[1] was an orphan. He had no kith or kin at home, so he took to wandering to look for good friends. He went along and went along—wandering. A mouse ran up to him and called out, "Godspeed, Bladder-Blatherskite. Take me with you!" "And who are you?" "I am Mousey-tufted-ear." "Well, come on!"

They went along and went along, Bladder-Blatherskite and Mousey-tufted-ear—wandering. They were met by a frog. "May God speed you! Listen, you are two and I am alone in the world. Take me with you!" "And who are you?" "I am Froggy-gabbler." "Well, come on!"

They went along and went along, Bladder-Blatherskite, Mousey-tufted-ear, and Froggy-gabbler. They were met by a snake. "Godspeed you! Hold on, take me with you, too!" "And who are you?" "I am Slips-through-the-grass!" "Well, come on!"

They went along and went along, Bladder-Blatherskite, Mousey-tufted-ear, Froggy-gabbler, and Snake slips-through-the-grass. They were met by a rabbit. "Godspeed! Take me with you, too!" "And who are you?" "I am Hops-in-the-forest!" "Well, come on!"

They went along and went along, Bladder-Blatherskite, Mousey-tufted-ear, Froggy-gabbler, Snake slips-through-the-grass and Rabbit hops-in-the-forest. They were met by a fox. "Godspeed! Take me with you!" "And who are you?" "I am Godmother fox!" "Well, come on!"

They went along and went along, Bladder-Blatherskite, Mousey-tufted-ear, Froggy-gabbler, Snake slips-through-the-grass, Rabbit hops-in-the-forest, and Godmother fox. They were met by a wolf. "Godspeed! Take me with you!" "And who are you?" "I am the trumpeter of the hills!" "Well, come on!"

They went along and went along, Bladder-Blatherskite, Mousey-tufted-ear, Froggy-gabbler, Snake slips-through-the-grass, Rabbit-hops-in-the-forest, Godmother fox, and Wolf, the trumpeter of the hills. They were met by a bear. "Godspeed! Take me with you!" "And who are you?" "I am the mutterer of the seas!" "Well, come on!"

As though on a pilgrimage, they made their way, Bladder-Blatherskite and Mousey-tufted-ear, and Froggy-gabbler, and Snake slips-through-the-grass, and Rabbit hops-in-the-forest, and Godmother fox, and Wolf, the trumpeter of the hills, and Bear, the mutterer of the seas, and they came to a little house in the desolate forest where a witch was hosting a wedding.

"Hey," they told themselves, "let's show what we can do!"

Then they stood in line in the yard and Bladder-Blatherskite here, as everywhere, stood to the fore. Bladder-Blatherskite blew himself up and prepared such a din that it roared; Mousey-tufted-ear whistled; Froggy-gabbler gabbed away; Snake slips-through-the-grass scraped like a bow on a fiddle; Rabbit hops-in-the-forest hopped about in front of them and wove smartly among their legs; Godmother fox, as though she were at a christening, drew herself up and sang; Wolf, the trumpeter of the hills, trumpeted; Bear, the mutterer of the seas, muttered. The forest echoed with it far and wide and those inside trembled: what kind of musicians had come to the wedding? Now Bladder-Blatherskite wanted to make an even bigger impression and blew himself up quite right again. With that a great Pop! rumbled out. His friends broke into such giggles at that, and those inside were so frightened by the clatter and giggling that they scattered in all directions. And the witch, when she saw the wedding guests gather themselves to leave, disappeared before them.

The friends then went inside, sat around the covered table, and ate and drank from what was prepared. And so that the wedding would not be simply before a sheaf of straw,[2] they appointed the bear the elder, the wolf took the fox as his wife, and they finished the wedding off in proper order. The wolf and fox are still living today—if they haven't died.

Notes

1. Slovak: Mechúrik-Koščúrik. The name is derived from *mechúr*, meaning "bladder," and *koštúr*, a glass pipe for drawing wine from a barrel for tasting. The derivation of the second half of the name is obscure today even for many educated Slovaks, and I have taken the poetic properties of the name as primary. Other names in the story, in order of appearance, are *myška-chocholuška, žabka-rapotačka, had po tráve šmyk, zajac po lese skok, lištička-kmotrička, vlk horský trubač,* and *medveď morský mumláč.*—Trans.

2. For weddings it is a custom to prepare a sheaf of straw with a hat and a cloak and place it at the table in the place of the elder, if he is no longer among the living or is away somewhere. The custom of calling someone whose wife is away a straw widower, just as they call someone whose husband is not present a straw widow, probably comes from this.

❦ 19 ❦

Vintalko

*I*n a far-off country there lived an old king who could barely stand on his own feet, he was so weakened. He saw what was happening to him, and saw well that he wouldn't be blowing on his porridge much longer and that he had little time left in the world to rule. So one morning he summoned his three sons and announced to them: "My dear children! You yourselves see and know that I am already very old and it's not possible for me to live among you much longer. So, while I am still here, go out into the world to learn and experience something, for without experience one won't get anywhere. If the Lord returns you safely home, you will help me to rule so that after my death, with lessons in everything and practice, you won't have to struggle as I once did. I will give you money, as much as you need, and I will give each of you a horse Cyclone so that you won't have to go everywhere on foot and thus wear yourselves out so quickly."

The sons complied with their father's wishes and even set the date right away when they would set out on the long journey. When everything was prepared, they took their leave of their father and mother, sat on their Cyclones, and set out into the wide world.

They went and went together for some time, and thank God, it went well for them everywhere. But the two older brothers began to act unwisely, for wherever they went they lived magnificently and in fine style, so that soon enough they had spent all their money. With empty purses they lost their appetite to travel further, and said they would indeed be returning home. "Why should we wander about the world," they said, "when we'll be better off at home?" And they tried to persuade the youngest to return with them. But he was anxious to see the world and was not convinced in the end. When his brothers saw they could do nothing with him, they left him there and turned back alone.

Vintalko, the youngest brother, was sad that his brothers had left him so, but just strode on his way with his Cyclone. The sun was just setting when he came to an iron forest with an iron bridge in the road. Vintalko thought, "Eh, this wouldn't be a bad place to spend the night, for who knows if I'll find some house or shelter if I go on." And he simply went straight down under the iron bridge. He took off his saber and his other weapon and rested a bit. Then he went off into the forest to kill some rabbit or other for dinner, which task he accomplished. He then came back under the bridge, roasted the rabbit, and ate his dinner.

After dinner it occurred to him that his brothers could say any untruth about him easily enough, and his poor father would be filled with sorrow. Without much thought he took a piece of paper and wrote to his father not to believe his brothers if they say something bad about him, that he was alive and, thankfully, well. When he had finished writing, he rolled it up, placed it in his Cyclone's ear, and told him to hurry as best he could. He hurried indeed, but those two still arrived a bit earlier, and their father immediately asked where the youngest brother Vintalko had gone.

"Where indeed, Vintalko," they said. "Some wolves tore him apart there in the forest!" Just then the winded Cyclone ran straight up to the king and shook the paper from his ear. The king found that odd, but picked up the paper and read it. Then he became quite angry and ordered the two older brothers put to death without further ado, "So that you'll know," he said, "what it means to try to deceive your father like that!"

Under the iron bridge, Vintalko lay down and fell asleep. But at midnight a terrible wind, din, and crash broke out right over the bridge where Vintalko was resting. With that he awoke and immediately reached for his weapon. Turns out a dragon was flying along on a fairy horse, which had stumbled on top of the bridge. The dragon became enraged at that and started to curse his fairy horse: "I've been riding this way on you every day these seventy years and you've never pulled what you did today. Do you perhaps hear someone? Is Vintalko, perhaps, hidden here somewhere?"

With that Vintalko jumped out from under the bridge and announced, "Here I am, what do you want?"

"It's good that you are here," answered the dragon. "We shall fight, for I have long been looking for you and a place to have it out with you. But now all is well, since you are here! How shall we fight, with sabers or cudgels?"

"I don't care; perhaps as you prefer."

"Well, if you're leaving it up to me, then take your cudgel in hand and come!"

The quick Vintalko hurled his cudgel at the dragon and three heads flew right off. The dragon in turn worked himself up and hurled his cudgel, but with no effect. Then Vintalko grabbed his saber and cut off one head after the other. But when he was aiming at the last, our dragon began to beg, "Forgive me, Vintalko. Spare me my life, and someday I will be of service to you."

Vintalko obeyed and replaced the severed heads, which immediately grew together. The dragon thanked him, took hold of the claw from the large toe on his right foot, tore it off and gave it to Vintalko: "Here's this claw. If you are anywhere in any sort of danger, just think of it and of me: Right away seventy regiments of dragons just like me, with nine heads, will come to your aid." With that he left Vintalko, sat on his fairy horse, and went on his way.

Vintalko jumped down under the bridge and rested a bit until the dawn began to break, and when the sun was rising he was already on his way. He went and went over hill and dale, and he immediately was filled with sorrow when he thought of his two brothers, but he again took cheer soon enough and began to sing to himself.

Noon was approaching, but our Vintalko gave no thought to lunch. He just went on as if spellbound until the very evening. And just when the sun was setting he came to a silver bridge, and right beside it a silver forest, too. Vintalko simply went under the bridge. He laid down every weapon he had and took a breather. After a while he left for the forest, thinking that he might hunt some kind of rabbit for dinner, which he was lucky enough to do. He came back beneath the silver bridge, roasted the rabbit, ate his dinner, and finally lay down and fell asleep. But he couldn't sleep in peace for long, for again a great wind arose and a clamor twice that of the previous night. Another's hair would have stood on end in fright, but not Vintalko's, for he knew what it would be. He knew that the dragon had certainly come who was master of that silver forest. When the fairy horse was flying over the very bridge, he stumbled so suddenly that the dragon nearly blew off him. The furious dragon began to curse terribly, "Confound you, you worthless so-and-so! Why, I've been riding you here every night for a hundred and seventy years, but you've never pulled on me what you did today. Do you hear someone, or what the devil has got into you?"

"Indeed, I hear someone," answered the fairy horse, "and it's Vintalko, who overcame your brother last night." Enraged, the dragon called out, "Vintalko, come out! Shall we test with cudgels who of us is the better man?"

Vintalko called right back, "Let it be done as you wish!" With that he jumped out from under the bridge and hurled his cudgel at the dragon so that three heads immediately flew off. Then the dragon hurled his at Vintalko, but with no effect, for he missed and the cudgel flew off and burrowed deeply into the ground. Then the enraged dragon grabbed Vintalko about the waist and began to throttle him. But Vintalko was a brisk fellow and slipped away, and when he had swung a few times only one head remained. When the dragon saw that Vintalko was certainly not joking with him, he began to beg for forgiveness. Vintalko pardoned him, reseated his severed heads, and they grew back immediately.

When the dragon was again all together, he pulled out a fife and gave it to Vintalko: "Take this fife," he said. "When you are in some kind of danger, just think of me and blow on that fife! Right away seventy regiments of dragons just like me, with twelve heads, will come to your aid." With that he sat on his fairy horse, left Vintalko, and went on his way. And Vintalko lay down to sleep, for there was still a moment until morning.

When he had rested a mite from his great fight with the dragon he again set out on his way to try even more of the world. So the poor boy traveled all day, hungry and thirsty, until the sun was already making for its rest, when he came to a golden bridge, and right beside it a golden forest. He didn't look that beautiful forest over, but, since he was exhausted, he went straight under the bridge and rested there. But to what end? Hunger is a great master. He had to go to the forest to shoot something or other in order to strengthen himself a bit. After dinner he again lay down, but he couldn't fall asleep, and although he was brave as could be, he still felt out of sorts under that bridge.

When the wind began to stir he knew right away that it had to be some kind of dragon again and might even be the third and youngest brother of those other two. And he saw the dragon flying in the clouds on his fairy horse, enraged. He threw his cudgel so firmly to the ground that the whole earth shook and the cudgel bounced back up to the clouds. But just when he was flying over the bridge, even his fairy horse stumbled. With that the enraged dragon jumped to the ground and cursed his fairy horse, "Why, you worthless good-for-nothing! I've come this way with you every night for two hundred and seventy years. But you've never done to me what you did tonight. Perhaps you hear someone?

"I do, master, I hear someone, and it's Vintalko under the bridge who overcame your brothers yesterday and the day before."

The dragon immediately called him out, "Come out, brother Vintalko! Let's test with cudgels who of us is the better man." Vintalko came out and hurled his cudgel at him right away, and three heads flew off. The dragon threw his, but missed, and when the cudgel fell to the ground, the ground shook and the forests rumbled. Furious at that, the dragon grabbed Vintalko about his middle and drove him into the ground up to his waist. Vintalko jumped out, grabbed the dragon and drove him into the ground up to his armpits. Then he grabbed his saber and cut off its heads one after the other like some kind of poppy pods. When twenty-three heads were already lying on the ground the dragon finally began to beg, "Forgive me, Vintalko. You're better than me and my brothers after all."

Vintalko forgave him, placed his heads back, and each immediately grew together as if it had never been severed. The dragon thanked him, took out a fife, and gave it to Vintalko: "Take this fife!" he said. "When you are in an emergency and need help, just think of me and blow on that fife. Right away a hundred regiments of dragons like me will come to your aid." With that he sat on his fairy horse, blessed Vintalko, and flew on his way. Vintalko went to rest until it was light.

In the morning when the dawn began to break, he again set out on his way. He passed over a high mountain and a great plain opened before him, and on that plain in one meadow a very old man was pasturing a most varied herd: geese, ducks, cows, oxen, and who knows what else. He approached the old man, and the old man was overjoyed at the sight of Vintalko, for he recognized Vintalko's great strength and courage. He also finally recognized that he was his grandson. Both were overjoyed that they had come together this way, and they told what had happened to them, until in the end Vintalko said to him, "But grandfather, whose motley herd are you grazing? Why, it must be hard to herd such a band."

"Eh, sonny, why, I'm used to it already, and I only graze them each day until noon. For there in that castle lives a king who is the most powerful in the whole world, but is as small as an ant, and he's called Grošking, or The Black Ant. Well, he has a mother, and she comes here every noon and fixes one of her lips to the earth and the other to the heavens, and I have to chase the herd into her mouth."

"Grandpa dear," Vintalko responded, "do you know what? Chase *me* in there, it's just now noon, and I'll put her straight." Grandfather agreed to what his grandson said, and when the king's mother came, she fixed one lip to the earth and the other to the heavens, and the old man chased the herd into her mouth and with that Vintalko ran in with the herd. And he thought of the nine-headed dragon and his claw. Sure enough, seventy regiments of dragons stood before him and asked, "What is your wish, our liege?"

Vintalko said, "Scatter this witch around all the deserts so that there will never be word of her again." And the dragons did everything to a T right away. Then Vintalko went with his grandfather to his home, which stood on that very meadow, and he asked this and that about Grošking and whether he could go up to see his castle.

"You can," answered the old man, "everyone is allowed to go who wants, but please, just leave him be, even if you had twice the help you have, he would overcome you, for when he swings his little whip around but once, everything is dead." Vintalko couldn't wait, and right after lunch he went up to the Grošking's castle. When he reached the gate, Grošo was just returning from a hunt. Vintalko broke into great laughter when he saw the stooped, pitiful ant, and he couldn't get it into his head that there could be so much power in such a little monster. He became bold and hurled his cudgel, but he missed. And immediately after he blew on the fifes, one after the other, thought of the claw and all three dragons. His regiments stood before him right away and began to claw at Grošking. But he swung his whip about just once, and the dragons and Vintalko fell together like flies on the ground straight-away, and Grošo went into his castle.

Vintalko, who was only knocked out, came to in a moment and went straight to his grandfather, who was looking for him and waiting impatiently. When he saw him coming, he was glad. But it seemed strange to him that he was walking so slowly and listlessly, and as soon as Vintalko arrived he asked him, "So, you went after him, my boy?"

"I did, I did! A plague upon him! Why, he held us all off like flies with his whip." The old man immediately gave him something to drink, which had him healthy again in a moment.

The next day, early in the morning, the Grošking sent a servant to request that Vintalko come up to the castle forthwith. Vintalko got ready and went. When he was already in the king's room, Grošo began to shout at him terribly, "How do you dare revolt and attack me? Why I'll kill you right here, you no-account you. But you know what? If you steal me such and such a maiden, I'll give you your life. But if you don't bring her, death's your portion. I'll give you one day. Think it over and come to see me! I'll take care of all the arrangements for the trip."

Vintalko returned to his grandfather and informed him how boss Grošo had treated him and what he had ordered him to do. Could he advise him how to get such and such a maiden who lives beyond such and such a sea? His grandfather answered, "Go back to the castle and ask Grošking to have such a ship as has never been before in the world made for you, and to fill it with the finest goods possible since the world was thought of. And let him give you an army to lead you over the sea to that far country."

Vintalko thanked him for the advice and told it all to Grošking. The king, as the most powerful in the whole world, simply gave the order and it was all arranged right away. Vintalko boarded the prepared vessel and they sailed successfully to the other shore. The ship stopped under the very mansion where the pretty maiden lived. The next day he unloaded the most beautiful goods and in a moment the news had spread about town that there had never been such a merchant with such goods. Before he could even gather his wits, the pretty little maiden came to buy one thing and another, and Vintalko, as soon as he saw her, bounded straight up to her and spirited her off to the most remote room where they were among the finest goods. When he had led her into that room, however, he gave a sign for them to release the ship and to hurry across the wide sea as best they could.

The dear little maiden liked the goods very much and had already purchased so much that her purse wasn't adequate. She turned then to her servant to have her run home for money. But when she jumped out the door, she hopped into the sea.

The journey was not long for Vintalko with such a pretty maiden, and neither was it for her. She didn't even consider what was happening to her until they had crossed the sea and the boat docked. Then she sighed and told Vintalko, "Vintalko dear, I would rather marry you a thousand times than marry that disgusting ant once." But it was in vain. Vintalko led her off the boat and gave her to Grošking. The king praised and thanked Vintalko, and what's more, asked him to come to the castle every day when he went to hunt, for he didn't want to leave his young bride alone, so that it wouldn't be dull for her.

The next day Grošking left right away for a hunt and Vintalko went to his bride, and they talked about all kinds of things. And when Vintalko saw that she didn't want the Grošking after all, he told her to question him about what his power consisted in.

Grošo returned from the hunt and Vintalko returned to his grandfather on the meadow, where he remained until the next day. When Grošking stepped inside, his bride began to embrace him and kiss him, and then she asked him, "Darling, why just tell me, what does your great power consist in?" He tried to mislead her every which way at first, but when she didn't believe him and had annoyed him with all that questioning, he just stomped his foot once and she fainted away right there.

The next day when Vintalko came, she told him everything. But he simply advised her to question him once again. When he returned again, she treated him even more nicely. Grošo, who loved her very much, told her everything in the end. "There is a well in such and such a place, on such and such a meadow, under the mountain so-and-so, and it is completely covered in precious gems. I go to that well every God-given day at noon and a stag comes out of the well to meet me carrying a quart of wine and a towel. When I drink that wine and wipe with one side of the towel, I rule half the world. And when I wipe with the other side, I rule the whole world."

Grošking's bride told all of this to Vintalko as soon as he arrived. And Vintalko needed nothing more. He left straight-away at noon for the well on that meadow. A stag ran to meet him and called out in a human voice, "Thank God that I will no longer have to serve that disgusting black monster, but will have a master more worthy than others!" And it gave him the wine—he drank it—gave him the towel with which he wiped on one side, and he immediately ruled half the world. He wiped with the other side and ruled the whole world.

When he returned home, Grošking was just returning from the hunt. He stopped him and threw him from his horse, and he gave up the ghost. Then Vintalko was king in his place. He married the beautiful bride and wrote to his parents. They came and he joined the one kingdom to the other for one great kingdom. He took his grandfather and father into his castle, and they then lived and ruled, and rule today, if they haven't passed away.

❦ 20 ❦

Sítno

*P*rince Laktibrada went into the mountains to hunt, got lost, and roamed alone in the mountains for three days. On the third day he arrived in a very dark valley where he didn't see a thing about him; but he just walked upward along a burbling brook, knowing nothing of where he was going and where he would arrive. After much going, he caught sight of a great, brightly lit castle, but it was still far off. He gathered his remaining strength and hurried to it.

Before the gate of the castle he came upon a grey old man with a long beard to his waist. He bowed to him nicely and said, "My dear old honest man, tell me please, where have I arrived and what castle is this here? I hope you will receive me thankfully and provide for me?"

"Oh, welcome prince Laktibrada, welcome!" said the old man. You are in the new world here, where there never is heard a human voice." With that he took him by the right hand and led him into a great, spacious hall. And he treated him to select foods and drinks.

But there were three large tables in that hall: one golden, the second silver, and the third iron. A handsome lad constantly carried a large book from one to another and at each table he read out a few names from the book. The prince marveled at it all, but most of all at the book and the lad. In the end he asked, "What is this, here? What is going on here with that book?"

"This place, to which your legs have carried you," the old man said, "is Sitno. From here the souls that have yet to be born enter the world. The names of all are written in the book, and whomever's name the lad reads out, that soul leaves here immediately for the world and is embodied. Whosoever's name is read over the golden table will be fortunate and all will go well for him. Whosoever's name is read over the iron table will be unfortunate, no matter what he undertakes. But whomever we read out over the silver table will have average fortune in his life."

"If that's how it is," said the prince, "tell me please, over which table was I born?"

"We read your name out over the iron table," answered the old man.

"God forbid," sighed the prince. "But could you still help me out?"

"You can be helped out," said the old man, "but nowise other than if you marry your stove-boy's daughter upon arriving home."

The prince shook his head, but promised he would do so.

Meanwhile the old man gave Laktibrada a golden clew and told him to set it out ahead of him and to go whichever way it wandered, that in that way he would escape those mountains and arrive home. He did so and successfully arrived at his father's home.

But bad tidings awaited him at home! His father had died while he was roaming and had left his youngest, Laktibrada, out of the inheritance, thinking he had perished. His two older brothers had married, taking the daughters of other powerful kings to wife, and they lived opulently in royal palaces—and they wouldn't allow the youngest even a whiff. What could he do? He took his stove-boy's girl to wife and went to live with her in a distant cottage that his father had often visited and that now stood neglected.

Once his wife observed how some dogs were tussling by the cottage porch. "Just look at how those dogs are tussling!" she told her husband.

With that the dogs struck against the wall and some plaster fell off. A kettle full of gold fell over from within the wall. His miserly father had once set it there, and since he had died suddenly, could not inform his eldest sons about the treasure.

With the help of that treasure, Laktibrada won his inheritance back from his brothers, made them his subjects, and even became king over them.

🍂 21 🍂

The People-Eaters

*I*f I knew what you knew, I would tell what you don't know. Well, but you can hardly be expected to know yet, that once there was a poor father, and that father had three daughters. His wife died, and each day it seemed worse to him to leave those daughters without a mother. So he married for the second time and took a stepmother for them. But that only made it seem worse to him, for the stepmother hated those three daughters terribly and just harped constantly that they weren't capable of anything except eating and drinking what's prepared.

Once, moreover, a hard year fell upon the people, little grew, and profits were thin, so that they had nothing to put on or dine on. Only now did the stepmother really light into the father and the girls. She called the girls and told them that no more would they needlessly consume bread at home, but should go work, and she sent their father to lead them off somewhere, from whence they should never again cross her path. The father could no longer endure the great sin that his wife was endlessly committing on him in his home, so he told the girls to get ready, that he would lead all three of them off for work.

The three girls tied what dresses remained to them into bundles and were ready by evening, but they weren't to depart, mind you, until the next day. So the youngest one ran off to the village to an old godmother—and she was a prophetess. And she foretold, well and good, what the father and stepmother were planning for the girls. She told the youngest to take a measure of ash with her to sprinkle all along the way that they would go, so that, if it was necessary, they could find the way back.

The next day, the father led his three girls over hill and dale, and the youngest kept to herself and sprinkled that ash behind her wherever they went. At sundown they came to a great thicket, and made their way through it until it grew dark. When they could no longer see, the father said, "Well, my children, we'll get no farther today, but let's build a fire and spend the night here. And tomorrow we'll be on our way!"

The tired girls lay down by the fire and quickly fell asleep like logs. But their father did not fall asleep, instead he merely waited until the girls dropped off. And when they did, he took to his heels and sped home, hurrying so that they wouldn't spot him or catch up to him.

When dawn broke, the girls awoke and sought their father; they called and looked in every direction, but found nothing at all. "Oh, my lord," shrieked the two eldest, "he's left us! How shall we ever find our way home? Now we shall certainly perish here in this forest!"

"That's an easy enough job," said the youngest. "We shall go back the same way we came."

"Well, come on then, if you know and we don't," snapped the elder ones.

"Let's have a go at it," said the youngest, "just come on and don't quarrel so much!" And with that she set out and followed the ash with them behind her until they came to their father's little house. The father and stepmother only spotted them when they piled into the house. "What, back so soon from work?" said their stepmother, welcoming them. "Yes," replied the youngest, "you'll have to lead us better." The father excused himself, saying that he himself got lost, but that he would lead them better the next day.

They didn't even untie their bundles, but just awaited tomorrow's day to go to work. But the youngest ran off again to that prophetess. She gave her a ball of thread and instructed her to tie one end of the thread to the first tree, to cast the thread off the ball behind her, and thus to go. And so they went from dawn to dusk until they came to the middle of the forest. There the father again gathered them around a fire, and when they fell asleep, he went home.

The next morning when the sisters awoke there was so much wailing that the mountains echoed from it. But the youngest showed them the end of the thread and began to take up the thread on the ball again until they came to the edge of the forest, whence they easily made their way home.

"That way there'll be nothing left of us," said the stepmother to the father. "You'll have to better lead them astray."

"Well, fear not," said the father, "just send them off once again!" And she sent him off with them again, for the third time. The girls didn't want to go anymore, but they had to give in before their stepmother. The youngest went off again to the prophetess.

"Well, my girl," said the godmother, "be on your guard this time or things could go badly. Just for safety, here's a measure of peas, sprinkle it bit by bit wherever you go and you will not go astray."

In the morning, dawn had hardly begun to break when the stepmother roused them to pack to go into the world, and into the world it was indeed, for they didn't know themselves where. Their father led them over all kinds of barren land and over old ravines the whole day long, and the youngest sprinkled those peas wherever they turned. When it was getting on toward evening, they came to a huge forest, and when they could go no farther for the darkness, their father said, "Well, my girls, that's enough for us for today. Lie down and rest so that you'll manage tomorrow. We're sure to come upon some good people at some point where you will go to work."

He built a fire, and the girls lay down. And sooner than you could pray an Our Father, they fell asleep as if they'd been charmed. And the father lit out so that no one would spot him or catch up to him.

When the girls awoke in the morning, not for the world could they call their father back or wait him out. "Ah, why should we needlessly scratch our throats?" said the older ones. "Let's go home, why, he'll be at home again."

"Well then, let's go," said the youngest, and she set out after those peas. They went and went until they came upon the barren land. But here they lost the way, for the birds had pecked up the peas, and now they didn't know whether to turn left or right. They wailed and lamented until they'd had their fill, then set out whither their eyes led them.

The whole day long they went through the bare fields and through ancient forests, and of people there was nary a trace. It grew dark, and in the forest they couldn't even see a span ahead. What to do? Good advice costs a penny. "Wait here, sisters," said the youngest, "I'll climb up a tree here somewhere, maybe some little light somewhere will catch my eye."

So she climbed up a tree, and indeed, she saw a light in a deep valley, but it was quite far off. But so what if it was far? They set out already in the direction of that light, and so they came to a hilltop, and from it they saw the light far below them in the valley. "Well, let's just enter that valley, no matter what's there," said the sisters, and they went straight down the side of the mountain.

And they didn't know, until they stopped in the valley in front of a giant old castle. The gate was locked, and a light was shining from but one room. "God willing, whatever may be inside, we'll just knock on this gate," said the sisters, taking courage, and they knocked.

It was quiet for a long time in the entire castle, nothing even rustled. But after a long, long time they heard something crawling down to the gate. The gate creaked, opened, and a terrible female figure stood in front of it: thick as a log, a mouth to her ears, teeth like stakes, a nose like a fist had smashed her face, and eyes like plates, just rolling out.

"Welcome, I say, my girls, welcome! What brings you here? What would you like?"

"Oh, here's what we would like," answered the youngest, "we are seeking some bit of work. Won't you take us on?"

"Well, if that's how it is, come on in, my old man will rejoice at you. Don't worry about another thing!"

They entered the castle and passed through many rooms until they came to the one where the light was shining, and there at the head of the table sat one who was, by all indications, as old as the woman.

And guess what they were, my dear souls—people-eaters![1]

At the news the old man just muttered that it was fine and went off to sleep, and the old woman put our wayfarers to bed, too. In the morning the old man was no longer at home and the old woman divvied up the work to them. "You, the oldest," she said, "you'll delouse me and serve the old man as well. You, the middle one, will run the household, and you, the youngest, will go to the kitchen."

So far, so good. The work went like water off a duck's back for our girls, for a time. But they soon found out where they were, and what they were there for. They discovered that one of the rooms was full of beautiful damsels, locked in, which the old man had brought from the countryside, for they say he went about the villages with a basket and purchased children. Those damsels told them to be on their guard, for no servant yet had left the place alive—the old ones had eaten them!—that they, too, were shut up in that room just so that the old ones could have a feast whenever they pleased. Now there was fear enough among them, but what was there to do? They just endured as best they could.

Once the old man said to the woman as he was leaving in the morning, "Old woman, bake me one of our servant girls for dinner, the fattest one."[2] The youngest heard this and didn't say a word, but thought over what to do. The old woman simply told her to fire up the stove, that they were going to bake cakes, and when it was at its hottest she told her, "My dear girl, sit on the breadboard and I'll show you how to load the oven."

But she shrewdly replied, "Oh, why, I don't know how I should sit. You sit first and show me!"

The old woman heaved herself up on the breadboard, and swish! the girl slid her from the fireplace into the oven. There she burned into a piece of coal. With that her sisters got after her, asking what she had done, what would the old man say now? But she told them everything and ordered them to do nothing but to run about the castle and around the castle wringing their hands that the old woman had been lost. With that they began to run all about the castle and around the castle and wring their hands, "Alas, Lord, where can our granny have gotten to?"

Then the old man arrived home and asked them what had gotten into them. "Oh, what indeed," answered the youngest. "The old woman wandered off from the house somewhere and now we can't find her anywhere."

"Why, that's nothing, children," said the old man. "She'll come." Then he ordered them to search his head for lice and fire up the stove until the old woman would arrive. When the oldest was searching him, he fell asleep and his sconce nodded. The other two stole up quietly, unbelted the sword that he always wore, lopped off the old greybeard's head, and threw him into the oven too. He broiled as well and burned to dust.

Well, now there was joy aplenty! The damsels shut up in the side room thanked them for freeing them and ran off home in all directions. Our three sisters saw that no one was left in the castle and stayed there, managing all the wealth as if it were their own. They lived there peacefully from day to day and didn't worry themselves much about the world.

However, once while they were living there the rumor came to them that a young king from such and such a castle was preparing to marry, and that he was summoning all the maidens from the country on such and such a day to a dance, so that he could choose the one who would most please him to wife. Our three sisters needed only to hear that, and they immediately decked themselves out, one prettier than the other. But when it was time to leave, the older ones said, "One of us has to stay home to watch the house, and that will be you, the youngest; next time another of us will stay."

And so she simply had to stay home. The poor thing sat at home, and it seemed unfair to her that her sisters were already dancing somewhere and she wasn't. But that evening the doors suddenly opened and whence she came, thence she came, here came her godmother-prophetess. "What are you doing at home, goddaughter, when the others are dancing?"

"Why, I would love to go to that dance, but what should I do when they ordered me to watch the house?"

"Well, that's nothing, you'll have time enough yet there. Here you are, in this eggshell is a dress of star stuff. Put it on and mount my fairy horse. When the king there asks who you are, tell him nothing but that you are from Slipper's castle." So, she put on the dress, mounted the fairy horse, and was there straight-away, where she was the prettiest among the maidens.

The young king didn't take his eye off of her, but just circled her and danced only with her. Her sisters sat in a corner like wallflowers. They and the other maidens drank in the scene and wondered greatly who the star maiden could possibly be. But no one knew her. Once the king himself spoke to her, asking her to tell him who she was. "I am," she said, "from Slipper's castle," and not a word more.

It was getting on toward morning and the guests were dispersing, and our star maiden sneaked out and disappeared on the fairy horse. Her sisters came home after her, and she had to hear endless tales of the star maiden whom they had seen at the dance. But she didn't even reply.

Not long after that there was another dance at the king's. The two older sisters again got themselves up and left for the dance, and left the youngest at home to watch the house. When they left, whence she came, thence she came, here came the godmother-prophetess and sent her off on her fairy horse in a dress of moon stuff to the dance. "Why, I'll guard the house for the time," she said. "Just dance as before and don't say more than that you are from Slipper's castle."

And so it went again: her sisters were wallflowers and she danced herself out with the young king, and before dawn flew home on the fairy horse. When her sisters arrived, she again heard endless tales about the moon maiden. But she didn't say a word.

The young king again, for the third time, gave a similar dance, but this time he told his servants all around that if the pretty maiden tried to escape again, to catch her. The older sisters and many other maidens had long been dancing there, and the one on which all was waiting hadn't yet shown her face. Then the doors opened and she entered in a dress of sun stuff, and the hall rejoiced and all looked upon her. The young king immediately jumped to her side and never moved even a step away! He danced and entertained himself with her, and questioned her about who she was and where she was from.

"I am," she said, "from Slipper's castle," and didn't say a word more of it to him. But the time came to leave and the servants chased her, trying to catch her. She slipped away, it's true, but in her fright she lost the slipper from her right foot. "It's good," said the king, "that we have at least that."

And he immediately sent his servants to wherever any maiden was to test the slipper on her foot, and the one that it fit, to bring her to him, that she would be his wife. The servants had much to do to walk all over the country-side and test the slipper, and the slipper fit not a one. Finally they came to our three sisters and the two eldest quickly bared their feet, thinking it might fit. But their dear little feet were much too large. "Well, aren't there more of you here?" asked the servant.

"There's still our sister," they said, "but she didn't go anywhere, and it would be a waste to fit her."

"Well, no matter, bring her here! The king warned us not to skip a single one."

And so the youngest had to show herself and try the slipper. And it was as if the slipper had been poured on her foot! She herself made excuses enough, that she had watched the house and such, that the slipper probably belonged to some other maiden—but then she had to follow them to the king. He recognized her immediately, that she was the right one he had been searching for, and she admitted it to him.

And they lived a long time, the Lord God himself only knows till when.

Notes

1. In one variation of this tale, the sisters came to the castle while it was still light out and found the old woman at home alone. The old man was still abroad, where he blew as the Wind and devoured people. The old woman covered our travelers with twelve washtubs, but the old man sniffed them out anyway, but then let them be. They took them into service, all three of them served there, and what follows is the same as in the main story.

2. In the variation where the old man is represented as Wind, he says quite naively that he is leaving for the glass peak to dry clothes.

❦ 22 ❦

The Sorceress Queen

In times of yore there lived a rich and powerful king. He had no other children than his lone daughter Blossom, and she was already old enough to marry. And since she was very pretty, kings' sons came from every country to ask for her hand. First one, then another seemed pleasing both to her and to her father, and they would have quickly had a wedding, but her mother said that she was her only daughter and that she couldn't go so easily with just anybody, but only with the one who could sleep by her side three nights through without her disappearing from his side. Now the princes really began to pour in from all sides for Blossom, for it seemed easy enough to them to sleep three nights through by her side. But indeed, no one was able to do it, and each of them lost his head in proper order.

A king in the neighboring kingdom had three sons, and all three would have been glad to win Blossom, but which of them was to go courting first? They quarreled day and night over that. "Well, you know the saying," their father said at last, "the oldest first to the mill."

And so the eldest set out first. When he came to Blossom's parents everything was smiling upon him and the queen told him that everything would be as he wished if only he would sleep three nights through by her daughter's side without her disappearing.

Completely overjoyed, the prince asked Blossom to go for a walk with him, and she went. They walked through the royal garden and looked at the beautiful flowers, and Blossom plucked a few of them and gave them to the prince. He was so elated that his cheeks just burned with joy. From the flowers they went to the lake, where Blossom threw breadcrumbs into the water and the fish, hearing something falling into the water, came and fed.

Suddenly, whence he came, thence he came, a tramp appeared before the prince and begged alms. But the prince became angered and burst out at him, "What? You dare to stand in my way? Get out of my sight!" The tramp looked sadly at the prince and left.

From the garden the prince and princess went to dinner. Here again another tramp met them and asked for something from the prince. He drove him off needlessly as well, and the tramp looked sadly at the departing prince. The dinner was joyful and the banquet outstanding. After dinner the prince mounted his horse and went to ride in the fields. Here again a poor tramp stepped into his path and begged the Lord's grace, for mercy upon his plight. But the angered prince shouted at him, "Am I your brother that you keep crossing my path? Don't you know that I am a prince? Get out of my sight at once!"

With that he spurred his horse and off it went over hill and dale so quickly that the dust flew behind him, and the dear tramp sadly gazed after him for a long time. The prince only returned to the town late at night and lay down next to Blossom. And since he was worn out from riding, he immediately fell into a deep sleep. When he awoke after midnight he noticed that the princess was no longer at his side; so he arose and built a fire in the fireplace to see where she was, for he thought that she had hidden in order to scare him. He looked and looked, but there was no trace anywhere. He wanted to go out, but the door was well locked from the other side.

"She certainly didn't squeeze through the keyhole," he thought, and again looked in all corners. Again, nothing. Frightened, he lay down in the bed again, but couldn't sleep from fear.

In the morning the queen came to wish him good morning and asked him straight-away where the princess was. When he was silent, the queen just smiled maliciously and left. Blossom came in immediately afterward and entertained him the entire day. While they were playing, he asked her where she had been that night. But she only told him that she herself didn't know where she went from everyone's side who slept beside her.

The next night the prince decided that he wouldn't close his eyes. But no sooner did he lie down than he fell asleep and the princess disappeared. In the morning the queen entered the room with the same question: "Where is Blossom?" It's a wonder the prince didn't turn to stone right there. He made excuses, saying that there was no good in it if she could escape herself through locked doors, that perhaps parom himself had caught her.

The queen just laughed at that, but so strangely that the prince's hair stood on end. All day he walked as if on thorns, for he thought that the next day they'd behead him, and when evening came, he took the princess by the hand with the intention not to sleep the entire night. He succeeded for a long time, but his eyelids eventually fell and he was helpless.

He awoke toward morning and the princess was not at his side, so he wanted to escape. But the door was well locked from inside and out. He began to break it down, but his efforts were in vain and he sunk to the ground as if in a faint. With that the door flew open as if by itself and in stepped the queen. She didn't even ask him where Blossom was, but just laughed so that a shiver went through the prince's bones. In desperation he fell on his knees before the queen and begged her in the name of all the gods for mercy. But she pushed him away and, locking the door behind her, flew out like a witch. In a short while the executioners came, tied up the prince, led him out before the castle, and lopped off his head with a sword.

The sad tidings flew throughout the lands and came even to the prince's father. He was very aggrieved and didn't want to let his second son go to Blossom. But when he had mourned a bit, he let him go after much begging, and the second son, overjoyed, flew on his horse and only stopped at Blossom's. But it turned out sadly for him, for he didn't keep his eye on Blossom and where she went, and on the third day they removed him from the world in exactly the same way as they had his older brother.

When the tidings of that were broadcast as well, the father of the princes was even sadder and wouldn't even hear of his youngest son going to woo Blossom. But while the king thought one way, the son thought another. Once it happened that father and son went to the garden, but on foot, though they were royalty, for at that time people still didn't have carts or carriages, but just their own healthy legs.

When they arrived the king was in a good humor and his son began to beg him to let him go for Blossom. He had to beg for some time before he was allowed. But in the end, father had nothing against it. The prince prepared right away for his trip.

He was nearly ready, having only to throw his pouch over his shoulder, when someone knocked on the door. The prince opened and saw a tramp standing before the door begging alms. He immediately pulled out a groš and gave it to him, telling him to buy whatever he wanted with it. The tramp thanked him kindly and asked the prince to take him into his service, saying he knew a bit more than how to blow on his porridge. The prince replied, "Well, tell me, or show me now, what do you know?"

"People call me Long-legged," said the tramp, "for when I wish I can stretch to the clouds." With that he began to stretch and he grew by leaps and bounds, until he had grown so that the prince could no longer see his head, for it was way up in the clouds. Then he stooped and became as he was before. But afterward, saying he was a bit wearied, he lay down to rest. Meanwhile the prince set out on his way and left Long-legged to rest with other unnecessary things at home.

At one time or another, when he had rested up and stretched sufficiently, Long-legged awoke and heard that the prince had long before departed. So he stepped out the door and stretched to the clouds and took off like the wind into the fields. In an instant he disappeared from sight, for he traveled ten miles with each step, even over all the mountains and rivers.

As he strode along so, the sun beat down on his head, for his head was very close to it. But this he solved by catching a cloud in the sky and holding it over his head to veil it from the sun. He had hardly gone a few steps when he caught up to the prince, who simply wondered at what brought him there and why. But Long-legged assured him that he would be of use there, for he would need to step lively.

So they went on their way a mite and then were met by another tramp who begged something from them. The prince gave him a groš right away and wanted to go on, but the tramp stopped him and begged him to take him into his service, for he knew a bit more than how to eat bread. "What sort of thing?" asked the prince.

"Sir," he said, "I can see maybe a thousand miles, perhaps more. That's why people call me Sharp-eyed."

"That's something too," answered the prince. "But if you're such a master, tell me what my uncle is doing now in his country over the glass sea."

With that Long-legged took Sharp-eyed on his shoulders and stretched with him to the clouds. Sharp-eyed looked for a moment and then told Long-legged that the clouds were blocking his view. With that Long-legged began to blow so powerfully that trees on the high mountains broke as if a dragon was flying over them and whipping them with its tail. He didn't blow long and all the clouds dispersed and Sharp-eyed told Long-legged to stoop, for he knew already what was going on in the land beyond the glass sea.

"Eh," the prince said to them, "what kind of wind was that? Why it nearly took me and my horse!"

"I just blew the clouds off a bit," said Long-legged, "so that they wouldn't hinder Sharp-eyed."

"Well, and you, Sharp-eyed? What did you see?"

"Sir, they are preparing for war there now, for they are cleaning their swords and the king is walking among them with his two sons."

"It's true what you say," said the prince. "Come along with us, but on foot, for we have no horses."

"Small worry," added Long-legged. "Just come here, both of you!"

He took Sharp-eyed on his shoulder and the prince with his horse on his hand ahead of him, and in half an hour they were in the neighboring land at Blossom's.

The old queen promised the new suitor the princess right away if only he would accomplish what had cost his brothers their necks. But Blossom began to cry with grief as soon as she caught sight of the prince and heard that he too had to fulfill the conditions, for she fell up to her ears in love with his beauty. The prince cheered her, saying she had to be his, and entertained her in the garden and by the lake right up until evening. They didn't even know how the day had passed. That evening, when they were sitting in their room, someone knocked at the door.

"Who's there?"

Another tramp begging alms. The prince reached into his pocket and a thaler was on the tramp's palm.

"Thank you," he said, "for the advance. Take me in your service!"

"I'll take you," said the prince. "And what do you know?"

"When I want," the third one said, "I can eat and drink a great amount. That's why people call me Big-bellied."

"That too could come in handy!" said the prince, and Big-bellied stayed with him.

That evening Sharp-eyed told the prince to sleep soundly, for he had an eye one hundred times better for what would happen in the room than anyone else. So the prince slept without worries, and Sharp-eyed kept a lookout for what would happen.

At midnight he saw a golden rose fly from the prince's bed and squeeze through the door. He immediately awoke Long-legged and they went out together. Outside Long-legged took Sharp-eyed on his shoulders and stretched to the clouds with him. When Sharp-eyed looked about on all sides he said, "Well, dear brother, just head to the east and take big steps, for the princess is a hundred miles off."

Long-legged kicked up his heels and moved along so that his hair steamed. When they had come those hundred miles they saw a bush, and on that bush a lot of roses. But right in the middle was the prettiest golden rose, and that was the princess. Sharp-eyed plucked her and sat back on Long-legged's shoulders, and before long they were home again. They found the prince up already, gave him the rose, and he enjoyed it to his heart's content.

Soon it grew light and the queen came wishing good morning and asked the prince if he had slept well and where the princess was. With that the prince gave her the rose, and it's a marvel the queen didn't burst from wrath. She left with the rose, saying nothing. In a little while Blossom came and they enjoyed themselves the entire day again. That night they lay down together nicely and the prince dropped sweetly asleep, but Sharp-eyed kept a sharp lookout on everything. At midnight he saw a golden bird fly through the room and slip out of the keyhole. He immediately awoke Long-legged and they went out together. Sharp-eyed sat on the shoulders of Long-legged who stretched with him to the clouds.

When Sharp-eyed had looked around he told Long-legged to go to the north and quickly, for the princess was two hundred miles off. Long-legged went and took such steps as a genuine giant takes, or even bigger, for he was the biggest among all giants in the world.

In half an hour they were in a forest where the enchanted princess was flying like a birdie from tree to tree. It took a bit of work to catch her, but finally she was in Sharp-eyed's grasp. And it was high time, for dawn was not far off. Long-legged really hurried so that they were with the prince in a quarter hour.

No sooner had Sharp-eyed given the prince the bird than the queen trotted into the room with the question, "Where is Blossom?" The prince gave her the bird and she, in anger, ground her teeth together so that the prince's hair stood on end.

The queen again disenchanted the princess and sent her to the prince. With that Blossom asked him how he could do it, to have her by his side every morning. The prince told her not to worry about it, as long as he was succeeding. She was satisfied with that and they again walked and enjoyed themselves the whole day through.

That evening they again lay down and slept peacefully. But Sharp-eyed had his orbs open. There was a rustle at midnight and then it was quiet again. But Sharp-eyed and Long-legged squeaked out the door, and outside they stretched again to the clouds. With that Sharp-eyed looked around and said, "Stoop quickly and go get Big-bellied, for the princess is three hundred miles off, on a lake."

Long-legged stooped and went for Big-bellied. When he came out again, he took Sharp-eyed on his shoulders and Big-bellied under his arm and lit out with them into the wide world.

In an hour and a half they came to the lake on which a pure white swan was swimming and singing so beautifully that all three nearly forgot what they had to do. But that didn't last long: Long-legged jumped into the water to catch her, but it was so deep that, no matter how tall he was, only a tuft of hair stuck out.

So they went about it another way. Big-bellied lay down by the lake and began to lap up the lake water. When he had lapped a brave lot of it the bottom was showing and Sharp-eyed and Long-legged waited by his mouth to catch the swan when it went into his mouth on the water. The swan herself nearly ran into his gorge, but Sharp-eyed caught her wing right by his jaw and she was theirs. Long-legged took Sharp-eyed and the swan on his shoulders and Big-bellied under his arm and stepped homeward over hill and dale.

When they had gone quite a way, Long-legged suddenly said to Big-bellied, "My, brother, but you are heavy!"

Big-bellied responded, "Well, wait a bit. I'll be a bit lighter for you if I spit some out."

Long-legged stopped and Big-bellied spit. My, but wasn't that some spittle! It flooded whole fields and villages when it fell to the ground. He was a bit lighter then, but Long-legged had to stop numerous times until Big-bellied had spit out all the water.

After many steps they arrived home, and indeed, it was high time. For the queen had just opened the door and asked about Blossom. The prince gave her the swan, and when she saw it, she burst from spite. When the queen burst, the swan turned into a beautiful princess, threw her arms around the prince's neck and, kissing him, thanked him for her liberty.

Blossom's father didn't know what to do in his great joy. He immediately had guests summoned for the wedding, which was to take place in two days. The prince would have liked his parents as well to have come to the wedding. But they lived a few days' journey off. A messenger wouldn't have even reached them by the time the wedding started. So the prince asked Long-legged for help. Long-legged told him not to worry, that it was his job, after all. Before the wedding he set out and the joyous parents were there in a few hours. Blossom's father welcomed them royally and the joy of all joys, the wedding of all weddings, began.

There were many gentlemen, princes, and yeomen there. The music didn't cease for fourteen days, for the wedding itself lasted for as long as there was eating, drinking, and dancing.

After the feast the prince went with Blossom to the garden for a walk. The three tramps went with them and took leave of them. The prince didn't want to let them go at all, saying what would it look like if they had suffered together and now, in the midst of joy, they had to leave? But they wouldn't be delayed, saying they had to serve other good people. They shook hands in farewell and went on.

The prince lived for a long time with Blossom, and even told his grandchildren of the three good tramps who had not only saved his life, but had helped him win a good wife.

❦ 23 ❦

Heavenly Glory

Once there was a rich gentleman who had a single son called Vilko. The gentleman was already very old, grey as a pigeon and weak as a fly; given that, he only looked toward the grave. But Vilko was strong, healthy as a fish in water, and also a handsome lad, so that the girls just clung to him.

His father loved him an unheard-of amount, and besides him had no other joy in the world. The only thing that bothered him was that it seemed Vilko had no desire to marry, but just constantly roamed the world saying he would certainly not marry until he saw heavenly glory beforehand.

The father let it be for a while, for he thought the idea would fly out of his son's head. But before he knew it, Vilko was already twenty-five and still cast no glances at the girls. Then the father saw that nothing would come of waiting, and that he himself would have to interfere.

"Eh, my son, my son," he began to persuade him, but nicely, "you are already, thank the Lord, a fine lad, fit for the world, and lack nothing except to be happily married. Look, just look, nothing in the world will cheer an old man like me. But I really would be pleased if I could still enjoy myself at your wedding. Marry, my son, marry! You see, already twenty-five years have passed and you haven't even thought seriously."

"Why, I've thought indeed," said Vilko, "but I've always thought that I will not marry until I see heavenly glory." The good father became very sorrowful at such an answer and his heart ached terribly. Vilko was also sorry that he couldn't do his good father's will, but he had already set his mind. So now he went to his church where he was accustomed to pray to ask the Lord God to allow him, even if just through a keyhole, to look upon heavenly glory. His father and the family tried to persuade Vilko to marry even after this, but every God-given day Vilko just prayed on his knees in his church, and didn't marry, and didn't marry. Finally they let it be.

Months passed, and even years, but still Vilko's request remained unfulfilled. After a long, long time he himself began to think differently, and he promised his father that he would soon marry. The poor father, when he heard that from Vilko, immediately looked ten years younger. He didn't know what to do for joy that his final wish would someday be fulfilled. He immediately ordered unheard-of preparations for a wedding. The most beautiful girl in the whole country was to be his young bride. Wherever there was a gentleman, he was invited to the party. Barrels of money followed after barrels, for the old man didn't hesitate to buy everything that was expensive and valuable in the world. So it was to be a wedding such as the world did not remember.

Everything was at the peak of readiness . . . the priest stood before the altar, the bridesmaids were preparing a wreath for the head of the bride, and the groomsmen were waiting at hand to lead her to the wedding. With that dear Vilko, at the finest moment when everything was waiting on him, sneaked quietly out from between the wedding guests and ran to his church to pray one final time to the Lord God to let him, if just for a moment, into heavenly glory.

He prayed and prayed, kneeling on his bare knees. And while he was praying, an old, old little man came to him, and he was God's messenger. "Well, Vilko, why are you praying here?" asked the old man.

"Ah, why am I praying! I swore that I wouldn't marry before I saw heavenly glory. And look, now it's time for my wedding and I still haven't seen a thing, not even so much as a poppy seed."

"Well, and would you really like to see heavenly glory?"

"I would, I would, grandfather."

"Well, if you desire it so, sit on my back!" Vilko didn't have to be told twice. He seated himself, and no sooner had he done so than the world disappeared from before his eyes. No one saw what had happened; no one saw where they went, which way the old man flew with Vilko. There was just, they say, a rustle, and such a lovely odor spread throughout the world that people couldn't even manage to greet each other, they were sneezing so.

God's messenger flew with Vilko in a moment to heaven's gates. There he set him down, took off his clothes, dressed him in heavenly garb and sent him thus into heaven. But no man, even if he be a hundred times wiser than the wisest, knows how it went for Vilko in heaven, only it is certain that it had to go well, for he forgot about his father and his bride and everything that was dear to him below. And when God's messenger came to him to send him home, Vilko said, "Ah, I've only been here an hour. Allow me, please, to enjoy another hour." The second hour passed as lightly as a sweet dream and Vilko still did not want to go down, for when the messenger called him he said, "Ah, please, oh please, leave me here for a third little hour; why, I'll certainly go then."

The old man let himself be persuaded, and Vilko again enjoyed heavenly glory. He didn't even notice how quickly time was flying by until God's messenger came to him a third time: "Well, Vilko, that should be enough for you; now you must go down!"

And poor Vilko, willy-nilly, made his way out. The old man again changed his clothes before the gate, took him on his back, and flew with him back to the very place from which he had carried him off. Then Vilko again kneeled and thanked the Lord God that he had let him look upon heavenly glory.

When he had finished praying, he stood up. "Well," he said, "now I will go gladly to my wedding," and he went out. But what kind of miracle was this! Everything appeared differently to him than it had before. He wiped his eyes as though awakened from a dream; he looked around like one who doesn't trust himself. Had his eyes been so changed by the heavenly glory, or what?

The very church he had once helped to build. But now it looked blackened, pocked, as if the tenth set of shingles were already rotting on it. Three hours ago there was a graveyard in front of the church, and now winter corn was greening there. Where the mill stream had flowed before, now there was a heavily trafficked road upon which carts ran hither and thither.

Poor Vilko didn't understand the least of it. The whole landscape was foreign, unfamiliar, as if he were seeing it for the first time. Only the large boulders between the fields to the east stood unchanged and he recognized them as the same ones he had loved to look on as a child. "Ah," he thought, "the Lord God must indeed be very mighty if he could change everything so much in such a short period of time!"

He came to his father's castle. It, too, appeared old, grimy, as though it had been built before the world remembered when. He entered, and unfamiliar people were walking around everywhere. He bowed and spoke to everyone welcomingly, for it seemed that these were the guests that had come for the wedding. "Right away, right away," he said, "we can have the wedding. I've taken care of my business."

But people looked at him with their eyes bugging out, heard him with their jaws agape, and no one dared to ask him, "Who are you? Where are you from?" They just looked at the strange man, and Vilko wondered even more at their wonder. Luckily there was an old ashboy there who was more than three hundred years old. He recognized his young master and called to him by name.

"And who are you, good man?" asked Vilko.

"Well, don't you recognize me, your ashboy?"

"Ashboy!" recalled Vilko. "Have you, my ashboy, really aged on me so?"

"Aye, aged indeed! What should I do when the Lord God refuses to call me home?"

"And where is my father, my bride?"

"Ah, where indeed? Your bride married another and has long since passed away with him. You father has returned to dust. Why, three hundred years have passed since that time!"

At last it dawned on Vilko! Three hundred years! And it had seemed to him less than three hours! He looked toward heaven, looked at the earth, and from that moment grew visibly older and older. His eyes grew dim, his cheeks fell, his beard became as white as snow, and his body bent to the ground, so that in a few moments he looked not a mite younger than the ashboy. Two men over three hundred years old were looking eye to eye!

With that a quiet breeze blew over them and they both turned to dust!

♥ 24 ♥

Old Bodrík and the Wolf

The bača had a dog, Bodrík,[1] that had tended his sheep watchfully for years, at night as in the daytime, so that a wolf couldn't even approach the fold. But what good was that, when old Bodrík had already gone lame and hadn't a single tooth left? "An old dog is only good for the trash heap," said the bača. "Why feed the old cur when he's not up to it anymore?" Instead they fed a young pup, petted him, and sent him out to the fold.

Old Bodrík lay hungry on the trash heap and grieved over what had become of him. Night fell. The young dog crept into the building and stretched out there on a bed of tow. Old Bodrík slept attentively; even now he was aware of a wolf. He tried to jump the fence, but his legs weren't up to it because he was starved. He sadly lay down again and thought, "When I have none, let the wolf have his fare!" He didn't even bark.

Going to milk his sheep that morning, the bača noticed one was missing. After a bit, it dawned on him, "Hey, surely if old Bodrík had been on watch, the wolf wouldn't have carried one off!" And so he shouted for old Bodrík to come back to him, petted him nicely, and fed him well. Old Bodrík ran circles around him and jumped for joy. In the evening he didn't lie down on the trash heap, nor in the building, but circled the fold, for he knew that where the wolf had once been enticed, there he would certainly return. And come the wolf did, as though to a sure thing.

But Bodrík stood in his path, "What do *you* want here?"

"What do you mean, what do I want? I want a sheep!" said the wolf.

"If you run with wolves, the devil takes your sheep and bulls!" answered old Bodrík. "Yesterday my master didn't feed me. I was hungry and weak, so it was easy enough for you to carry off a sheep. But today my master fed me well, I'm strong enough again and you'll get no sheep from me."

"If you won't give me a sheep, then prepare for a scuffle with me! Do you know what that means?" goaded the wolf.

"Well, if you're going to be that way, prepare to scuffle yourself. As soon as I finish my sentry duty around the fold, first thing in the morning I'll oppose you there in the forest and we'll scuffle! If you know how!"

The wolf simply snarled and ran to the forest to scavenge up some support, because he wanted vengeance right away on old Bodrík. He convinced the bear and the fox to help him.

But the dog knew the ways of wolves quite well, and didn't go to the forest alone, but took with him the sow and the old tomcat, his long-standing retinue. He himself limped on one leg, and these two were no longer young, but for all that they were true and tested friends.

When the bear and fox caught sight of the approaching group, they became quite frightened. "Look, brothers," exclaimed the bear, "see how the first one constantly bends over. He's surely collecting stones to kill us with." The dog was hobbling and the bear thought that every time he veered he picked up a stone.

"Look at the second one," exclaimed the fox, "hacking about with a sword!" The tomcat waved his tail upward and the fox thought he was displaying a sword.

And then, when they heard the sow grunt, they knew her from her voice and that she was expecting and certainly would not be joking around. Well, they certainly didn't take it lightly either. The bear climbed up a tree and the fox jumped into some thorns.

When our friends arrived in the forest, the tomcat purred happily: "prrn-prrn." The fox heard "thorn, in the thorns" and thought they wanted to jump on her first. She didn't wait, but jumped out of the bushes and headed off. The sow began to grunt under the bear: "urp-urp-urp." The bear heard "up-up," indicating that she knew that he was up there and that she wanted to root up the tree, for she was fiercely rooting with her snout. He didn't delay either, but jumped down and was soon beyond hill and dale. The wolf was left alone and was pleased simply to skedaddle himself, with his skin intact.

Old Bodrík let out a bark and the whole forest echoed with it. He was glad that his friends had helped him and they had chased the savages far beyond the forest. Thenceforth and ever after he lived well in the fold, until his death.

Note

1. The dog's name comes from the adjective "bodrý," which means "lively."— Trans.

❦ 25 ❦

A Pair of Equal Beauty

*I*t happened. If it didn't happen, it will never happen, for the wonders that took place during the blessed memory of Kaukoň King have ceased. Once there was a king and a queen and they had so much wealth that no king in the world could equal them. But all that wealth pleased them little, and from year to year they became all the sadder, for they had no heir. "Ah, to whom, to whom should we leave this our kingdom and all our treasures after our deaths!" wailed the queen. "Who knows into whose evil hands it will fall and afterward everything will be ruined!"

The same thoughts also gave the king no peace, but he still comforted the queen, "Eh, don't worry my dear, don't worry. Everything can still be alright, the Lord God can still bless even us." And the Lord God blessed them indeed, for a year later the queen gave birth to a beautiful son. There was unheard-of joy! Emissaries ran in all directions to summon the nobility from the entire realm. The feast lasted three whole weeks and music played day and night, for the king wouldn't have wagered for the whole world that his greatest desire would be fulfilled.

The royal parents were pleased with their son, who grew into a strapping fellow. Now his father and mother began to persuade him to get married. "Give us the joy," they said, "of making merry in our old age at your wedding!" They recommended him this princess, then that princess, one prettier than the other, for him to chose from according to his own will. But not a single one pleased him, and when they still didn't give him any peace he said to them finally that he would not marry at all. That displeased the king very much. "How would it be," he said, "if you didn't marry?" Indeed, upon his death the kingdom again would be without an heir. And again they tried to persuade him and bargained with him every which way, but nothing came of it.

When the king saw that they would never get anywhere by dealing nicely, he tightened the strings up and began to deal with his doggone son more firmly. But all for naught. In the end the king became so enraged that he shut him up in a room where no one had ever lived and set a servant there to guard him.

In front of the door where the prince was shut up was a very deep well, and in that well lived a witch. Around midnight, when everything in the castle was sleeping, she pulled herself out and a flash shone in her eye through the keyhole, for even when the prince fell asleep a candle had to be burning beside him. This struck the witch as strange: "What? Is something shining in that room? I'll have to see for myself."

She peeked through the keyhole and saw the prince in bed. She immediately turned into a fly, flew inside, and looked and looked at him, shaking her head. "My," she said, "aren't you a pretty one!" When she had looked her fill, she again flew out and wandered the earth.

While she was wandering hither and thither, she met up with a tall, thin man, and he was a wizard. They recognized each other right off. "Where are you coming from?" the wizard asked her.

"From my beautiful prince," answered the witch. "And you from where?"

"From my beautiful princess!"

"From your beautiful princess?"

"From my beautiful princess. And so that you know, there's none more beautiful in the whole world."

"Come on," replied the witch, "my prince is a hundred times more beautiful, and if you don't believe it, run and fetch your princess; then you'll see."

The wizard was off like a shot and flew back in a moment with his princess. Well and good. They carried the princess to the prince's room and laid her in the bed beside him. Then they began again to screech: "The prince is more beautiful! The princess is more beautiful!" And this took a few moments. In the end, the wizard became fed up:

"Well, wait," he said, "I'll put an end to this argument." And with that he stomped his foot so that the whole room shook. In the middle of the room a fathomless abyss opened up and the supreme judge from hell stood before them.

"Well, what do you want?!" he said. "Why have you disturbed my peace again?"

"Don't be angry, don't," the witch pacified him. "We just were quarreling a bit over which of these two is more beautiful. I say the prince, and he says the princess. What do you say?"

"That will be clear right away," rumbled the judge from hell. "We'll see how they behave toward one another." All three of them turned into flies and the judge from hell buzzed under the prince's nose, so that he immediately awoke. When he spotted the princess beside him, he was quite surprised and did not believe his own eyes, for it seemed to him that he was dreaming. After he had looked around better, he saw that he was not dreaming after all. Then he began to wail at his parents. "What are they thinking?" he said. "Why didn't they show her to me during the day?" And he looked and looked at her, and the more he looked, the more he liked her. "Eh, if they had shown me this one," he said, "I wouldn't have said a word. My, isn't she beautiful, isn't she fair!"

While he was saying this, he exchanged his ring with the princess's. With that the fly buzzed again: the prince fell asleep, and now they awakened the princess. She, too, when she saw the prince beside her, at first was very surprised and then complained about her parents, asking why they didn't show him to her during the day. She looked and looked at him, and the more she looked, the more she liked him. "Eh, if they had shown me this one," she said, "I wouldn't have said a word. My, aren't you beautiful! Aren't you lovely!"

With that she wanted to swap her ring for the prince's, but she saw that they were already changed. Then the fly buzzed and the princess fell asleep. The flies changed back into what they were before.

Now the judge from hell gave his judgment that the two were equal in beauty. With that, he vanished and the wizard flew off with the princess to where he had taken her from. The witch descended into her well.

In the morning, as soon as the prince awoke he asked the servant who was the one who had slept beside him that night. The poor servant, who knew nothing of what had happened, for he had slept like the dead, avoided answering however he could at first, and finally said, jokingly, that it was probably just a dream.

But the prince became enraged at that, grabbed the servant, and tried to throw him into the well in front of the door. Only with great difficulty did the servant claw his way out of his grasp and ran all affright to the king's chamberlain, saying that the prince's wits were not in order, that he had told him of some maiden who had slept beside him during the night and when he couldn't tell him anything about it, that he had tried to throw him into the well.

The chamberlain didn't take this lightly, but went straight to the prince: "Good morning! How did you sleep?"

But the irritated prince cut him off: "Why should you ask? Instead you tell me who it was that slept beside me this night."

"I know of no one," the amazed chamberlain excused himself. And when the prince just firmly insisted that he say, for if he didn't, things would go badly for him, he too began to think that the prince must have lost his wits a bit, and he hurried straight to the king himself.

When the king heard what had happened with the prince, he was terrified and wrung his hands. "My Lord, my Lord! What have I lived to see in my old age? This will finally lead me to the grave! Ah, if only I hadn't dealt with him so severely! If only I hadn't shut him up in that room!" Lamenting thus he came to his son. "How are you, my dear son? What has happened to you?"

"Why, you well know what has happened to me," answered the prince.

"But father dear, I would never have guessed that you would play such jokes on me." The king tried in vain to make excuses, saying that he knew of nothing, but the prince would not be calmed and believed only when the king swore to him on his crown.

No sooner had that happened than the prince fell ill and took to his bed.

The princess who had been beside the prince that night was also the precious only child of wealthy, royal parents. When she was old enough to wed, rich princes from all over requested her hand, but she did not like any of them.

In the end her father became angered and also locked her up in an isolated room with a servant. After that night, as soon as she awoke, she immediately began to ask after the prince. When no one could tell her anything and in the end the king swore upon his crown, she too fell ill and took to her bed.

The king and queen were terribly frightened for the princess and immediately called doctors, each of whom gave his best advice. But all of that helped not at all and the princess worsened from day to day.

Luckily the old servant woman had a son, a soldier. He seized upon an idea and asked the king to give him leave, saying he would go straight to the ends of the earth and would be sure to find such a doctor as could cure the princess. Well and good. He started off right the next day.

He had already traversed the seventy-sixth country and still hadn't found the doctor he was looking for. But in the seventy-seventh he came to the town where the sick prince was lying.

"What is new here?" he asked people.

"Sad news!" he was answered. "The king's son is sick unto death." And they told him the whole story. Elated, he immediately set out for the king's castle and announced himself, that he was so and so, a doctor from the seventy-seventh country, and promised to cure the prince.

"Come on," the king said to him, "there have been doctors here aplenty and none of them could help." After some time, though, he did allow him to test his luck. "Fine, then," he said, "just step back a bit and leave me alone with the sick one!"

Everyone left the room and he sat down by the prince's bed. Then he began to tell about the princess, and whatever he knew, he told. When the prince had heard that, he needed no other medicine and gained enough strength to sit up. The king and queen then returned and saw that their son was already sitting. They cried like children for great joy. In a week the prince was a man fit for his place.

Then the doctor told the prince that it was time to be on their way, for in the meantime the princess could easily die from her great grief. They conferred right away about what to do and how to do it. They furtively prepared two sets of clothing and requested the king to allow them to go on a hunt. Then they saddled their horses, took with them one servant, and went to the nearest forest. When they had gone in a good distance they jumped down and tied their horses to a tree. Then the prince turned to the servant and told him to go collect dry wood, that they would build a fire.

When the servant had left, they cut his horse to pieces, quickly changed clothing and splattered those they had worn from home in blood. They then sat on their horses again and galloped on. When the servant came with the wood he saw the horse strewn all over and the bloody clothing. He was frightened out of his wits, for it seemed that a wild animal had torn them apart. He was even afraid to return home, but just roamed hither and thither.

Noon came and they were expecting the prince and doctor at home. Evening came, and still nothing. The king and queen were terrified and couldn't close their eyes the whole night; and no sooner did it begin to lighten than they sent twelve men to search for the prince. The men soon returned and told what they had seen and found. Then there was crying and lamenting throughout the royal town.

But the prince and the doctor were flying day and night, until they came to the castle where the sick princess was lying. The soldier entered the room first, alone. There the princess lay on the bed, already more dead than alive, and the king and queen were crying, wailing over her.

"Well, don't cry," the soldier began, "I've found a doctor already and he will certainly cure her."

"And where is he? Why didn't you bring him right away?" the king and queen asked together.

"He's here, don't worry," replied the soldier. "But he asks that you step back, for he says he must first speak with the princess alone." The king and queen stepped into the side room and the soldier called the prince.

No sooner had the prince stepped in than the princess recognized him and stretched out her arms toward him and spoke in a weak voice, "That's him! That's him! Ah, welcome, welcome! I'm glad you've come. An hour more would have been too late!"

Eh, that was a doctor! The sick one visibly regained color, and when her parents returned they didn't know what to do for joy that their daughter had come around in such a short moment.

The prince sat constantly beside his dear, but did not tell her parents, and he also told the princess to remain silent. Only when she had become entirely well did she reveal to her parents that it was he, of whom she had spoken, and he introduced himself as a king's son. In a short while they celebrated the wedding of the pair *of equal beauty*!

And when they had celebrated a bit, everyone, young and old, set out for the prince's parents, who were still weeping over his death. Well, now there was certainly joy, welcomes, feasts, music, dance, and whatnot!

After the death of the old kings, both kingdoms fell to the young prince.

On the willow hangs a bell, that's all there is to tell.

❦ 26 ❦

Klinko and Kompit King

*I*n Kompit King's land there was a village, and in that village
lived a father with three sons who wouldn't amount to anything.
Once he led them into the forest to test them and see which of
them, after all, would turn out to be worth something. While they were walking in the forest, the oldest one spotted a crooked hornbeam tree and called
out, "Hey, father, wouldn't that hornbeam be great for a wheel rim!"

"Well, good," said the father, "you're going to be a wheelwright."

A bit later the second one spotted a maple and called out, "Hey, father,
wouldn't there be good troughs from that maple!"

"Well, good," said the father, "you're going to be a trough-maker."

And finally the youngest one spotted a wild apple and called out, "Hey,
father, have a gander at that apple. I'll make some cuts, and won't it make a
fine cudgel!"

"And what do *you* need a cudgel for?" said the father. "You're not thinking of committing highway robbery with it?"

"Perhaps even highway robbery!" said the son, and he immediately made
cuts for the cudgel.[1]

The father began the other two on their trades straight-away. And the next
spring, the youngest cut his cudgel from the wild apple, bleached and fired it,
and also left to ply his trade. Which ways he wandered, we don't know, but it's
enough that in the early autumn our Klinko, for that was his name, once again
appeared at home, saying he would continue to ply his trade there.

Kompit King, too, heard something of what trade our Klinko had learned.
He had him summoned, and Klinko stood boldly before him. "You, Klinko,"
he said, "is it true that you've taken up highway robbery?"

"If I may be permitted a word," answered Klinko, "I have not yet taken up
highway robbery, but I have learned that trade."

"Hm, hm," said the king, shaking his head, "and do you know your trade?"

"Do I know it? Test me if you like."

"Why, that's what I intended to do, to test you. And so, behold, today my harvesters are harvesting the winter corn with four oxen. If you steal the two lead oxen without hurting any of them, they're yours, but if not, I'll send you to the cooler as a highwayman, since you've admitted to the trade, and you'll wait long before seeing the light of day again." Well and good, the bet was made.

Klinko scared up a number of black chickens in the village and hid from the harvesters beside the fields in the bushes. When they approached along the furrow to his hiding place, he released the chickens in front of them. "Aha, young thrushes! Aha, young thrushes!" called the harvesters, and they began to chase the hens through the bushes.

In the meantime, Klinko left the bushes, cut off the tails of the two lead oxen and stuffed them in the jaws of the two behind, unhitched the two maimed ones and didn't stop with them until they were at home in the barn. The harvesters opened their traps to no avail, for the hens scattered and hid from them in the bushes. But it's a wonder they didn't perish from surprise when they returned to the team. Why, only the tails of the lead oxen stuck out of the mouths of the two behind! They immediately ran off like a shot to their lord, saying it had to be that the two oxen behind had devoured the lead team, for when they came back after a moment, they were just gnawing on the tails.

"Indeed, they have devoured your reason, if you didn't drink it away somewhere first," said the king. "Didn't I warn you that Klinko was coming to steal the lead oxen, and you still let yourselves be bamboozled by him?! Well, but it's too late to waste words over," he added, when he thought about it. "Why, we'll slap him silly the next time, since he's started it!"

The oxen were Klinko's, but to what end? The king again had him summoned before him. "You, Klinko," he said, "that was nothing clever with those bulls, but if you don't cart off all my grain by morning from the threshing floor, where my threshers have threshed it into a pile, well, then you'll just end up in the best place for little birdies like yourself." Klinko agreed once again, and in the meantime, the king warned his threshers not to sleep the entire night and to beat Klinko with their flails if he were to show.

The threshers didn't sleep; in fact they watched so sharply on all sides, it's a wonder their eyes didn't pop out. All at once something, in all its actions like Klinko, crept in from the side into a corner of the threshing floor and straight to the pile. Well, they weren't idle! They grabbed their flails and whop! whop! they struck its head, its legs, its body; it resounded like no entrails ever had. Well, its legs and arms moved no more. When they had rung him off like that, they lay down and slept till morning like they were safe. In the morning the pile of grain was gone! Had a sprite carried it off, or the wind caught it? No, the rascal Klinko had slaughtered his oxen for salt curing and had taken their entrails and wound them in straw in the shape of a man and had shoved it in the area in his clothes. They convinced themselves of what they had been flailing and it didn't need to be said that while they were sleeping, Klinko had waltzed in and carted off the whole pile of grain. Now he had something for meat and for bread!

But King Kompit now thought, "Wait, you rogue, you won't come by it that easily! I'll have to entice you into my home." He had Klinko summoned and told him, "Either you give up your skin now, or steal all my bacon. Look, here it is, curing in the chimney!" Klinko indeed looked it over and left. But the king placed a guard under the chimney from the evening on and ordered them to pack in the powder and fire away at the slightest rustle in the chimney.

The sharpshooters were definitely on the lookout, and suddenly they heard something rustling down the chimney, going "oh!" The three of them immediately shot up the chimney, and it just sighed, as if steam were pouring out of it, and tumbled down the chimney. It sprawled at their feet like a body without a soul. With the shots, the king himself burst out of the room with a lamp. They looked at the soulless Klinko—and saw bagpipes with a deflated and shot-through bag, for Klinko had lowered those bagpipes into the chimney from above, and they had oh'ed when the bag had touched the walls, and they had sighed out the steam when they had been shot. They shined the lamp up the chimney, and the bacon was already gone! Klinko was somewhere at home licking his fingers from the fat. The king sent from the other end of the house to the roof right away to catch the highwayman. But Klinko had only left them an empty ladder leaning against the house. They could only sing, "As soon as you snooze, the bacon you'll lose, and the lard." Klinko and his father would certainly have enough grease for the winter!

The king was vexed, but he wanted to try again, to see how he himself would measure up with Klinko. Well and good. Kompit had hussars in his court, and they were trained to be on the lookout, whether at war or wherever, and probably the devil himself couldn't put one over on them. Each of them kept a saddle horse and would probably let his eyes be plucked before giving up his horse. The king entirely relied on and trusted them, and so he just told Klinko, "Eh, Klinko, Klinko, you're a dirty dog indeed! But if you don't steal my head hussar's horse from the stable this night, I'll have you quartered. You've taken me for so much already!"

But he warned the head hussar, "Look, you, if you let that horse be stolen, you'll walk behind the others forever!"

Well, now the hussar's honor was at stake as well. So he placed a guard by the gate, in front of the stable, and three in each corner of the stable. Yet another was to hold the horse by the bridle, another by the tail, and the boss himself sat on the horse, thinking he would see the one who stole his horse if he were sitting on it. And so they watched for that dog Klinko with sabers drawn and carbines on their shoulders.

Toward evening some shopkeeper came that way with his wheelbarrow. "Halt, man, what are you carting?" said the guard, stopping him.

"Ah, well, what indeed? A little slivovica and a little borovička in these two barrels. But let me pass, for I have to get home to the next village and I'm afraid to travel in the dark, lest that dog Klinko rob me."

"And do you know Klinko?"

"Do I know him? Why, he drank the nights through at my place with his friends until he learned his trade. But I'd like to skin him alive, because for all he drank all year he put me off, saying he would pay me for the rest at the next carnival."

"Aha, sir, then we are friends!" said the guard, and wouldn't let him budge until he had word from his boss. The word was that the shopkeeper should come in, that at least he would recognize Klinko if he came with his friends, for they needed only to slap Klinko himself silly. The shopkeeper resisted, but they tore his harness from his neck and cast him inside with all his things to wait for that dog Klinko.

Klinko didn't come. He didn't need to, for he was already there. But he played another and just waited until the fruitless watch and wait really got on everyone's nerves. Then he said, "Boys, why we're crazy! To have so much and not to use it!"

"Indeed, you're right," said the chief himself. "Here I am, going mousey from hunger and thirst on that horse. Give me a glassful!" The shopkeeper gave him a glassful of powerful liquid. But when he had drunk his glassful and the boys brightened up, then glass followed glass. By midnight, each was snoring in his corner and the one on the horse teetered from side to side, so that it's a wonder he didn't fall and break his neck. Well, our shopkeeper didn't want that on his conscience, so he quietly brought a trunk and sat him on it from the horse and tied him on with straw bands so there would be no accident. He also stuck straw bands in the hands of the one holding the bridle and one with the tail in his hand. With that he himself sat on the horse and galloped off like a hussar. Why, they had quite a sight in the morning when they wiped their eyes!

"Klinko, Klinko, you are a branded rogue! Let hell itself vie with you! But we'll keep to our own," said the king in the morning when he assured himself of how Klinko had nicely comported himself, even against his hussars.

But it soon came to vying with hell itself. One of Kompit King's daughters disappeared soon after, and they said devils carried her off. He sent after Klinko three times to steal his daughter from hell. But he now got no response until the king announced that he would give his girl to wife to whomever leads her out of hell. Then Klinko requested from him chalk that would write in triplicate, three pounds of incense, and three bricks, and left with that.

When he arrived in hell, he made a circle around himself with the triplicate chalk, lit the incense, and set up those three bricks. As soon as the devils smelled that incense, they swarmed about him. "Klinko, what do you want, why are you burning incense?"

"Well, you know, I'm building a church here and burning incense so that you know ahead of time what it will be like when the priests will burn incense under your noses."

The devils were sneezing like mad from the incense, they couldn't endure it, let alone allow someone to build a church. "Eh, Klinko, don't build it! Instead, we'll give you what you want."

"Well, you crazy devils, you should have known right off what I've come after. Give me my lord's daughter!" They led before him some girl without arms. "Ah, you jackasses, you think you'll get rid of me with such a thing!" said Klinko, and he burned the incense more intensely and continued building the church. Then they led him another girl without legs. "Ah, you brutes, you," Klinko inveighed against them, "Give me the proper one instantly!" The devils shoved twelve identical maidens toward his circle, screeched, "Choose the right one!" and ran off to the other end of hell, for they couldn't stand the incense there.

Klinko just looked over the maidens: all of them were sputtering from the incense except for the last one. He took that one and went on his way with her. He walked and walked over hill and dale, and the first devil caught up to him. "Stop, Klinko, the maiden isn't yours."

"And whose is she?"

"The one's who runs off and gets lost beyond that summit first."

"Fine, brother, but I'm not your equal. I'm tired from the long walk, but there, under the hazel bush, is my brother, all rested. Knock on the bush and run with him!" The devil pounded on the shrub, and out jumped a hare, and by the time the devil gathered his wits, it was already over the summit.

He walked on and on over hill and dale, and the second devil caught up to him. "Stop, Klinko, the maiden isn't yours!"

"And whose is she?"

"The one's who first throws the other to the ground."

"You must be mad to think I'd tangle with you, since I'm making a trip both there and back, and you only here. I'm beat. But there, where you came out from under that outcropping, is my older brother. Tangle with him!" The devil ran off to the cave! There an old bear welcomed him with his paws and hurled him so deep into the ground that he only stopped just above the pit of hell, if in fact he didn't grind his way through.

He walked on and on over hill and dale, and the third devil caught up to him. "Stop, Klinko, the maiden isn't yours!"

"And whose is she?"

"The one's who whistles the loudest." The devil let out such a whistle that the tops of the trees shook and it echoed back from way off the seventh peak. Klinko then began to fell small birches all over the mountain.

"Why are you felling those trees?" asked the devil.

"I have to secure my head and the maiden's and even the head of all of hell, so they won't shatter when I whistle. Wind yourself a lash, brother, if you like, so we can get it over with!" The devil became frightened at that and left Klinko there.

Then Klinko successfully made his way home with the maiden. The king, as he had promised, right away gave her to him to wife and with her half the kingdom. Klinko hung his trade on a nail, since he had won Kompit King's daughter and he had more to defend, rather than buying at the price of his five fingers a sixth palm.

Note

1. The cuts are made on a young wild apple or pear tree, usually bent at the base and of suitable size for a cudgel. With a knife or valaška, cuts are made all around and as deep as the wood, about one foot high. The young tree remains on its stump thus for a year or even two. Large knots develop from these cuts. Then they cut the tree, dry it, bleach it, and fire it, and the cudgel is fit to hand.

❧ 27 ❧

Kinglet, Cooklet, and Ashlet

*I*t was during that blissful time when pigs wore boots and frogs walked about in bonnets and magpies wore hats; when donkeys jangled their spurs in the streets and hares trumpeted for the dogs. Back then the girls had it good: the dogs washed the dishes, the pigs oiled the stoves, the geese swept out the rooms, and the fish: the carp washed the rags for them in the Hron River and the crayfish rinsed them out. Don't worry, girls! The pigs have already begun to wear boots, the frogs to walk about in bonnets, and the magpies to wear fastened-on hats; the donkeys again jangle their spurs in the streets and the hares trumpet for the dogs. The good times will come again!

So, during those blissful times there was a king and he had a very pretty wife. But his pretty wife had no children. So the king had it proclaimed throughout the land that whomever could be found that could advise his wife as to what would give her a child, that person would receive a large reward. The queen was given all sorts of advice, but to no avail.

Finally an old dame came and brought her a fish and told her to eat it, but not to allow anyone even to taste of it.[1] The queen ran straight to the kitchen, ordered the fish fried, and warned the cook not even to take a sniff of it.

"Eh, the devil if I'm going to cook food and not even taste if it's salty or not!" the cook said faced with the food, and she tasted it.

When the food was ready, she carried it to the queen, who ate it up straight-away. The cook carried the plate out to the kitchen, where the ashgirl, who fed the stove, was fidgeting about. And the girl licked the plate from that fish. So, then, the queen, the cook, and the ashgirl all became pregnant at once, and they all gave birth at once on the same day, and each had a fine boy.

They later named those boys according to their mothers, Kinglet, Cooklet, and Ashlet, and the king had all three of them raised and educated the same. But Ashlet was the smartest and the finest of them all.[2]

The three boys grew up steadily, and finally grew into strapping young lads. With that they all stood as one before the king and asked him to let them go try the world. The king let them go, but warned them not to lose one another and to stick together.

So they sat on their fairy horses and that same day cantered over a fair chunk of the world until they stopped in a large valley where they spent the night. They awoke at dawn and Ashlet took his cudgel in hand and threw it as far as he could. "Well," he said, "we'll breakfast where that cudgel fell!" So they went, and it took some time until they came to the cudgel. There they breakfasted. After breakfast Ashlet took his cudgel and threw it on further. "Well," he said, "we'll lunch there!" They went, and around noon they rode up to the place where the cudgel fell. They immediately sat down, let their horses graze, and ate their fill of lunch. After lunch Ashlet took his cudgel and threw it as far as he could. "Well," he said, "we'll sleep by that cudgel!"

The cudgel fell right by an iron bridge. That evening they all arrived there and made a lean-to, saying they'd spend the night there. "But this iron bridge here must mean something," said Ashlet. "We'll have to keep watch for what will happen. Who of you is of a brave heart that will guard my sword till morning on the bridge?" and he fastened his sword in the middle of the bridge.

"Well, I'm the one!" said Kinglet. "You sleep peacefully and I'll keep a good eye on everything." But to himself he thought, "You just go to sleep, then I'll lie down as well. I'd be a madman not to get a good sleep!" The other two lay down by the fire and Cooklet began to snore right away. Only Ashlet didn't sleep; but he pretended that he, too, was already snoring. When Kinglet heard those snores as well, he lay down by the campfire and wheezed like a bag. Ashlet was just waiting for that. He quietly got up and stood watch on the iron bridge.

At midnight a gale blew up, the water splashed and the bridge shook. A three-headed dragon flew up on a fairy horse. But the dragon's fairy horse stumbled before the iron bridge. "Ho, what are you afraid of, horsey?" spoke the dragon. "Why, Ashlet is a good man, but I'm better. Soon you'll bathe in his blood."

"Maybe you will, maybe you won't!" said Ashlet, and he took his saber, drew it three times over the sharpening steel, and made his way toward the dragon. Snicker-snack! At once the three heads were off! The dragon's body fell into the water and was carried off. Then Ashlet, too, slept peacefully until morn.

"Well, what happened during the night?" those two asked Kinglet in the morning.

"What could happen?" he said. "Nothing!"

"Well, if there's nothing here, let's go on," said Ashlet. "Maybe there something will come up."

And so they set out and in the evening arrived at a silver bridge. Ashlet again fastened his sword in the middle of the bridge and said, "Well, which will undertake to guard this sword for me till morning?"

"I'll undertake it!" spoke Cooklet, and he remained beside the sword. Kinglet and Ashlet were snoring sweetly by the campfire, but Ashlet only for show. Cooklet envied them, and lay down beside them and dropped off right away.

Ashlet arose immediately and stood on the silver bridge. At midnight a gale blew up, the water splashed and the bridge shook, for a six-headed dragon was flying toward the bridge. But the dragon's fairy horse stumbled before the bridge. "Ho, horsey, what do you fear?" said the dragon. "Maybe it frightens you that Ashlet killed my brother? Never fear, you'll soon bathe in his blood!"

"Maybe you will, maybe you won't!" said Ashlet taking out his sword and drawing it across the sharpening steel.

They fought. The dragon's heads fell into the water and his body after them; the water carried it all off. Ashlet slept well until the bright morn.

"What did you spy this night?" the brothers asked Cooklet, who had arisen before morning and stood like a brave fellow on the bridge.

"Nothing!" he said.

"Well, if nothing, then let's go on!" said Ashlet. They went, and in the evening they came to a golden bridge.

"Now I shall be on watch," Ashlet said to the others, and they agreed, especially as they had caught sight of a hut not far off, and it was empty. "Just keep watch," they thought, "we'll at least get a good rest in bed; for we've already had enough of roughing it." But Ashlet knew that if it had been bad till then, now it would be worse. So he hung his cuffs in the hut over the bed and told them, "Look that you don't sleep until midnight, and if blood runs from these cuffs, come to my aid, but if water runs, you can sleep in peace." The brothers promised and Ashlet went on watch.

He watched and watched and counted stars to pass the time. At midnight the earth rumbled, a tempest roared, the water sprayed and the bridge shook. A twelve-headed dragon was flying toward it. The dragon's fairy horse stumbled and stopped before the bridge. "Why are you standing, horsey?" asked the dragon. "Fear not that Ashlet did my two brothers in, he'll not do me in; soon you'll bathe in his blood!" But the fairy horse didn't budge.

"Let me pass over the bridge, Ashlet!" roared the dragon.

"Come on then!" said Ashlet, welcoming him with a sharpened saber.

The dragon entered the fray, and the first six heads fell just like that. But the remaining ones fell only with suffering. Ashlet hewed away firmly, and blood began to drip from the cuffs, but his brothers did not awaken. After that misery, he relieved the dragon of three more heads, and blood already ran from the cuffs in a trickle. But still no one came to his aid. He gathered his remaining strength and lopped off the dragon's three remaining heads.

But with that he fell unconscious to the ground and slept there.

The sweet little sun awakened the brothers in the morning. They found themselves covered in blood. "Oh!" they said, "things are bad for our brother!" They jumped to their feet, took their sabers and ran to his aid. On one side of the bridge they found their brother sleeping, and the body of the dragon strewn over the other. They were afraid to awaken Ashlet, but he himself awoke and laughed how they had come to his aid. They held their tongues, for they had to. They threw the body of the dragon into the water, which foamed terribly and carried it off. Then they sat on their horses and went on.

They had already run a considerable stretch of the road when it occurred to Ashlet that he had forgotten his cuffs in that little hut. "Wait, brothers!" he said. "I'm going for those cuffs. I'll be right back." And so he went to that little hut. But he heard straight off that someone was talking inside there. He immediately tied his horse to a tree off to the side and himself made his way on tiptoes to under the window, where he could overhear what was going on inside. An old witch was sitting at the table with her three girls and they were discussing the following:

"Well, we'll just have to wipe them off the face of the earth, since Ashlet did in our husbands," one of the maidens spoke up.

"If it weren't for Ashlet, we'd bring the other two to ruin more easily," said the crone.

"We'll take care of them anyway. I'll change into a pear tree. They'll be hungry, and when they pluck of my fruit, I'll poison them," said the eldest.

"And I'll change into a well, and when they drink of me, I'll tear them apart," said the second.

"And if that doesn't kill them, I'll turn into the sun and burn them up," added the youngest.

"Well, that will be fine!" the crone said to them, and they continued to conspire about one thing and other.

With that, outside Ashlet turned himself into a black cat and jumped up on the window. "Aha, mama, what a pretty kitty in the window; let her in to me," said the youngest maiden.

The old crone opened the window and the cat jumped in and ran straight into the lap of the youngest. She petted the cat, just petted it until suddenly it jumped to the ground and began to meow from under the bench. Then it leapt over the bed, grabbed the cuffs and with two jumps was out the window.

"Hey," said the old crone, "that's no good. That was Ashlet himself here. Get after him right away, before he catches up to his brothers."

But Ashlet, being Ashlet, had already mounted his horse and caught up to his brothers at once.

Those three traveled well and good through the forests. Around noon they were already hungry and thirsty, for the sun was beating down bravely. Then they came upon a green meadow and in the middle of the meadow stood a pear tree, so heavy with fruit, it's a wonder its branches didn't break.

"This was just made for us," said Kinglet. "Our horses will graze and we'll eat and quench our thirst on those pears."

"Don't you dare touch a thing!" said Ashlet. He jumped up to the pear tree and hewed into it crosswise with his saber. Blood spurted from the pear on all sides.

They went on until they came again to a green meadow with a well on the edge from which fresh water flowed. "Well, at least here we'll finally get a drink!" said Cooklet, and he dismounted to drink.

"Wait a bit!" Ashlet called out, and he jumped from his horse and hewed three times to and fro at the well. Now only pure blood poured forth from the well.

They went on again, and they had hardly gone a hundred steps when they found themselves in a clearing and the sun began to beat down hotter than a white-hot iron rail. "This is the straits we've come to; there's nowhere even to take shelter," said those two.

Ashlet advised them to make a tent out of their jackets, and they hid themselves under that tent, but to no avail. With that Ashlet leapt out from under the tent and slashed three times with his sword criss-cross above the tent. The bloody tent fell down on him and the heat passed.[3]

They continued on safely then and came to a place where the road divided three ways. "Brothers!" Ashlet said to them, "I've traveled quite enough with you. Now let us each go his own way. One of you go to the left, the other to the right, and I'll go along the middle road, straight as a cut. We'll meet up here again in a year and share what we've each accomplished." That pleased them all, and so each went his own way.

Dear Ashlet just as he had said went along, straight as if you had cut it. One evening he came to a house. A smith lived in the house, and he was a werewolf, and the smith's wife a witch, the same one whose daughters and sons-in-law Ashlet had done in.

"Just wait, little birdie," thought the crone, "now you're in my cage; you shan't fly away so easily."

"Wouldn't you shelter me this night," asked Ashlet, "along with my fairy horse?"

"Indeed, quite thankfully!" said the old crone, bustling around him.

She told him to tie up his fairy horse in the stable and led him into the shack, fed him well, and put him to bed. But in the morning when he arose and asked for his fairy horse, the crone was completely changed.

"You so-and-so," she said, baring her teeth at him, "who did in my sons-in-law and daughters! Why, I'll give you a fairy horse! You'll get an old flax brake, not a fairy horse! But if you're such a man, bring me a maiden with golden hair, a golden duck with twelve golden eggs, and a golden nanny-goat, then you'll get your fairy horse. But in no other way, so that you know! Run off now this way and that to that town, you'll find them there."

"Well, that's nothing," said Ashlet. "Why, I'll go even to that town." But it was not so easy as he thought. He trekked a long time through forests, over all kinds of desolate lands where there was neither hide nor hair of anything, let alone any human. Once he came upon a very old path, and went along it for a long, long time. A little old fellow was sitting by the path and Ashlet paid him reverence: "Godspeed you, old fellow!"

"And you, dear son! Where are you going, where?"

"Ah, well, here and there, to that town for the golden maiden, golden duck, and golden nanny-goat. Wouldn't you advise me which way to go and how to get them?"

"Just take this old path, my son, and you'll soon arrive. Those things have long been waiting on such a champion as yourself. When you come to the town, a drum will be hanging over the gate. Don't fear a thing! Take the drum down, strike it and go drumming through the town to the tallest palace. Stop there and drum until they give you everything."

Ashlet thanked him for the good advice and, arriving at the town, did everything as the old fellow had ordered. When he was drumming before the palace, the king sent to ask what he wanted.

"Nothing," he said, "just the maiden with the golden hair, the golden duck with the twelve eggs, and the golden nanny-goat." And on he drummed.

The king again sent to ask who he was that he dared make such a request. And he replied, "I am Ashlet!"

Then they gave him the golden maiden, golden duck, and golden nanny right away. With great joy he then went back to the smith's.

Meanwhile the smith had been contriving a way to do in Ashlet if he managed to return from that town. In the stable where they kept Ashlet's fairy horse he dug a deep, fathomless hole and filled it with water, thinking to push him in there when he went for his horse. Ashlet arrived with the golden maiden and the duck and nanny-goat and handed everything over to the smith and the witch, telling them to give him his horse.

"Why, give him we shall," they said, "just go get him! He's there in the ninth stable." And the smith went at his heels as if to show him the stable. But Ashlet had already divined that something was afoot. He opened the stable door and spotted the hole right away. All he had to do was spin around and the smith was in the hole and drowned. Then the witch attacked him, saying, "You so-and-so who killed my husband! Assistants! Heat up the tongs and tear him to pieces. I'll give you each a ducat!"

And the assistants were already at him with white-hot tongs. Ashlet quickly called out: "Assistants, grab that hag! I'll give you a golden nanny-goat!"

And since they were already angry with her, they caught her for him and tore her to pieces with the hot tongs. Ashlet gave them the golden nanny-goat and himself sat on his fairy horse with the golden maiden and the golden duck and proudly rode off.

There at the three roads his brothers were already waiting for him, and they were very ashamed that they had accomplished nothing and that he was returning with such nice things. "We shan't even go before father," they said.

But he convinced them to go, so they went. But it vexed those two day and night that they were returning home without a thing. So they agreed behind Ashlet's back to kill him and one of them would take the maiden, the other the duck. And so they did: they lopped off Ashlet's head at night while he was sleeping and went proudly home. No one but his fairy horse remained behind with the dead Ashlet.

The fairy horse grazed sadly around the dead one in the meadow and couldn't help him. Once he spotted a little snake with an herb in his mouth, hurrying through the meadow. "Where are you hurrying to, my little snake, with that herb?" asked the fairy horse.

"Where else," replied the snake. "They trampled my father's head and I'm going to revive him."

"Give me that herb immediately!" he said. "Can't you see there's a man been killed here?"

"Eh," said the snake, "look yourself if you want one."

"Well, won't you give it to me?"

"I won't!" he said.

The fairy horse stomped but once and the herb flew from the snake's mouth. The fairy horse took it, rubbed his master's neck with it, and his head grew back and he came to life.

"Eh," he said, "did I ever sleep well!"

"Why, you would have slept forever," said the fairy horse. "Just mount up and let's go!"

Ashlet flew on his fairy horse and arrived at his home town. It was draped half in red, half in black. "What's new here?" he asked people.

"What else," they answered, "both joy and sorrow. We are celebrating that Kinglet brought a golden maiden and will be wed to her and Cooklet's golden duck is laying him golden eggs; we are grieving that Ashlet, who was the best among them, perished somewhere in the world!"

He needed to hear no more. He simply spurred his horse and stood directly before the church where they were going for the wedding. As soon as the golden maiden spotted him, she leapt up to him and embraced him before everyone, saying it was Ashlet who deserved her. When the king learned about everything, he immediately gave Ashlet not only the golden maiden and golden duck, but also the kingdom. They had the whole town draped in red cloth and celebrated such a wedding as will never again be, so long as the world is the world.

The other two had to serve Ashlet forever as their punishment, for Ashlet was the greatest champion.[4]

Notes

1. A white snake, according to other versions.

2. O. Chriašteľ names the three sons Doglet (Pesúčin), Cooklet, and Kinglet. The first was born of a bitch that licked up the foam from the ground when the cook, who was boiling up the snake, forgot that no animal was allowed to eat even the foam from the dish.

3. According to Chriašteľ's narration, the three daughters turned into a meadow, water, and a bed. The three brothers were to pasture their horses in the meadow, drink of the water, and lie down in the bed in the evening, so that the last could suffocate them, if they hadn't already perished in the meadow or of the water. Ashlet, naturally, slashed it all to pieces.

4. According to the narration of Chriašteľ, the tale ends in this way: the three brothers came among a bunch of beggars who called out to them from every side, and they had to throw them money, but were not allowed to look around at them. Cooklet and Kinglet looked around, though, and perished. Only Doglet (Ashlet) returned home. At home, according to this narration, only the queen was still alive, and she had the town half draped in black cloth as a sign that they were half celebrating and half mourning for her sons. In the end the youngest [sic—Trans.] became king.

❦ 28 ❦

The Old Maid and the Devil

Sit down, boys, and I'll tell you a yarn. Where there was, there there was, once there was an old maid! Her parents would have married her off in her youth ten times, but back then she didn't want anyone; when she had grown old like a mushroom she would have agreed to marry anyone, but suitors no longer came.

"Go find a husband yourself already if you want one!" her parents told her. So she got ready and left. The Lord Jesus met her. "Whither away, my maiden, whither?" he asked her.

"I'm going to find a husband!" she said.

"Why, if that's the case, come follow me! For every soul is my bride."

"And who might you be?"

"I am the Lord Jesus Christ!"

"I don't want you. You're God, and God is a dandy of a debtor; everyone just calls out to him, 'Oh God, give, give!' And he gives but cannot satisfy. Why, you yourself had nowhere to lay your head here on earth, so you would have no place to shelter your wife."

"Well, go on then," the Lord Jesus said to her.

And on she went. The devil met her. "Whither away, my maiden, whither?" he, too, asked her.

"I'm going to find a husband!" she said.

"Why, if that's the case, come follow me! For in the end you'll find yourself on my path anyway."

"And who might you be?"

"I'm the devil!"

"I'll take you, for everyone gives in to you and says, 'The devil take me!' And they say you have money like chaff; it would certainly be Parom's curse if you didn't have the means to keep a wife!" And before she had even finished speaking she leapt onto his back.

"You wait, you hag. You'll see what the devil is!" he thought, and indeed he began to devilishly drag the maid to and fro, to shake her up and jiggle her, and to trip on every mound with her. My, but didn't he find out what an old hag is! For she latched directly onto a tuft of his hair, slapped him silly from one side and the other, called him every kind of blackguard, and cursed him so that the entire realm of hell would have heard enough. And the more he tried to shake her from his neck, the tighter she grabbed him at his throat. Why, the old devil grew weary indeed of carrying the old maid!

Well, he just turned aside beneath her and trudged on quite unhappily. A young student met them. "Why are you so stooped?" the student asked the devil.

"Why, you see what weighs upon my shoulders!" moaned the devil. But what the maid didn't notice was that he whispered to the student that if he would defend him somehow from that old maid, he would be well paid.

So they went along together and came to some water, deep water. They could in no way cross it. The student allowed that he would lead them across if they would help him to weave a wattle fence. When he had finished weaving it he called out to the maid, "Run off and get me that twig there, so I can finish weaving!" While she was running, the student took the devil with him on the wattle fence and they rowed across. The maid remained across the water, the deep water!

Those two fellows then left. The devil asked, "Well, brother, what should I give you for freeing me from that old maid?"

"Why, I don't know what you should give me!" said the student.

The devil took him along to a pub in a town, had a quart of wine poured, and said, "Well, brother, you sit here with the wine and I'll go and possess the greatest gentleman in the town so that he sicken unto death. Then you let it be known that you'll heal him. And give him but the broth from this vegetable and he'll get better straight-away and they'll pay you well. Then we'll both have peace!"

The devil went about his business and the other sipped his wine. Then hubbub broke out in the entire town that the greatest gentleman in town was deathly ill and would pay handsomely whomsoever would help him out. "If that's all, I can take care of that," said the student to the innkeeper. And the innkeeper ran off straight-away to let the gentleman know, and even for that he received a handful of ducats. They came directly for the student.

The student gave him the broth from the vegetable to drink; and straight-away there was nothing wrong with the gentleman once the devil ran out of him. They showered the student with silver and gold.

He went outside and there stood the devil. "Well, brother, did they pay you and are you at peace?"

"At peace!" answered the student.

"Well, but you see, I still cannot be at peace," said the devil. "For they didn't send me out of hell to be husband to that old maid, but rather to do in that gentleman, for he has lived enough. So you look well and run away so they cannot catch up to you, for it will go poorly for you if we meet again by the side of that gentleman."

The student ran off, but they caught up to him immediately to make him return to the gentleman, for now he was worse. They would not release him until he returned. When they entered, the devil called out to the student, "Didn't I tell you not to come, that it would go poorly for you? Now you shall perish here!"

"Well, it's nothing, brother!" said the student. "Why, I just came to tell you that the old maid is waiting for you here at the gate!" The devil didn't wait for a moment, but leapt out of the gentleman and God himself only knows where he vanished to now. But the gentleman, became well again and only now did they really reward the student so that it was enough for his whole life!

The Tale of the Foolish Woman

man had a foolish wife. One time she asked him, "Hubby dear, what good is all that flour up there in the loft and so much pork and bacon in the chimney to you?"

"Wifey dear," he answered, "you know, you can mix up that flour if you need to, and that pork and bacon will go with the cabbage."

"And what do you have in that old jar beneath the bed?"

"Oh, those are pumpkin seeds. When the potter comes by we'll swap them for a new jar." But it was money in the jar. Knowing, however, that his wife was not all there, the man didn't want to reveal anything to her about money.

The next morning the man left for work and told his wife to wash and dry their get-up and put everything into order, that he would return in the evening. "I'll wash everything, hubby, don't you worry," said the woman, seeing him off.

Hardly had the man gone when the potter passed the hut with a wagon full of jars. As soon as the woman saw him, she snatched the old jar from beneath the bed, the one with the pumpkin seeds, ran out the door, and called after the potter, "Hey mister, mister, wait! I'm coming with you for a swap!" "And what would you like to swap for?" asked the potter. "With these pumpkin seeds. My husband has been saving them for a long time, for you to exchange them for a new jar for us."

The potter, seeing money instead of seeds, knew immediately what kind of customer he had before him. He praised the seeds, saying how pretty they were and that there would be a lot of beautiful pumpkins from them, and unloaded half the wagon of jars on the ground. And the woman nearly jumped out of her skin for joy. The potter left with the money and the woman began to place the jars on the fence posts, one alongside the other. One small one didn't fit on the fence. She began to call to the jars, "Move over, make room! Can't you see that this little one has no place?" But the jars didn't want to move. She took a stick and lit into them, thrashing them so that the shards flew. When she had broken them all up, she stuck that little one on a post and looked it over with approval at how nice it looked there, how prettily she had done it.

Then she went to the kitchen, took the meat from the chimney, taking even the bacon, and carried it all out to the garden and covered the heads of cabbages with it. It wasn't long before dogs came and devoured the meat and bacon. The foolish woman became angry with them, took up a club, and chased the devils from the garden. But her own dog she caught by the ears, led into the basement, and tied to the tap on the barrel. "You'll stay here, chained up in the cold as a penalty, understand?" she said.

But she had hardly finished saying that when the darn dog tore off the tap and was soon out of the cold. And the wine? That poured from the barrel like a spring! The dumb woman ran to the loft for flour, carried it down, and mixed it all in.

When she had managed all of that so well, she remembered that she was to wash her husband's clothing as well. So she went to the room, gathered all the coats, pants, jackets, caps, capes, smock frocks, and overcoats, soaked them, soaped them up, and placed them in the vat. She topped it off with ashes and boiled it thoroughly in a cauldron of water. Then she rinsed it all good, gave it an honest washing with a pestle, wrung it all out, and hung it on the fence.[1]

Soon her dear hubby was on his way home. She ran out to meet him and boasted to him of what she had done all day and how she had put everything in order. Her husband's hair certainly stood on end when he heard and saw everything. But what to do to her? Kill her, or chase her out into the world, or what?

"Ah, woman, may Parom strike your soul! Why, you're as dumb as a ram's horn!" he exclaimed crossly and as best he could spelled out to the letter what she had done. "Ah, but what's the use," he added when he had recovered himself a bit. "Now quickly, let's see if we can't catch that potter. That would make up for all the damage. You go to the left, I'm going to the right. If you see him first, call me, and if I see him first, I'll call you."

They ran off. A moment later the woman began to shout, "Yippee, dear, come quickly, I've got him, the rascal!"

The man ran at a breakneck pace, and when he came upon his wife, he saw that she had the scarecrow in the poppies in her embrace. "Alas Lord, this foolish woman has me on the verge of defeat. What am I, a sinful man, to do with her?" While he was moaning over her, something came to mind. "My dear wife," he began with a careful voice, as though he had nothing in mind except her happiness, "my dear, haven't you heard that there's to be a war with the Turks and that the women as well must go under fire?" "Oh, mercy, my dear, sweet husband! Really, is it so?" exclaimed the woman and she shook like an aspen leaf. "Yes, really. And would you be afraid to go against the Turks?" "Would that the heathen vanished—I certainly would be afraid!" "Well, never fear, I'll hide you where they'll never find you." "Oh, hide me, hide me, my dearest, sweetest hubby!" she begged him and clasped her hands.

So he took her by the arm and went with her into the forest. There he dug a hole and buried his wife in it up to her neck so that only her head stuck out. Then he tore up moss, collected leaves, and placed it around her and sprinkled it over her head. Then he ordered her to make neither a sound nor a move and went home.

The poor woman really stuck out there like a stump in the mountainside, but she didn't make a peep. Night even came, but she was quiet, mute, and she thought that it could not be otherwise. Then suddenly she heard voices and saw a light glimmer and approach nearer and nearer. They were highwaymen and were returning straight from a robbery. When they came to her they stopped and the leader said, "We're safe here and can even count our money and divide it up. Put that lantern there on that stump!" But the stump on which the highwaymen set the lantern was the woman's head.

The robbers poured a pile of money onto the turf and counted how much of it each was to receive. When they were in the midst of counting, not far from them a cry began to sound: "Ay-ay-ay!" Fear came upon them, they put out the lantern, left everything there, and everyone took the shortest route to the thickets; they ran off in all directions. That ay-ing, however, came from the buried woman. The lantern on her head had heated up and had begun to burn her. She was ay-ing from pain. But it had seemed to the robbers that from under the ground who knows what kind of ghost would jump out on them or that they were surrounded on all sides. They let fear get the best of them, just like anyone with a bad conscience. They never again returned to that place.

But the man had no peace at home. He couldn't even fall asleep for thinking of what his wife was doing in the forest. He was somehow sorry for her. He got up like a shot and at dawn was already in the forest. When his wife saw him approaching, she called out to him joyfully, "Look, hubby dear, haven't I made more money than I gave the potter?!" When the man saw the piles of golden money there, he forgot everything that had happened between them. He dug his wife out of the ground and walked her home.

They bought plenty of flour again, and wine, pork, and bacon. They bought new attire and a new home. And since they had plenty of money, they had—for it cannot be otherwise among the rich—plenty of sense ever after, both of them.

Note

1. This method of washing is suited to sheets and bedclothes, not to men's woolen pants and similar items, which it would destroy.—Trans.

❦ 30 ❦

Johnny Pea

O nce there was a woman, but she couldn't have any children. She
always begged the Lord God to bless her after all with some kind
of child. Once she was picking peas, and well, she complained,
"Alas, if the Lord God would bless me with at least a child like a little pea,
that would lighten my heart after all."

Once, when some time had passed since then, her old man went to plow
the fields and she was cooking something to eat at home. When noontime
came, she ran in and out of the kitchen incessantly, pulling her hair and
moaning, "Oh, Lord, who will take my old man his dinner?"

"I will, Mama!" something called out from behind the stove.

The woman looked around but didn't see a thing. And she said under her
breath, "But who are you, where are you, a pox upon you?!"

"Ah, don't you see me?" it answered and jumped out from behind the
stove onto the stove shelf, from the shelf to the bench and there began to
dance. It was as tiny as a pea and had eyes like saucers that flashed quite
charmingly. "I am it, your Johnny, your sonny!" it shouted.

And when the mother looked on closely, very closely, she finally saw
what the Lord God had sent her, that it was the one like a pea, her true son,
Johnny Pea.[1]

"Well, Mama, just give me something to eat quickly, then I'll take father
his," Pea called.

His mother brought him a full bowl of halušky and he didn't leave it until
the bottom peeked out. Then his mother tied a covered bowl of halušky on
his back for his father and stuck a fork and spoon under his arm. He took the
bowl of soup in hand and went out into the fields to search for his father.

He went along with happy thoughts, whistling, until he came to a little
brook. Then he began to scratch his head, not knowing how to cross the
water. In the end he took the fork and spoon from under his arm, sat in the
spoon like in a boat, rowed with the fork and so crossed successfully to the
other side. Then he kicked up his heels and ran as if being chased. But he lost

his balance and tripped over a mound and fell and went boom! into a ditch. The bowl broke and he began to drown in the soup. But he quickly pulled out the fork and propped himself up on it like on a pole and waited until the soup flowed off. Then the greatest calamity occurred, for he couldn't climb his way out of the ditch. You know what he did then? He made a bridge from the halušky and so freed himself from the ditch, then gathered the halušky again and went on his way.

He caught sight of his father and called out from far away, "Papa, papa, papa of mine, I'm bringing you something to eat!"

And the peasant wondered greatly when he saw the bowl and no one carrying it. And he said, "Where are you? What are you?"

"Eh, can't you see me? I am it, your sonny, your Johnny!"

The father wondered at these words, for he had left no son at home. But as it is, so shall it be: when Johnny showed himself to him, he just pressed him and kissed him as if he wanted to choke him.

When they had enjoyed themselves to their heart's content, Johnny gave his father the food. But his father only asked, "Didn't you bring me any soup?"

And his dear son answered, "No indeed, papa, for a dog came along and broke mother's bowl, so she sent you none."

The father began to eat his halušky, but they were quite crunchy between his teeth, so he asked what was with the halušky. But Johnny quickly cut him off, "Really, they crushed the poppy seeds poorly, that's why they're like that."

But his father noticed that something was afoot, for he saw sand and dirt on the halušky. So he began to take his belt from his pants to tan Johnny's hide. Johnny didn't wait long, but kicked up his heels and ran to the oxen, for he sensed that it would hurt him.

The peasant, when he had eaten, returned to his work and paid no attention to the fact that his son had run off. But when he began to plow, Johnny began to shout in the ox's ear, "Geddup there, geddup!" Then his father noticed him. He approached him and pulled his hair thoroughly for rousing his oxen. But Johnny paid it no mind. He was glad the issue of the halušky had cooled off. After that, Pea drove his father's oxen so well that his father came to love him.

Then a gentleman passed by that way and wondered greatly when he heard a voice but did not see the drover, and he asked the peasant to tell him what was shouting so. The peasant told him everything and showed him his son in the ox's ear. The gentleman marveled at the boy and determined that he must get him by whatever means, for when he was leaving home he had promised his wife that he would bring her something unlike anything before. So he began to bargain with the peasant to release the boy to him. But he would not sell his own blood even for all the treasures in the world. He said, "Why, it is

God's gift and my entire joy in my old age." And he shook his head and simply wouldn't sell. But when Johnny whispered in his ear, "Just sell me, papa, I'll get away from him," and when the gentleman promised him a hundred ducats, why, he sold him and sent him on his way.

The gentleman locked Pea into a partition in his case among ducats galore. He stuck the case in his saddlebag, mounted his horse, and spurred him on. In a short while, Pea removed a knife from his cloak and drilled a hole in the case and the saddlebag, and he released all the ducats one by one along the way. Then he let himself out. It was easy for him to find the way back since the ducats showed him the way. He could hardly gather them all and carry them home.

"Look, papa," he said, "wasn't I right to tell you to sell me? Now you have both the money and your son at home." And it was a wonder his parents didn't suffocate him out of joy.

Once his mother was cooking halušky, and Pea sidled up to her and took from the pot a little haluška that was floating on top. With that some soldiers who served the gentleman Johnny had run off from came inside, looking for him. Johnny hardly had time to whisper to his mother to hide him, that they had come for him. So she quickly grabbed the lid, and as he was sitting on the handle of the pot, she shut him in it. The soldiers turned the house inside out but didn't find Pea anywhere.

The soldiers left and Johnny crawled out from under the lid, but entirely burnt. He just staggered from side to side and it's a wonder he didn't fall over somewhere. But as they say, a good dog will lick himself well, and Johnny not only got clear of that, but was tempered by it like steel. Then he stood before his parents and told them, "You have enough to live on now; you don't need my help. But I have nothing more to do here, for they will not leave me in peace. So I shall go into the world to seek my fortune. Stay well, then!"

And his parents really didn't want to let him go and they cried like children. But Johnny wouldn't be persuaded. He went far, far from his parents into the wide world.

So he went, day and night, wherever his eyes led him. He suffered much from hunger and thirst. In the end, he became fed up. He went into a tavern. There he drank until he could no longer stand on his feet and he thought about his lot. In the end, he decided he would go in for highway robbery. But where? That he didn't know. And how, when he didn't even have the least little cudgel? He chewed this over well, then went along his way.

Once he came to a hill with a castle road beneath it. So he rolled the entire hill down on that road. In a moment some carters came along the road, carting heavy iron. Well, they were quite aggrieved when they saw that they couldn't pass on the castle road. They moaned greatly, for they did not want to return. They scratched behind their ears, blasphemed, and did God knows what out of anger and grief.

With that our Pea crawled up to them laughing and called out, "Fellas, what will you give me if I carry that hill off?"

And the carters called back, "Who, you? A hundred gods plague your mother! Why, one can hardly tell you from the ground!"

But Johnny wasn't frightened. He began to bargain with them, saying if they would give him as much of the iron as he could carry off on his shoulders, he would roll off that entire hill. The fellows just laughed at that. But one of them finally called out, "Fellas, the devil doesn't sleep. Promise him. I imagine he'll do something, if he promises so much!" So they promised him what he wanted.

Pea just went behind the hill, leaned into it with his shoulders, and at once it rose and rolled down. The carters' eyes simply bugged out and they began to worry about their iron. And they said, "Welcome, lad, what will you have to drink?"

"Nothing to drink," said Pea, "but give me my iron."

What could they do? They just scratched behind their ears and let him take the iron. And Pea took the iron from all twelve carts nicely onto his shoulders and left them, whistling.

The carters just watched him go for a moment like calves, but then they began to curse him and throw rocks after him. But he paid it no heed and just went his own way, until he stopped by a forge. And if that hadn't presented itself to him, he wouldn't have stopped until somewhere in the seventy-seventh country. Then he tossed the iron to the ground, which shook so that the windows on the smith's house just tinkled. The trade master himself ran out of the cottage to the forge and began to curse the journeymen, "Zounds, fellas, what are you doing?" And he would, perhaps, have beaten them too, but Johnny couldn't stand doing anyone a bad turn. So he went to the smith and told him that he had made that boom with the iron he had carried here to be worked. The smith looked around and laughed at Pea, "Damn you, you Gypsy frog! How could you carry so much iron? Why, you don't even resemble a human!"

At these words Pea became enraged. He took all the iron and began to spin it like nothing on the little finger of his left hand. Then he began to threaten the smith, who fell on his knees and begged him to forgive him. Johnny said, "So it shall be, but you will forge me a cudgel from that iron, do you understand?" And the smith agreed to everything.

Twenty-four journeymen then forged the cudgel. Pea and the smith drank like barrel staves, so that even a Turk couldn't catch them. They shouted and sang and quarreled, sometimes even pulled hair, but always made up again.

When the smith became very drunk, Johnny teased him for all his worth. Once, when he couldn't stand on his own legs, he nailed him to the wall by his hair. Another time he led him around the room by his nose like a bear and played all kinds of trifling tricks on him.

Twenty-four days passed and the twenty-four journeymen completed the cudgel, which weighed nine hundred ninety-nine hundredweights. Johnny paid for the work and for all his debts that he had accumulated drinking with the smith and journeymen, and set out into the world, spinning the cudgel over his head until the air sang.

He traveled long over rocky paths in the forest until he had worn his boots completely out so that they pinched him terribly. He threw his cudgel to the ground, sat under a mushroom that gave him shade, pulled out an awl and some wire from his pouch, and began to mend his boots. Meanwhile a very tired man was passing by. He tried to sit on the very spot where Johnny was sitting. Johnny called out, "Don't sit here, there are people here!"

But the man just looked around and around, and when he didn't see anything, he again tried to sit. Johnny again called out, "Don't sit here, there are people here!"

But the man didn't pay it any mind and just tried to sit. Johnny turned up the awl and stuck it into the man up to his hand. The man began to yell from the extreme pain and ran away from there, for it seemed to him that something was haunting him there. And Pea called out, "You deserve it, for not listening to the advice of wise people!"

When he had mended his boots, he lay down to sleep and slept until morning.

In the morning when he awoke, he went further and deeper into the forest. All at once he saw a great fire. Eleven highwaymen were standing around the fire and cooking an entire ox. Pea was terribly frightened and climbed up a thick, tall pine. Then the highwaymen ate and began to drink. But as each began to lift his cup to his mouth, Johnny poked a pine cone in right in front of his nose. The highwaymen became quite enraged and began to shout and look for the evil person who was playing such pranks. But they couldn't find a thing.

"Well, you know what, lads," said Johnny when he came down from the tree and stood before them, "I'm the bad one you're looking for."

"And who might you be? What are you?"

"A highwayman, like yourselves!" Pea called out.

With that they all began to laugh, "Aha, have a gander at him! A highwayman like us, and you can hardly tell him from the ground!"

He didn't respond to that, but just grabbed his cudgel and began to swing it over their heads so they had to leap back. They saw then that it was no joke and welcomed him among them like their equal. "Curse it all! Why, offer me some of that meat, since you've taken me in," said Pea.

"Well, cut off a portion. No one is going to serve you," they answered him. And so they were friends entirely. They even drank together, and the eleven drank like dwarves, and Johnny alone was quite sober.

So they put him on watch. Johnny was so assured that in these distant forests nothing of any kind would come to them that he didn't even take his cudgel with him, but just stood in his place, walked back and forth like a soldier behind the highwaymen's heads, and whistled to himself. But then a wolf ran up and swallowed him at once like a dog a fly. There he would remain perhaps for all eternity!

But his wise head was of help here as well. He took his knife from his cloak and began to cut the wolf from inside. The wolf twisted and writhed from pain. Johnny just cut away until he noticed that the wolf had turned back with him. Then he cut him somewhat less fatally. So then the wolf carried him back to the watch place and coughed him out. Then the wolf took off so that his heels jingled, and Johnny rejoiced that he had even outwitted the wolf.

In the morning the highwaymen just laughed at him when he told them how unexpectedly it had happened there. Only now did a shiver go down his spine when he thought how he had nearly smothered in the wolf's belly.

"Listen Pea," the highwaymen then said to him, "if you want us to really let you join us, you'll have to carry off a master job. You know what? In Trhanová one farmer has four nice oxen. Bring them here, and we'll let you join."

Johnny had a heart of iron. He thought that so long as his cudgel was alive, he would be alive, and as long as he was alive, he had nothing in the world to fear. So he agreed to everything. As soon as dusk fell he took the four best men and went to Trhanová. There, on the edge of the village, stood the house of the rich farmer they'd heard of. The stables stood somewhat off from the houses so that it was easy for Pea and his friends to enter. But no sooner had he entered, than he began to raise a din. The highwaymen shouted at him, asking what he was thinking, they might get caught. But Pea answered, "Leave me be! I'm doing this so they won't say we are thieves who want to earn their honorable bread by secret thievery."

But his boldness didn't bring any good, for the owner, hearing the ruckus, took his axe on his shoulder, lit a lantern, and went to see his oxen. The other four ran off, but Pea stood in the middle of the stable. The owner entered and wanted to go further, but something shouted out at him, "Halt!"

He wondered at that and called out, "Who are you? What are you?"

And it called out again, "Halt! I'm a highwayman, if you want to know!" And Johnny, who was not idle, grabbed the farmer by the breast, shook him like a wild pear, and shoved him into a corner. The farmer didn't see anyone, so it seemed to him that he was being haunted. In great fear he went inside and meanwhile Pea led off his oxen as is fit.

When he came to the forest and the highwaymen, they began to praise him as a worthy fellow. He said, "It's true. But a good man is neither here nor there, because that joke should have cost me my life. Why, that stupid farmer should have trampled me. Was he blind or stupid that he didn't see me?" Everyone broke into laughter, but Pea wasn't in a laughing mood; he was spiteful that they took him simply as some kind of boy. But he thought, "Just wait, frost will come to the dog!"

While Pea was out stealing the oxen, the others had pillaged some coins, and they brought a great lot of them. When they began to divvy them up, they tried to outwit Johnny. Just when the ox was done baking over the fire, they sent him to wash out the intestines so that, in the meantime, they could fill themselves at Johnny's expense and divvy up the money. But he was not as dumb as he looked, and he thought the entire matter through. He took the intestines on his shoulder and when he came to the stream, he threw them into the water and began to beat them terribly with a stick, shouting, "Ow, it wasn't me, but them over there! Ow, why, I didn't do anything; it was them!"

It seemed to the highwaymen that the rangers had come to catch them and were already thrashing Pea. They up and ran away as fast as their legs would carry them. Johnny knew how to touch a vein with them. Then he came to the fire, ate his roast like a man, took the highwaymen's money in his pouch, and went home to his parents, thinking that now he would really shower them in money.

But he found his father and mother laid out on boards. He cried, shouted, and gave them his money, but they would never again awake for him. It's no use to call on one who has been in God's court. So he had them nicely buried like a good child should.

After the funeral, the priest and schoolmaster left the cemetery along with the people. Only the grave-digger and Johnny stayed behind. He wanted to have another look at his parents and leaned over the hole, but lost his balance, and plop! fell into the hole. Lumps of clay flew down behind him and shut him in for all eternity! But he didn't want to lose his young life just any old way. He shouted, cried, and begged the grave-digger to come to his aid, saying he would give him both gold and silver.

The grave-digger had once been a soldier, so he had a very hard heart. He just called back, "Lie there if you like it!"

My, my, our Johnny was in a hurry now! His only companion on the road was his cudgel, and he didn't have it now. Then he recalled his mother's only legacy, his knife. So he pulled it out of his pouch and cut the lumps into pieces. Once he was out from under the clumps, it was nothing for him to jump out of the hole, although new clumps of earth were falling on him, since the grave-digger had begun to fill in the grave. Then Johnny took terrible revenge upon him. He threw him into the hole and buried him there alive, shouting, "Aha, a pox upon your mother—lie there if you like it!"

From that time on he was as alone in the world as a finger. He had neither father nor mother, and nothing pleased him. So he gave in to worldly vanities. He drank like a Turk, fought with everyone he met, and so made only mischief. Then, when he'd had his fill of that, nothing was sweet for him. So he again went in for highway robbery.

He long roamed through great forests without seeing either hide or hair of anything. At night he had to sleep in the trees so the critters didn't eat him. One evening he was sitting that way in a tree, but he spotted a light in the distance. He rejoiced greatly and ran there straight-away. There were eleven highwaymen cooking over a fire there. Johnny crawled up to them slowly and called out, "Godspeed you!"

"Godspeed you, too!" they answered him.

Then they slowly made friends and a council was held, for they had to chose a captain for the next day, and since there were eleven of them, they let Johnny join them and talked him into trying his luck as well.

They discussed how, then, to choose the captain. One advised one way, one another, until finally Johnny Pea spoke up, "Why should you argue so? Let each toss his cudgel into the air, and the one whose falls the last will be the captain."

Everyone agreed to his wise counsel and began preparing for work right at dawn. Everyone tossed their cudgel into the air. Pea spun his huge cudgel around his head a few times until the air sang. Then he tossed it high, so high! The highwaymen waited and waited for it to fall, but they couldn't wait long enough. Only the next day at noon did Johnny's cudgel fall down, and it ripped into the ground so that not a spec or trace of it remained.

Then he was chosen as the leader, but he was nonetheless just sad for his cudgel and said to his friends, "We're nothing until we get my cudgel out."

In the end he had his lads dig it out. They worked for three days, but by then only the end of the cudgel peeked out. But Johnny needed no more. He grabbed the end in his fist and with one jerk the cudgel was out.

In that country there was a lovely royal palace. Its walls were gilded in gold and silver. In its cabinets and cellars there was much treasure hidden. And the king of the castle still had nothing to fear from thieves, though he never placed any guard on the walls, for, lo and behold, there had never been in the world what they had here! On the roof of the house sat a rooster that would crow right away whenever any thief came within a mile of the castle. Pea's friends had wanted to pillage that castle many a time, but that rooster always betrayed them. Many times they paid no attention to the rooster and went to the castle. But men stood there prepared and made a bloody soup of them as a welcome. But since they had frequently attempted the castle, the king wished to endure them no longer and promised his daughter to wife to the one who would kill those bold highwaymen. This news had also reached Pea's ears.

Meanwhile the highwaymen, since they had obtained such a worthy captain, begged him to go pillage that castle with them and to kill that rooster somehow beforehand. Pea let himself be convinced and immediately ordered ten of them to take his cudgel on their shoulders and carry it. He himself sat in the pouch of the eleventh, for he didn't want to go on foot. Along the way, Pea wanted to have a laugh, so he always jumped out of the pouch wherever any stone lay along the way and put it in the eleventh's pouch. There was a full pouch of stones and Pea sat on top of them. And when the eleventh felt inside for what was so heavy, he always warded off his hand, telling him not to touch him. And when he could no longer bear the great burden and his knees were giving, Pea bounded out onto his cap and laughed his head off at him.

They came as close as the point where the castle was exactly a mile and a step away. Then they stopped. Johnny took his cudgel and threw it, and knocked the rooster from the roof of the castle so that it never was heard from again. The highwaymen came unnoticed to the chambers of the castle. The captain squeezed through the keyhole to the basement, opened the window, and the highwaymen began to crawl through one by one. But Pea cut off the head of each and pulled the body in. Then he cut out all their tongues. He hid the tongues in his pouch and went on his way.

In the morning the king's steward went to the basement on some errand. His eyes just bugged out at the dead bodies and what had taken place! He was so terrified that he nearly fell over. Only when he had better wiped his eyes did he see that all the fellows were armed and someone had done in those forest birds here. He was overjoyed, for the king's promise occurred to him. He thought about how to pull it off right away.

Then he stood before the king and told him that he had done in those highwaymen during the night and requested his reward straight-away. In joy that he would have peace from those forest men, the king promised him his daughter immediately and ordered preparations be made for the wedding.

It was time for the wedding. Whence he came, thence he came, here came our Pea among them and raised a shout of alarm to the ceiling, though they would have to look under their feet not to trample the shouter.

"What, you think perhaps this moron killed twelve highwaymen here?" he said, pointing at the young son-in-law.

"Yes, this brave man showed us the heads of eleven highwaymen," said the king, "so you just shush here!"

"Yeah, I'll shush when he also shows the twelfth head. And of those eleven, where are the tongues?" shouted Pea, and he cursed the dear son-in-law as a world-class liar. The king immediately ordered the heads collected and examined. There wasn't a tongue in any of them. "Well, your highness," Pea now said, "There can't be a head without a tongue. Now ask that prime young son-in-law where the tongues went!"

And our prime son-in-law went mute and shook like an aspen leaf. Then Pea pulled out the proper tongues from his pouch, compared them to the heads, and everyone guessed right away what was up. Pea was justly declared the husband of the princess and they whipped that world-class liar out, telling him never to show himself again.

The princess didn't want to marry Pea, for he could hardly be told from the ground. But the king had given his word and so neither he himself nor anyone else could retreat. Johnny was married to the princess.

After the wedding, Johnny considered his sins. And he swore on his faith that he would do penance. He confessed to the priest. Then, when the priest had absolved him and said, "amen," something rumbled as if thunder had struck. And it was Johnny's skin, which was pulled tight, that popped. A dashing lad, lovely as a rose and tall as a fir tree, returned from confession.

The princess couldn't believe her eyes at what had happened to her Pea. She nearly jumped out of her skin for joy that she had got such a handsome husband. Then there was really a wedding like the world had never seen, and never again will. It was all merry-making, rejoicing, singing, dancing, and feasting. And young Johnny lived a long, long time with his little wife; I guess they're still living now, if they haven't passed away.

Note

1. The tale of Johnny Pea was also recorded by A. Ghillányi and Jožko Bela from Liptov county and P. Dobšinský from Gemer. But with these versions, except for the beginnings which are similar to Kalinčiak's version, the remainder of the tale passes into the plot of "Lomidrevo or Valibuk." Just as Lomidrevo is born an unusually large child, in these versions he is born unusually tiny and only later turns into a dashing and strapping lad. The birth of Pea according to these versions also deserves a hearing:

According to A. Ghillányi, a wife desirous of a child was cleaning her trunk, found a pea in the corner and said, "If I had at least a son as big as this pea, all would be well." She placed the pea on the hearth, and when she was cooking lunch for her husband sighed, "Ah, Lord, who will take this lunch to my husband in the field?" Then from whence it shouted, thence it shouted, "Mama, give it here! Why, I'll take it to father." With that a boy little bigger than a pea jumped out from behind the stove. He was Pea because he had come into being from a pea. The pot was as big as a cauldron and Johnny—he could hardly be made out from the ground. But he made nothing of it, just took the cauldron or pot, threw it on his shoulders, and took it to his father in the field. Then he went straight-away to earn money, to thresh, etc., like Lomidrevo.

Jožko Bela narrates how the mother, distressed over the fact that a dragon had devoured her two sons who were seeking her daughter, went to an old woman for counsel on how she could have another son. The woman told her she would find a pea among her clothes and to eat that pea. After some time the woman gave birth to a boy, the tiny Pea. She nursed him for three times nine years until he grew into a man who could tear the thickest oaks out of the ground like the thinnest hemp. Then he went into the world, like Lomidrevo.

According to P. Dobšinský, the father, who had seen not a crust of bread on his table for a year, in sorrow that his wife was about to give birth to his ninth, went to plow his fields. With that the ninth son entered the world happily, but as tiny as a pea. Right away, though, he showed who he was and what he was. He provided a heifer for the christening for the godfathers and godmothers, carried his father his meal, and drove the oxen for plowing. Then he went to a gentleman's with his father and brothers for the threshing, provided them a livelihood, and went alone into the world, where he was joined by Mixstone and Mixiron, and liberated the king's daughters with them, as we read in the Lomidrevo tale.

❦ 31 ❦

The Man Who Never Sinned

In a little village there once lived a very poor, but at the same time also very honest and devout man, for though he was already as grey as a dove, still he had never yet sinned, never harmed anyone even with the slightest word, never trespassed against anyone, nor wronged anyone. And this vexed the devil in hell, who scratched behind his ears and said, "Why, one could just explode over that person! Another person, though he be honest, will at least serve me once in his life, but this one will die today or tomorrow and he still hasn't done a thing according to my will. But you just wait, I'll show you yet!"

The poor man knew nothing of this and least of all of what the devil was making ready for him. He lived peacefully in his little home, prayed to God every day, didn't harm anyone, didn't covet his neighbor's things, and acted in all things according to God's command.

Then one day—whence he came, thence he came, it had been better if he'd vanished to the depths at Sitno!—the devil pattered into his room just as the Lord God had formed him: he had teeth like stakes, legs like a horse, horns on his head and—I beg you—even a tail on his behind. And he began straight-away: "Well, well, do you know who I am? Ever since your birth I have followed you constantly, and not once have I been able to catch you at a sin. Now choose what you would like: either you kill a man or blaspheme against God or get drunk. Of those three sins, like it or not, you must commit one! I'll come again tomorrow to hear what you've chosen."

When he had finished saying this, he flew up the chimney. And what of the honest man? He wasn't terribly frightened after all, for he knew that whoever is with God, the Lord God is with him, too. So he thought and thought all day long about what he should do, but thinking was not his trade and did not go well for him. He read the whole God-given day in pious books and in the end prayed and sighed: "Lead us not into temptation, but deliver us from evil."

But to what end? The next day in the morning the devil again slid down the chimney and stood before him. "Well, have you thought it over already?"

"Eh, I've thought it over, thought it over well! If you're the devil, then go to hell where the Lord Jesus shut you up and leave honest people in peace. I shall not sin according to your will!"

"But I tell you again that you will not avoid it, for there is not and shall not be a person who never sinned once in his life. If you resist that, I shall ensure that you commit all three sins. Decide you well! Tomorrow I shall come again!" With that, off went the devil up the chimney.

The poor man remained alone at the table with his head in his hands. He thought and thought about things. The more he worried his head the more he became convinced that what the devil said had something to it. "Why, he was right after all," he reflected to himself, "we are all sinners after all; why, the Lord Jesus did not die in vain for me as well, and I have not yet sinned. Why, that devil could be right after all! Well, I shan't quibble with him. But to kill a man? Eh, that would be a great sin. Why, I haven't harmed a soul my entire life, not even the smallest child, nor even touched someone with my little finger, and now suddenly to kill a man? Nothing will come of that! To blaspheme against God, that would be a great sin, too! Why, since childhood I have even avoided saying a bad word to people, and now in my age I should blaspheme against God? I shan't do that either! Get drunk? Hm, that would probably be the least sin, for I shan't trespass against anyone with that! Why not? I'll get drunk, I'll come home, sleep it off, and that will be the end of it and the devil will leave me in peace!"

Thus the honest man deliberated, and with those words he stood up from the table and went to the inn, where he drained many a full glass to the dregs.

He came home, and then, contrary to his habits, he began to raise a ruckus. Unfortunately, a small grandchild began to cry, and he wanted to pat him on the back—but he hit him in the head and the child blacked out forever. With that suddenly there wasn't thunder, or parom, or a saint, or even God whom he didn't recall and against whom he didn't blaspheme.

Behold what drunkenness does! If he had not gotten drunk, he could have died a saint, and then he wouldn't have become such a muckraker, thief, and highwayman! For, they say, the hardest is to get drunk just once, after that it goes like clockwork. And the black one in hell rejoiced over him, and is rejoicing even today that he didn't think up firewater for naught!

❦ 32 ❦

Beautiful Ibronka

*I*n a certain village the girls went to spinning parties, and all of them went to a house on the edge of the village. All of them had boyfriends already, all, that is, except beautiful Ibronka. She was sorry that she alone had no one to speak to while the other girls joked and made merry to their hearts' content with their beaus. And the others teased her, saying she should weave him from straw if she hadn't any beau. And you know what they did once? They took a sheaf from the roof, put a smock on it and stuck a hat on it, and stood it by her on the bench, saying it was her beau.

Annoyed, Ibronka shot back, "If only one would come already, even if he be the devil himself!"

And just look at him! That very evening a bonny lad came to the spinning party and sat beside beautiful Ibronka. After that he came every evening and conducted himself like a gentleman, giving them all kinds of things for spittle.[1] He even supplied candles for light for everyone. But he just hovered around Ibronka and courted her nicely. The other girls began to envy her. Ibronka grew to the heavens out of sheer joy whenever she looked upon the bonny lad. Only one thing bothered her about him, the fact that she could never get out of him who he was, where he was from, and the fact that every time he escorted her home from the spinning party, before midnight he disappeared from her sight and she never noticed in which direction.

She sought advice from an old woman about how to manage to find out who he was and where her boyfriend was from. The old woman advised her to wind a large clew of spinning material, and when her boyfriend was leaving, to attach the end of the thread to his clothing and to follow the direction the thread comes off the clew.

Ibronka did so the very next evening when her dear beau escorted her home. While she gathered the cast-off thread back onto the clew behind him, it led her to the cemetery, right to the door of the ossuary. She peeked through the keyhole inside. And you know what she saw? Her dear beau, whenever he found a bit of flesh on the bone, pulled it off and made crackers and what not for the spinning party, and from the bones he made candles. She became extremely frightened and ran away home. Never again did she show her face at a spinning party![2]

But there was no use in trying to hide from her boyfriend. Suddenly at midnight he stood himself beneath the window of her room and called out:

He: "What did you see, what did you see,
                   when you ran to the cemetery behind me?"

She answered: "What should I say, when nothing I saw?!"

He: "If you don't say, your brother will die!"

She: "And when he dies, he will rest."

That very night her brother passed away before dawn and they buried him. After the funeral, at midnight her boyfriend stood again in her window.

He: "What did you see, what did you see,
                   when you ran to the cemetery behind me?"

She: "What should I say, when nothing I saw?!"

He: "If you don't say, your sister will die!"

She: "And when she dies, she will rest."

That very night her sister passed away before dawn and they buried her. And so beautiful Ibronka's father died after that, and then her mother. She remained alone in the world, as alone as an herb in the field.

Ibronka called on her neighbors after that and gave them the following final orders, "Look, my dear neighbors. When I die, don't carry my coffin out over the doorstep through the door, and don't even strike the coffin three times on the doorstep, but have a hole dug under the doorstep and pull my coffin out of the house through that hole.[3] And hitch the pony that remains in the stable to the cart and bury me where the pony stops with me!"

What was bound to happen came to pass. The boyfriend stood beneath the window a final time.

He: "What did you see, what did you see,
                 when you ran to the cemetery behind me?"

She: "What should I say, when nothing I saw?!"

He: "If you don't say, you too shall die!"

She: "And when I die, I will rest!"

That very night beautiful Ibronka, too, passed away before dawn. The neighbors dressed her as she herself had ordered. Then they put her in the coffin and pulled it out under the doorstep, loaded it on the cart, and set the pony off with her, wherever it wanted to go. The pony pulled the coffin to the crossroads and stopped there as if welded to the spot. So there on the crossroads they buried beautiful Ibronka.

And that was in winter.

When spring began and the flowers began to bloom, Ibronka too grew out of the grave. She grew into a beautiful lily and bloomed into a lovely white flower. A young gentleman was passing in his coach and spotted that beautiful lily.

"Hey, driver, stop! And you, Miško," he called to his lad, "jump down from the coach and pluck that lily there!" The lad jumped down to the grave, but when he tried to pluck the lily, it disappeared before his very eyes.

"Sir," he said, "there's no flower here!"

"What, perhaps it seems so to you, or you've got the wolf's blindness?" said the gentleman. "Why, I see the lily from here. Driver, you show him! And be sharp about it!"

But the driver jumped down from his box in vain. It was as if darkness arose in his eyes when he approached the grave. And the lily still gleamed whitely in the gentleman's eyes. So he himself jumped down for it and plucked it straight-away, as if it had placed itself in his hands. He put it in his hat, and when he came home, he hung his hat along with the everything else on a nail. He dined well, leaving nothing behind, and lay down to sleep.

Around midnight the lily in the hat shook and turned into a beautiful maiden, and began to look over the table and cupboards, saying,

    "Here they drank and they dined;
    naught for me they left behind."

And when she found nothing, she shook again and was a lily as before in the hat.

In the morning the gentleman arose and here everything on the table and in the cupboard was overturned. He immediately took his lad for strict questioning about who had roamed about in the room at night. But he knew not for the life of him, nor did anyone else know a thing.

"Well, why, it will out, whatever it is!" said the gentleman to his lad. "But if it happens another night and you know nothing about it, well, you'll be a head shorter!"

The next night the lad watched everything from a side room through the keyhole. At midnight he saw a light around the hat, the lily shook and turned into a beautiful maiden. She scoured all the cupboards, and when at last she found a piece of cake, she spoke:

> "Here they drank and they dined;
> aught for me they left behind."

She nibbled it lustily. Then she bent over the sleeping gentleman and kissed him three times. But once she shook again, she was a lily as before in the hat.

In the morning the lad told the gentleman everything. The gentleman shook his head, but said nothing; only that evening he had the cook prepare good food and good wine for the table. He thought, "You'll have to convince yourself." At night he pretended to sleep, but did not sleep. When midnight came, it started glowing, from the lily came a beautiful maiden that lit up the entire room. When she saw the food and drink on the table, she spoke up overjoyed,

> "Here they drank and they dined;
> look at all they left behind."

She ate and drank her fill and went straight to the gentleman's bed. When she bent over him, the gentleman grabbed her around the waist and wouldn't let go. She turned into a toad, a lizard, a snake, and all kinds of creatures in the world, but he wouldn't let go and said, "I won't let you go, my dear, I won't until you become such a maiden as you were before and until you promise to wed me!"

After some time she again became the beautiful Ibronka, and promised him on the condition that he never take her to the church. They were even married at home.

They lived together nicely, as the Lord God had commanded. And they even had a child—a beautiful girl as alike to her mother as if she'd fallen from her eye. That's why they named her nothing else, but after her mother, beautiful Ibronka.

But the dear mother never, but never went to the church. After much time her husband began to persuade her, asking why she still avoided the church at a great distance. He said that every honest mother takes her children herself to church before the Lord God, except her. After much persuasion she herself said, "Well, God willing, I'll go too!"

When she was praying in the church—but she could hardly pray for fear—she caught sight of her boyfriend of long past peeking out at her and guffawing from behind the altar. She knew right away that it meant no good! And indeed, when she exited the church he stood at her side, as when he used to escort her home from the spinning parties, and he whispered to her, "I've looked in seventy-seven countries and in all churches for you. Finally I know where you are. We'll see each other this evening!"

When midnight arrived, he stood in her window and asked:

He:	"What did you see, what did you see, when you ran to the cemetery behind me?"
She:	"What should I say, when nothing I saw?!"
He:	"If you don't say, your child will die!"

She became so terrified, the heart in her nearly burst. And now she told him everything that she had seen in the ossuary. When she finished her tale, she gave up her spirit straight-away and the boyfriend disappeared, and nothing was ever heard of him again. Ibronka lies buried at the crossroads again. Whoever goes that way gives a sigh for her. But at home an aggrieved father comforts a small girl, saying when she grows up, she won't be ashamed indeed of her mother, but she will also become such a big, beautiful Ibronka.

Notes

1. When spinning by hand, the spinner moistens her fingers with saliva.—Trans.

2. According to Kaderiak and my own mother's telling, the thread led the girl to the church door, through which she saw the devil, her boyfriend, baking a child on the altar over wax candles. She vowed never again to go to the church.

3. The rituals surrounding a person's death are too complex to describe fully here. It was generally believed that with the first ringing of the bells, the deceased's spirit left the body, but remained in the vicinity of the home. The deceased's body was placed in a coffin in the home, feet to the door and head to the icon corner. The coffin was left open as long as possible since it was believed that the deceased's spirit was in the vicinity and could see and hear. The coffin was carried out feet first and struck three times against the doorstep so the spirit would take its definitive leave of the home. When the deceased was considered a potential vampire, the coffin was carried out of the home through a hole under the doorstep instead. Potential vampires included anyone with supernatural powers, such as witches and seers, someone who exhibited various bodily and spiritual peculiarities during his life, a suicide, etc. In this tale it is probably the unusual nature of the heroine's death that prompts the inclusion of these precautions. (Cf. entries "pohreb" and "upír" in the *Encyklopédia ľudovej kultúry Slovenska*.)—Trans.

The Shorn Nanny Goat and the Hedgehog

'Twas a nanny goat with horns,
halfway up her side was shorn;
she ran off to the mountain glens
and hid herself from den to den.

She hid in the fox's den.

Then the fox came home and wanted to go into her den. But a strange animal was in her lair. It rose up and stamped its feet and called out:

"I'm a nanny goat with horns,
halfway up my side I'm shorn;
pitter-patter with my feet,
with my horns it's you I'll beat."

The fox took fright, ran off and wailed all over the forest. A wolf met her:
"Why are you crying sister fox?"
"Oh, brother wolf, why shouldn't I cry? Something's there inside my lair!"
"Come along, I'll run it out for you!"
They went together to the den and the wolf called out:

"Who is it there,
in fox's lair?"

And the nanny goat stomped:

"I'm a nanny goat with horns,
halfway up my side I'm shorn;
pitter-patter with my feet,
with my horns it's you I'll beat."

The wolf took fright as well. They both ran off and wailed all over the forest. A bear met them: "Why are you crying, sister fox?"

"Oh, my dear bear, give me your paw; why shouldn't I cry? Something's there inside my lair!"

"Come along, I'll run it out for you!"

They all went to the den and the bear called out:

> "Who is it there,
> in fox's lair?"

And the nanny goat stomped:

> "I'm a nanny goat with horns,
> halfway up my side I'm shorn;
> pitter-patter with my feet,
> with my horns it's you I'll beat."

The bear took fright as well. They ran off and wailed all over the forest. A hedgehog met them: "Why are you crying, sister fox?"

"Oh, why shouldn't I cry? Something's there inside my lair, and none of us can chase it out!"

"Come along, I'll run it out for you."

"Oh, you hedgehog, little runner, what would you do? Why, *we've* already been there, kings and gentlemen, and accomplished nothing," they said.

But it replied, "Though I'm a hedgehog, little runner, I'll beat you there!"

And it ran and ran, for it curled up in a ball and rolled down the hill. They just ran after it. It came to the den and called:

> "Who is it there,
> in fox's lair?

And the nanny goat stomped:

> "I'm a nanny goat with horns,
> halfway up my side I'm shorn;
> pitter-patter with my feet,
> with my horns it's you I'll beat."

It called back:

> "The hedgehog, that's me,
> will beat *you*, you'll see!"

And it rolled into the hole and began to prick that shorn side. The nanny goat bleated in pain and jumped out.

With that the others ran up. The wolf caught the nanny goat and tore it to pieces. They all had supper: the bear drank up the blood, the wolf devoured the meat, and the fox and hedgehog gnawed the little bones.

Ever since, the fox has lived peacefully in her den. The wolf and the bear went to track prey over the hills. But the hedgehog had its den not far off, and it lay down in comfort there and gnawed the crab apples it had gathered in the fall.

Children (addressing the teller):	And how did it gather them when it doesn't have hands?
Teller:	Well, children, there's a way for everything!
Children:	But how?
Teller:	Well, it balls up and rolls under the crab apple, where there's all kinds of apples in the fall in the forest. They get pierced on his spines. Then it softly sticks out its legs and goes carefully to its den. When it stuffs itself in, probably some crab apples fall off, but they're already by the door. It carries them one by one in its muzzle. But it needn't run to the apple tree for each one.
Children:	And how does it ball itself up into a ball?
Teller:	Well, you'd like to see everything, and you should see this once. Wait until the mud dries up, then it'll be summer. If you're good, I'll catch you a hedgehog out behind the barn. It'll be balled up, but we'll put it in the manger by the well and pour in water. It'll stick out its legs right away, and we'll have an edgy hedgy. Then we'll let it go and it'll ball up before your very eyes.

Children (clapping
and cheering):

Yeah, hedgy will ball up for us!

Teller:

And it'll roll around and around with its spines, scattering little children and pricking them in the side! (The teller meanwhile pokes the children under their arms and they scatter in all directions.)

❦ 34 ❦

The Old Man and the Twelve Sheep

*L*isten children! I'm going to tell you a fairy tale like you've never heard before; but pay attention so that you remember it well.

Well, once a poor father had three sons with whom he lived in dire want. Often it came to the point where they barely kept themselves alive. So once the father called all three together and spoke to them thus: "My dear sons, in the final analysis we won't get anywhere this way, but we will perish if we don't find some other way to be counted among people. I've concluded that if one among you went into the world, perhaps he might earn something with which we could ward off this misery at least for a while. What do you say to that?"

"What should we say?" his sons spoke up. "We are of one mind with you and would even all go together." But their father didn't want to let all of them go at once, saying what would he do, an old man, at home alone. So they sent the eldest off first.

The oldest son went, the poor fellow, and walked for a long time and saw neither hide nor hair of a living soul. After some time he met up with a little old man.

"Where are you going, my son," he said, "where?"

"You see, grandpa, we are three brothers at home with an elderly father and we're very poor. Well, I set out into the world to look for a bit of work."

"Good, my son, good," said the oldster; "you could even work for me if you're so willing."

"Well, and what kind of work would you give me?"

"Nothing, my son, but to pasture twelve sheep. You certainly know how to pasture sheep?"

"I do, grandpa, I do."

"Well, if you do, then come with me!" And he set out after the little old man.

Right away the next day the oldster took his servant and led him to his twelve sheep. "Well, my son," he said, "these are my sheep; so look well and pasture them and don't let them out of your sight. After all I shall pay you decently for your labor. And don't drive them in any way, but let them go freely wherever they like. Why they will pasture themselves for you. Here's a pouch; you'll find in it everything you need. And take this fife as well, you can play on it."

The servant led the sheep out to graze and went, tooting on the fife, dragging his feet along behind them wherever they grazed, until, bit by bit, they arrived at a river. With that the dear sheep took off and ran straight into the water and swam to the other side. The servant would have liked to follow them, but he couldn't: the river was wide and very deep. Well, in fear for the sheep he burst out crying, saying what will he do if they don't return. He walked up and down the bank a long time and looked sadly at the other side. Then he fell to the ground and fell asleep well and good, and slept and slept, only awakening in the evening. When he awoke, the first thing he did was look to the other bank, and lo and behold, the sheep were just approaching the bank and swam well and good back over.

"Ah, the dear Lord be praised, you've returned to me safely!" he sighed, and piping happily, walked slowly behind the sheep all the way home.

The oldster had been watching for him for a bit. "Well," he said, "have you pastured my sheep?"

"Indeed, I have pastured them, grandpa!"

"Well, and how did it go? Well, go on, tell me something!"

The servant told about everything that had happened: that he had gone along piping on the fife behind the sheep until they came to a river; there, that they crossed the water on him and went off somewhere, and he couldn't cross by any means; that he cried a lot and fell asleep in torment, but in the evening when he awoke, he saw the sheep, well-pastured, crossing the water; but that he certainly did not know where they had been so well pastured or even where they went.

"Well, fine, my son, fine," said the oldster. "And now tell me what you want for your service, for a year has passed. I'll give you what you choose: either eternal salvation or money?"

And the servant responded, "Ah, grandpa, that eternal salvation would also come in handy indeed; but we are very poor, so give me the money instead!" And he gave him as much money as he could carry off.

When he arrived home, everyone was overjoyed to see him, for he had earned good money.

Not long after, they sent the middle one out, and everything occurred for him in the same way it had for the eldest.

Finally the youngest set out, saying, "If it went so well for you, I'll try my luck too!"

He took the same road his brothers had walked, and while he was walking, he thought about what it would be like for him in the next world. Suddenly, he too met up with the little old man.

"Where are you going so pensively, my son," said the old man, "where?"

"Ah, where am I going, grandpa! I'm going into the world to seek some kind of work among good people. We are three brothers at home with a father who's already old and we have no way to support ourselves. Well, my two older brothers have already worked, and each brought home money; now I've undertaken to try my luck."

"Good, my son, good," said the oldster. "You could even work for me if you would like to come."

"Wouldn't I like to come? Of course I'd like to, only would I understand the kind of work you'd give me?"

"Do you know how to pasture sheep?"

"I do, grandpa, I do."

"Well, if you do, then come with me!" And he led him to where he lived.

The next morning the oldster took the servant and led him to his sheep. "Well my son," he said, "these are my sheep. There are twelve of them, as you see. Pasture them well and don't let them out of your sight; after all, I'll pay you decently. But don't drive them in any way, just let them go freely wherever they themselves would like. And here's a pouch for you and a fife to pipe on behind the sheep."

The servant set out after the sheep, and they went nicely along their way; they didn't break into a run or anything, and he just walked slowly behind them, piping on the fife. Then they came to the river, and the dear sheep went straight into the water. But the youngest brother didn't think much. He quickly grabbed one sheep by the fleece and swam well and good with it to the other bank. And he again stepped along at a distance behind the sheep, piping on his fife.

Somehow or other the sheep came to a meadow, and in the meadow there was grass up to one's waist and it was full of sheep, but they were as thin as grayhounds. "My," thought the youngest brother, "dear God Almighty, what is the reason that these sheep are so thin in such fine grass?"

But he again simply set out behind those sheep, for they didn't even look about there, but as if they were being led on a leash, they continued on to another meadow on which very little grass grew, but it must have been very beneficial, for the sheep that grazed on it were so beautiful, so lovely, as if they had been chosen individually from a thousand flocks. Then those twelve sheep stopped to graze as well, and it was a sight to look upon. And wherever those sheep moved, a very sweet bird flew over them everywhere. When the sheep had grazed their fill, they turned about of their own accord and set out along the way they had come. So they came again to that river, and when they crossed the water, the youngest brother grabbed one sheep by its fleece and so crossed to the other bank. He returned home just before evening with well-pastured sheep. In a moment the old man caught sight of him.

"Well," he said, "have you pastured my sheep well?"

"Indeed, the Lord be praised, I have, grandfather, well!"

"Well, and did you follow my order? How did it go? Well, go on, tell me something!"

"Well, yes, I did everything just as you told me, for I just slowly followed a short distance behind the sheep." And then he told him everything that had happened: how he crossed the water, how they came to the meadow where the grass was luxuriant but the sheep thin, and that his sheep didn't even stop there; how they went straight to another meadow where there was just a bit of grass, but the sheep grazed their fill. And that a very lovely bird flew over them constantly.

"Well, good, my son, good," the oldster praised him. "I'm pleased with you. Now just tell me what you want for your service, for a year has passed already. I'll give you what you choose: either salvation or money?"

"Ah, grandpa," answered the servant, "it's true that we are three sons with a father who's already old and we're very poor; but after all, my older brothers already earned something and we can get by somehow: just give me that salvation."

"Good, my dear son," said the oldster, patting his back. "If you desire salvation, you should have it, for you are an honest man to whom salvation is worth more than money. And you shall receive money besides. You see, my dear son, I am Christ; those twelve sheep that you pastured, those are my twelve disciples; that meadow with the luxurious grass is the vanities of the world and those thin sheep on it are the sons of this world; the meadow with the low grass is virtue and the sheep on it are honest people. Just as there is no benefit on the first meadow, there is much on the second. And the bird that flew over the sheep was I, for I am with my disciples eternally."

Thus spoke the little old man. Then he blessed the youngest brother and gave him as much money as he could carry.

So, behold, the youngest brother received for his honesty both salvation and money, and his brothers only money, for that is all that they desired.

❦ 35 ❦

The Twelve Months

O nce there was a mother who had two girls: one of her own and the other a stepdaughter. She loved her own very much, and she couldn't even look upon her stepdaughter, but that was only because Maruška was prettier than her Holena. But Maruška knew nothing of her beauty. She couldn't possibly imagine why her mother wrinkled her brow whenever she looked upon her. She thought that perhaps she had done something to displease her stepmother. But while Holena just primped and preened herself, dallied about the room, or strutted through the yard, or paraded about the streets, she put everything in the house in order, tidied up, cooked, laundered, sewed, spun, wove, carried hay, milked the cows, did all the work, and her stepmother did nothing but curse her and rebuke her every day. Nothing did any good, and she suffered like a beast. Day by day it got worse for her. And, mind you, that was only because day by day she became prettier and Holena uglier. Then her mother thought, "Why should I allow a beautiful stepdaughter in the house? When the boys come courting, they'll fall in love with Maruška and won't care to love Holena." She even consulted with Holena about it, and they came up with things that would never even occur to a decent person.

One day, and it was just after the New Year, in the bitter cold of winter, Holena suddenly felt like smelling violets. And she said, "Maruška, go to the mountain and gather me a bouquet of violets. I want to wear it under my sash, for I so wish to smell some violets."

"My Lord, dear sister, what has come over you! Who ever heard of violets growing beneath the snow?" said poor Maruška.

"You trollop, you clod, you! How dare you talk back when I give you an order!" Holena shouted back at her. What's more, she threatened her, "Get out of here, and if you don't bring violets from the mountain, I'll kill you!" And her stepmother pushed her out, banged the door behind her, and closed the lock.

The girl started off, weeping, for the mountain. There were walls of snow and nowhere even a human footstep. She wandered and wandered for a long time. Hunger tormented her, the cold shook her, and weeping even more, she begged the Lord God rather to take her from this world. Then she spotted a light in the distance. She followed the glow until she reached the summit of the mountain. There a great bonfire was burning, about the bonfire were twelve stones, and sitting on those stones were twelve men. Three were white-bearded, three younger than they, three younger still, and three the youngest. They sat quietly, mutely, numbly staring into the fire. These twelve men—they were the twelve months. Great Sečeň now sat up on the highest stone. His hair and beard were as white as snow and he held a cudgel in his hand. Maruška was frightened and stood as though she, too, were numb. But she grew bold, came closer, and begged, "Good people of God, let me warm myself. The cold is shaking me."

Great Sečeň nodded his head and asked her, "Wherefore have you come, my child? What seek you here?"

"I have come for violets," answered Maruška.

"It is not the time to gather violets. There is snow, after all," said Great Sečeň.

"Oh, I know that, but my sister Holena and my stepmother ordered me to bring violets from the mountain. If I don't bring them, they'll kill me. I beg of you kindly, uncles, tell me where I can gather them."

With that Great Sečeň rose, approached the youngest month, placed the cudgel in his hand and said, "Brother Brezeň, seat yourself up in my place!"

The month Brezeň sat on the highest stone and waved the cudgel over the bonfire. The fire flamed up to a great height, the snow began to melt, trees began to bud, beneath the birches the grass grew greener, in the grass the flower buds began to darken. It was spring. Among the shrubs hidden beneath the leaves, violets bloomed. Even as Maruška looked on, it was as if the ground was being spread with an azure covering. "Gather them quickly, Maruška, quickly," the young Brezeň instructed. Elated, Maruška soon plucked and put together a large bouquet. Then she thanked the months nicely and hurried home.

Holena was amazed and her stepmother, too, when they saw her hurrying home with violets. They opened the door to her and the scent of violets filled the entire house. "Wherever did you pick them?" asked Holena defiantly.

"Oh, high up on the mountain they are growing beneath the bushes. There's really quite a lot of them," answered Maruška quietly. Holena tore the bouquet from her hands, fastened it under her sash, sniffed it herself, had her mother sniff it, but didn't tell her sister, "Take a whiff!"

The next day Holena was sitting beneath the stove and she suddenly felt like having some strawberries. She called out, "Maruška, go and bring me some strawberries from the mountain."

"My Lord, dear sister, what has come over you! Who ever heard of strawberries growing beneath the snow?"

"Oh, you trollop, you clod, you! How dare you talk back when I give you an order! Go quickly, and if you don't bring me strawberries, I'll kill you!" Holena threatened. Her stepmother pushed Maruška out, banged the door behind her, and closed the lock.

The girl started off, weeping, for the mountain. There were walls of snow and nowhere even a human footstep. She wandered and wandered for a long time. Hunger tormented her, the cold crushed her; and she begged the Lord God rather to take her from this world. Then she spotted in the distance the same light as the day before. The glow led her again to the bonfire. The twelve men—twelve months—sat around it again today. Great Sečeň, white and bearded, the highest, with a cudgel in his hand.

"Good people of God, let me warm myself please! The cold has crushed me to smithereens," Maruška begged them.

Great Sečeň nodded his head and asked her, "And wherefore come you again, my child, and what seek you?"

"I have come for strawberries," the girl answered.

"Oh, but it is winter, and strawberries do not grow on snow," said Great Sečeň.

"Oh, I know that," said Maruška sadly. "But my sister Holena and my stepmother ordered me to gather strawberries. If I don't bring them some, they'll kill me. I beg of you kindly, uncles, tell me where can I gather them?"

With that Great Sečeň rose, went to the month sitting opposite him, gave him the cudgel and said, "Brother Lipeň, now you seat yourself in my place!"

The month Lipeň sat on the highest stone and waved the cudgel over the bonfire. The fire flared up three times higher, the snows melted off in a moment, the trees unfolded their leaves, the birds chirped and sang all around, and the flowers were everywhere—it was summer. The undergrowth looked as though it had been strewn with white stars, and the white stars changed perceptibly into strawberries and ripened until they were fully ripe. Even as Maruška looked on, it was as if blood had been poured over the ground.

"Gather them quickly, Maruška, quickly," dear Lipeň instructed. Delighted, Maruška soon gathered an apronful of strawberries. She thanked the months nicely and hurried home.

Holena was amazed and her stepmother, too, when they saw her hurrying home with strawberries. They opened the door to her and the smell of strawberries filled the entire house.

"Wherever did you gather them?" asked Holena defiantly.

And Maruška simply answered quietly, "Oh, high up on the mountain they are growing beneath the bushes. There's really quite a lot of them!"

Holena took the strawberries and ate until she was sated. Her stepmother ate her fill as well, but they didn't say to Maruška, "Take one."

Holena was developing a sweet tooth and on the third day she felt like biting into an apple. "Go, Maruška, go to the mountain and bring me some red apples," she ordered.

"My Lord, dear sister, what has come over you! Who ever heard of apples ripening in the winter?"

"Oh, you trollop, you clod, you! How dare you talk back when I give you an order! Go quickly to the mountain, and if you don't bring me some red apples, I will certainly kill you!" Holena threatened. Her stepmother pushed Maruška out, banged the door behind her, and closed the lock.

The girl started off, weeping, for the mountain. There were walls of snow and nowhere even a footstep. She wandered and wandered for a long time. Hunger tormented her, the cold crushed her; and she begged the Lord God rather to take her from this world. Then she caught sight in the distance of the same light and the glow led her again to the bonfire. The twelve men— twelve months—were sitting around it, sitting as though welded to the spot. Great Sečeň, white and bearded, sat the highest with a cudgel in his hand.

"Good people of God, let me warm myself please! The cold has crushed me to smithereens," Maruška begged them.

Great Sečeň nodded his head and asked, "And wherefore come you again, my child?"

"I have come for red apples," answered the girl.

"It is winter, red apples do not ripen in winter," Great Sečeň said.

"I know that," said Maruška sadly. "But Holena and my stepmother threatened me that if I don't bring red apples from the mountain, they will kill me. I beg of you, uncles, help me just once more."

With that Great Sečeň rose, went to one of the older months, placed the cudgel in his hand and said, "Brother Rujeň, take my place!"

The month Rujeň sat on the highest stone and waved the cudgel over the bonfire. The fire blazed up, the snow disappeared, but the leaves didn't unfold on the trees, rather the yellow slowly retreated from them—it was autumn. Maruška didn't see any spring flowers this time. She wouldn't even have looked for them. Instead she looked over the trees, and in fact there was an apple tree and high on the ends of its branches were red apples.

"Pluck them, Maruška, pluck quickly!" Rujeň instructed.

Maruška shook the apple tree and an apple fell; she shook again and another fell.

"Grab them, Maruška, grab them quickly and run home!" Rujeň called out.

She snatched the two apples, thanked the months nicely, and really did hurry home.

Holena was amazed and her stepmother, too, when Maruška arrived home. They opened for her and she gave them two apples. "And wherever did you pick them?" asked Holena.

"High up on the mountain they are growing, and there's really quite a lot of them," Maruška said. Well, she had to say no more to Holena than that there were a lot of them there.

"And you trollop, you clod, you! Why didn't you bring more? Or perhaps you ate them along the way?" Holena lashed out at her.

"Oh, dear sister, I didn't even eat a smidgen. When I first shook the tree, one fell; when I shook it again, another fell, and they didn't let me shake anymore. They called to me to go home," Maruška said.

"May parom slay you!" Holena swore and tried to strike Maruška. And her stepmother, who wasn't idle, took after her with a stick. Maruška didn't want to let herself be beaten and ran into the kitchen and hid herself somewhere beneath the stove.

The sweet-toothed Holena soon stopped cursing and devoted her attention to her apple, giving one to her mother as well. They had never in their lives eaten such sweet apples. Only now did they really develop an appetite. "Mom, give me my fur coat! I am going alone to the mountain! That trollop would just eat them along the way again. I'll find the place sure enough, even if it were in hell, and I'll pluck them all, if there are so many, though the devil himself call to me!" Holena hollered in this way, and her mother dissuaded her in vain. She took her fur coat for her body, a covering for her head, wrapped herself up like a granny, and started off for the mountain. Her mother just wrung her hands on the threshold, looking after her, wondering what the girl was in for.

Holena walked to the mountain. There were walls of snow and nowhere even a footstep. She wandered and wandered and her desire for apples kept pressing her on as if it was chasing her. Then she spotted a light in the distance. She started after it and came to a bonfire where twelve men—the twelve months—were sitting all around. But she didn't pay her respects to them, didn't ask them, but simply stretched out her palms to the fire and warmed herself, as though the fire was just for her.

"Wherefore have you come and what do you seek?" asked Great Sečeň, becoming vexed at her.

"Why do you question me, you old fool, you? You have no need to know why I come or where I am going!" Holena said curtly. She started off into the forest as if the apples were ready and waiting for her there.

Great Sečeň wrinkled his brow and waved the cudgel over his head. At that instant the heavens clouded over, the bonfire died, the snow fell thickly, and a cold wind blew. Holena couldn't see even a step ahead. The further she went, the larger were the snowdrifts into which she stumbled. She cursed Maruška and the Lord God. Her muscles stiffened, her knees gave, and she collapsed.

Her mother was waiting for Holena, looking out the window, even stepping out the door to look. Hour followed hour, but Holena simply didn't come. "Doesn't she want to leave the apples, or what is going on? I'll have to have a look for myself!" the mother said to herself. She took her fur coat, wound herself into her shawl, and went after the girl.

The snow was falling thicker and thicker, the wind colder and colder, the snowdrifts like walls. She stumbled through them and called out to the girl, but not a soul answered her. She became lost, no idea where she was, and began to curse Holena and God. Her muscles stiffened, her knees gave, and she, too, collapsed.

At home Maruška cooked dinner, fed and milked the cow, but neither Holena nor her stepmother returned.

"Where are those two amusing themselves for so long?" worried Maruška, sitting down that evening at the distaff. She sat there until night, her spindle long filled, but not a word came of those two. "Oh Lord, what happened to them!" the girl grieved and anxiously peered out the window. There wasn't a soul to see out there, just the twinkling of the stars after the blizzard, the light of the earth from the snow, and the snapping of the roofs from the cold. Sadly she shut the window and prayed for her sister and mother. In the morning she waited with breakfast and lunch, but she'll never wait out Holena or her stepmother. Both froze to death on the mountain.

The hut and cow and garden and fields and meadows around the house remained after them for Maruška. Before spring came round, a manager was found for all of this: a bonnie laddie who married Maruška, and they both lived well and in peace.

Holy peace and love are above all else!

❦ 36 ❦

The Wooden Cow

Once the world was different than it is today, when everyone just looks down his nose and frowns and grieves from dawn till dusk. Once people didn't pinch their pennies so, didn't fret so in the name of prosperity: but they ate and drank what they had and laughed. That helped their digestion. Back then if you didn't know a joke to tell, you did better not to show yourself in public, because everyone was joyful, talkative, and joking. Well, it will be that way again some day!

Back then there lived a king's daughter. But God forbid that *she* laugh, even for her suitors. And she would have had ten for every finger, she was so rich and beautiful. Her parents didn't know what to do with her. Finally they had it trumpeted throughout the land they would give his weight in gold to the one who would get her laughing. You can bet that the wags from all over swarmed in, but they all left with their heads hanging. Finally no one even undertook it anymore. But they say a master is always found for any trade.

The worried king had just sat down beside the maiden to engage her in a little conversation when the door opened a bit and someone stuck in a disheveled head: "I humbly beg, is his lord the king at home?"

"And who are you? What do you want here, you knave?" the king shouted at him.

"I humbly beg, I've come to have justice confirmed!"

"What kind of justice? Don't you have a magistrate on the bench at home?" And he would have chased the dear guest out if the serious maiden, who only now opened her mouth a bit for the first time in three days, hadn't said more or less that the king is the king in order that no one be turned away.

"Just tell me, what's the predicament?" he said.

"Well, after all, look, that's why I came!" answered Kubo, for it was him, Kubo, our cowherd from the village. And indeed, he now took off his lambskin cap from his disheveled head, hung it on his stick, and stood himself just as he was, in his cloak, belt, wool trousers, and peasant boots, before his lord the king and before his daughter. He began to speak in his own simple manner, but the king listened now, since his daughter, who turned everyone away, was also listening when he opened his mouth. Let's listen as well!

In the village it was proclaimed that everyone, whether he had a cow or not, had to pay the cowherd regularly, so that it would be fair for all.

"The devil if that's fair to me," thought Mr. Krajec, "when I have no cows, not even a poor little calf. You wait, buddy, why I'll make it hot for you! I'm not going to stuff good money down your gullet for nothing!"

He designed a cow out of wood and gave it to the herder to pasture; he even warned him to pasture it well and lead it home nicely every evening like the others.

"That'll be a pain!" the cowherd reflected, scratching behind his ears. But he had to take the cow, for he was being paid for it. He had no choice but to carry the cow nicely on his shoulders behind the herd and carry it home to Mr. Krajec every evening.

Things took a turn for the worse in the fall when the frost came on and got under the cowherd's nails. There was no wood in the whole field. So he grabbed the wooden figure, cut it and placed it on the fire. He warmed up, but it got even warmer later on!

"Where's my cow?" called out old Krajec in the evening when no cow came.

"Why, I cut it up out there in the field," said the cowherd.

"You just wait, Kubo, why, you'll pay for it!"

The cowherd just shrugged his shoulders, for what would be would be; but old Krajec, the sly fox, ran straight to the magistrate while the iron was hot.

"Mr. Magistrate," he said, "I had a cow. I paid regularly for it, as you ordered, and Kubo pastured it nicely for me all summer with the others. But you know what he did today? He hacked up my cow in the field and didn't even bring me a trace of it. What do you say to that?"

"Well, indeed, my dear Krajec, I'll say simply what the Lord God commanded: a cow for a cow!" They sent a constable straight to the cowherd to have him bring his cow before the esteemed court. "She's not fit, constable, after all she's not fit to go before the esteemed court. Ask them to indulge me a bit and allow me to comb her and clean her up!" With that the cowherd sent the constable on his way and thought to himself, for he had gathered what was up, "Curse the magistrate! You're not going to grease your muzzles with my calf. I'll grease under your noses with a different feather!"[1]

He led his cow out behind the barn and killed it there. He hung the meat on hooks, planning to sell it the next day, and stretched the skin over wooden shanks, since after all, even Krajec's cow stood on just such wooden shanks. But then the magistrate issued an order that whoever dared to buy something from the cowherd, even for the least sum, would lose both the meat and the money and would also be put in the stocks. The poor cowherd didn't earn a bit of profit, for people were afraid to break the magistrate's prohibition. But some were found who were not afraid of that, namely the priest's Rover and his friends. They stood beneath the hooks behind the barn and licked their muzzles, looking up at the meat and wagging their tails.

"Aha," said the cowherd, "you'd like to buy but don't have the cash? Well, never mind, I'll entrust it to you if you agree to the debt and will pay when I come to collect?" With that he took down an entire shin from the hook and his friends bared their teeth at it: "Aha," he said, "you can't even wait for me to give it to you. Well, then we are agreed!" And so he tossed them the shin, and the priest's Rover was the first to sink his teeth into the roast; he didn't have to offer any to the others.

But what about the rest of the meat? There was an easy end to that as well! "I'll have it cooked," he thought, "roasted, and fried, and I'll invite all my neighbors to the feast. Why, maybe then I'll just have to raise my eyes and they'll entertain me one after another along with my wife and children. That way somehow I'll get through the winter."

As he thought, so he did, and he encouraged and encouraged his guests, "Eat up, my dear neighbors, eat like at home, help yourself like it's yours: the Lord God provided me with meat, and now I am providing you!" The dear neighbors ate and drank their fill, said their thanks and went their way. But they didn't look in on the cowherd again.

He finally had peace from his neighbors, but at home his wife sang the same song every godforsaken day: "Now give me something for the pot, since you wasted the cow! Can't you see that your children are nearly dying on the stove from hunger?"

It's a wonder the dear cowherd didn't go grey right there! After some time, he recalled that, after all, he had a debtor at the priest's. He went straight there and searched and sought for him like for a needle all over the yard, the shed, the barn, the stables, and in every corner. But the dear little pup had hidden himself well. "If you won't show me your face," thought the herder, "why, I'll easily outwit you; you wait, I'll accuse you before your master!"

Just as he stuck his head in over the priest's door he spotted Rover, blind in one eye, stretched out beneath the table. "So you're here, you blind dog?" he called out. "Pay me what you owe!"

But the priest was also standing at the table, and you have to know that the priest was also blind in one eye and couldn't see out the other, and so he could only think that the herder was shouting at him. It was as if lightning had struck him, he leapt at the cowherd so: "Well, you're even going to call me a blind dog! Don't you know who I am? And what do I owe you, you beggar, you wastrel?!"

My! The herder was no longer standing in the door, but had already lit out of the house, and the priest sicced Rover on him who nearly tore off his heels. But that was nothing yet, that he had chased him out of the house with a dog for his just debt. The priest would have had the cowherd stretched on the rack for his discourtesy if he hadn't taken to his heels. "Just wait, you rogue!" said the priest. "You haven't escaped me yet."

And he went straight before the esteemed bench and didn't stop accusing until the gentleman in charge had sentenced the cowherd to a hundred blows with a knotty club. The poor cowherd didn't find out until the bailiff and six men stood in front of his house to lead him under bare pitchforks before the bench. No help was to be had except by taking the back door out into the fields and from the fields into the wide world.

He walked and walked in that wide world from village to village, from town to town. Once he stopped in a town, leaned on his stick and marveled, just marveled, for he had certainly never seen such a tall, and what's more completely green, building.

"My," he reflected, "what strange lime must grow here, if they whitewash to such a shade of green. And those windows, they're like our doors. Yeah, and don't they go high, one on top of the other! Now, can the hens really manage to fly up to the beam when it's so high? And wherever are the pig pens and barns for the cows when there's not even a proper gate or yard or anything?!"

With that people who were standing by him began to giggle behind his back that he marveled like a calf at a new gate, and what didn't they hear while he babbled! "Well, you dolt," they said to him, "don't you even know where you are? Why, you're standing before the king's palace!"

"But I . . . before the king's palace? Eh, well glory be, tell me something about the king as well!"

And you should have just heard them laugh then, saying that, after all, even little boys knew already that the king promised his weight in gold to the one who would make his daughter laugh—and they left him standing there like a madman.

"My weight in gold, that wouldn't be bad! After all, you've got nothing at all and your children at home are crying!" thought the cowherd, and he just wondered how to get inside! There was a wide gate leading in, but to what end? In front of the gate a champion walked back and forth with a bare saber, just flashing for him, it was so polished; and he'd heard long ago that such a champion would just say to the saber, "Cut, little saber!" and right away everyone's head would be off. Why, he wouldn't have stepped through that gate for the world!

But so what? He still dared to try to outwit such a champion. "Let him guard this hole," he said, "the birdie will fly over a different way!" And he began to walk around the building, thinking there would have to be a yard and garden, that there he would slip over the fence more easily and then into the yard even if a hundred dogs guarded it, for a good herder doesn't fear them. He'd just give a whistle on his fingers and right away they'd all wag their tails around him. But the further he went, the worse it got.

Why, there wasn't a proper fence around the home like at home in the village, just gate after gate and beneath each one as many as two champions with flashing sabers. Once, finally, but far off, perhaps at the tenth neighbor's, there was a bare wall.

"Here goes! From one neighbor's to another's you'll jump your way to the king's," he thought, and was over the wall. And there was, believe it or not, a garden there. But just consider the stupidity: not a bit of barley or carrots anywhere, like a good farmer needs, just flowers and all kinds of grass and shrubs. Well, and sand was spread out all over there! Our entire village wouldn't begin to carry it away; but how nicely they kept it, smoothed it out, that useless sand!

"Eh," he thought, "that's certainly no joke, you daren't step there in your dusty old scuffs!" So he went through the grass and among the flowers. Well, you've never seen such a thing as how those three who were pottering around in the flowers—were they weeding them or blowing off the dust or what?—got angry at that! They came at the cowherd from three sides, barking like dogs, "You blackguard, you good-for-naught! You'll tramp in our flowers here!?"

Well, and they would have worked him over good with their sticks if Kubo the cowherd hadn't had legs ten times better than the likes of them, raised on fat. When they came at him from one side, he jumped to the other; when they came from three sides, he escaped via the fourth. At least he danced them through the garden a bit. But he'd had enough even of that, so he left them a few hundred steps behind him and, when they weren't looking, slipped through a little door out of the garden.

He didn't even know of his fortune, that he was now in the courtyard of his lord the king. Well, zounds! That was a yard! Not a bit of dust on it! His old woman never swept the house like that. Well, but after all, where do they put the dust from such a large home? Why, they don't keep it in the wardrobe, do they? And the manure, I ask you, where do they take it? Why they couldn't just hide it like a needle! So he went to look for the dust heap and dung heap in every corner. But that was the worst thing he could have done. Just then he was suddenly surrounded by five men who grabbed him by his locks and shouted at him, "What are you doing here, you hundred-legged beast, poking about the king's palace? Shoot the spy! To the gallows with him!"

Why, that wouldn't have even happened with the church's rules, to take a man to the gallows for no reason at all! "But people," he said to them, "you've not been eating crazy mushrooms, have you? Why I, the cowherd from our village, am just looking for where you take out the dung for such a lord as our lord the king. And then I would like to go to his lord the king to make his daughter laugh."

With that they quieted their strings. Everyone stepped back and only one remained, the most nicely dressed of them all. "Well, that's nothing, good man; why, I won't let them hurt you," he began nicely to ply the cowherd. "Why, I'll take you straight to the king," he continued, "if you just promise me one-fourth of what you get when you make the king's daughter laugh."

"Why not?" said the cowherd. "Just wait for me here!"

So he sat down to wait and sent the cowherd along the right way, and even told him how to pass the three guards. He went nicely and boldly on. But he nearly fell off his feet every time the guard thundered at him, "Halt! Who goes there?"

But he grew bold and said to each, "I'm going to his lord the king's daughter for a laugh!"

With that each guard began to ply him, begging a fourth of what he would get when he made the king's daughter laugh out of him.

"And so, here I am, your Kingship," he now said. "For Kubo the cowherd from our village, is none other than myself, as you see me here. And I've told you everything that happened to me, and I'm happy that your daughter at least here and there during the story lifted a corner of her mouth in a smile."

"You've done well, my son," said the king, patting his shoulders. "Now what do you ask for that tale?"

"Well, as I told you from the start, I've come to have justice confirmed. Justice, my Lord, only what is just, confirm that for me: my hundred blows with a knotty club, adjudged to me by the esteemed court!"

"Kubo, Kubo," said the king, "stop joking already! I mean it, really, I'll give you your weight in gold since you've made my daughter happy."

"Eh, my Lord, I mean it as well, for you to confirm with your seal my hundred blows with a knotty club as my portion for having cheered your daughter, so that I shan't remain indebted to those four outside who each begged a fourth of it out of me."

"So it is, Daddy, confirm it," said the king's daughter, breaking into laughter and clapping her hands. "Why our shameless guards have long deserved the lesson!"

And so it was. The king signed the sentence and confirmed it with his seal, a hundred blows with a knotty club for the wag Kubo, but on the trousers of those four who had each begged an even fourth of it when they wouldn't let our Kubo before the king any other way. And Kubo, the cowherd from our village, just laughed under his moustache when they dusted their trousers well and good.

But they didn't want to let our Kubo leave them so unceremoniously. The king had him shown where his barn was, and what belongs to it—I beg your honorable heads—the dung heap. They drove him out behind four steeds to the fields. There on the edge of the forest stood the king's barn, and in it, a whole herd—a hundred beautiful cows. They told him that from that time on he would be the king's cowherd and that he could bring his wife and children. Kubo was well off from that time forward, along with his wife and children. And what's more, the king gave him his choice of one of those cows. And that cow had a bell, that's all there is to tell.

Note

1. Goose feathers were used to wipe butter on top of baked goods to give them a shine.—Trans.

❦ 37 ❦

A Woman's Wit

Once, but like as not long ago, there were two neighbors: one poor and the other rich. The poor one didn't have but one little pig, and there was nothing to slop him with, for the entire household was bare. The rich one had ten odd sows and often slopped them with barley, and there was always something in the trough to feed on. Because they shared a yard, the little pig would run in among the rich neighbor's herd as much as three times a day and would snatch some barley, would even eat from the trough. But once this so irked the rich man that he grabbed a club and smacked the pig in the forehead. It immediately collapsed in the dust and breathed its last.

The poor man went to the magistrate to complain of the damage that he had incurred. The rich man countered with the damages that he had been incurring and refused to pay for the pig. The magistrate couldn't square their accounts. "Well," he said finally, "both of you incurred damages and they will be recompensed to the one of you who can solve this riddle tomorrow morning: What is the fattest, what is the fastest, and what is the cleanest?"[1] Both went home with their heads hanging.

The rich one was welcomed by his wife: "Well, why are you walking about like one thunderstruck?" "Oh, at least *you* could leave me alone," he snapped. "Why, the devil himself wouldn't have thought of it! He went so far as to pose us a riddle, and justice will go to whomever solves it." "So, what riddle?" "What is the fattest, what is the fastest, and what is the cleanest?" "And you're racking your brains over that, you dunce you?! Why, you could have thought of it right away: what could be fatter than our fatling that we've fed these three years; what could be faster than our horse that we fodder every day; and what could be cleaner than our well into which we toss two hundredweights of salt every year?!" "In truth, you're right, my dear!" And the face of the rich man brightened as though he had already won justice and the gentleman had patted his back for being a wise man.

When the poor man stepped through the door, his sixteen-year-old daughter stood up from the table to meet him and immediately read in his eyes that all was not well. "Well, what's wrong, pappy? It'd be a heck of a fix, and no joke, if you'd lost!" "Lost? I haven't lost yet, but I don't know if I will be able to play it out," the father said, and told his daughter all about it. "Don't worry about a thing, pappy. Why, I'll think it over till morning," said the daughter, and with that they each lay down in peace.

In the morning, the daughter simply whispered something in her father's ear, and cheered he went directly before the magistrate. The rich man was already waiting there and proudly stood himself to the fore. My, if you only could have seen how he retreated when the magistrate, upon hearing his guess, simply told him never to come even to his house with such trifles.

"Well, and you? What have you contrived?" he said, turning to the poor man. "I beg the indulgence of the highborn gentleman. Let me just say that the fattest is our mother earth, for we all fatten ourselves from her; but the fastest is the moon, because it circles the earth and heavens every four weeks; and the cleanest is the sun, for it shines just as prettily for all the ages."

"What a man!" said the magistrate, patting his back. "Your rich neighbor had no reason to kill your pig over a bit of barley. In compensation, I give you the fatling that they've been feeding these three years." And with that, justice was done. The rich swaggerer left quietly, without even a sound. He hadn't even dreamed that the magistrate would shame him so and then wipe his mouth of the fatling. But when the poor man thanked the gentleman for the ruling and began to leave as though it were all over, the fine gentleman nodded him back for another word.

"You," said the gentleman, "you didn't contrive your answer to my riddle by yourself, for many wise men and women have racked their brains over it and couldn't come up with a thing. Tell me once and for all who taught you the answer!" The poor man had nothing to hide, so he said right away that his own daughter had pondered it overnight and in the morning had whispered in his ear. "Well, if you have such a wise girl," said the gentleman, "here, take her this handful of flax; they just brought it to me from the fields. In the space of three days, let her pull it, ret it, dry it, scutch it, comb it, spin it, and weave a cloth from the yarn and bleach it. From that cloth let her sew a pretty white shirt for my wedding. If she accomplishes this, I will escort her to that wedding. If she does not, I will treat her as one who interfered with justice and trespassed in my court. And now get out of my sight!"

And get he did! He would rather never have gone to that court or to have lost three times. From a handful of flax an entire man's shirt, and on top of that to have to complete it in three days! It was also unheard of! But when he told the girl at home, she made nothing of it, but simply broke off one little branch of new growth from a tree and placed it in her father's hand. "Take this, Papa dear," she said, "and go once again to that gentleman and tell him I said to make from this branch for me by morning a brake, a distaff, a spindle, a reel, a bobbin, a loom, a spinning wheel, and whatever else is necessary, before I complete everything he has ordered."

The dear gentleman only now realized with whom he had crossed swords. By hook or by crook, we don't know, but it's enough that he completed everything as she had ordered. Then she, too, sent him the wedding shirt on the third day.

"Well," said the magistrate to the father, "if your daughter is such a master, let her come right now to the wedding. But let her come to me neither in the day nor at night, neither by foot nor by coach nor on horseback, by the road and not by the road, neither dressed nor naked, and let her also bring me a gift that is not a gift!"[2] Oh, that was all he needed to hear! The father just shook his head at such work, but his daughter calmed him, saying he should leave this, too, up to her. And the gentleman from that hour on never even left the window, but looked for her constantly. He couldn't wait, for he knew that her equal in beauty didn't exist far and wide.

On the third day in the morning the whole world was still sleeping, because it had only just begun to lighten, but the dear gentleman was already standing in the open window. And he saw a young girl approaching his palace, and certainly, thus, neither in the day nor at night, for it was dawn; she came neither by foot nor by coach nor on horseback, for she sat on a billy goat and while she sat, she still walked with her feet on the ground; she went by the road and not by the road, because the billy goat stepped along in a rut; neither dressed nor undressed, for she had on a net belted with only an apron; and in her lap she had something hidden—the gift that was no gift, for sure. He immediately sent his chambermaid to meet her with a beautiful wedding dress and requested her to bring him the gift and no gift.

Beautiful as a rose in bloom, she entered his room and gave him two doves. When he tried to take them in his hands, she let them go. They fluttered and flew out the open window into the wide world. Thus she had given him a gift and no gift, for he had them, but immediately did not. "Well, my dear," said the gentleman, "from this hour on we belong to each other. But just because you are so wise and I, too, have my own mind, you know that it would go badly for me if you continued to interfere in my court. So I say to you, even before the wedding, don't ever trouble yourself about my court. If I notice even the slightest thing, I will send you from the house that very day." She consented to that and they went directly before the altar.

If only you had seen that pair of doves, for thus they lived while she didn't trouble herself about his magistrate's mace. But what was bound to happen, finally did. Once two wayfarers were before the court. One had driven a herd of horses from the market, the other a herd of oxen, and both passed the night together. During the night one of the horseman's mares foaled, but he didn't notice. The foal went astray among the oxen. The ox-keeper found him beneath an ox and didn't want to give him up. The magistrate awarded the foal to the ox-keeper, I guess because he could better grease a palm.

"The devils take that kind of justice!" muttered the annoyed horseman to himself when he met the lady in the yard. "What's wrong, good fellow?" asked the lady. "Well, look my lady, we came here for justice and here justice says that the ox foaled and not the mare." And he told her all about it.

"Now don't worry about a thing, good fellow," said the lady. "Just listen to me and everything will turn out fine. This afternoon my husband will go for a walk there on the meadow by the stream. Take a scythe and a net with you. When he approaches, grab the scythe and cut in the water, then jump out on the bank and make with the net like you are catching fish in the grass. When my husband sees that, he will take interest and curse you as a jackass. You just say, 'Ah, Mr. Magistrate, it's more likely that I can cut grass in the water and catch fish in the grass than that an ox should foal.' When you say that, you'll see that the foal will be yours. But, for God's sake, don't betray me, because I could then remain no longer in his house, and you see that I only wish you well and seek justice." Having said that, she ran in to her husband and took on such a holy look as if she knew of nothing.

Toward evening the gentleman went out for a walk. And you know what he saw? That horseman mowing in the water and setting a net for fish in the grass! "Well, what are you doing here all topsy-turvy, you jackass of the Lord Jesus Christ?" "In truth," he answered boldly, "your name-calling, Mr. Magistrate, is ill-fitting, for it is more likely that I can mow in the water and catch fish in the grass than your idea that an ox foaled." As he said that, it became clear to the gentleman what he wanted here. But it also became clear who could have set him to it.

"So that's how it is?" he said. "You have the gall to correct my judgment? That didn't come from your head! Tell me right now, who instructed you?" "Ah, well, look . . . Mr. Magistrate . . . well, um . . . that is . . ." "Now you're muddling it! Can't you come out with it? Tell me, or you'll get no foal. Was it my wife who instructed you?" When he could no longer extract himself from the hempen cords, the man admitted that it was the gentlewoman who had gotten him tangled up.

"There, you see," said the gentleman, "you could have steered clear of trouble. Anyway, I knew it right off. Now go to that ox-keeper and tell him to give you back the foal, that I order it, understand?" "I understand and beg the indulgence of the gentleman." And he jumped up and ran off, joyous over his just foal.

But the gentleman's veins didn't quiver in happiness. He would rather have lived to see I don't know what than this. Because the longer he had his dear, cooing turtledove the more he loved her, and now his lot was no other than to put her out of the house, if he wanted to keep his word. And in truth, when he went home, he forced her to leave the house. "Take what you like the most," he spoke with finality, "and get out of my house!"

She didn't answer a thing, except to request in the end that she be allowed to prepare dinner, the most perfect kind, so that they could dine together once more. He consented. The dinner was tasty and with good wine. She herself poured for him "one last time" and the gentleman drank the pint to the dregs . . . and fell asleep. You could have torn strips from him and he wouldn't have awakened.

But the lady had a coach already prepared. She set the gentleman in the coach and sat down herself beside him and ordered to be driven to her father's yard. She jumped from the coach, readied her farmer's bed, and laid her husband in it.

In the morning the gentleman magistrate had reason to wipe his eyes: where was he, what happened, had his gentleman's palace really turned overnight into a farmer's dwelling? Then she came to him and said, "You slept well, didn't you, my dear? You see, one can sleep well even in a farmer's house. Indeed, it will be fine for us here. We can stay here forever if we wish." "But, but how . . . what have you done with me?" "Now, don't forget, my dear, that just yesterday evening you sent me away. You allowed me only to take with me what I like the most. I took you!"

"Well, no one will ever get the better of my wife!" said the gentleman, and all was well again. They returned home and took her father with them. And this time the gentleman really led his bride proudly into the house!

Notes

1. According to the account of Šparnensis, the questions were: What is dearest to a person, what is sweetest, what is the most clever? The rich man solved it thus: Dearest to a person is his wife, sweetest is honey, and the most clever is the mill wheel, because it turns forever. The poor one guessed: Dearest to a person is his life, sweetest is a dream, and the most clever is a thought, for it flies from the earth to heaven in a moment.

2. According to Reuss's account: "let her come in daylight and not by daylight, on horseback and not on horseback, dressed and undressed, bringing a gift and no gift." According to Dobšinský's account, she was to bring the fruit of a tree that was already blooming while the old fruit on it was still ripening—and that was to be juniper berries (juniperus communis).

❦ 38 ❦

The Toad's Godmother

*T*hree sisters were walking through a green meadow. Suddenly they came upon a huge toad that looked at them with huge, bulging eyes as if it wanted to eat them or bewitch them.

"Ugh, how disgusting! How it frightened me!" shouted the oldest sister.

"Let's kill the beast so it won't wander about under foot!" the middle one responded. And both of them were quite ready to kill the toad, but the youngest wouldn't have it.

"Eh," she said, "not that way, sisters, no! Even a worm struggles against death, so let's leave the toad, let it live." The sisters broke into guffaws at that and the oldest told her provocatively, "You can take it with you for all I care and even sleep with it."

"Why, it seems to me to be expecting: you can offer to serve it as godmother!" the middle sister said, badgering her.

"Why not! Even a toad is God's creature," said the youngest—and a tear fell from her eye.

Seven weeks passed after that and the sisters had long forgotten the toad. But now suddenly one morning a beautifully dressed young man stepped into their room, turned to the youngest with a deep bow, and said, "My lord and lady request the honor of your service and that you come to see them for a short time. A coach is waiting for you before the door." So the youngest quickly got ready and sat in the golden coach. Four jet-black horses flew like a storm and the two oldest sisters watched her go as if in a trance, until she disappeared from their sight.

The golden coach stopped before a tall castle. There were four and twenty windows on the east side of the castle and four and twenty on the west. Before each window was a golden tree and on each tree sat a golden bird. When the youngest sister got out of the coach, the air shook with the song of the golden birds welcoming her.

She entered into a gorgeous room where everything glimmered with gold. The toad was lying in a golden bed in silk sheets moaning deeply, heavily; but no sooner did it see the arrival than it turned to her and said, "You promised to serve me as godmother. I would like to know if you stand by your word."

Only now did the youngest recall all that had happened on that walk. But she remembered well what she had said, and now replied, "Why not? You, too, are God's creature!" At that moment the toad gave birth to a beautiful son. An old woman was standing by, who bathed and swaddled the boy. "Take the child, my dear godmother, take him to his baptism," the one on the bed requested. The beautiful godmother took the lovely boy in her arms and went with him to the church. The priest in the church had hardly finished christening and blessing the boy when the toad at home burst its skin and a beautiful lady jumped out.

The godmother emerged happily from the church with her godson in her arms. But right in the doorway she was stopped by a stooped old woman who stretched out a withered arm to her. "Oh, don't pass a poor beggar by, my dear!" she begged in a piercing voice. She reached into her pocket and withdrew a silver coin. The old woman smiled at her and said, "God reward you, my dear, may God reward and bless you one hundred times as much. But beware, in the palace they will offer you gold and silver. Take nothing, my dear, or you would turn into a toad. Only after much insisting should you request a handful of sweepings! Take nothing else, and you will free yourself and the child's mother."

With that the old woman disappeared like the slap of a palm.

The youngest then carried the child to the golden palace without further obstruction. There the elated beautiful lady met her with arms open wide: "Welcome, my godmother, welcome! My, whatever shall I give you for your service? Take gold, take silver! Take whatever your heart desires!" But the godmother didn't want to take a thing, saying she had simply done her Christian duty. "Oh, how's that, my dear godmother? Can I leave you go with empty arms?" the lady bargained. "You must take something. Ask for whatever, and I will give it to you."

"Well, if that's how it must be," the toad's godmother said finally, "then give me a handful of sweepings from under the broom."

The lady wouldn't have it and quibbled with her every which way, but in the end did what she had asked.

No sooner had the dear toad's godmother stepped out of the door than the sweepings that she had wrapped in her kerchief began to jingle beautifully: each bit of powder had turned into a glittering heavy nugget of gold! And behind her the air shook with the singing of the birds: "You have freed us! You have freed us!"

❦ 39 ❦

The Kids

"**C**ome, children, come. I'm going to tell you a little story. Annie, Susie, Mary, where are you? Sit around the fire. And you, Andy, bring some wood, and you, Johnny, put some on the fire so that we can see better. There, that's good. Now listen!"

The mother called her children to the hearth around her in this way, then she continued:

There once was a hill, and on that hill a meadow, and on that meadow a little house, and in that house lived a nanny goat and she had kids. When she went to find them some milk, she instructed them, "My children, don't let anyone in, because they would slay you."

A wolf was listening beneath the window. As soon as the nanny goat left, he began to sing beneath the window:

> "Kiddies, kiddies, won't you let me in?
> I've milk in my udder, a mouth full of water,
> and my horns are loaded with hay."

"Certainly we will not, for our mother has a thinner throat," replied the kids, and didn't let him in.

The wolf ran to the smith: "Smith, smith, forge me a thin throat!" And the smith forged a thin throat.[1] The wolf ran to the kids below the window and began with his narrow throat:

> "Kiddies, kiddies, won't you let me in?
> I've milk in my udder, a mouth full of water,
> and my horns are loaded with hay."

"You're surely not our mother," said the oldest kid, who was already wiser, "we won't let you in!"

"But that's our mother for sure," said the younger kids.

"It is not!" argued the oldest.

"Yes it is!" quarreled the youngsters.

"Fine, but we are not going to let anyone in for a little while longer," said the oldest and stood in their way.

"No, we will let her in right away, because we are hungry!" said the youngsters and pushed him away from the door.

And open the door they did.

In jumped the wolf with claws and teeth bared. The kids scattered, one this way, one that—and the wolf after them! They hid from him, some beneath the bench, some below the fire, some in the stove, some in the vent. But he sniffed them out and swallowed them up. Only the oldest immediately stuffed himself under the stair and the wolf didn't find him there.

Later, the nanny goat came home and found the door open. "Oh my God," she cried, "what has happened here?" She searched, bleated, and called out to her children until the one under the stair stuck out his head and recognized his mother:

"Mommy, mommy," he called, "is it really you?"

"Yes it is, my child. Where are the rest of you?"

"Oh, mommy dear, where are they indeed! The wolf came and they opened for him and he ate them up. Only he didn't find me beneath the stair."

And the nanny goat dashed off to the smith: "Smith, smith, forge me a knife!" And the smith forged her a knife and she went after the wolf. He hadn't gotten far. He wanted to take a drink at the well to chase down the meat. She butted him with her horns and opened him with her knife. She took out the kids and washed them in the well and gave them water. Soon they came to themselves. But it would have been too late if the wolf had had time to drink his fill. And it was lucky that he didn't crunch them, but simply swallowed them whole. They certainly listened to their mother after that and never again opened the door to the wolf.[2]

Notes

1. According to Dobšinský, the smith forged a recorder on which the wolf played.

2. With this fairy tale mothers quiet their children and call their attention on the one hand to the faithful care of a mother and on the other to the results of children's disobedience.

During the second singing of the song with the "narrow throat," the wolf sings an octave higher than the first time. The kids answer him quickly in chorus.

❦ 40 ❦

Salt over Gold

A king had three girls whom he guarded like the eyes in his head. When his muscles had weakened and snow had settled on his head, it often crossed his mind which of his three girls should be queen after his death. It was difficult for him to choose between them, for all of them were fair and he loved them all the same. Finally it occurred to him to appoint as queen the one who loved him the most. He called his girls before him and told them:

"My dear girls, I'm old, you see, and I don't know if I'll be with you much longer, so I want to name the one who will be queen after my death. But first I would like to know, my dear children, how each of you loves me. Well now, my eldest, you say first. How do you love your father?"

"Ah, father dear, you're dearer to me than gold," answered the oldest daughter and kissed her father's hand nicely.

"Very well. And you, my second, how do you love your father?"

"Oh, my dear father, I love you like my green maiden wreath!" said the second, putting her arms around her father's neck.

"Very well. And you, my youngest, how do you love me?"

"I love you like salt, Daddy!" said Maruška, looking sweetly at her father.

"What, you little good-for-nothing, you love father only as much as salt?" her older sisters shouted at her.

"In truth, I love him as much as salt," Maruška confirmed and looked at her father even more tenderly.

But she failed to win even him over. Her father became terribly angry that a child should love her own father only as much as that worthless salt that everyone takes between their fingers and spreads.[1]

"Go! Get out of my sight," he snapped at her, "if you don't value me more than a bit of salt! If the time should ever come that salt is worth more than gold, then report here and you shall be queen."

Maruška couldn't speak for sorrow that her father so undervalued her love. She was used to following her father's words to a T, and she knew that she wouldn't be able to hold out against her sisters in the house any longer, so she gathered her rags and started off. She followed the wind over hill and dale until she came to a dark forest far away. There—whence she came, thence she came—an old woman stood in her path.

"Maruška, Maruška, tell me. Where are you going and why are you so teary-eyed?"

"Oh, you dear old woman, why should I tell you when you can't help me?"

"Well, little girl, you just tell me your tale and perhaps you'll even find some good counsel in me. Don't you know that where they're grey, they know the way?"

Maruška told the old woman her reason for crying and wished only to live to see her father convinced that she truly loved him. The old woman knew ahead of time what Maruška would say, for she was a wise woman, a foreteller. That's why she confirmed everything Maruška said and asked her to come immediately and work for her. Maruška was glad that she had found someone she could complain to, and thankfully followed the old woman to where she lived, in a small cottage beneath the forest pines. One gives what one has, and the old woman fed Maruška with what she could. Maruška certainly needed a bit of refreshment, for she was both hungry and thirsty by now.

"And now," said the old woman, "hop to it. But do you know how to spin, to spool, to clew, and to weave? Can you tend my sheep and will you also milk them?"

"I don't know how yet, my dear old woman, I don't. But I'll soon learn if you'll just show me once," Maruška said.

"Well, then, I'll show you everything, and when the season comes, you'll be handy with it all."

And so Maruška took to the work like a wasp, and though she didn't yet know how everything was done among the poor, she quickly adjusted to everything. Her rolled-up sleeves and white apron even suited her, like a maiden fit for the world.

At home during that time the sisters lived opulently. They continually caressed their father, wrapped themselves around his neck and would, it seems, have eaten him up out of sheer love, because whatever their wild desires, he fulfilled them. The eldest dressed every day in more expensive dresses and wrapped herself in gold. The second hosted banquets and dances; both indulged in whatever crossed their minds. Soon the father noticed that gold was dearer to the eldest than her father, and when the second made it known that she wanted to marry, he knew that her love for her father would wither with her green maiden wreath. Suddenly Maruška crossed his mind, but to what end? Of her they'd heard nary a tale.

"Well, and so what?" he sought her in his memory. "After all, she only loved me like worthless salt."

Once there was to be another big banquet in the castle, and it was rumored that suitors were to come to the second daughter. And here came the cook, pale and all out of breath.

"Your highness," he stammered, "a great misfortune, a great misfortune!"

"What's with you, have you lost your mind?" asked the king.

"This . . . this, your highness, brings my mind to a halt. Of all the salt that we had, whether it got wet or maybe just disappeared into the ground, there's none left, not even a grain. With what shall I salt the food?"

"But you're a fool! Send for some more!"

"Wherever I send, it so happens that in every house and in the entire kingdom, there's no salt!"

"Well then, salt with something else, or else cook food that doesn't need salt!" said the surly king, sending the cook away finally.

The cook thought, "as the lord commands, so must it be done," and cooked food without salt; at first, whatever came to mind, and then only sweets. Those were strange, saltless banquets! And the guests soon left the king and new ones came no more. And why should they, when even here they didn't have what was found elsewhere even among the poorest: "bread with salt and good will." The king wandered around wearily, and his daughters were as though thunderstruck. Where had the good times gone? Indeed, of gold there was enough, but not a grain of salt though they send to the end of the earth for it. It disappeared and disappeared.

Slowly, the people began to lose their appetites for food, but wished instead for just a bit of salt, like a mere poppy seed, on their tongues. Even the livestock suffered. The cows and sheep stopped giving milk because they had no salt. The people wandered about in a daze and began to fall ill. The king and his girls were mere shadows, and he wouldn't have even known them for illness. It was God's rebuke to the whole country. The one who would bring them a grain of salt would be worth his weight in gold.

Now the king understood what a precious gift of God salt is, but could have endured his misery if he hadn't had Maruška on his conscience and the injustice he had done her!

Meanwhile, all was going quite well for Maruška. There was no work which she couldn't learn and to which she could not get accustomed. She knew nothing of misery. She didn't even know what was happening in her father's house and in his country. But the wise woman knew all, including when it's time for what. One time, therefore, she called Maruška and told her, "My dear girl, I told you, after all, to everything there is a season. Your season has come and it's time for you to return home."

"Oh, my dear, good old woman, how can I go home when my father doesn't want me?" asked Maruška and she began to cry.

"Don't cry, my dear girl, everything will be fine. Salt has become dearer than gold there; even you may report to your father."

And with that the foreteller told of everything which Maruška hadn't known, and added, "You've served me honestly, so tell me now, what do you wish for this loyal service?"

"You've advised me well and raised me well, granny! I just thank you for everything. I wish for nothing, just a handful of salt to take to my father as a gift."

"And you don't wish anything else? Don't you know that I can do anything for you?" again asked the wise woman.

"I wish nothing more, just the salt!" answered Maruška.

"Well then, if you value salt so much, may it never be lacking to you," the foreteller said finally. "And I won't give you anything else, just this little wand. Go with the wind as it blows from the north, across three valleys and three peaks. Then stop and strike the ground with the wand! Where you hit it, the ground will open; go in! Everything you find there is yours; it will be for your dowry!"

Maruška thanked her for everything, took the golden wand and a full bag of salt, and sadly started off—sadly indeed, for life had been good with the old woman. But she consoled herself that, after all, she wasn't saying goodbye forever to the old woman, that she would yet come for her, if only her father at home would be appeased. The old woman just smiled at that and told her, "Just stay good and honest, my dear girl, and things will be fine forever. Don't worry about me the least bit!"

While they were talking, they came to the edge of the forest. And when Maruška wanted to thank the good old woman one more time, she wasn't there anymore—where she'd gone, there she'd gone, but Maruška was left alone as a finger. For that reason she longed even more for her father and hurried briskly in the direction of his castle.

She arrived among her own, but, partly because they had not seen her for a long time, partly because she had her head wrapped in a kerchief, they didn't recognize her and didn't want to allow her before the king. "Eh, just let me go," insisted Maruška, "why, I'm bringing the king a gift greater than gold, and one that will be medicine for his certain recovery!" They told the king and he immediately commanded them to allow her in. When she came to him, she requested that they give her bread. The king ordered it brought to her, but at the same time sighed deeply. "Bread we have, but we have no salt!"

"What we don't have, we can have!" said Maruška, and she cut off a slice of bread, opened her bag, sprinkled it, and gave it to the king.[2]

"Salt!" rejoiced the king. "Hey, little woman, that's a valuable gift; how can I repay you? Ask for whatever you want and you'll get it!"

"I don't want anything, Daddy, just love me like this salt!" said Maruška in a sweet voice like she used to use with her father, and uncovered her head. It's a wonder the king didn't swoon from joy when he recognized his dear Maruška. He begged her not to dwell on what had happened. She just kissed and hugged him and didn't leave her dear eye off him. "After all, as they say, everything turned out well."

The news spread immediately through the castle and town that the king's youngest daughter had come and that she'd brought salt. Everyone rejoiced at that. Even Maruška's sisters rejoiced, not for their sister, but for the salt, that they might at least get a lick. And Maruška had forgotten the injury done her by her sisters and welcomed them also with a salted slice of bread. And she shared the salt from her bag with everyone who came. And when her father, in fear that they not be left again without salt, reminded her not, for God's sake, to give it all out, that "they say, slowly with what's good," she always answered simply, "There's enough here yet, Daddy!" And indeed, however much she took, she always had enough left for everyone, as though it were eternally in that bag. Everything was replenished, as on the sun.

And all the illness left the king, just as though it had been taken off of him. In joy, he called together the elders of the town and country and appointed Maruška queen. Then, when they proclaimed Maruška queen beneath the high heavens, she felt a warm breeze blow in her face; it was blowing from the north. She immediately confessed to her father about what and how the wise woman had advised her. She went with the wind, and when she had crossed three valleys and three peaks, she stopped with her wand and struck the ground with it. As she struck, the ground split open and Maruška entered straight into the ground.

Suddenly—she didn't even know how she'd got there—she came to an immense hall, which seemed to be completely of ice: the ceiling, walls, and floor, everything shone and glimmered as though showered with sparks. Along the sides were shiny galleries and from these poured out tiny dwarves with burning lanterns, welcoming Maruška. "Welcome here, welcome, queen. We've been waiting for you; our lady has commanded us to lead you everywhere and show you everything, because it is all yours!"

They chirped around her, gamboled about with their lanterns, spun, climbed up and down the walls like flies, and the walls glittered all around like gems. Maruška walked as if blinded by so much beauty. The dwarves led her along halls and galleries where ice orbs hung from the ceilings, glittering just like silver. They also led her to the garden where there were red ice-roses, daisies, and all kinds of astonishing flowers. The dwarves plucked the most beautiful rose and gave it to their new queen. She sniffed it, but the rose had no odor.

"But what in the world is this?" asked the queen. "Why, I've never seen such beauty!"

"It's all salt!" the dwarves answered her.

"But really? That's salt growing?" wondered the queen and thought that it would be a pity to take the least bit of it.

But the dwarves guessed what she was thinking and called out, "Take it, just take it, Maruška, just take as much as you like. You'll never take it all, never again will you lack!" Maruška thanked the dwarves nicely, left them, and came out of the ground. But the ground remained open behind her.

When she returned home and showed her father the rose and told him everything, the king saw that the old woman from the cottage truly had given his daughter a richer dowry than he could have outfitted her with. But Maruška hadn't forgotten the old woman from the cottage either. She had a beautiful coach harnessed and started off with her father to search for the old woman, saying they'd never let her leave them again.

Maruška knew the way, she knew every path in the forest well, but though they crisscrossed the forest a hundred times and looked as if for poppy seeds on all sides, there was no sign of the cottage and not a sound of the old woman. Only now were they persuaded what kind of old woman she was and that any search would be for nought. They returned home. In the bag Maruška had been given, no salt remained, but Maruška knew now where salt grows: they took and took and never took it all, never again were they lacking.

Notes

1. In Slovakia salt is often on the table in a small bowl and is spread with the fingers.—Trans.

2. Bread and salt are a part of the traditional welcoming ceremony in many Slavic countries.—Trans.

The Tinkers and the Evil One

Once six tinkers were returning home from their trades, to Rovne. They hummed along the way, whooped and hollered so that everything around echoed from it. And while they were going along, here and there they even gamboled and skipped about. And why not? After all, each of them carried a few hard-won gold pieces in their packs, so that now they could have their way a while and put their households in order, and they weren't far from home now.

It seems they passed over Javorina,[1] coming this way from Moravia. At the very summit, such a thick fog came down on them that they couldn't even see one another. Well, they just joined hands and walked on, going by memory. Even so, they only fell on their faces, roamed about, and were constantly stopping. So they sat down and waited for it to lighten a bit. After a long wait, the dawn began to break and they saw that they had strayed from the path and were lost. Fear gripped them, for in the undergrowth it's no cinch to find a path. The more they searched, the more they were led astray and haunted.[2] All of them were hungry, but in their pack there weren't even poppyseed crumbs. Then one of them, all tired and annoyed, said, "If only we'd come upon some kind of cabin, even if the evil ones themselves lived there!"

No sooner did he open his trap than a little light suddenly flickered ahead of them. They followed that little light until they came to an isolated yard. They knocked on the door and it opened to them all by itself. They went in and . . . gadzooks! A black man came to meet them, asking them what brought them his way. They asked him for a night's lodging and something to eat.

"Oh, I'll give you a bed and a good dinner," said the black man, "but you must agree to solve the three riddles that I pose." They agreed readily. "But," he said, "if you don't guess it will go badly for you."

"My, but what riddles they would have to be," they said, "that we couldn't solve them!" And they followed their host into the cabin.

Five of them went, but the sixth one, the youngest, whom they always took for a fool, didn't go. He recognized the evil one from his horse's hooves and saw that things ain't good. He crossed himself and asked God for help and advice there under the heavens where he remained. When he had finished praying, he entered behind the others and stuffed himself behind the stove. My, but those at the table ate, drank, and caroused. They laughed at him for not joining them. But when they had eaten and drunk their fill, the evil one came and sat among them and began to lay out his riddles.

"Well, boys, guess what this table is made of."

They guessed, the dear boys, they guessed. One said it's made of linden wood, another that it's maple, a third that it's oak, the fourth that it's hornbeam, the fifth that it's ash. But the evil one just shook his head, that it sure ain't that. Then the youngest tinker spoke up from behind the stove, "The table is made of horsehide!"

The evil one just looked at him and furrowed his brow. He had guessed it!

"And what is the table's base made of?" said the evil one, posing his second riddle. The tinkers guessed that maybe it's iron, or copper, or perhaps brass, or some kind of metal. But the evil one just laughed at them. Once again, the youngest spoke up from behind the stove, "The base is made of horses' shin bones!"

It's a wonder the devil didn't explode in anger. He'd guessed that one, too!

"Fine, but what are these glasses made of?" the evil one riddled the third time and lifted a full glass from the table. Our tinkers finally understood whom they were faced with, and they trembled like aspen leaves. One guessed glass, another silver, the third gold, and they couldn't call anything else to mind. So the youngest called out, "Those glasses are made of horses' hooves, and you're the evil one!"

And our evil one opened his gob, twisted up his face, and broke out into such inhuman guffaws that everything shook all around. Then he grumbled, "You're lucky. I would have torn you to pieces!"

Suddenly not a trace of anything remained except a deadly stench.

When the tinkers got their wits about them, they thanked their friend for saving their lives. They were amazed that he had been able to guess everything, and said, "Boy, it must have been Lucifer himself testing us."

"No, brothers," said the youngest, "but the Lord God put the answers in my mind when I asked him nicely."

Before dawn they took to the road again and arrived home successfully. For as long as they lived, the name of the evil one never passed their tongues again. They'd learned their lesson. In fact, ever since that time, whenever any tinker is about to say the name of the evil one, he immediately spits on the ground and adds: "A plague upon him!" or "May he perish!"

Notes

1. Javorina is a mountain on the border between Slovakia and Moravia—at the time of the tale's recording between Hungary and Austria—just west of Trenčin, Slovakia. Rovne is Lednické Rovne, to the north-east from Trenčin, a town known for its tradition of tinkers.—Trans.

2. Local superstitions included supernatural forces, perhaps the spirit of a drowned person or a wood sprite, or simply a small light, which led travelers from the path and into the swamps, where they drowned. A nonsuperstitious mind would likely assign the cause instead to alcohol.—Trans.

❦ 42 ❦

The Honest Valach

In a farmer's room around a white linden table there once sat a few good neighbors, and they were speaking about farming matters. One was complaining that his horses weren't worth a rap. "I don't even know," he said, "what the deuce got into them, if the servant overworked them, or if they're overfed, or what's wrong with them! But what can you do—you can't follow in your hired hand's footsteps all the time to see how he treats the animals."

"Yeah, well, my oxen are great!" another said. "My Ďuro seems quite clumsy, but he's good to the animals, and my oxen have been gaining weight so this past half-year, it's as if he were loading something on them."

"You already know, my neighbors," said the owner, "that I don't like to speak much, but what I say has weight. Since we're talking about servants, why, let me just tell you that compared to my valach, there's none in the world more honest, that would serve more loyally and never deceive his master in a thing. And, why, its simply a joy to look upon those sheep that he pastures, and so far not a thing has ever been wrong with them."

"Nice, they're nice, those rams of yours," said the neighbor, "for everyone already agrees that valach of yours knows his work. But if he's deceiving or not, well, now and then. If it came right down to it, believe me, your valach too would be as much a slyboots as any other."

"Really, my Janko?"

"Indeed, your Janko—he's as much a slyboots as any other."

"Ah, no, not him!" said the owner.

"Ah, yes indeed, him! But if you think I'm just being mealymouthed, how much will you bet, eh?"

"Perhaps a hundred gold pieces for me!"

"Good, it's worth the hundred gold pieces," said the neighbor, shaking the owner's hand. "If your valach doesn't sell me the nicest ram and tell you that a wolf caught it or something like that, then I'll give you the hundred gold pieces!" The other neighbors confirmed the bet, saying, "It's a dishonest man who won't pay."

Three days later, when dawn had hardly begun to break, the dear neighbor was already over hill and dale. He was climbing the path to the sheep farm. "Yeah, a hundred gold pieces—a pretty penny for a peasant!" he said, giving a little skip. Indeed, it's a wonder he didn't jump out of his skin for joy, for he practically held them in his fist. "And how? I'll give him a nice word and a hard thaler—that should sparkle nicely in his eyes as well!" He could see in advance how the valach would hand the ram over to him. And among such thoughts the time passed so easily that he didn't even know where he was until the dogs began to bark at him before the shepherd's hut itself.

"Godspeed, Janko! How are you?"

"Godspeed, Godspeed! I'm well, thank you very much. And welcome!"

From chit to chat, they began to talk, just like normal on the sheep farm. They chatted about God knows what, just not about the ram, for the honesty of the valach appeared in every word he spoke. And that honesty itself, it seemed, had so scared off the dear buyer from the start that he didn't dare raise his business out of the blue. He even began to be afraid that he would lose those hundred gold pieces. And in his fear, he forgot everything that he had thought about on his way there. He had no idea what to say further and how to broach the subject.

Perhaps he even would have simply left out of honesty, but that irritated him, and those unhappy rams began to bleat in their fold, undoubtedly in anticipation of the time when the valach usually let them out. And as the dew had already dried, the valach went to chase his sheep out into the green pasture.

"It's now or never!" thought the neighbor, and got right down to business.

"My, what nice rams! How many have you got?"

"There ought to be fifty and a hundred, but really, it's been so long since I counted them."

"Eh, look at that one there with the bell. Isn't he a beauty! Couldn't you let me have that one?"

"Well, why not? Yes indeed, I'll let you have him. I'll even choose a nicer one, but first I have to tell the owner."

"Eh, what's he have to do with it? Does the owner really have to know about everything? Janko!" he said, patting his shoulders and looking into his eyes, "Janko! Me . . . and you!"

"Me . . . and you? Hmm!" Janko looked up at the sky as if he wanted to count the stars in the middle of the day, for he didn't get what that meant.

"Why, I'm certainly not asking it for free," said the neighbor, giving him a hard thaler. "So, here you go, take it! What are you waiting for—it'll come in handier for you than for the owner. And just give me that ram, and I can do you a good turn someday. Why, it's certainly not the whole world, one little ram, just give it to me!"

And thus he persuaded him on and on, talking as pretty as he could. The good valach five times already had wanted to give him the ram after being pestered so, but God knows what wouldn't allow him to do it; he wanted to enough, but still couldn't. And in the end he simply wouldn't give up the ram, so the neighbor had to return home with empty pockets.

He arrived at home and was more sour than milk! Gloomy and irritated, he couldn't rest or relax; he didn't want to eat, couldn't sleep; he was sorry for tempting the valach, but irked that he hadn't accomplished what he'd set out to do. "God . . . you! You . . .! Why it's unheard of! The devil himself must have whispered the entire bet in my ear!" The household was sorry for its master, for they loved him. But his beautiful only Hanka was the sorriest, for she loved him the most.

"But Daddy, pretty please, do tell me what happened to you? Why, you left the house this morning so happy and now you're like one thunderstruck!" And she pestered him so and followed him around until he told her everything that had happened. "I don't care anymore about the hundred gold pieces," he said, "the devil take them, but if only I could get my hands on that ram. Why, I'd be sure to compensate the honest valach somehow."

Green mountains and a beautiful wood! Beneath them in the deep valley one can hear the burble of a rushing stream, above them the bells of the rams, grazing on the green turf. They are nice rams, as obedient as children, for a good lad grazes them—a just lad that never deceived his master. "Heigh there, not there, my rams, not at the edge of the thicket! The dew hasn't dried there yet; come here on the clearing, this way! I'll play to you on the bag-pipes so you graze better!"

The bagpipes sounded and the valach played. But even though he played beautifully, still voices a hundred times more beautiful echoed back to him near the thicket. "Eh, are my pipes able to play so nicely?" thought the lad, and he approached the thicket. And behold, on the edge of the thicket he saw the neighbor's Hanka singing and gathering ripe strawberries around the bushes. The bagpipes fell silent and Janko, as though nothing had happened, bent over to pluck a nice strawberry at his feet, then another, and a third, and who knows how many, all the nicest strawberries. Only when he had a nice bouquet of them did he grow bold and give them to the lass. She smiled at the pretty strawberries, and the lad was elated at the lass's smile. The bouquet and smile so acquainted the two souls that they then collected strawberries side by side along the edge of the thicket.

And when the basket of strawberries was already full and the heart of the lad was full of the lass's beauty, they both sat by the peacefully grazing herd in the shade of a spreading beech tree. The girl played with a white ram, and the lad enjoyed the pretty lass. The lass kissed the beautiful ram, which let itself be kissed; but when the lad wanted to kiss the pretty lass, she moved her head. "Give me," she said, "give me that ram instead!"

"Ah, I sure would give him to you, my dear! Not only one, but even more nice rams if they were mine, as they're not. But what would the owner say to me then?"

"Why, the owner needn't know. You can easily tell him that it died."

"Well, that's how it is. Aha, but that wouldn't be any good. Why it would be gypping him! Oh, just go away, go away! Better not to kiss you than to have to gyp someone for you."

Hanka entertained herself no more with the quiet ram, and Janik no more enjoyed the pretty lass. She left sadly for home, and the lad looked after her sadly for a long time. "Come," he called, "come tomorrow! Perhaps we shall decide differently, either you or me."

Hardly had the newly arisen sun dried out the cold dew than the valach chased his herd out to pasture above the thicket, and he awaited the beautiful Hanka. And come she did, and fidgeting around the lad, she petted and hugged the white ram. And when he wanted to embrace her, she slipped away like a fish. "Give me," she said, "give me that ram instead; why, you can easily tell the owner that he died."

The poor valach thought and thought about what to do, and couldn't decide either way. "He will believe me, my good master, he will. Why shouldn't he? But if only it could somehow be done properly. Eh, go away, go away! Better not to kiss you than to have to deceive my master for you!"

The lass stopped petting the ram and sadly started away. But the valach looked after her even more sadly. He was sorry both for the lass and the ram, and he nearly called her back to give it to her, but that unfortunate gypping completely dissuaded him from that. "Come," he called after her, "come in the morning, and if it's no different, maybe I'll give it to you, that ram."

On the third day in the morning it seemed to our valach both that the sun had changed its attire into prettier flashes and that his rams were prettier and more obedient. So he too put on a clean shirt, got himself up as if for church and thus chased his herd out onto the green pasture by the thick beech. The rams sought soft grass. In a short while the lass came and looked for ripe strawberries along the edge of the thicket, together with the good valach. When the basket was full of strawberries and the lad's heart was full of love for the lass, they sat down beneath the old spreading beech. The girl stroked the white ram, and the lad stroked the girl's cheeks; she kissed the quiet ram, but when the lad wanted to kiss her, she quickly moved her head. "You promised," she said, "you promised me that ram."

"Ah," good Janko heaved a sigh, "I promised him to you, I did. Well, here goes, if there's no other way, just take him!" And behold, the girl became as quiet as a lamb and no longer tilted her head away from the good lad.

So far so good. After a while night came and a cold breeze cooled the hot blood of the valach. The poor valach! Yesterday, while he played at the side of the pretty lass, love tormented him; and today, when he had just awakened, right away his old honesty began to spin him around, calling out to him ceaselessly: "Valach, valach, where's your ram?!"

He let the herd out of the fold so sadly, it was as if he hadn't eaten a thing for three days. Had it really happened with the ram? He began to count the flock, but whatever's missing is missing: he never could count to a hundred and fifty! The more he counted, the more forlorn he became. He looked back and forth from the rams to the valley and the thick beech. But there was no ram there, and no lass. "Eh!" he threatened the thicket with his fist, "if you came now I wouldn't give you that ram, even if you were a hundred times prettier! But so what? On Mitra there will be a counting, and no ram! How will you tell the owner?"

He leaned on his valaška and thought and thought for a long time. Now and then he would scratch behind his ears, now and then nod his head, but nohow could he come up with anything. Then he suddenly jumped up, overjoyed: "Well," he said, "now I know. So: the master will ask me: 'Valach, where is that ram?' And I'll say to him: 'Ah, sir, where is the ram! When I was grazing the flock in the sun the ram wandered into the thicket and the devil took him!' But, after all, the devil didn't take him, I gave him myself. Well, that's no good, I won't say that. That would be gypping him!"

As before, again the poor valach began to think. When he wasn't chasing a ram, he was leaning on his valaška thinking. He thought: "I'll say that a wolf caught him. Hmm, that would be something, when no wolf has ever caught a ram. But after all, no wolf caught it. Well, that would be a gyp, too. I won't say that. But I have to tell him something after all. The owner asks me: 'Valach, where is the ram?' I'll shrug my shoulders. 'Did they steal it?' 'No!' 'Did a wolf take it?' 'No!' 'Did you sell it yourself?' 'No!' 'Well, where the devil is it then?' Well, what will I say now? Why, I'll say that I gave him to a pretty lass so she would let me kiss her. Why, my word, look here, that's it. At least it's not a gyp. That's what I'll say, even if the owner takes it out of my pay, at least I'll still be a man!"

Along came Demitra and the owners gathered to check their inventory and question their bačas and valachs. But our honest valach told the truth indeed, and the dear neighbor had to fork over the hundred gold pieces. "Hey, buddy!" the other neighbors called out, "that was an expensive ram!"

❦ 43 ❦

Auntie Death

$\mathcal{W}$here it was, where it wasn't, don't worry about it, just so it was the way I tell you.

There was once a maiden and she lived with other people in a little house somewhere far away in a dark pine grove. She was already fully grown and fit for work, but what good was that when she took such a fright from every rustle that she could hardly breathe for fear. She wouldn't for the world remain home alone or go somewhere without others—even if it were in the middle of the day. And when evening came on, she wouldn't even peek out the door!

But one Christmas everyone was going to the midnight mass. It didn't suit our coward to journey to the distant church that way at midnight, nor to remain home by herself. "But it's nothing, after all. Just stay at home, and when you are about to become very frightened, go out on the stoop and call out: 'Somebody, somebody, come to me!' Then someone will come and you'll be two." These words of the household members were agreeable to the maiden and she remained at home, for she was afraid of the midnight mass and if somebody really came, they would be two without fear.

She sat by the fire, sat alone by the hearth and added twigs to the fire. Suddenly something in the fire began to hiss and splutter. She came to rapt attention, as if every wicked witch was swarming down the flue. "Well, but it's nothing. I won't be alone," she thought. As the household members had told her, she ran out and called from the stoop three times: "Somebody, somebody, come to me! Somebody, somebody, come to me! Somebody, somebody, come to me!"

"I'm coming, I'm coming! Just cook up some porridge!" echoed out to her from the dark pine grove.

She ran inside, gathered the grain, washed it and set it on the fireside. She covered her eyes with her palms so as not to see anything around her; only from time to time she would peek out between her fingers when she stoked the fire or stirred the food in the pot with her other hand. Suddenly the porridge began: voo—voo—foo, fooch, fooch! She froze, but then came slightly to her senses and thought that no doubt the porridge was finishing cooking and was fooching. So she ran outside and called: "The porridge is fooching, the porridge is boiling; somebody, somebody, come to me!"

"I'm coming, I'm coming; just add the fat!" echoed out to her again from the dark pine grove.

She ran inside, poured the porridge into a bowl, added fat, and ran outside again and called: "Our porridge's in the pot; somebody, somebody come to me!"

"I'm coming, I'm coming; just set the table!" echoed out to her for the third time from the dark pine grove.

She went in and set the table. No sooner had she placed the bowl on the table and lifted her eyes than she saw an old auntie sitting at the table who said, "My dear girl, sit down!" So the maiden sat and they ate the porridge together.

While they were eating, the question kept buzzing in our maiden's head: how ever did that auntie come in? And so she asked, "But auntie, which way did you come in?"

"Ah, my dear girl, there are no castles in the world that I cannot slip into."

"Well, but how did you slip in when the door didn't even squeak?"

"Ah, my dear girl, the way I walk there's no rustle, there's no bustle, and no one notices!"

While they were finishing eating, the maiden looked the auntie over from head to toe and said, "Why auntie, what long legs you have!"

"Ah, my dear girl, they'll step at once from one end of the world to the other!"

"Why, auntie, what long arms you have!"

"Ah, my dear girl, there's no one in the world far enough that they can't reach them!"

"Why, auntie, even what big eyes you have!"

"Ah, my dear girl, they can spot every little worm, let alone a person, no matter where it is hidden!"

And when, at that moment, our auntie swallowed the last spoonful of porridge and it rattled in her mouth, why our dear maiden already was shaking like an aspen and shouted out, "My, auntie, you have terrifying teeth!"

"Just so you know, they eat everyone: I'll eat you up too—chomp!"

And that was all for the maiden! The household found her soulless and neither hide nor hair of the auntie.

❦ 44 ❦

Petor and the Heavenly Father in the Wide Vale

1. Petor's Cap

*W*hen Saint Petor and the Heavenly Father walked in the *wide vale*, once they came to a christening in a village. The women gathered around Petor, saying he should bestow something upon the baby. But since he had nothing to give, one woman took his cap and placed it on the boy's head. Petor became angry; however, the Heavenly Father said unto him, "If that is the custom, let the child have the cap." Then they left.

The boy grew up and was a lad of unheard-of beauty. When he was fully grown, he pastured his mother's herd. Once Petor and the Heavenly Father again passed through the field where the boy was herding. Then Petor said to the Heavenly Father, "Heavenly Father, how many years have we wandered the wide vale, and yet I have truly never seen such a handsome lad as that shepherd!"

"That's the lad whose christening we were at when the woman took your cap," said the Heavenly Father.

"Cursed woman!" said Petor in anger, and he asked the Heavenly Father to change the lad into an ugly one. The Heavenly Father did according to his will.

The boy chased the sheep home and went to his mother to ask for his supper. His mother's eyes just bugged to see what kind of lad came into her house and even asked for supper. And when he told her that he was her son, she grabbed the stove broom and smoked him out, calling after him, "Get out of my sight! My son was a dashing lad, beautiful as can be, and you're just a monster!"

Crying, the boy went to the forest. He came to a hermit there and asked for God's mercy, be it only a crust of bread. The hermit questioned him about who he was, and where he was from, and when the lad had told him everything, he gave him some bread and put him to bed.

In the morning when they'd had a good sleep, the hermit said, "But my lad, if they won't recognize you at home, you could also stay with me. I also have a flock of sheep you could pasture for me. Well, shall we make a deal?"

They agreed that the old sheep would remain the hermit's, but afterward half of the lambs and young would always be the boy's. With that, the boy went to pasture, and he had some talent: the old sheep gave birth to lambs with fleeces to the ground. When the hermit saw that the lad took such good care of the sheep, he left on a long journey and told the boy only, "Look after everything as well as you have so far, so that no sheep dies. I'll see when I return if you tell me the truth!"

The lad continued to pasture and care for the sheep. It was a fine flock indeed. Then Petor and the Heavenly Father passed by the flock. Petor wondered at the fine herd, but when the Heavenly Father said that the flock was pastured by that lad in his cap and that half of the beautiful lambs belonged to the lad, Petor asked the Heavenly Father to make it so that the lad's lambs would perish. The Heavenly Father did according to his will.

The lad endured this tragedy as well. When the hermit returned, he told the truth about what had happened; he returned the hermit his sheep and showed him just the skins of his own. And the hermit advised him to go to town, sell the skins, to buy grain with the money from the sale, and to sow it. The lad followed this good advice.

With God's blessing everything grew by leaps and bounds, and he had such a good sowing that its equal wasn't to be found in the whole wide vale. Petor and the Heavenly Father again passed by, and Petor wondered at the fine sowing. When the Heavenly Father told him that the beautiful grain was that lad's who had his cap, Petor asked the Heavenly Father to send hail upon it. The Heavenly Father did according to his will.

A storm came and the hail destroyed everything in the fields. Not even a stalk remained to the lad. But he endured this accident as well.

And the hermit advised him to go to the king in the town, who had three daughters, to boldly ask for the hand of one of them so that he would still become a king's son-in-law. The lad also followed this advice of the hermit.

He went straight to the town, stood boldly before the king, and asked for one of his girls to wife. The king led him to his three daughters and said, "Well, girls, which of you would care to marry this dashing lad?"

"Eh, I'd rather hang myself on a poplar than bind my world together with such an unkempt boy!" the eldest responded and turned away.

"I'd rather jump into the Váh River than call such a monster my own!" said the middle one, not wanting even to look on.

"Oh truly, father, I'll take him; if he's not handsome, he'll be good!" responded the youngest, and she took him.

There was a wedding party. Petor and the Heavenly Father passed through that town and came to the party. They were made welcome and generously hosted. And Petor asked the Heavenly Father why they had stopped at just that wedding party and who was the young son-in-law.

"That lad who the woman gave the cap to; don't you recognize him?" answered the Heavenly Father.

When dear Petor feasted his eyes on the lovely face of the bride and looked at the ugly face of the groom, he asked the Heavenly Father to make him as handsome as he had once been. But the Heavenly Father made him twice as handsome as he had been, so that the whole chamber lit up with the beauty of the fair young groom. The bride's proud sisters became so vexed at that, that one hung herself on a poplar and the other jumped into the Váh. But the dashing lad reigned happily with the youngest.

2. Petor the Early Bird

Once when Petor and the Heavenly Father were again walking in the wide vale, they couldn't get a place to sleep. Finally a peasant took them in for the night and appropriately provided them with a good supper. After supper he pointed out the stove, and Petor hurried to lie down by the breadboards, saying it's warmer there. The Heavenly Father just lay down on the bench by the stove. Petor gave praise inwardly that he was lying on something warm, had a good supper, and in the morning, perhaps, they would be entertained even better.

Dawn had just begun to break when the peasant arose and called out immediately to the wayfarers, "Get up! Get up!" Petor waited to see if the Heavenly Father would arise, but he didn't move, so he too continued to lie. A moment later the peasant called out again, "Get up, boys! Since you've had both supper and a night's rest, get to work as well!"

And when Petor again didn't move, the dear owner grabbed a breadboard and beat him. That seemed unfair to Petor and he regretted that he had lain down by the breadboards. In the meantime, as if nothing had happened, Petor asked the Heavenly Father to change places and lie in the warmer spot, by the breadboards. The Heavenly Father even in this did according to his will.

After a bit the peasant returned and swore, "Curse you, why the one by the breadboards is still sleeping like a bear in winter! And what about the one on the stove bench?" He struck that one bravely in the back, thinking that the other one should also get something as a lesson. But when Petor still didn't move, the irked peasant went about his work alone.

But Petor begged the Heavenly Father to leave the dwelling of that bully where they were being entertained that morning as soon as possible. The Heavenly Father had already arisen and didn't say either way but just smiled a bit and left, Petor after him. And so they went on.

3. Petor the Miser

While they were further roaming the wide vale, once the Heavenly Father sent Petor to buy a roasted goose. Petor bought the roasted goose, but the miser licked it, developed an appetite, and ate an entire thigh along the way. And the Heavenly Father asked of him, "Petor, where is the other leg of the goose?"

"She didn't have another!" Petor replied curtly.

"My, have you ever seen a goose with just one leg?" answered the Heavenly Father.

"Aha, Heavenly Daddy, there's a goose standing on one leg!" said Petor, pointing to a flock of geese, among which one was standing on only one leg on the ice. The Heavenly Father said neither this nor that and on they went.

They came to a great forest and found a treasure there. The Heavenly Father took the treasure out of the ground and divided it into three parts. Petor stared and stared at those piles, his eyes ran from one to the other to the third until he asked the Heavenly Father, "Whose is the third part, Heavenly Father, when there are only two of us?"

"One shall be mine, the other yours, and the third goes to the one who ate that leg!" said the Heavenly Father.

"Well, Heavenly Father, I ate it, since I was hungry," admitted Petor. The Heavenly Father became somewhat vexed at Petor, since he had gypped him, but he became reconciled again right away and gave him the third pile, for he loved Petor.

4. Petor's Shirt

But Petor must have managed his treasure dreadfully, for when they were again roaming the wide vale, he tore his shirt and had nothing with which to purchase a new one. They came to a certain fence on which there hung a few shirts that belonged to a *poor* woman. Petor said unto the Heavenly Father that he would take one of them. The Heavenly Father didn't want to consent to that, but Petor said, "Eh, well I'll still take one!"

And so he did. The Heavenly Father shook his head, but said only, "Since you've taken it, have it, but in the evening you'll go to hear what the woman has to say."

When the woman came to collect her shirts from the fence that evening and saw that one was missing, she said, "Eh, what's done is done. May the Heavenly Father bless the one who took it."

Petor, listening behind the fence, was cheered at such words and went to inform the Heavenly Father. But the Heavenly Father ordered him to hang the shirt on the fence again right away, for he said they couldn't keep the stolen item in a place where they bless a thief. Willing or no, he obeyed and they went on.

They came in the meantime to another fence on which there hung many shirts belonging to a *rich* housewife. Petor again said unto the Heavenly Father that he would take one of them, since there were so many of them there. But the Heavenly Father didn't want to consent to that. Still, Petor took one.

"Well, since you've taken it, have it, but in the evening you'll go to hear what the woman has to say," the Heavenly Father said unto him.

Petor went that evening to listen. When the woman came to collect the shirts and saw that one was missing, she began to swear, "The devils drag to hell the one who stole my shirt!"

When Petor let this be known unto the Heavenly Father, the Heavenly Father told him to keep the shirt. This was so because the woman had cursed Petor to hell, so that Petor knew how serious it was to keep a stolen thing.

❦ 45 ❦

The King of Time

O nce there were two brothers. Though they were of the same father and the same mother, their relationship did not look like it does between brothers. The older one was miserly and stingy, and therefore also rich, while the younger one was poor, but no one in the village could match him for honesty. More than once the younger one went to his rich older brother to beg for help, for need often oppressed him so that he had naught to place in his mouth. He didn't ask much, just begged, for God's sake, for a bite to eat. But the rich one, as if he were not even his brother, took offense at him and said, "You think I'm going to take care of such sluggards here?" and pushed him out.

One time his brother again pushed him out mercilessly, and he had never before been in such straits as just then. He didn't know, finally, what else to do, so he took to the forest to see if he couldn't find some kind of roots. He looked and looked, roamed all through the forest, but couldn't find a thing except for some wild apples that had fallen under one tree. He paid no mind to the fact that they were sour and put his teeth on edge, but ate his fill of them, then collapsed on the ground and fell asleep without knowing how. And while he was sleeping, he dreamt that his left arm was itching and that he saw a fire in his hut.

When he awoke he was frozen entirely; he shook like a leaf, and night was already beginning to fall. "Alas, where shall a sinner like me warm himself now," he said to himself. "My brother will not allow me into his home and it is a long time since there was a fire in my hut." He stood thinking about what he would do, until he had a bright idea. "I'll try," he said, "to go to the glass mountain. They say that a fire has burned there forever. Here goes! If people here won't have mercy, perhaps there someone will have mercy on me." And he got ready and left.

Already from afar he saw a great fire blazing on the glass mountain and twelve strange people sitting around it. When he approached nearer and caught sight of those people, he stiffened in fear and began to think all kinds of things. But in the end he thought that, after all, the Lord God would be with him there, too, and he went straight on. When he arrived, he paid his respects and began to beg, "Oh, good people, have mercy on me. I am a poor man and no one even pays me any mind. I am terribly cold and in my hut I have neither fire or wood. Allow me to warm myself a bit at your fire here."

All twelve of them looked him over and spoke, "Son! Seat yourself among us and warm yourself from any one of us." So he sat among them, and since they were all silent, he too was afraid to speak a word. He just looked into the fire and glanced around at the twelve. As he watched, he noticed that the twelve were changing their places in order. And when they had gone once around the fire and when each of them was again in his place—wonder of wonders! An old man with a grey beard to his waist and a balding head rose out of the flames and spoke unto him: "Fellow! Do not shorten the days of your life here. Make an effort and act honorably! Take some of this glowing coal, perhaps, for we would use it all up otherwise."

With that the twelve arose, loaded coals into a large sack and lifted it to his shoulder. He thanked them kindly and walked off along the path with a full sack more easily than coming there empty-handed, for he had warmed himself and the sack seemed very light to him.

He arrived home overjoyed that now he would at least have a fire and began to pour out the coal in the middle of the room. But what wonder was this again! Each little spark, no sooner did it fall to the ground than it turned into a gold coin. You can imagine how he felt, and he didn't stop dropping until he had unloaded it all. A heap of coins stood in front of him and all of it was his. He didn't believe his own eyes; only when he had taken a fistful of ducats did he believe it was true after all. Then he fell on his knees and thanked the Lord God for blessing him in such a miraculous manner and assisting him out of all his misery.

Then he had the desire to weigh the heap of coins, but he didn't have anything to do it with. So he went to his brother and asked him to lend him his scale. "Lend my scale!" the rich one began to laugh. "Well, what are you going to do with it, you ragamuffin?"

And he answered quite meekly, "A neighbor owed me a measure of grain and gave it to me now, and I'd like to weigh it."

His brother did not believe him, but gave him the scale to find out what he was going to weigh with it, and to that end he spread its bottom with pitch. The younger brother weighed and weighed those coins, weighed up a lot of them. When he finished, he took the scale and carried it back to his brother. But the rich brother caught sight of a few ducats stuck to the bottom right away and shouted at his brother in great anger, "You dirty, rotten so-and-so! You wanted to deceive me, but it didn't fly. You thought I would become greedy for your ducats? If they were worth trying for. But tell me really, where did you get the money, or else I'll run right off and accuse you of stealing it." The younger brother, as an honest man, told everything about how he came into the money.

That way the younger brother had blessings enough, too. He purchased land and cattle, and farmed with the help of God as best he could. But for the household he needed a manager, so he married. He took a fair maid to wife and lived with her in peace and happiness.

But the older brother envied his brother's riches endlessly, and though he himself had enough, he still always desired more and more. You know what he did? He left for the glass mountain, thinking it would go as well for him as it had for his brother.

He came to the glass mountain, approached the fire and began to speak to the twelve: "Good people, allow me, a poor man, to warm myself at your fire. The night cold has crushed me, I can't go any further and have no place to warm myself."

But one of the twelve answered him, "Son, you were born in a happy hour and have riches enough, but you are wicked and stingy. You mustn't lie to us, and because you have lied you shall not be spared a penalty." The rich one was terrified as if thunderstruck and sat among the twelve, but was afraid thereafter even to murmur.

The twelve again changed places, and when each returned to his own spot, an old man with a grey beard to his waist and a balding head arose from the flames and spoke thus: "Badly it goes for bad people. Your brother is an honest man, so he is blessed; but you are wicked, so you will not be spared punishment." With that one of the twelve seized our rich one, clawed at him mercilessly, and passed him to another. The second abused him even worse and tossed him to the third, the third to the fourth, the fourth to the fifth, the fifth to the sixth, and so on in order until the last, and when the last had clawed at him and abused him sufficiently, he tossed him to the old man. That one grabbed him and tore off and ate meat from him, and the godless rich fellow shouted, "Thirteen is an unlucky number, but I am even more luckless."

The twelve ate the glowing coals, and when the cock in the village crowed, everything disappeared. The next day they searched for the rich fellow and called out to him, but nowhere could they find out anything about him. The younger brother sensed, to be sure, what could have happened, but he spoke not a word.

The younger brother lived in peace with his little wife. They were full of praise that they were so well off, and they thankfully helped others as well. But their happiness did not endure for long. Once our dear fellow left for the fields and when he returned that evening he could not find his dear wife anywhere. He walked to and fro, called out to her, inquired about her, and sought her, but there wasn't a trace of his wife. Worried to death, he searched for her and sought her day after day, but always in vain. After that, nothing could cheer him and he never had peace. In his sorrow, he went out into the world, saying that he would find his dear wife, no matter where she be.

He walked, the poor sad man, wherever his eyes led him. He walked for many days until in the end he came to a lake where a cabin stood. "I'll rest up a bit here," he said, "and perhaps I'll overhear something." And he entered. But they welcomed him poorly. There was no one in the cabin but a single woman who cried out in fear when she saw him: "God Almighty, sir, what do you want here, what do you seek? If you show yourself to my husband, he'll eat you straight-away."

"And who is your husband?" asked our wayfarer.

"Well, don't you know?" answered the woman. "My husband is the water king, who has everything wet under his power. Run away, for God's sake, run, for no sooner will he come than he'll devour you straight-away."

"Alas, have mercy on me. Where should I go in the night? Hide me somewhere where he won't notice me." The wayfarer begged in this way until he had entreated her and she hid him behind the stove.

In a moment the water king came and before he had entered the doorway, he shouted, "Woman, it stinks of human flesh, retrieve it for me straight-away, or it will go badly for you as well." In vain would she have kept him secret. Willy-nilly, she handed over the unlucky one. The poor man shook like a twig and began to make excuses, saying he had done nothing wrong but had simply come to inquire if there were any tidings of his wife.

"Well, if you are so honest," grumbled the water king, "I'll just let you go. But I cannot help you, for I have no tidings of your wife, except that yesterday I saw a pair of ducks swimming on the water, and wonder if she wasn't among them. But meanwhile, you know what? Go to my brother, who is king of fire. I imagine he'll have more to say."

Our wayfarer was glad that after so much fear he could rest up in peace. Straight-away the next day he went on until he came to the king of fire. But he, too, could tell him no more and sent him to the third brother, who was king of wind. When he arrived there and said where he was going and why, the king of wind grew pensive, shook his head, and couldn't say anything for sure. Finally, he at least hinted that it seemed to him he had seen a woman like such and such beneath the glass mountain.

No sooner had our wayfarer heard that than he returned at once the same way he had come, for the glass mountain was not far from his village. He didn't even peek in at home, but turned up at the stream that ran below the glass mountain. Many ducks were bathing in that stream and they called out after him, "Good fellow, good fellow, don't go there for you shall perish." But he wouldn't be led astray and simply went on until he arrived at the very foot of the mountain.

At the foot of the mountain an opening was revealed to him that led into the mountain, and he entered that opening and went further and further until he came to a number of cottages. He passed all the cottages, one after the other, until he came to the biggest. With that a bunch of witches and warlocks surrounded him from all sides and snapped at him, "What do you want, what do you want?"

"I have come," he said, "to seek my wife, for they told me she had been seen here."

"Eh, she's here alright," shouted the witches around him. "But you shan't have her unless you recognize her from among a hundred womenfolk."

"Well," he said, "why shouldn't I recognize her!?! Aha, lo and behold, she is here!" and he had hardly said that when his arms were around her neck. And his wife embraced him and caressed him and they both were glad to be together again. And while they were caressing, his wife whispered into his ear, "This time you recognized me, but I don't know if you shall tomorrow, for we shall be two hundred, all dressed alike. But you know what? Go up on the glass mountain tonight. The king of time is there and he has twelve servants. Ask him how you can recognize me. If you are good, they will help you, but if you're wicked they'll devour you so that not even the tiniest bone will remain of you."

"Good, good," he answered in her ear, "I'll go and ask. But tell me first of all, why did you run off from me so unawares?"

"I didn't run off," said his wife. "But a hunter lured me to the stream, and when I arrived he splashed us both with some water and wings grew upon us. He beat his wings and in that instant we turned into ducks. Willy-nilly, after that I followed him until he led me here and I was turned back into a woman. But now I will go with you, if you are good, for only in that way will you be able to recognize me."

With that they took leave of each other. She went among the others and he set out for the glass mountain. The servants of the king of time sat around a fire, and when our wayfarer came to them, they immediately recognized him and asked what he wanted. "I would be glad to know," he said, "how to recognize my wife in the morning among two hundred womenfolk."

"Alas, good man, we know no assistance in that. But wait a bit, maybe our master will know." In a moment an old man with a grey beard to his waist and a balding head rose from the flames, and when the wayfarer submitted his wish, he answered, "Grandson of mine! They all shall be dressed alike, but only your wife shall have a black thread in her boot on her right foot."

He thanked him kindly for the good advice and hurried down. The next day he found his wife among two hundred who were dressed alike and recognized her by the black thread. Once he had guessed what he was to guess, not even the witches could deny him her. So they gave her to him and sent them off as one should: they gave them money, goods, and a cow. And on the cow a bell, that's all there is to tell.

❦ 46 ❦

The Bača and the Dragon

Once there was a bača, and since he was bača, he had to live way up in the mountains on the sheep farm. When he had scalded the whey and locked the cheese and boiled whey into storage, he would sometimes leave the hut to be guarded by one of the shepherds, and he himself would go out after the sheep to toot on his fife and look around at the hills and dales and at the wide, azure sky.

Once, in the autumn, when the snakes go into the ground to sleep, the dear bača stopped by a fir tree, leaned on his staff and gazed down into the thick forest before him. It's a wonder his knees didn't give at what he saw! Legions of snakes were gathering from all directions and slithering toward a great boulder right before our bača's eyes. When they slithered up to the boulder, each snake took some kind of herb that was growing there on its tongue and touched the rock with the herb—and the rock opened for it all by itself. Snakes, one after the other, disappeared into that rock as if they had simply vanished.

The bača brooded and brooded over what it could be, until he finally struck upon something. He ordered his dog, Dunaj, to drive the sheep back home and himself set out straight for the boulder. "I need to examine that herb and see where those snakes are crawling to," he said to himself. The herb was an herb like any other—he didn't know what kind; but when he tore it off and touched the rock with it, the rock also opened for him. He entered and found a spacious cavern whose walls simply glittered with gold and silver, as if it had been strewn with stars. In the middle of the cavern was a golden table, and on the table lay a gigantic old snake, all coiled up. The other snakes lay similarly around the table and about the cavern. They were already sleeping and didn't even move when the bača entered.

The bača liked the cavern and looked it over from all angles. But then he thought of his sheep and the farm. "Well," he said, "I've seen what I wanted to. Now I'll go back." It was easy for him to say "I'll go," but how to get out? The boulder closed behind him as it had behind the snakes, and he had no idea what to do so that it would open for him. The sweet little birdie in the cage tried this way and that, but the rock was unrelenting.

"What now? Since I can't get out, I too shall sleep," he thought finally, and wound himself into his cape, which fortunately he had brought with him, lay down, and went to sleep.

It didn't seem to him that he had slept long when some kind of rustle and hum awakened him. He started and wondered what devil was rustling under his hut, for it seemed to him that he was sleeping in his hut on the sheep farm. But when he wiped his eyes, he realized where he was. The walls of the cave and the golden table in the middle glittered at him. The old snake was still lying coiled on it, but the other snakes were moving their heads, licking the golden table, and now and again they hissed, "Is it time yet?" The old snake heard their hissing and finally raised his own head and said, "It is time!"

After he said that, he stretched out from head to tail like a stick, slithered down from the table, and went out. All the snakes slithered after him. The bača also stretched out to his full length, managed even to yawn a couple times, and set out after the snakes, thinking to himself, "Wherever they go, I'll go too." It is easy to say, "I'll go too," but how? The old snake touched the rock and it opened and the snakes slithered out. The bača wanted to go after the last one, but the boulder rolled back in his face so that his eyelids fluttered. And the old snake outside hissed in a whistling voice, "Eh, human, you have to stay here!"

"Eh, what would I do here?" replied the bača. "You have no farm here so you can't give me work, and I won't sleep forever. Let me out. I have sheep on the farm and a wicked wife at home: she'll curse me if I don't drive them home on time."

"You won't leave here until you swear three times that you'll not say where you were and how you got there," hissed the snake. What could the bača do? He thankfully swore to God three times that he wouldn't tell, just so they would let him out.

"If you don't keep your promise, things will surely go quite badly for you!" the snake threatened the bača when he let him out.

Only then, when he stepped out into the wide world, did the bača's knees begin to give. He was frightened by what he saw. Why, instead of autumn, there were budding beeches and hoed fields greening with spring pasture! "Woe is me!" he said, wringing his hands. "What have I, little half-wit, done! Why, I slept the winter through in the cave! Alas, my sheep, where shall I find you? Alack, my wife, what will she say to this—she'll torture me to death right here!"

Lamenting in that manner, he went in the direction where his hut stood.

Nearby he saw his wife cleaning something. Fearing that she would light into him straight-away, he hid behind the fold. While he was squatting there, mind you if he didn't see a good-looking man pop up out of nowhere who began asking her where her husband was. The bača's wife began to cry and told the gentleman that her husband had left way back in the fall with the sheep and still hadn't returned. That the dog, Dunaj, had led the sheep home in the evening, but there had been neither hide nor hair of the bača. "Surely the wolves devoured him, or witches scattered pieces of him over the hills," moaned the bača's wife.

"Eh, don't cry, dear wife," the bača spoke up from behind the fold, "why, I'm here! The wolves didn't devour me and the witches didn't scatter me over the hills; I simply laid myself down here, see, under the wattle fence, and fell asleep, and I slept the winter through in the fold."

Well, the dear bača had acted unwisely! No sooner did his wife hear his words than she left crying be and began vainly cursing until the hills echoed with it: "May a hundred bolts of thunder strike your soul, you ninny, you wretch! Are you an honest man? What kind of bača are you? You put your sheep in God's hands and yourself lie down by the fold and sleep like a snake in winter! Who ever heard of such a thing?"

The bača thought to himself, "Why, she's guessed it!" but remained mute as a stump, for he couldn't tell the truth. The good-looking man said to his wife, to cheer her, that it couldn't be true what her husband said, that he had to winter elsewhere; but that it would still turn out well if only her husband would say where he had been. Well, then the bača's wife really began to lay into him to say immediately where he had been wandering and where and with what types he had wintered. Who knows what would have come of it if that good-looking gentleman hadn't slipped something into her fist and convinced her to be quiet and instead to go home to the village, saying that she wasn't needed here on the farm anyway when the bača himself was here and would put everything in order.

When the bača's wife left, the good-looking gentleman took on his true appearance, and then the bača saw in front of himself the black magician from the hills. He recognized him right away, because the magician has a third eye in his forehead. The magician is a very powerful man and can give himself any form whatsoever; and whoever tries to oppose him, he turns into maybe a ram or a billygoat. No wonder the bača became terribly frightened. He was more afraid of him than of his wife.

And the black magician just set his sights on the bača telling once and for all where he had been and what he had seen. The bača fell mute and still; one could have hewn him like wood and he wouldn't have even moved at the blow, for he still feared the old snake and feared to break his oath, so he said nothing. But when the magician asked a second time and a third, already in a terrifying voice, where he had been and what he had seen, and when the figure of the black magician grew before him by leaps and bounds, then the bača forgot the snake and his oath. He admitted where he had been, how he had gotten into the rock, and what he had experienced there.

"Well then," said the black magician, "come with me. You'll show me this rock and the herb." The bača had to go.

When they arrived at the boulder, the bača tore off an herb and lay it on the rock, and the rock opened. But the black magician didn't step in, and didn't allow the bača to either; he just pulled out some kind of book and began to read from it, and just read and read. The bača's entire body shook like a twig.

Suddenly the earth shook; a hissing and whistling echoed from the rock, and out crawled a cruel dragon, which the old snake had turned himself into. Flames lashed out from his muzzle, his head was huge, and his tail slashed from left to right and shattered any tree it touched.

"Throw this halter on his neck!" ordered the magician, giving him some kind of leading rein without lifting his eyes from the book. The bača took the halter, but was afraid even to approach the dragon. Only when the magician ordered him a second and a third time, willy-nilly, he listened.

Alas, woe to the bača! Just as he was about to throw the halter on his neck, the dragon spun around once and the bača didn't even notice how he ended up on the dragon's back, and the dragon took off with him over hill and over dale. At that moment it turned pitch black and only the flames that lashed out from the dragon's muzzle and eyes lit their way. The earth shook and rocks were pouring down from the peaks. The dragon whipped his tail about terribly on all sides, and every little beech or fir he touched snapped like a little twig, and so much water gushed out of him onto the ground that it flowed down the sides of the mountains like the Váh River. It's terrifying even to think of such a thing. The bača was neither dead nor alive; it just seemed a bit to him that he was still alive.

Slowly, gradually, the dragon's anger died down after all; he didn't brandish his tail about anymore, stopped releasing water, and no flames lashed from his muzzle. The bača immediately breathed easier, sighed, and just waited for the dragon to begin to descend. But it hadn't been enough for the dragon. He had in mind to begin to punish the dear fellow only now. Slowly, ever so slowly, he began to rise with him from the earth to the mountains, always higher and higher until it seemed to the bača that the great peaks and ridges were no more than anthills, and still the dragon flew higher until the bača saw nothing but the sun, stars, and clouds. Then the dragon stopped with him and hung in the air.

"Alas, Lord, what shall I do now, hanging here in the air? If I jump down, not even a scrap of me will remain, and I cannot fly to heaven!" lamented the bača, and he cried like a baby.

The dragon didn't even peep.

"O dragon, powerful Sir Dragon, have mercy!" he begged, so that even a stone would have been moved at his request. "Oh, fly, fly down. I swear to God not to anger you again in your lifetime."

The dragon just sniffed and snorted, but didn't even say b or c or move a bit. Then suddenly the voice of a skylark rose to the bača's ears. He rejoiced at that. And the dear skylark flew nearer and nearer to him. When its wings were finally beating above him, the bača begged him: "O skylark, bird dear to God, I beg you, fly up to the Heavenly Father and tell him of my plight! Tell him that I greet him a hundred times and am calling on the Lord's help!"

The skylark flew to the Heavenly Father and told there how the bača was calling on God's mercy. And the Heavenly Father had mercy on the poor bača, wrote something in gold letters on a birch leaf, put the leaf in the skylark's beak, and ordered him to release it on the dragon's head.

The skylark flew in the windy heights, landed on the dragon's head, and dropped the leaf with the golden letters. At that instant the dragon flew down gently to the ground with the bača.

When the bača came to his senses, he saw that he was standing by his hut on the sheep farm, that Dunaj—as if nothing had happened—was returning the sheep to the fold for milking; on the branch saw a bell—that's all there is to tell!

❦ 47 ❦

The Golden-Horned Stag

*I*n a desolate land not far from the mountains, there was once an old lady who had but one son. He regularly went hunting, and when he returned from the hunt on his jet-black horse, his mother always came out to welcome him joyfully and lead him home.

Once, when this young gentleman was walking in the garden, he saw a golden-horned stag. Strange to say, the stag, instead of running away from him, came closer to the youth and enticed him on, but did not allow himself to be caught. And this happened more than once. Blahoslav, for that was the youth's name, went home for an arrow, had his black horse saddled, and chased after the stag at a run. The stag no longer waited in place, but ran further and further, from the garden to the grove and from the grove to the forest. Blahoslav set out after him until at last he had come so far that he would not have been able to find his way out of the forest. Now he began to consider what to do, whether to return home or to follow the golden-horned stag even further. He even began to look for the way back, but only made his way deeper into the thickets. Nothing remained but to follow the golden-horned stag, which was continually enticing him on. He crossed all kinds of hills and dales until he suddenly found himself in the courtyard of a castle that was encircled by high walls.

"You won't get away from me here, you golden-horned beast!" Such were his thoughts as he once again drove his spurs into his horse's side to catch the stag as quickly as possible. His exhausted horse was on its last legs, but even now obeyed its master and ran as fast as it could. But wonder of wonders, what should happen!? He neared the wild stag, shot his arrow, and the arrow pierced its side! When Blahoslav came to the place where he had last seen the stag, you know what he saw? His arrow was sticking out of some kind of board on which it was written that he should enter the castle, put his black horse in the stable, and go up and into the room and take whatever he finds there, that there is no need to be afraid.

"Well, isn't that nice!" he said to his horse, which stood sadly beside him, completely exhausted. "But never mind. Come, you good animal; why, we'll find a place somewhere to spend the night."

He led his horse into the stable, and you know what he found? Oats, hay, straw, and clover—everything a horse could need was there in sufficient quantity. "Here you are, my friend, eat what you will and drink as much as you like."

Having told his horse that, he entered the room where, this time, everything was prepared for *him* to eat. He immediately sat down and ate and drank whatever he wished. When he had eaten his fill, he thought: "But I've spent my entire day on that stupid stag! Ah, but wasn't he pretty, the old nag! Well, I'm bushed, but where shall I sleep?" He looked around and saw a nice bed all made up. As though he knew that the bed had been prepared for him, he lay down directly upon getting undressed. Everything was running around in his head, and he fell asleep in the midst of the most various thoughts. But there wasn't anyone to say goodnight to him.

Soon three maidens came to his bed and begged him with clasped hands to pass three days there. They told him that they were the daughters of a king and that they had to remain here until someone came who would suffer for them. And they begged him to endure heroically a few days, and then left him.

Right away everything in the room began to shake. The terrible uproar and rattling woke him up. He got up, but he didn't see anything. Quite frightened, he just sat quietly and listened. Suddenly it even approached his bed and beat him and bore down on him so that he couldn't even breathe. But thankfully the time had come when all spooks had to return home, and, completely exhausted, he again fell quietly asleep.

In the morning he arose, got dressed, and already food was awaiting him on the table. He ate his fill and went to see what his jet-black horse was doing. The horse was behaving well, for he had enough of everything. So Blahoslav left him to eat and went to explore the entire building.

He came to a well with clear water. He so desired a drink that he lay straight down and took the water directly into his mouth. But the ground broke away under his hand, and his hand and hair got wet.

"Ah, I can't even drink the water here now!"

But he rejoiced greatly when he looked at his hand, for it was completely covered in silver, and the same had certainly happened to his hair which had also gotten wet. He immediately wrapped his hand and hair in a kerchief and continued through the garden, looking at everything. When he had looked everything over, he went to the room to have lunch.

In this manner he lived quite well for three days in the castle. But at night the spooks wouldn't leave him alone and treated him worse and worse every night. He would have run off if the three maidens hadn't reminded him each time to remain there for three nights and thus to free them. On the third night, however, he could remain in the room no longer, but went to the chapel to spend the remainder of the night in prayer. But as soon as he knelt and said a few words in prayer, he stopped, for he was faint for lack of sleep the first two nights. Then he saw, in his dream, the three maidens step into the chapel, and each in turn knelt at the altar and prayed. When they had finished, the youngest came to Blahoslav and wrote on his sword the name of the castle where her father lived and said that, if he wanted her, he should come to her father's. Then the three of them left, for they were now free, since he had remained for three nights.

Blahoslav, as soon as he awoke, saddled his horse and galloped off into the wide world, the sooner to arrive at the castle of the father of the three maidens. He went at a run the whole way, the horse himself setting the pace, as though he were carrying him home. When he approached the castle, he didn't want to enter on his horse, "for who knows if it was true or if it was just a dream, and maybe they won't remember me, and does the youngest really want me?" He dismounted and released his horse to go forth in the world wherever he liked. And the jet-black horse ran off to his mother and happily whinnied that the master was still alive and not to worry about him any longer.

But Blahoslav walked into the castle with his head and hand wrapped and asked for work. A cook's assistant was the only position open. He had to add wood to the fire constantly and do whatever the cook ordered him to do. But he did it all gladly, waiting breathlessly for the moment when he could join the young princess.

The princesses also frequented the kitchen, but in a particular order. Each week another learned how to cook. When Blahoslav came to the castle, the oldest came every day. And when she arrived, she always looked at him, for she wondered that such a good-looking young fellow could become a cook's helper. But she never addressed him, nor he her. The same with the second princess.

But when the youngest began to come to the kitchen, he could restrain himself no longer and showed her the silver-covered finger. The next day he let some hair stick out from under the kerchief so that she could see it. And see it she did, but she still didn't say anything. Not until the third day did she tell the cook to have his helper bring her food. Which he did.

When Blahoslav passed through the door into the room of the youngest, he immediately saw that everything would be fine. She was wearing the same dress she had worn in the chapel in the enchanted castle. He showed her his silver hair and fingers. She continued to promise him to be his wife. But she told him, "You have to wait until my sisters and I choose our husbands, for they are also waiting for you. Once they choose, then it can be."

So he continued to wrap his head and hand and served as a cook's assistant.

Soon after that the father of the three maidens announced that on a particular day his daughters would choose their husbands, that whoever they tossed a golden kerchief to, that would be the one. No sooner had it been announced around the country than gentlemen and princes already began to arrive at the castle, and on the appointed day all stood before the old king. Now the two older princesses each tossed the kerchief to that prince that they like the best. The youngest refused to throw hers for a long time, until she saw the dear cook's assistant looking on from the doorway at how they were choosing their husbands. She immediately gave her kerchief to her dear cook's assistant.

Her father became angry and wanted to chase the assistant out, saying that such a bandaged cook's assistant would never be his son. But he didn't want to go out. The king grabbed him by the head to throw him out, but he pulled off his wrapping and the silver hair glistened. Then it became clear that it was the same lad who had endured three nights in the enchanted castle and set the maidens free. After that, they simply sent for Blahoslav's mother and held a great wedding at which everyone ate and drank to his heart's content. There was no lack of anything!

Blahoslav still lives with his youngest princess, unless they've passed away.

❦ 48 ❦

Right

Once there lived three brothers, and they lived nicely together while their father, who subdued and reconciled them, was alive. But when their father died and they buried him the next day, the oldest immediately began, "Let's divvy up!"

And the second one, who was willing, only asked, "Well, how shall we divvy up?"

"How else should we? By right! To me the same as to you!" retorted the oldest.

They didn't even ask the youngest how to divvy up and what, for they had always said of him that he carries chaff beneath his cap. And when it really came to the distribution, "to me the same as to you," the two oldest chose: one the room in the front of the house, the other the bed-chamber in back to live in, and they gave the youngest the old barn. And when, for the entire distribution, he received from each room only those things that we call "the handle from the axe," and when he complained about it, they both upbraided him, "Hush! Don't you hear that with each thing we trumpet in your ear, 'To me the same as to you!'—and that's the truth!"[1]

And the doggone distribution continued as it had before until each had received something from everything. However, of cows their father had left them but one. How to divide it so that it could remain whole? For a long time they pondered it this way and that, to sell her or not to sell, until the older, wiser ones resolved that they would build new barns next to the old one that they had given the youngest, and whichever barn the cow would go into of its own accord, its owner would keep her.

In a few days two opulent new barns stood in the yard next to the old one, and those two brothers were proud ahead of time that they would win, for, they thought, even a cow doesn't have bran in its head and would rather enter into a new barn than an old, shabby one. They even stocked the manger with hay and oats so the cow would have something to stop at. The youngest had neither oats nor hay; he stuck some green beech sprigs over the door so that at least something would be there. When the cow came in from the fields that evening, she happily bellowed at the green sprigs, stuck them in her mouth, and stood in her long-familiar place in the old barn, although in front of an empty manger.

"That's not right!" yelled the brothers. "The cow made a mistake, but we'll do it by rights this time." And so, first thing the next day, they slaughtered the cow, took the tallow and meat for themselves, and threw the youngest the flayed skin. What could he do? He took the right they had given him and spread the skin in the sun. A host of flies, mosquitoes, wasps, and hornets sat on the stinking skin. "Well now, just light and lively!" thought the youngest. He snatched the skin, sewed it shut, threw it over his shoulder, took his walking stick in hand, and off he went into the world with that right of his.

In the evening he came to a mill and asked for a night's shelter. But the mill-woman wouldn't hear of it. She said more or less that she was alone, the servants had run off when the man of the house was gone, and that he had gone somewhere beyond the Hron River for a millstone, and that she didn't like to keep strange men overnight. "Oh, don't think that way, my dear mill-woman, no!" begged the wayfarer. "You see, this is my entire estate, all my right. And they would rob me of it yet, if night were to take me somewhere in the fields. Please, just protect me along with it! Why, it's all the same to me if I have to crawl into a corner somewhere, as long as my right is in safekeeping."

And with that he threw his dear right under the bed, and it just droned away. The mill-woman, whether frightened by the din or what not, finally gave in to him if he would crawl into the loft, into the remotest corner, and wouldn't make a peep until morning. Just as well! He crawled into the loft and curled up there.

But with that he began to hear happy chatter and giggles beneath him and something shone in his eyes. He looked down out of the corner of his eyes and in the room the mill-woman was already at the table with some petty gentleman or other. They were eating cakes and roasts, drinking wine, and joking and giggling for joy. "Aha!" he thought, "that's why she ran all the servants out of the house and me into the loft, saying that she's afraid of men!"

With that, however, someone began to bang on the door from outside and shouted, "Woman, open!" And the wife inside with her suitor didn't know where to split to. "It seems all the devils are carrying my dear one home just now," she said. "Just go there into the bedchamber, my dear, sweet suitor! Hide in that barrel with feathers by the door, at least it will be soft for you there, and my old man won't sound you out. After that, what happens, happens. I'll take care of it."

The dear, sweet suitor really jumped into the barrel in the bedchamber, but in fright and in the bustle, he jumped into the barrel of tar, and only when he had climbed out of that one with much ado did he find the other and conceal himself in the feathers. The wife hid the cakes beneath the comforter, the roasts and wine behind the stove. The old man outside had to bang away at the door until his wife came to unlock it.

"Oh, just don't be angry with me, my dear, sweet, beloved hubby!" she said. "I had drifted off a bit and was frightened by the pounding. Well, I didn't come to my senses straight-away and suddenly, what's going on! But now all is well, now that you are here!"

"Eh, I'm here for you! My bones all rattled, my cart broken on the horrible road, my head full of pain—what's more, I've been scurrying home for my soul since the third village limits. We forgot the axe, so we couldn't even repair what had happened to the cart. Three carts couldn't even take me now, I'm so incensed—and hungry; you should have realized that!"

"Ach, well, what should I give you after all? You know well that when you aren't here I don't cook anything for myself. Nothing would even taste good to me without you. Besides a bit of sour cabbage soup from the head you snipped off when you left, I don't have a bit of anything."

"You have nothing?! And what kind of bagpipes are those sticking out from under the bed? Do I need to trip over that, too, or isn't it enough that I beat up my legs on the road?!"

"Goodness! Just don't be angry! After all, it's nothing! Some wayfarer laid it there, said that it was all his right."

"And where is this wayfarer?"

"Sleeping up in the loft somewhere."

"Call him here! I want to talk with him a bit about that right. At least I'll chase these whims out of my head."

The wayfarer called out from the loft, "God keep us and keep badness away, my dear host!"

"God grant it us both! Come here! What kind of right do you have?"

"The rightest right! It tells all and keeps nothing secret. You just have to strike it with this walking stick."

"Well, strike it. See what it says." The wayfarer struck the skin with the walking stick. The hornets-spirits roused and droned so that it clamored.

"What the deuce is droning in that right?" asked the miller.

"My dear host, why those are prophet-spirits that speak the rightest truth."

"Well, and what are they saying?"

"Hmm, indeed, they smell the cakes that are hidden under the comforter."

"Oh, stop your babble! Cakes even—where would they have come from?"

They lifted the comforter and saw the assortment: poppy-seed rolls, jam-rolls, cheese-rolls, white cakes, horseshoe cakes, pretzels, twists, and bundt cakes. They immediately sat down at the table and ate their fill. The right was still droning, though only quietly. "What else is droning in that right?" said the miller. The wayfarer struck it, knelt down, and placed his ear on it, and jumped for joy, "We're doing great, mine host. There's wine and roasts behind the stove!"

They went and found nearly an entire pig on the frying pan garnished with kasha and a full pint of Tokaj wine. My, if they didn't dig into that with gusto like good friends, though the mill-woman looked at it like a turkey: with a long nose and ruffled feathers. But when they had brightened up a bit through the wine, the miller said, "Well, my friend and brother, won't that right prophesy something else?"

"Oh, why not? Why, it would guess for you things that you hadn't even dreamed of." The wayfarer struck the right and it droned. But he simply shook his head when he placed his ear on it.

"Well, what is it? It's nothing bad I hope?" asked the miller.

"But with everything else, it's nothing good. I guess we should leave things as they are!"

"Not that, either. When it's right, out with the truth!"

"Well, if that's the way it must be, out with the truth! In your bedchamber is a black, feathered devil in a barrel!"

"Why, could that be?" said the miller, shaking his head.

"It can't be otherwise. But let's take the cudgel to mash his back so that the tomcat loses his appetite for others' bacon!"

When they shined a light into the bedchamber, they dragged the tarred and feathered devil out of the barrel and thrashed him until his bones popped and until he begged them, "Ow, don't beat me anymore, don't beat me! I'd rather give you one hundred gold pieces!" When he paid up out of his pocket, in twenties like hoarfrost, they let him go. And that mashed-back fellow knew well where the miller put the door when he built the house.

After that they slept as if in clover. But when the wayfarer took his bag-pipes on his shoulder the next morning, the miller wouldn't hear of letting the right go as if it were nothing. "Brother, sir," he said, "I might have difficult times at home without that right, God forbid. Won't you sell it to me?"

"Gratefully, brother, sir! After all, my trade is to distribute right around the world—there's little enough of it."

"And what will you take for it?"

"I'll take, after all, what we made with it." And immediately the miller counted out those one hundred gold pieces which the devil had paid for his beating and they parted: the one in this direction toward his wagon, completely assured that he had right on guard at home, the other home, pleased with his sovereigns. But he wasn't even one hundred steps from the mill when the mill-woman called out after him, "Stop, brother, sir, stop—at least for one word!"

And already she was at his back. She didn't cause him trouble, but fell at his feet saying that life at home with that right would not be good, and why should her husband know immediately about every little intrigue, and how can she get quit of that right, that she wasn't requesting this for nothing. "Since my husband gave you one hundred gold pieces," she said, "which you earned anyway, I'll give you two hundred, just get rid of that right!" And she forced a pouch with twenties into his pocket. Well, he didn't resist much, but told her to cut a small hole into the skin, just big enough to take the end of a funnel, and to have boiling water ready on hand to scald those hornet-spirit-prophets, but that she must do it carefully, for if they escape, they will drone the rightest truth in the house for ever and ever. "If that's all, then I'll take care of that darned right!" she said, and hurried to do it.

The youngest had gone with his bag and returned with a ready penny, and he built a brand-new home with a bedchamber. It sprung up from the ground as if overnight! He also bought a cow from his profits, while the others had to dig into their father's sovereigns if they wanted cows. They envied him and only asked, from whence had he procured it all?

"Oh, and where are the gentlemen of the manor headed?" he replied. "The right that you allotted me brought it to me. Why, you don't even know that on the other side of the mountain you can scare up a dupe who is ready to buy. For a trifle, let alone your right, they'll pay well, but you have to use your head."

Those two weren't idle, but killed their cows, threw the meat to the dogs saying, what good would it be to them when even so they would get rich, spread the skins in the sun, and when the hornet-spirits flew up, they sewed them shut, took them on their shoulders, and set out for the mill. "Would you like to buy a right?"

"Humph, why don't you buy it from me!" thundered the deceived miller, and flew at them with a post. And behind the farmer whoever had arms and legs, and with whatever fell to hand, they drummed the rights off the backs of those fellows and even sicced their dogs on them.

"Well, we tried it your way!" snapped those battered and bitten ones at the youngest when they finally crawled home. "My oh my, have you ever heard of such shame, such a disgrace! Not only to lose the cows, but to cash in so on the skins!"

"Well, it's certainly not my fault," said the youngest, "if you are stupider than the stupidest and can't even sell ready goods."

"Don't you start in on us."

One word led to another, and they would have killed him if he hadn't shown his heels. But they did vent their wrath; they shattered everything in his home into bits: windows, glasses, jars, bowls, casseroles, whatever could be shattered. They left only a heap of shards from the household of furnishings. The youngest didn't grieve over that very much, but thought, "Don't expect wise deeds from a madman. And after all, it's never so bad that it can't get better." And he planked up the shards in barrels, placed it on his cart, hitched up the horses that he had procured in the meantime, and "giddyup" set out into the world to seek his new fortune.

He traveled over the mountains the way that the most notorious men travel, among the beeches, and by morning came to an inn in those mountains. "What goods are you carting, driver?" asked the innkeeper.

"Forsooth, my dear innkeeper, sir, that's the king's money in those three barrels. The lords ordered me to stop for the night only at your inn, so that they would know where to search if anything happened to me. We would do well to store the barrels for the night in your basement and lock it up. You know that the lords will later give something for it, if you protect the king's property like that." He immediately placed the barrels in the basement. The innkeeper dropped the bar on the door and our driver then just saw to his horses, entered his room, and pretended to sleep.

But he didn't sleep. He had a sense of what would go on in such a den. About midnight there came twelve ruffians, the kind of good ol' boys who know every path in the mountains. They hauled in a barrel of money and said immediately to the innkeeper, "Hide this one along with the other two full barrels that we have behind the door in the basement there. In the morning we'll divide it all up. And give us something to eat and drink, for our stomachs have crawled up our backs and pips are growing in our gullets."

They ate and drank and had a merry old time, and near morning they all fell asleep. With that our driver awakened the innkeeper and said to him, "Get my barrels out! You know that with that kind of goods a fellow can't afford to be a bit late or the army will come in search of me."

"Alas, fellow, how can I give them to you? If those fellows catch me even moving, they'll be on our heels. It cannot be until those fellows leave."

"And I have to be on the other side of the mountain by the time those fellows awaken. But do as you will, if you prefer the king's army to come here to find me."

"In that case, I'd rather give you the keys and let you take the money yourself."

Our driver obeyed the innkeeper to a T, opened the basement, loaded the highwaymen's barrels on his cart, turned the shaft of his cart around, and lit out so that they wouldn't even catch him on three horses. When the highwaymen got up and set to divvying up, they found nothing but shards in the barrels. They chased after him thoroughly, spread out on the way he would have continued on, but all for naught. Somehow it didn't even occur to them that the driver could turn around the shaft of his cart; it mystified them that a master over the masters had appeared.

And our master didn't stop until he had reached his own yard and immediately sent to his older brothers for a scale to weigh the money. They both appeared immediately with a scale and they aahed when he brought measure after measure from the cart, and all thalers and ducats that appeared to have just been stamped. "From whence have you procured so much money again?" they asked.

"I've long told you that a man doesn't get a thing until he uses his head. You know the inn in the mountains there? The innkeeper has determined to make new things from old. That's why he paid me for those shards in ducats, for he said that none were fit for his new trade like mine."

"Is that all," thought the brothers, "why, from our dwellings there will be even better shards!"

They broke and smashed everything in their houses into a little pile, barreled up the shards, loaded them on their carts, and "heeyaed" like mad one after the other to the inn. The highwaymen lying in wait needed nothing more than to see the barrels and immediately they surrounded them. "Aha, birdies, now you're in a cage!" They took everything, including the carts and their property, and stripped them nearly naked and whipped them into the mountains. "Are you so crazy that you had to get caught in our trap?" said one. "You should be happy that we're letting you go alive!"

The youngest merely smiled, "To me the same as to you—and that's the truth," when he saw them dragging themselves home, barefoot, naked, and whipped. But the next day he wasn't laughing when those conspirators burst into his home at daybreak and before he could react, tied him up so that he couldn't move a limb.

"You won't escape this time, you hundred-legged so-and-so!" they said to him. "You cost us everything—and nearly our health and our lives, just like your life is in the balance. To me the same as to you! Do you understand? Just what kind of death do you choose?" What could he do? He simply told them to do with him as they wished, just not to shed his blood as the same mother had all suckled them all. "As you have chosen, so shall it be. We don't want your blood, but we'll throw you into the Hron River," replied the oldest. And the second one added, "Let's sew him into a sack so that he can't see the way there and back, if he should somehow swim out, even though he's tied up. Won't that be wise?"

"Yes, brother, wise," added the eldest. "Bring the sack here!" And so they stuck him into the sack and carried him to the very banks of the Hron.

"Eh, brother," said the second one, "let's not make a mistake this time! How should we throw him in, headfirst or feet first? Which way is better?"

"Why you're right, which way is better?"

"Let's go consult with some wiser people. After all, we've got him in the bag. In the meantime he can at least pray." And they lit out for the village to the wise folk! And the one in the bag called out like mad, "I won't be king, I won't!" A bača came along tending his flock of sheep. "What are you saying in that bag there?"

"I won't be king, I won't!"

"Even so, king? Who wants you for their king?"

"Oh, lord, who else? The king here in the castle died and they don't have another, so they want me as their king, for they say I am the wisest. But since I've resisted they want to throw me in the water. Still, now more than ever, I won't be king, I won't!"

"If that's all," said the bača, "I'll be king. I'm sick of the same thing day after day, just following the sheep. Let's swap!" The swap took place immediately. The bača crawled into the bag and the other sewed him in so that they would be sure to find him there. Then he threw the bača's new cloak over his shoulders, took the axe and fujara, chased the sheep behind a little hill where he found a ford, so he herded the sheep to the other side of the river. The brothers returned as if to a sure thing and heard a shout from the bag, "I'll be king now, I'll do it!"

"Listen to him, he even wants to be king over us; wouldn't that be right!" said the eldest.

"Here's his right: headfirst into the Hron when he wants to be bigger than his britches," said the second one. And they grabbed the sack at both ends and threw the bača headfirst into the Hron. But to be sure they watched for a long time after, to see if the one thrown in wouldn't somehow swim out. But he certainly made friends with the fish and frogs for a longer time than those two could wait.

Suddenly they heard bells and bleating from the other bank of the river. They lifted their eyes and saw their true brother there. He had just chased the herd of sheep to the water to pasture and was playing beautifully on the fujara. "Look at him, look, why he's already there!"

"Why, he's there! Brother, is it you, or not?"

"Indeed, it's me, just as you see me!"

"And where did you get that herd, cloak, and fujara?"

"Gifts, brothers, gifts! Why, I was burping on an empty stomach since you didn't give me anything to eat and today is Monday . . . But what are you asking for? Haven't you heard what the world is like under the water? There are beautiful green meadows, groves, and fields. And such herds as this pasture on them. The bača himself offered me this herd, for my own profit, since madmen tricked me to my end."

And the dear madmen looked into the water once again to see if it what he said was right about what is under the water! And indeed, the flock and green meadow from the other bank was reflected in the wide plane of the water and it seemed to them as if it was all under the water. They didn't even wait long enough to discuss which way to jump, but simply jumped headfirst into the water. They're herding sheep there even today on Abraham's meadow!

But the wise one chased the flock of sheep home and later married, when he had the means. And he told his children, "Madmen are madmen—they dig their own holes!" and "The greedy one loses all!"

Note

1. The title of the story in Slovak is "pravda," which means "truth" in the contemporary language, but could also mean, "something just or right" in an older sense, closer to the contemporary "pravo." The story plays on the wide meaning of the word, so that this phrase could just as easily be rendered "and that's what's right!" or "and that's by right!"—Trans.

❦ 49 ❦

The Dead Suitor

Once there was a bonnie laddie and a fair maiden. They liked each other very much and in a short while were to marry. But at that moment, war broke out. The laddie had to strap his sword to his waist and go with the others to war. When he left his sweetheart, he entreated her on bended knee to wait for him seven years and seven weeks, and only then to marry.

The war ended happily, and the gladdened girls welcomed home their lads. Hanka, too, stepped outside the door and watched and watched for her Janík, but dear Janík didn't come. She inquired about him, asked everyone, one after the other, who had come back from the war, but no one had any news about him. The poor girl was very sad, and was seen more than once with eyes red from tears. Time ran its course, and one by one the girls got married, only Hanka wouldn't even think of it. Men from all over asked for her, but she wouldn't even hear of another and simply waited for her own. Seven years had nearly passed without a sign of her dear one. Then they came again to ask for Hanka, and she didn't know what to do. She both wanted and didn't want to get married, for she thought, "If I go with this one and he returns, it will be bad, but if I reject this one and he doesn't return, that won't be good either."

With such thoughts in her head, she set out to see one old woman who understood all kinds of things. "God grant you a good evening, granny!" she said, paying her respects.

"God grant it, God grant!" said the old woman with thanks. "Why have you come to us, my dear?"

"Ah, why? Tell me please, just tell me if I will ever see my dear one again? When he left for the war he entreated me on his bare knees to wait for him seven years and seven weeks, and if he didn't return, that then I could marry another. The seven years have already passed and those few weeks will pass quickly. Oh, just tell me, tell me, should I wait longer?"

The old woman just listened and listened, and then asked her, "Well, do you love your dear one, do you love him?"

"Oh, yes!" sighed the girl.

"Well, good," she said, "good, there's easy help for that. In the old cemetery on the right, at the base of the wall, there's a human rib bone. Go take it, my dear, and then go to the ford and fill a pot with water, pour in three handfuls of sand, and set it on the fire in front of the mouth of the stove. Add grain until it is thick and stir it with that rib bone from eleven until midnight. He will come to you, my dear, he will come, no matter where he be under the earth."

Hanka walked straight to the old cemetery. At the base of the wall she saw the human rib bone. Her heart began to thump and a shiver went over her whole body. But she boldened, picked up the rib bone, wrapped it in a white handkerchief, and ran off with it, ran until she reached home. Then she took a pot and went to the ford, filled it with water, and poured in the sand. At eleven she lit the stove, added the grain, stood it before the stove mouth, and stirred it with the human rib bone.

The fire blazed in the stove and the porridge cooked, and she simply stirred. Until suddenly it began to mutter from the pot: "Back, back, back! Back, back, back!" And her dear, buried in a far-off land, heard it; he started, jumped out of the grave, mounted a white horse, and off he went, following that voice. Hanka just kept stirring and the porridge muttered: "Back, back!" Until the horse stamped in front of the house and the dear one banged the window with his fist: "Open for your dear, my dear!"

She ran out and said, "Welcome, welcome! Oh, it's been so hard waiting for you. Come on in, come!"

The wind howled, the shutters were banging away, and a gale roared over the house. But the dear one paid it no heed and simply ordered her, "Take what you have here, dear. We have a long trip ahead of us yet today."

She begged him, "Oh, just wait a bit, enjoy yourself until morning!"

He didn't respond, but just pressed her and said that he had to return to the army by midnight. So, what could she do? She swiftly gathered her bags and mounted up behind him.

The white horse leapt forward, and didn't bother about hill and dale, but simply flew unceasingly, as if in a tempest. And the dear one turned to his dear and said:

> "The moon is shining, sadly shining—my soul is flying.
> The stars are twinkling, sadly twinkling—calling my soul.
> Hanka, aren't you afraid?"

"Oh, dear Janík, what could I be afraid of when I'm with you!" And with that a shiver passed over her.

On they flew over mountain, over water, over crags, the wind whistling. And again he spoke:

"The moon is shining, sadly shining—my soul is flying.
The stars are twinkling, sadly twinkling—calling my soul.
Hanka, aren't you afraid?"

"Oh, dear Janík, after all I'm with you, what should I fear?" And her whole body shook like an aspen leaf.

They flew on and on and the wind blew stronger and stronger until the beeches and oaks began to break. He again called out:

"The moon is shining, sadly shining—my soul is flying.
The stars are twinkling, sadly twinkling—calling my soul.
Hanka, aren't you afraid?"

"Oh, I'm not afraid, I'm not!" and she clung to him tighter, for they were flying quite high and the tempest nearly caught them.

They came to a cemetery. The white horse jumped the low fence like it was nothing and disappeared from beneath them like fog—the dear one stood with his dear above an open grave. Hanka stood terror-struck, her teeth chattering. And her dear pointed to the grave:

"We are home now, my dear;
Lie down in the bed
From which you awakened me."

"I'll lie down, I will," she said, "but you go first, so I know which side to lie on."

And hup! he jumped into the grave, and plop! she threw in her bags; but she took to her heels and ran and ran as fast as her feet would carry her. When she had run a good piece she thought she would rest a bit, for she was all out of steam, her clothes torn and her legs bloodied. But with that she heard the stamp of a horse so loud the earth trembled. She knew right away what it was and off she ran again. Luckily she saw a light in one little house.

"Goodness, just quickly inside!" and she locked the door behind her.

With that, horror and fright! There was not a living soul in the room, but one corpse lay in the middle on two white boards—and he had once been a sorcerer. A shiver passed over her entire body, but she regained her senses, climbed up on the stove, and curled up in the corner.

Just then her dear one galloped up on the white horse and banged on the door with his fist, saying, "Let the dead open for the dead who is coming for the live one!"

"Wait, let me move my leg!" answered the one laid out on the boards, and he let one leg down. Hanka recognized the voice of the dead one and cold shook her every limb.

"Let the dead open for the dead who is coming for the live one!" shouted the one outside even more terribly as he banged on the door.

"Wait, let me move my arm!" answered the one inside, and he hung his arm down.

"Let the dead open for the dead who is coming for the live one!" he thundered for the third time until the whole house shook.

"Wait, let me lift my head!" answered the dead one.

And with that he began to slowly raise his head, rise to his feet, and went to open the door. A cold sweat broke out on Hanka's brow.

The door was open and the dear one and the corpse were climbing the stove, he just had to reach out once more and she would be in his grasp. But with that the cock on his perch flapped his wings, stretched his throat, and cock-a-doodle-doed. At that moment, the dear one collapsed to the earth and the sorcerer dissolved into pitch. But Hanka, too, was overcome by fear: in the morning they found her there dead and buried her with her dear in the same grave.

❦ 50 ❦

Popolvár, the Greatest in the World

$\mathcal{W}$here there was, there there was, in the seventy-seventh land, beyond the red sea, beyond the glass mountain, and beyond the wooden crag, there was a town in which there lived a king who had three sons. The two elder sons were fine young lads to behold, but the third, he was just a Popolvár who never even peeked out from behind the stove. One day their father stood them before him and said unto them, "My dear sons, the Lord be praised, you are already fit young lads. You should try the world and see if anything becomes of you. Go forth according to your ages!"

And the eldest, ready for that right away, requested from his father a significant sum of money, a good horse, and a glittering weapon. He set forth and went on his way! All year he traveled over hill, over dale, and through desolate lands until he came to the copper forest. "I've wandered about enough," he said. "But I shouldn't be sorry if I took a small memento from this forest with me." He studied and studied that copper forest and broke off a small branch from it.

When he was coming home he called out to his father from afar, "Father, Father dear, I was quite far off indeed! See you, this little branch is from off there at the copper forest!"

But his father answered, "Why did you abandon home and wander about so? Why, your mother and I once used to travel to the copper forest for breakfast. I see that the world will get little benefit from you. You go now, my second son; what will you take for your journey?"

The second one also chose a good horse and a glittering weapon. He took money for the journey, left home well and good, and went! In a year he too came to the copper forest and broke off a small branch for a memento. But he continued on, for he knew that his father would just shame him if he only tried as much as his brother. He went along and wandered over hills, over dales, and through desolate lands until after another year he came to the silver forest. "Fine," he said, "my brother was never here. Such a wonder no person has ever known, such a beautiful silver forest!" He studied and studied that forest and broke off a small silver twig so that they would believe him, that he had been so far off.

When he was coming home he called from afar, "Father, Father dear, I was even farther off! Behold, this twig is from way off there at the silver forest!"

But his father answered, "Why, you have nothing to brag about either. Your mother and I once used to travel to the silver forest in the forenoon. I see that nothing will come of either of you. And what of you, the third one?!"

"What God grants will be!" answered the third one. "If it's my turn already, I too shall try my luck!" It's a wonder his two dear brothers didn't pass out from laughter at that, that even Popolvár wanted to go out into the world, when he hadn't even been a step away from the stove yet. But their father, who was strangely pensive, didn't stop him. With that our Popolvár became saddened that they took him for nothing, and he left them there.

He roamed regretfully about the courtyard and didn't even know how he came to the dung heap. A mangy pony was warming himself on the dung and he spoke unto Popolvár thus: "Popolvár, don't regret a single thing! We shall be good friends together. Stand before your father boldly once again and request nothing more for your journey than me and that rusty saber from the chimney, your father knows which one. He won't want to give it to you, but you insist and everything will be fine." Popolvár thanked the little pony for the advice and stood before his father again.

"Well, what of you, how about you, Popolvár? Perhaps you would like to go into the world after all?"

"I would, Father!" answered Popolvár bravely.

"And what would you like for your journey?"

"Nothing, Father, but that rusty saber from the chimney and the mangy little pony on the dung heap!" His father shook his head and at first didn't want to give it to him, asking what good it would do him, but then he allowed him everything.

Popolvár slung the rusty saber at his waist, caught the horse on a straw band, and led him off. Now his brothers really did pass out from laughter, and people about the town stood and stared at how the horse's knees were giving, how it would get caught in the mud and Popolvár had to pull him out himself every third step. But he pulled him out faithfully and made nothing of it.

With much ado, they dragged their way out of the town.[1] Here Popolvár alighted, rather to lead the little pony. But our pony just shook himself and straight-away became a beautiful fairy horse.

"Eh," he said, "don't you think, Popolvár, that I'm just any old horsey; why, I'm your father's fairy horse. And that saber isn't like any other saber, but whatever you order it, it will cut it to its knees. You'll have to fodder me, give me a trough of oats and a trough of fire!"

Popolvár was glad to have such things and immediately brought his fairy horse a trough of oats and a trough of fire. The horse gulped it down quickly and its veins quivered. "Mount up, Popolvár, for we have a long journey ahead!"

Popolvár mounted and just flew over dale and over hill, so that they just swarmed like anthills beneath them. In a moment the fairy horse stopped: "Here," he said, "is the copper forest that your oldest brother reached in a year and to which I used to carry your father and mother for breakfast. Dismount and give me a trough of oats and a trough of fire!"

He wasted no time, but fed the fairy horse and they flew again so that hill and dale alternated before their very eyes. In a moment the fairy horse gave a stomp: "We're here," he said, "at the silver forest that your older brother reached in two years and to which I used to carry your father and mother in the forenoon. Dismount and give me a trough of oats and a trough of fire!"

No sooner had the fairy horse gulped down the oats and fire than they were flying again; the hills and dales flew by below in the wink of an eye. In a moment the fairy horse stopped again: "Well, here we are at the golden forest where your brothers never arrived. But fodder me once again and I will take you to your father's friend's for the night!"

Popolvár foddered the fairy horse with oats and fire. They made a few leaps and were already in the courtyard of a huge castle. Popolvár went inside and paid his respects to the gentleman as a friend of his father.

"My, my, son," the king said straight to his face in wonder, "can it really be that in my last days I am seeing a living person again and that you are the son of my friend? Well, but you look good to the eye and if you passed over three forests today, then only my friend could send his son to me in such fashion. Eh, why there were never such friends, and never will be, as your father and I were when we fought that witch as youngsters—I imagine your father told you of her?"

"He told tales, but never of any such thing," said Popolvár, "but he gave me his saber to carry!"

"Eh, why that saber gobbled up that hag's army! But to what end? The more it gobbled up, the more swarmed forth from the earth. In our old age we let it all be!"

"Well, my young hands will try it," said Popolvár. "Of course, provided you have nothing against it?"

"Why, yes, I'd rather save you and your young blood. Return home instead! For the witch has gathered all her armies against me and will strike us by morning. As for me, what of it if I perish, but will you, young man, survive? At least you can take word of me to your father."

But Popolvár didn't retreat. Hardly had it dawned when he sat on his fairy horse and set out with the king's army against the witch's army that was spread out on a meadow like some kind of sea. In the middle of the army the witch stood alone on a pedestal from which her eyes sparked and she gave orders.

"Just boldly attack!" shouted Popolvár, and he himself set out in front. He ordered his saber to chop away, and it cut everything to its knees. Heads fell like poppy pods, but it was of no use when the hag's armies grew out of the ground, and the more he beheaded, the more came on. Nonetheless, Popolvár cut his way with the saber to the witch's pedestal and ordered the dear saber to cut it down. The witch fell straight to the ground and her regime fell. Popolvár ordered her cut into smithereens. When the witch was done in, her army disappeared as well, as if the ground had swallowed it up.

The old king was glad indeed that he could rest from that witch in his old age and wanted to keep Popolvár as his guest for as long as he would stay. But Popolvár would not delay, for he thought that, after all, he had accomplished something in the world with which he could stand before his father. So he left straight for home and spent no time along the way except to fodder his fairy horse with oats and fire by the golden, silver, and copper forests, and to break off some new growth from each.

When they arrived before the family home, the fairy horse changed back into a mangy little pony and his legs began to weave together. People stood and stared and passed out from laughter. His brothers made fun of him. But his father asked seriously, "Well, my son, where did you travel to?"

"Behold, Father dear!" Popolvár finally spoke. "I was where this little copper branch is from by breakfast; I was where this silver twig is from by noon; I was where this golden shoot is from in the afternoon, and by evening I had settled for the night beyond the golden forest with your friend. He greets you warmly!"

"Thank you for the greeting! And you, my son, are a man for bringing it to me. But is my old friend still alive? That cursed witch that we battled hasn't been his end? Well, say, say!"

"She wanted to be, but she'll do nothing to him anymore. We even demolished her pedestal, and the saber cut her to smithereens, and her army was swallowed up by the earth!"

His father was put at his ease entirely by this and even told his dear son about his friend's three daughters, of whom one was prettier than the next. But he said that the witch's sons, dragons, had carried them off somewhere and were keeping them in a lair. It would be a real hero who would free them.

That was all Popolvár needed to hear and he was straight-away ready for anything. His father would have preferred that he had never mentioned it, for he wanted his worthy son by his side and it was a dangerous undertaking. But when Popolvár himself wanted it, in the end he allowed him to go and try his luck.

Popolvár went directly to his fairy horse and said, "My dear little pony, let's go once again on a journey!"

"I know what you want," said the fairy horse, "but you are undertaking a lot. For no one has ever overpowered those dragons, and I don't know how you will manage."

"As God grants, so shall it be," said Popolvár. "They hadn't overcome the witch yet either, and we ruined her nonetheless. Let's go, my fairy horse!"

"If that's how you want it," the fairy horse said finally, "let's just set out!"

They left in the morning with the first light exactly as they had before: they barely dragged themselves through town and people laughed at them. Well, but outside the town the fairy horse shook himself, gulped down the oats and fire, and they were flying, and they flew over the copper and silver and golden forests, and stopped again for the night at his father's friend's in the large castle. They were well received there and the king would have carried Popolvár about in his arms for the sheer joy of seeing him again. But he just insisted that he have a seat, make himself comfortable, treat himself to something, and enjoy himself there.

"Oh, I'm not here for treats or enjoyment," said Popolvár. "Rather I think it only matters to you as well that I liberate your daughters."

"Better not to even mention them," said the king, growing sad. "They are already elsewhere and no one can wrench them from the claws of those dragons. Don't even you undertake it, my son, for you shall perish."

"Well, perish or not, here I go. But at least show me the way to those dragons."

The king long shook his head over whether he should allow it. But in the end he promised Popolvár that so far as it was possible he would see him off and show him the way to the underground lair where the dragons lived.

The next day they set out and traveled for a considerable time through the very countryside that they had won from that witch until they came to the very border. Then the king pointed to a den off in the distance and said, "You see, there my oldest is with a dragon with three heads. If you manage to thrash that one, she herself will show you the way to her sister. God speed you on your way!"

"You as well, and don't forget me!" Thus Popolvár took his leave of the king and his retinue and continued on alone into that den.

He poked around in it to and fro to poke out that dragon somewhere, but to no avail. Then suddenly he caught sight of a light. He went toward that light and arrived at a beautiful castle. He entered boldly and was met by a lovely princess, the king's oldest daughter, and she welcomed him, but not happily: "My, good fellow, what brings you here? I have been bewitched here so many years and haven't seen a human figure yet! But it's a pity for a bonny laddie, a pity! If my husband comes he will devour you immediately!"

"As God grants, so shall it be!" said Popolvár. "But I would just like to test my mettle against him and liberate you." With that a twenty-five-hundredweight cudgel thundered in the courtyard so that the ground shook.

"Alas, that is my husband and now no one can leave or enter," shouted the horrified princess. "Take this ring. If you twist it on your finger, you'll have the strength of a hundred men. And now shelter yourself someplace so he won't snatch you straight-away."

No sooner had she said this than the dragon stormed in, sniffed about on all sides, and roared, "Woman, it stinks of human flesh! Where is he, who is he, I'll eat him up." ·

"Ah, my dear sweet hubby, what would bring human flesh here? Why, you know that there's no hide nor hair of anything here, let alone a person."

"No matter, woman! It stinks of human flesh, out with it! Else I'll eat you right up," roared the dragon even more terribly, and with his tongues extended he licked his gaping chops. With that Popolvár stood himself before the princess so that the dragon wouldn't snatch her somehow and said, "Here I am, what do you want with me?"

"Rather what do you want with me? Are you such a man that you answer so boldly?"

"If you don't believe, come and wrestle!" said Popolvár.

"If you want, I won't refuse. Come out on the threshing floor where at least we will have more room," said the dragon.

So they went out on the threshing floor. Popolvár drew his saber and twisted the ring on his finger. He immediately felt the strength of a hundred men within him. The dragon mumbled something bad, seized Popolvár, and thrust him into the clay up to his knees. But Popolvár jumped briskly out, seized the dragon, and dashed him into the ground up to his waist. The dragon pulled himself out with an effort and then thrust Popolvár into the clay also to his waist. Only now did Popolvár gather himself and in a single jerk hurled the dragon into the clay so that only his heads remained sticking out. The dragon didn't move, but just licked his open chops with his tongues and shot flames from them so that Popolvár was lucky not to burn up. But he gave the order to his saber and it lopped off the dragon's heads so that the blood surged on all sides like from any old beast.

When Popolvár approached the princess, she kissed him for joy and would have been ready to depart for home with him immediately. But Popolvár couldn't wait for her to show him the way to her younger sister. She tried in every way to convince him otherwise, saying that the dragon there was more terrible, with six heads, but he just continued on his way.

He came to the second castle and entered. The second princess was there. And she just wrung her hands in wonder: "My, my, good fellow, what brings you here? I have been bewitched here so many years and haven't seen the semblance of a human yet! But flee, bonny laddie! My husband will be right here and devour you!"

She hadn't even finished saying this when there was a rumble in the air and a fifty-hundredweight cudgel crashed in the courtyard so that the ground shook.

"Alas, that is my husband and now no one can leave or enter," shouted the horrified princess. "Quickly, take this ring. If you twist it on your finger, you'll have the strength of two hundred men. Just be on your guard!"

Popolvár had just enough time to shelter himself, for the dragon burst in, sniffed about on all sides, and roared, "Woman, it stinks of human flesh! Where is he, who is he, I'll eat him up."

"Ah, my dearest hubby, what would bring human flesh here? Why, you know that there's no hide nor hair of anything here, let alone a person."

"No matter, woman! It stinks of human flesh, out with it! Else I'll eat you right up," roared the dragon even more terribly, and with his tongues extended he licked his gaping chops. Popolvár stood himself alone before the princess so that the dragon really wouldn't snatch her somehow and said, "Here I am, what do you want with me?"

"And you, little worm, what do you want? But are you really a man that you answer so boldly?"

"If you don't believe, come and wrestle!" said Popolvár.

The dragon just mumbled that he had to waste his time with such a scamp, but they went out to the threshing floor and open space. The dragon grabbed our laddie and thrust him up to his waist in the ground. But Popolvár had already twisted the ring and had the strength of two hundred men. So he leapt out like it was nothing. He squeezed the dragon about his waist so that his bones popped, and he hurled him suddenly into the ground so that only his heads stuck out. In fear and rage the dragon stuck out his tongues and from his open maws shot smoke and flames at Popolvár. Well, Popolvár called out to his saber, which lopped the heads right off, and the blood surged like from a beast. In the hot flames even the saber grew tired, but Popolvár called to it constantly so that it kept after it until all six heads had been chopped off.

Popolvár breathed a sigh and returned to the princess. She hugged him warmly and would have been ready to depart for home with him immediately. But he wouldn't rest until she showed him the way to her youngest sister. "How could we show our faces to your father," he said, "if I didn't bring all three of you?" With that he continued on his way.

Long he traveled over old mountains, by ore roads, until he came to the third castle, where the youngest was kept by a twelve-headed dragon. And she was just horrified and wrung her hands: "My, good fellow, what brings you here? I have been bewitched here so many years and haven't seen a human shape yet, and now I guess I'm seeing you for the first and last time! Ah, flee, bonny laddie, flee! My husband will be right here and devour you!"

She hadn't even finished saying this and already a hundred-hundredweight cudgel crashed in the courtyard. It rumbled and everything shook so that no one could leave or enter anymore. "Alas, that's that, now we're trapped! But here, take this ring quickly, when you twist it on your finger you'll receive the strength of three hundred men. And be on guard already!"

The dragon already was opening the door, and he sniffed about on all sides and roared, "Woman, it stinks of human flesh! Where is he, who is he, I'll tear him limb from limb!"

"Ah, my dearest hubby, what would bring human flesh to you?" she said, calming him. "Why, you know that there's no hide nor hair of anything here, let alone a person!"

"You won't talk your way out, woman! It stinks of human flesh here, out with it! Or else I'll eat you right up!" roared the dragon like a hundred peals of thunder, and with his tongues extended he licked his twelve gaping maws.

Popolvár jumped in front of the princess so that the dragon really wouldn't snatch her somehow. And he spoke, "Here I am, what do you want with me?"

"And you, little worm, what do you seek? But are you really a man that you answer so boldly?"

"If you don't believe, come and wrestle!" said Popolvár.

The dragon just mumbled that such a knave was interfering in his affairs; but they went out well and good to the threshing floor and open space. "Well, seize me you little bore worm," said the dragon, "for if I seized you, you would never blow on your porridge again, and I would never know if I had ever been in anyone's hands or not."

And indeed, our Popolvár seized the dragon so that its eyes flashed a bit, and dashed it into the ground up to its knees. Alas, what was that to the dragon? It jumped out and thrust Popolvár into the ground up to his waist. Popolvár gathered himself and once again twisted all three rings on his fingers; immediately he gained such strength as he had never had before. Now he seized the dragon about his middle so that it just popped, and thrust the monster into the ground so that only its heads stuck out. Its maws fell open and its tongues stuck out, but smoke and flames also rolled out from them on all sides. Popolvár himself passed out from the heat. But the saber jumped out of the sheath itself. When Popolvár saw that, he just called out ceaselessly and encouraged it: "My golden little saber, hew away, chop away until you chop it all off!"

The saber, too, had a time of it in the flames, but the more heads it lopped off, the less it was burned; in the end it chopped them all off.

Only now did Popolvár really heave a sigh and he approached the princess. She just looked upon him with a sweet eye, and when he looked upon her, she was pleasing to him indeed, for she was far more beautiful than the others. But they had no time to delay. They took whatever was valuable from the castle, loaded it on the fairy horse, and went. They went for the second and oldest sisters, everywhere gathering riches aplenty, and the fairy horse carried them along with everything well and good to their father's castle.

The old king grew youthful from joy when he saw his daughters before him even more beautiful and more grown up than they were before. He wanted to hear about nothing else but a wedding and encouraged Popolvár to choose the youngest. But Popolvár wouldn't even hear of it. He was hurrying to his father's to tell him what had happened, and then it would be up to his father to do what he determined would be best.

And so he set out and flew on his fairy horse over hill and dale, stopping only at the golden, silver, and copper forests to break something off the familiar branches and fodder his fairy horse with oats and fire.

When they arrived outside the town, the fairy horse turned into a mangy little pony and dragged along like a broken one to the king's castle. But the father had already seen his son, catching sight of him while looking out the window. He immediately called out, "Praise the dear Lord, my dearest son is coming!" And overjoyed, he ran to meet him in the courtyard.

Of joy and questions there was no end until Popolvár had told of everything, how he had defeated three dragons and led the three princesses home. "Well, you're a man!" said his father, slapping him on the shoulders. "Now it would be proper to have a wedding. You are three and there are three princesses as well, one prettier than the other!"

And the other two, who had managed nothing, instead of lowering their eyes to the ground as they should have, got themselves ready immediately. The left at once for the king's friend's where they requested the two older princesses' hands and led them home as their brides. And they celebrated and made merry as though the whole world were theirs.

But Popolvár just shook his head at it all and walked about pensively. "What's wrong with you?" his brothers asked him. "Perhaps the hens pecked up all your bread?" But he didn't answer such talk with a single word.

Once his father asked him, "Eh, dear Popolvár, what's wrong with you that you are so gloomy while the others make merry? You be merry for me as well. Why, you've already accomplished much in the world!"

"Much . . . too much, my dear father," said Popolvár, "but I cannot be at peace without knowing if there isn't someone in the world who is greater than I."

His father pretended he didn't hear the end and began to convince his son that it would be nice if he led home a bride and lived and made a life with her in sweet love and sincerity as the Lord God had commanded. But Popolvár again simply shook his head and asked, "Father dear, is there someone in the world greater?"

"There is, my son, there's the Iron Monk," admitted his father, saddened, after much questioning. "But no one will overcome him, for he knows everything whatsoever you think of or that you would like to know, and with a word he turns whomever he likes into whatever he likes. Beware, for you cannot even approach him."

"Eh, no one dared approach the witch either, nor her sons the dragons, and they are already somewhere in hell's greatest depths. Let me just go consult my fairy horse about it," said Popolvár, and he went straight to his fairy horse.

The fairy horse stood sadly in the courtyard, his head hanging, for he already knew what his master had taken into his head and that it wasn't likely to end well. "Well, my fairy horsey, why are you so sad?" Popolvár asked him.

"Eh, my master," said his fairy horse, "why shouldn't I be sad when you are going to where I cannot even stand with you. You *are* going to the Iron Monk, aren't you? We will be far away still and he will change us into whatever he wishes and we will lose all our power. I will not go with you before the Iron Monk."

"If you won't go before him, at least promise me that you will carry me to his dwelling," said Popolvár.

"That much I can still promise you, but ask no more of me," said the fairy horse.

Popolvár asked no more and went back to pester his father. His father tried and tried to put different thoughts into his head. But in the end he didn't want to thwart his will and he let him go. He had the entire castle draped in black cloth straight-away when Popolvár stepped out of it. and he said, "And the cloth will never come off unless my Popolvár returns."

Popolvár flew over the copper, silver, and golden forests and only descended finally at his father's friend's castle. He found that castle draped in black cloth as well. "Dear God, what's this?" thought Popolvár. "Why, the happiness should not have ended yet and here they are already mourning!"

And there was mourning indeed at his father's friend's, for while they were making merry there the youngest princess went for a walk—and with that, they say, the Iron Monk descended on her and carried her off. Popolvár couldn't have waited even without that to get to where the Iron Monk lived. His fairy horse carried him to the nearby castle of the Monk, but stopped there and told him, "Behold how it is shaking there on chicken legs; that's the Iron Monk's castle! You still have time to go back, for I know for certain that you will fall into the Iron Monk's power. But do as you will; I'll wait for you here to see what becomes of you!"

"God knows what will be, but here goes!" said Popolvár, and he went straight to the castle.

The Iron Monk was just thinking about Popolvár, and he already knew all that was happening. He awaited him out in the courtyard with the princess. The princess looked sweetly upon Popolvár, but the Iron Monk scowled at him and said, "You will not escape me now! Become millet grain!" At that instant Popolvár sifted into millet. There was a dust heap not far off and a rooster was scratching in it. The Monk called out to the rooster, "Rooster, peck up the millet!" The roster pecked the millet clean and that was the end of Popolvár's power!

He would have perished there, too, if it weren't for the princess. But she thought and thought and thought, what to do now? Then she came to the Iron Monk and presented herself more sweetly and pleasantly than ever before: "Lo, you are pleasing to me now when you work such miracles, for I see that you have no equal in the world. But listen, it would really be something if you could take something that had changed once and change it back again to what it was before."

"Oh, go on now!" said the Iron Monk and he left her. But she followed and didn't stop pestering him until he let it be known that in a room in such and such a place two sabers hang on the wall, and those two sabers hack against one another day and night, and when a bewitched thing is tossed between them, they cut it to smithereens, but those immediately grow together and become what it was before.

She needed nothing more. She slipped out into the yard and called, "pee, rooster, pee, pee, peep, tuk, tuk, tuk!" enticed the rooster to her, caught it, and killed it. She ripped the millet out of its crop, wiped it, and took it to the room and tossed it between those two sabers. The sabers cut the millet to smithereens, but Popolvár leapt out twice as handsome as before. She didn't allow him to thank her or even to whisper a word so that, God forbid, the Iron Monk wouldn't notice the slightest thing or think about a thing. She simply led him into a deep, dark chamber, telling him not to even breathe until she made the way clear. With that she returned to the Iron Monk as though nothing had happened.

She fawned upon him even more sweetly. And all she wanted to find out was from what he had his power. But nothing came of it. The Iron Monk constantly pushed her away if she even broached the topic. And if he had given it a moment's thought why she was trying to find out, well, he would have known about everything straight-away and that would have been the end of it. But as luck would have it, it didn't even cross his mind, even though he constantly became annoyed around her.

But the princess was always at his heels. She fawned upon him until he finally said, "Well, if you can't fall asleep without it, I'll tell you. Every seven years a golden duck flies over the sea there. Whoever catches that duck, takes golden eggs from it, and eats them, he will receive the power I now have: whatever he thinks about or wants to find out, he will know; he will change whomever he wants into whatever he wants by speaking the word. Today is the end of those seven years and the duck will fly over the sea now, toward evening. Tomorrow, God grant it, I will become master again for seven years and only then will you be mine forever."

"There, my golden little Monk, there, there!" the princess said, lulling and cooing until he fell asleep. Meanwhile it had grown dark and she went to the sea to seek that golden duck. And she caught sight of it swimming on the wide sea. She ran immediately to Popolvár with the news and told him everything.

"Go, Popolvár, go," she added, "through these doors out of the dungeon. Anyway, it is nearly midnight. But be my master by dawn, otherwise it is the end of both me and you!"

Popolvár slipped out of the dark chamber like nothing and just flew to the sea. The golden duck was swimming about the sea, and when he began to lure it, "ducky, ducky, duck," it came itself to meet him. But to what end? No sooner had he caught it and taken its eggs than the Iron Monk stood over him and clawed at the eggs in his mouth. But Popolvár was a quick lad! He warded off his hand from his mouth and had hardly swallowed the eggs when he called out, "Become a wild boar!" At that moment the Iron Monk turned into a wild boar and ran off into the forest.

Popolvár was finally the greatest in the world, for he knew everything about which he even thought or wanted to know, and to stand against him . . . well, perhaps no one ever had such a reign, or ever will!

Happily he went to the freed princess and she, smiling, came to meet him. They belonged to each other forever. They collected enough riches to satisfy maybe even the entire world.

And the fairy horse just neighed happily when he carried them home. They stopped first at her father's who already beforehand, when he saw them coming, had the black cloth ripped down and the castle draped in red. All the subjects made merry there. The young pair immediately left with her father for Popolvár's father's, where the news arrived ahead of them, and here, too, as a sign of joy the town and castle were draped in red cloth. The old kings and friends embraced warmly then, and when they saw that their children were happy, they retired entirely in peace and entrusted all their kingdoms to the youngest, Popolvár.

Popolvár, the greatest in the world, ruled gloriously thereafter—and still rules today if he hasn't passed away.

Note

1. According to other versions, Popolvár makes his way through town before the onlookers on a pig, and the fairy horse awaits him outside town. The pig, here, also has its mythic meaning; it is, according to the legends of our forebears, a representative of the earth in its winter season and aspect. Popolvár and the fairy horse represent the sun in the heavens. Popolvár sitting on the pig, therefore, would mean the closest approach of the sun to the ground, or rather of the earth to the sun at the Christmas solstice.

Classifications and Commentaries to the Tales

The notes to each tale include, first of all, a classification of the tale according to tale-type indices, then a list of the names of those who recorded versions of the tale. This is followed, for some tales, by a commentary on the tale. A word about each of these sections is in order, as well as about the numbered notes to the tales given in the text.

The classification of the tales according to the Aarne–Thompson catalog, *The Types of the Folktale* (Helsinki, 1964), was prepared by Dr. Viera Gašparíková, who generously shared with me the results of her painstaking work on the tales. I have also indicated where the particular variant of the tale is listed in Jiří Polívka's index, *Súpis slovenských rozprávok*. For legendary tales and others that could not be catalogued exactly in the Aarne–Thompson catalog, Gašparíková provides reference to Julian Kryżanowski's *Polska bajka ludowa w układzie systematycznym*, Hanuš Máchal's *Nákres slovanského bájesloví*, or Thompson's *Motif-Index of Folk Literature*.

As I have noted elsewhere, Dobšinský documented his sources by listing the names of those who recorded the manuscripts of the tale from which the final version was compiled. With each person's name he gives the region that person was from, implying in general that the version they recorded came from that region. But in most cases this is left as an assumption without further information available. The narrator of the given version is also named. In some cases, this indicates which manuscript variant Dobšinský used as his primary text. In others, it is the name of the compiler himself, Dobšinský, Škultéty, or one of the other early collaborators. Often Dobšinský reworked even these tales without indicating that fact.

The short commentaries to the tales, when they are provided, are by no means meant as an exhaustive treatment of the tale. Rather, they are intended to point out how a certain number of these tales fit into what is generally known about such tales worldwide. My two sources for such information are Stith Thompson's already rather dated volume *The Folktale* (1946), and Viera Gašparíková's excellent and extensive commentaries on another collection of Slovak tales that she edited and published with Božena Filová—*Slovenské ľudové rozprávky* (1993). Neither volume covers all of the tale types represented in this selection from Dobšinský's tales, and so many tales have remained without commentary. Obviously the first source for anyone wishing to do further research on any particular variant is the Aarne–Thompson index. However, when reference is provided to Gašparíková's commentaries, the researcher would do well to consult them. In addition, Gašparíková's *Catalogue of Slovak Folk Prose* and Polívka's *Súpis slovenských rozprávok* are the two most important indices of Slovak tales. The latter catalogs all the manuscript and published tales available by 1920, while the former catalogs the extensive manuscript collection accumulated by participants in Professor Frank Wollman's folklore seminar at Comenius University in Bratislava from 1928 to the beginning of World War II and includes an English summary of all the tales cataloged.

The numbered notes to the tales come from three sources: Dobšinský's own notes or those of his collaborators that accompanied the original publication (left unmarked), those of Eugen Pauliny, who edited the edition from which this translation was prepared (marked E.P.), and notes I have added myself for this translation (marked Trans.). For my own notes I have often relied on articles in the *Encyklopédia ľudovej kultúry slovenska* and suggestions made by my tireless collaborator, Dr. Marta Botiková.

1. A–T 303 (+ 612 + 774A). JP 1Ba #1. Recorded by Samuel Ormis and Gustáv Reuss from Gemer county, Eduard Skultety from Novohrad county, Aurel Kellner and Daniel Bodický from Liptov county, and Štefanovič from Zvolen county. Narrated by August Horislav Škultéty. This tale is a typical combination of the Dragon Slayer (A–T 300) and Two Brothers (A–T 303) tale types. Moreover, it reflects a combination of two common redactions of the Dragon Slayer plot. First, the Murder redaction, in which the dragon slayer is murdered by an imposter and then revived, which spread from Germany to the Czechoslovak area. Then, the Spring redaction, wherein the dragon guards a spring. According to Thompson, this redaction spread from the Balkans to Hungary, Russia, Poland, and the Baltic states, but Thompson doesn't list Czechoslovakia as reflecting this redaction (Thompson, *The Folktale*, 30–31).

2. A–T 1525 N + 1654. JP 106 #1. Recorded and narrated by Samuel Ormis.

3. A–T—. JP 151 G + H + Ľ #1. Máchal p. 174 cf. p. 175. Krzyżanowski 3040. Narrated by Ján Rotarides in the common rural dialect of Novohrad and Hont. This wizard is clearly a trickster and no magician. The inconsistency in the name Galgína/Balgína may not be a typo, but rather a clue to the wizard's true nature. On the other hand, he *does* struggle with an evil spirit in the third tale, but that spirit is alcohol.

4. A–T 767. JP 75. Told to Božena Němcová by Janko and Miko Sochorík, Juro Šulek, and Štefan Márton from Trenčín county.

5. A–T 500, JP 93A #1. Recorded by Pavol Michalovič and Pavol Dobšinský from Gemer county; narrated by Janko Kmeti in the way they speak in Veľká Paludza in Liptov county. Rumpelstilzchen to the Germans and Tom-Tit-Tot to the English, the supernatural helper of this tale is always Martinko Klyngáš, or some variation thereof, to the Slovaks. The relatively numerous recorded versions vary but little in their details, and so it is possible to speak of a national redaction of the tale, a phenomenon that is rare in spite of the nationalist programs of so many tale collectors (see Filová, *Slovenské ľudové rozprávky*, 669–70).

6. A–T (1739 + 1319 +) 1060 + cf. 1049. JP 89 B #1. Recorded by Janko Rimavský from Malohont county. In this tale the devil plays numbskull, and a woman and the Gypsy tricksters. The deception in the contest to press milk from stones (A–T 1060) is one of the oldest of this type, dating to the *Panchatantra*, and occurs commonly in Slovak variants (Thompson, *The Folktale*,197; Filová, *Slovenské ľudové rozprávky*, 723–24).

7. A–T 313 C (+ 327). JP 19 #2. Recorded by Samuel Reuss and Pavol Dobšinský from Gemer county, Jozef Bela from Liptov county, and Daniel Maróthy from Novohrad county. Narrated by Pavol Dobšinský. The tale of a girl who helps a hero to perform impossible tasks and escapes with him (A–T 313) is one of the oldest in the world, and among the most widely distributed. With the additional incident of the forgotten fiancée (A–T 313 C), the tale is largely restricted to Europe. Gašparíková lists thirteen versions in the Slovak tale fund (Filová, *Slovenské ľudové rozprávky*, 686–87).

8. A–T (cf. 303 A +) 327 B, resp. 1119 + 531. JP 24Aa #4. Recorded by Samuel Reuss and Mikuláš Ferienčik from Zvolen county, Ladislav Gustáv Gáber from Novohrad county, Pavol Dobšinský from Gemer, the Važec collection and Juro Krmeský from Liptov county. Narrated by A.H. Škultéty. The "Hero with a radiant horse sent to a sorceress for valuable things and a princess," as Polívka described this tale type, is a common tale in Slovakia. Gašparíková lists no less than twenty-five recorded variants (Filová, *Slovenské ľudové rozprávky*, 638–39), including one from the repertoire of Jozef Rusnák-Bronda (see Introduction). In this variant, the hero collects the title objects, which motivate his return to the sorceress, in the course of an obstacle flight (Motif D672) from that same sorceress.

9. A–T 720. JP 114 a #1. Recorded by Samuel Ormis, Ľudovit Reuss, and P. Dobšinský from Gemer county, and Jonatan Čipka from Malohont county. Narrated by Janko Botto. This tale centers about the song through which the murder is revealed, and surprisingly, it seems to exist primarily in oral tradition with little ties to literature, although Goethe's use of it in *Faust* is a notable exception. It is known throughout Europe, although it generally appears infrequently among the Slavs. The Slovaks are the exception here, with more than twelve versions in the recorded tale fund (Filová, *Slovenské ľudové rozprávky*, 641–42).

10. A–T (650 A +) 301 B. JP 2 Aa #1. Recorded by Samuel Reuss, Ľudovít Reuss, Pavol Dobšinský, and Ondrej Návoj from Gemer county, Karol Venich from Malohont county, Eugen Špamensis from Liptov county, and Horislav August Krčméry from Zvolen. Narrated by Pavol Dobšinský. The tale types 301, "The Bear's Son," in which a hero of supernatural strength and his companions rescue three princesses from the underworld, and 650, "Strong John," in which the strong hero enters into a bargain for his labor, are closely related. In *The Folktale*, Thompson laments, "Any distribution study of Strong John is made difficult [by this close relationship]. One is not always quite sure whether cataloguers have been careful to discriminate between the two types" (86). Such discrimination is made all the more difficult by variants such as the

present one, which clearly combine both types (Polívka also includes several versions under this heading in his catalog that do not include the bargain over payment for labor). The situation is further complicated in the Slovak tale fund by tales in which an extraordinarily small hero plays the role of the "Bear's Son" (see "Johnny Pea").

Dobšinský appends the following note to the tale: We don't intend to provide reflections or judgments upon our tales here, but we'll make an exception for this one and allow a small opinion, which the honorable late gentleman Samuel Reuss appended to it in his manuscript. It goes like this:

> The simple folk, who love their hearths, fields, and pastures, know how to speak about all life's circumstances and particularly about the creations of their minds simply, and without ornamentation. Such are the ancient Slavs and the creations of their spirits. Doubtless a higher degree of sincerity can be attached to this creativity of the Slavs. And we are truly convinced that this beautiful attribute is present in the Slavic national character.
>
> The description of our three heros, Lomidrevo, Miesiželeza, and Kopivrch [see note 2 following the text—Trans.] is simple and sincere, even though these figures are miraculous and giant. The originator of this fairy tale wanted to present the *non plus ultra* of physical strength, and although he described a bizarre and miraculous event, he reached the limit of the ideal and the sublime. We find the ideal in the attributes and characteristics of the characters, the sublime in their noble goal of liberating three princesses from the power of a dragon.
>
> We will add that the preparation of the heroes for their wonderful and unusual deeds is not awkward, although it is taken from ordinary life, and the frightening task is fitting for such monstrous strength. [The original text was in German.—E.P.]

11. A–T 157. JP 145 C #3. Recorded by Jurko Molnár from Kameňany, Gemer county.

12. A–T 450. JP 46 #1. Recorded by P. Dobšinský and S. Ormis from Gemer county, Ján Čipka, Karol Venich and Janko Rimavský from Malohont county, the Važec collection from Liptov county, and Adolf Reuss from Šariš county. Narrated by A.H. Škultéty. This is a fairly typical version of the tale of "Little Brother and Little Sister," which is well known in Europe and the Near East. The tale type is well represented in the Slovak tale fund—Polívka gives fourteen recorded versions.

13. A–T 1930 + 852 (resp. 1960 G + 1889 E) + 1882 + 1889 (resp. 1881 + cf. 1889 G) + 1930 (resp. 1965) + (852) + cf. 1882. JP 116 C #1. Recorded by Bojoslav Martin Šebek from Novohrad.

14. A–T 756B. JP 78 #4. Recorded by Štefan Marko Daxner from Malohont county, Samo Ormis from Gemer county, and Jozef Jančo from Šariš county. Compiled by A.H. Škultéty. This tale, The Devil's Contract (A–T 756B), is one of the most popular in Eastern Europe. Polívka lists nine versions from the older part of the Slovak tale fund.

15. A–T 314 (+ 532). JP 17 Ab #2. Recorded by Janko Rimavský and the Važec collection. Narrated by A.H. Škultéty. This version of the very popular *Goldener Märchen*, as it is known to the Germans, includes the motif of a restriction placed by the horse upon the hero about what he can say (A–T 532). Thompson notes that this version is popular in Russia, Finland, and Hungary (*The Folktale*, 59–61).

16. A–T 360. JP 85 A #2. Narrated by P. Dobšinský in the dialect of the village of Sirok in Gemer county. This tale is a variant of the Grimm's tale of "The Three Journeymen," with the difference that the devil does not save the boys in the end.

17. A–T 402. JP 13B #1. Recorded by Lukáčik in the Važec collection, Janko

Rimavský and A. Ľud. Gál from Malohont county; narrated by A.H. Škultéty. The Slovak folktale fund also includes variants of tale type 402 in which the enchanted princess is turned into a frog. Versions of this predominantly European tale with a cat do not appear to be extant further to the east than Slovakia (see Filová, *Slovenské ľudové rozprávky* Filová, 694–95).

18. A–T 130. JP 145 B #1. Recorded by Dr. Gustáv Reuss from Gemer county.

19. A–T (cf. types 550 or 551 + 300 A + 2028 + 531 +) 302. JP 9 #1. Recorded and narrated by Samko Jamriška from Malohont county. This tale, which combines elements of the dragon-slayer tale with motifs from several other tales, finishing like tale A–T 302, The ogre's heart in the egg, is found infrequently in the Slovak tale fund. When it appears in later Slovak collections, the influence of this version from Škultéty–Dobšinský is frequently evident.

20. A–T—. JP 126 F #1. Máchal, pp. 82–3. See MI N 115 and MI M 302.8. Recorded by a correspondent unknown to us in the collection by various authors (Codex diversorum auctorum) from before 1848. Although this tale cannot be specifically classified according to the international catalogue, it is not unique to Slovakia. As Gašparíková observes, it belongs generally to the class of tales about fate, A–T 930–949, and its motifs of a book of fate and prophecy from books can be found in the Motif Index (Filová, *Slovenské ľudové rozprávky*, 653).

21. A–T 327 A + 510 A. JP 51Bc #1. Recorded by Janko Rimavský from Malohont county. The combination of two tale types here, the children led into the woods and the classic Cinderella tale, is typical for the Western Slavs. As Gašparíková writes, "This combination is known in the literature as *Finette Cendron* after the version of the Countess d'Aulnoy (1650–1705). It came to our region in a Czech translation from a German intermediary in 1761, was frequently reprinted in folk readers, and exerted an influence not only on the Czech but also on the Slovak tradition" (Filová, *Slovenské ľudové rozprávky*, 640).

22. A–T 513A. JP 16 #1. Narrated by Pavol Križko. The supernatural helpers of this tale are related to a host of such helpers that appear in a variety of tale types (Motif F601ff.). There is wide variety in their names and in the types of tasks they perform, but a common plot involves, as in our variant, tasks that help to win a princess (A–T 513A). This tale type is known worldwide and is as variable in its details as such a distribution might suggest. However, even the Slovak variants of this tale exhibit great variety, and it is not the case, as it was with "The Spinner of Gold," that one can speak of a typical national variant (Filová, *Slovenské ľudové rozprávky*, 672).

23. A–T 470. JP 73 B #1. Recorded and narrated by Štefan Marko Daxner of Malohont county.

24. A–T 101 + 104 + 103. JP 146 Aa #2. Told to Božena Němcová by Janko and Miko Sochorík, Juro Šulek, and Štefan Márton from Trenčín county. This tale combines three types (A–T 101, The old dog as rescuer of the child (sheep); A–T 104, The cowardly duelers; and A–T 103, The wild animals hide from the unfamiliar animal) in a way that is not uncommon, particularly in Slavic countries. It is characteristic of the Slovak variants of the tale that the wild animals hide because they misinterpret the sounds made by the domestic animals (Filová, *Slovenské ľudové rozprávky*, 724–25).

25. A–T cf. 562. JP 29 D. Recorded and narrated by A.H. Škultéty from Malohont county. This tale is perhaps most closely related to tales of magic helpers, like Aladdin's lamp (A–T 561). It is unique in the Slovak tale fund—Polívka gives no other versions, and no related tales are indexed in the *Catalogue of Slovak Folk Prose*.

26. A–T 1525 A, P + 804 B + (cf. 313 or 554 +) 1072 + 1071 + 1084. JP 104 Ab #2.

Recorded by Bojoslav Martin Šebek, and Ján Banšel in the Banská Štiavnica *Folk Anthology*, and Pavol Dobšinský. The tale of the Master Thief (A–T 1525) is known in hundreds of variants the world over. This particular variant combines the core of the Master Thief narrative with a quest for a maiden in hell that results in a series of contests with the devil (see "The Gypsy Duped the Devil"). Such a combination is characteristic of numerous Slovak variants of the tale, but has also been recorded among Slovakia's neighbors: the Poles, Hungarians, Ukrainians, Belarusians, and Russians. Even the highwayman character's name seems connected to this structure— he's known as Klimek or Klementy among the Poles and Kilinkó, Tillinkó, or Fillinkó among the Hungarians (Filová, *Slovenské ľudové rozprávky*, 645–47, 734–35).

27. A–T 300 A (+ 531 + 612). JP 8 A #3. Recorded by Ondrej Chriašteľ from Zvolen county, Karol Venich from Malohont county, Adolf Ghillányi from Liptov county, and an unknown writer in the Levoča *Folk Almanac*. Compiled by P. Dobšinský. Various motifs from this tale are already familiar to the reader from "The Enchanted Forest" "Vintalko," and "The Golden Horseshoe, The Golden Feather, and The Golden Hair." Polívka refers to eleven versions of various degrees of similarity in his index under the rubric "The Hero with a Radiating Horse Struggles with Three Dragons on Bridges and Then with Their Wives." However, the later *Catalogue of Slovak Folk Prose* shows no closely related tales.

28. A–T (cf. 1476 B +) 1164 D. JP 88 B #1. Recorded by an unknown writer in the Važec collection from Liptov and Ján Hajšo from Dúžava by Rimava.

29. A–T 1387 + 1386 + 1385* + 1293 A* + cf. 1318 + (alternatively cf. 1381 +) cf. 1653. JP 133 Ca. Heard by Božena Němcová from the servant Marka in Balážske Ďarmoty, Trenčín county.

30. A–T 700 (+650 A +304). JP 7 B #4 (cf. 2 Ab). Recorded by Janko Kalinčiak from Sv. Jan in Liptov county, in that county's dialect. The tale of Johnny Pea in the Slovak tale fund is closely related to the tale of Lomidrevo, the pea-sized hero growing into the giant's place (see the note following the tale and those to "Lomidrevo or Valibuk"). However, in this variant the adventures are more typically those of a small protagonist.

31. A–T 839. JP 127 G. Narrated by Štefan Marko Daxner from Malohont county.

32. A–T 1476 B + 363 + 407 B. JP 54 A #4. Recorded by Janko Kaderiak from Asód near Budapest and Ľudo Reuss from Veľká Revúca. This tale is closely related to both "The Old Maid and the Devil" and "The Dead Suitor," but the explicit vampire motif distinguishes it from both. The tale is common in the Slovak tale fund.

33. A–T 2015. JP 146 B #1. Recorded by Samuel Ormis and P. Dobšinský from Gemer.

34. A–T 471. JP 73 A #1. Recorded by Janko Rimavský.

35. A–T (403 B, alternatively 480 A). JP 52 C #1. Recorded by Božena Němcová in Trenčín county from the servant Marka, who worked for her in Balážske Ďarmoty. This version of the kind and unkind sisters tale (A–T 403) published by Dobšinský differs only slightly from the version Němcová herself published. The tale is a favorite among both the Czechs (through Němcová) and Slovaks.

36. A–T 1642. JP 43 B #1. Recorded by Samo Ormis from Veľká Revúca, Amália Sirotková née Šidlay from Hájnik in Zvolen county, and Štefan Lukáčik from Hont county; compiled by Pavol Dobšinský.

37. A–T 875. JP 122 Da #2. Recorded by Adolf Reuss and Pavol Dobšinský from Gemer county and Eugen Vrahobor Šparnensis from Liptov. The tale of the clever peasant's daughter is found almost throughout the world and is very popular. There are

more than twenty versions in the Slovak tale fund. The two most common openings to the tale, are the majority of the Slovak versions resemble this version in opening with a court judgment, rather than with the peasant bringing a golden mortar to the lord, who requests the pestle to accompany it. Gašparíková indicates that this is typical of the Slavic versions in general (Filová, *Slovenské ľudové rozprávky*, 739–40).

38. A–T 476*. JP 14 #1. Recorded and narrated by Jonatan Čipka from Malohont county. While in the German, Czech, and Polish traditions the toad in this tale is typically the wife of a water sprite, and similar versions are also found in the Slovak tale fund, this variant is representative of others in the Slovak tradition that are closer to the known Hungarian versions, including the motif of the sweepings turning into coins (Filová, *Slovenské ľudové rozprávky*, 651).

39. A–T 123. JP 146 C #4. According to the version by Samuel Ormis from V. Revúca.

40. A–T 923. JP 51 D. Told to Božena Němcová by a servant at the spa Sliač.

41. A–T 812. JP 86 Aa #1. Written in the dialect of the Bošácká valley on the border between Trenčín and Nitra counties by Ľ.V. Rizner, according to Božena Němcová's version.

42. A–T 889. JP 127 H. Recorded by Štefan Marko Daxner of Malohont county.

43. JP 61. There are no related variants known in Slovakia for this tale, which lies on the border of the wondertale and demonological traditions. It can be loosely associated with the subtype A–T 333 B, "The Cannibal Godfather (Godmother)," but for the questions directed at Auntie Death and the typical outcome, one should also take into account type A–T 336. "Death Washes his Feet," which, in the international catalogue, is noted in the Hungarian tradition.—Gašparíková. Recorded by Pavol Dobšinský from Gemer county. The reader will recognize the relation between this tale and Little Red Riding Hood (type A–T 333).

Dobšinský appends this note: "While narrating and saying that 'chomp!' the teller opens wide his mouth and spreads his arms and fingers and chomps at the closest and most fearful of those who were listening raptly to the tale. The children will certainly freeze and be frightened; but with time they'll grow brave and will even joke about the legs, the arms, the eyes, and that chomp!"

44. (1) Petor's Cap: A–T 846*. JP 70 Fb #1. (2) Petor the Early Bird: A–T 791. JP 70 Fa #2. (3) Petor the Miser: A–T 785 A + 785. JP 70 A ab #1. (4) Petor's Shirt: Krzyżanowski 751 C. JP 70 Fd. Recorded by Božena Němcová from Trenčín county in her work *Slovak Folk and Fairy Tales*, 1858.

45. A–T (cf. types 403 B + 676 +) 400 (+ 313 or 554). JP 53 #2. Narrated by Janko Rimavský. This tale is closely related to "The Twelve Months," except instead of two sisters, there are two brothers. The Aarne–Thompson index does not treat the male and female versions independently, although their separate existence is generally recognized. In Slovak versions, the tale with male protagonists almost always includes the motif of weighing gold and the envy between the brothers, which can also be found in the tale of Ali Baba (type A–T 676). In this particular variant, the hero also loses his wife and must find her, as in tale type 400 (Filová, *Slovenské ľudové rozprávky*, 644–45).

Our text follows the later publication of Dobšinský; it differs from the first edition only insignificantly.—E.P. [Dobšinský published this tale twice and referred to it often in his writings on the wondertale.—Trans.]

46. A–T—. JP 150 #1. Told to Božena Němcová by Janko and Miko Sochorík, Juro Šulek, and Štefan Márton from Trenčín county.

47. A–T 401 A (cf. 401) + 314 or 502. JP 12 A #3. Recorded by Gustáv Pivko from Stará Turá in Nitra county in the local dialect, edited by Hostimír Šmid. This is another tale of largely European provenance. Thompson notes that "it seems to be most popular in Italy, among the south Slavic peoples, the Czechs [with whom he probably includes the Slovaks], and the Flemish" (*The Folktale*, 94).

48. A–T 1535 (+ cf. 1681). JP 125 #1. Recorded by Samo Ormis from Gemer county and Drahotín Belohorský from Turiec county. Arranged from their versions and narrated by Pavol Dobšinský. This is a fine Slovak version of a tale that is known and popular worldwide: the rich and the poor peasant (A–T 1535).

49. A–T 365. JP 54 Ba #1. Recorded by Samuel Ormis and Gustáv Reuss from Gemer county, Štefan Daxner from Malohont county, and Karol Venich from Liptov county. Narrated by A. H. Škultéty. This tale type is well known in Europe from the literary ballad tradition, especially G. A. Bürger's "Lenore," and to the Czechs and Slovaks from K.J. Erben's classic ballad, "Svatební košile." The type has been the subject of special study in Slovakia by M.A. Huska, and some thirty Slovak variants are thus known. While Thompson reports the prose version primarily in the Baltic states (*The Folktale*, 41), Gašparíková indicates that more recent study inclines to positing a Slavic origin for the tale, perhaps among the Russians or Ukrainians, if the place of origin was not northern Germany. Slavic redactions tend to show a more developed motif structure, including the spell-casting that calls the dead suitor, the magical deliverance of the girl, her hiding on the stove, the dissolution of the suitor into pitch, and the crowing of a cock, all of which tend to be absent in other European versions. Of these motifs, this variant lacks only the magical deliverance of the girl (Filová, *Slovenské ľudové rozprávky*, 726–28).

50. A–T (cf. types 550 or 551 + 300 +) 302 (+ cf. 325). JP 1 C #2. Recorded by Adolf Reuss from Muránska valley in Gemer county. Popolvár is another in a series of Slovak dragon slayers, like Lomidrevo and Vintalko, and even his namesake, Ashlet.

Appendix

Tale Collection in Nineteenth-Century Slovakia and the Origin of Traditional Slovak Folktales

Slovakia in the Nineteenth Century

The people who came to be known as Slovaks and the territory of present-day Slovakia were a part of the Hungarian kingdom, minor historical deviations aside, since its inception in the year 1000. They were long the beneficiaries of an ancient tradition of ethnic tolerance within the kingdom dating from its first king, St. Stephen. However, the advent of linguistic nationalism in Europe introduced forces that would eventually tear that kingdom apart. The Emperor Josef II's (reigned 1780–90) attempts at Germanizing his subjects were resisted in the Hungarian half of the Hapsburg empire and gave impetus to the development of the various vernaculars of that kingdom. In the early 1780s newspapers appeared in both Hungarian (Magyar) and Slovak. The Catholic priest Anton Bernolák became the first codifier of Slovak grammar in 1790, and in 1803 a Chair in Czechoslovak Language and Literature was established in the Lutheran lyceum in Pressburg (Bratislava). The Slovaks, just like the Hungarians, Croats, and Serbs, as well as other nations in the diverse kingdom, were experiencing their national revival.[1]

While arguing for the rights of the Hungarian kingdom within the Habsburg monarchy, the Hungarians used their control of administrative powers to suppress the linguistic and cultural development of other ethnic groups. This trend became particularly acute in the 1840s, when Magyarization became the rule in the Hungarian kingdom. In 1843–44 Hungarian was declared the exclusive language of legislation and, at least in principle, the language of public education.[2] Often Hungarian oppression was carried out in the name of rooting out Pan-Slavism, which, though it began as a politically neutral cultural ideology among Slovaks and Czechs in the 1820s, was quickly gain-

Map: Slovak Counties in Nineteenth-Century Austro-Hungary.

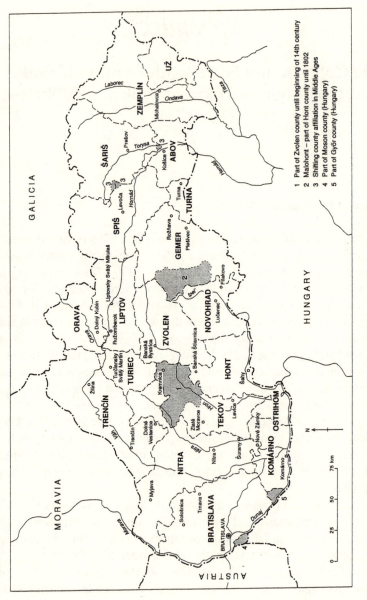

Legend:

1 Part of Zvolen county until beginning of 14th century
2 Malohont – part of Hont county until 1802
3 Shifting county affiliation in Middle Ages
4 Part of Moson county (Hungary)
5 Part of Győr county (Hungary)

Source: A History of Slovakia, Stanislav J. Kirschbaum, St. Martin's Press, 1995. © Stanislav J. Kirschbaum. Reprinted with permission of St. Martin's Press, LLC.

ing political overtones in the 1840s. Surrounded as they were by the Slavs who also populated their kingdom, the Hungarians probably had genuine reason to fear Pan-Slavism: the Slavs at the Slav Congress in Prague in 1848 certainly were not entirely friendly to the Hungarian cause. But the Hungarians' fear led them to see the vilified Pan-Slavism everywhere, and they used the accusation of it to halt even the purely nationalist activities of other groups.

The various Lutheran lycea in Slovakia, where Dobšinský's contemporaries studied and taught, became the frequent objects of Magyarizing attacks. Always a minority in Slovakia, the Lutherans at this time occupied a position of political and cultural influence out of proportion to their numbers. Many of the leaders among the Lutherans in Slovakia had been educated in Germany, where they were influenced by German Romanticism and the ideas of Johann Gottfried Herder. They brought the spirit of German Romanticism, with its ideology of the *volk* as the basis of the nation and its new esthetics, into the Slovak National Revival. But their real coup was linguistic. Though far more Czechophile than Slovak Catholics, the Lutherans, led by Ľudovít Štúr, proposed a successful codification of Slovak that led to the final break from Czech as a literary language. They proposed the dialect of central Slovakia as the basis of the written language, rather than the more Czech-like western dialect advocated by the Catholic priest Bernolák, not only because this dialect would be more central to all the dialects of Slovak, but also because they felt this greater separation would be a political advantage in asserting their national identity against the Hungarians. Štúr himself, who studied at the university in Halle, embodied the cultural and political leadership of the Slovak Protestants: as the author of *A Grammar of the Slovak Tongue* (Nauka reči slovenskej) (1846), he is considered the codifier of contemporary Slovak; and in 1847 he became the only Slovak representative to the house of the Hungarian Parliament.[3]

With the outbreak of the Hungarian Revolution in March 1848, the Slovaks found themselves in an unusual position. When the Slav Congress in Prague was broken up before any common program could be reached, Slovak leaders Štúr and Jozef Miloslav Hurban began to confer with the Croats. And when the Croats began their military campaign against Hungary, the few Slovak detachments that could be assembled under the conditions of martial law attempted to join in. That is, eventually the Slovaks found themselves fighting with the Habsburgs against the Hungarians. They preferred to take their chances with the Austrian monarchs rather than leave the Hungarians free to govern as they pleased. The Slovaks appealed to Emperor Franz Josef for political recognition in return for their involvement in the war, but were answered noncommittally. In the end, the Slovaks and other nationalities that had supported the Habsburg crown against the Hungarians had to suffer punishment along with the Hungarians: under Minister Bach's ten-year administration, Germanization became the rule in Austro-Hungary.[4]

In the 1860s, under Schmerling's "Provisorium" administration, the Slovaks were able to negotiate with the more liberal Viennese for some protection against the continuing Magyarizing tendencies of the local administrators. They established three Slovak gymnazia as well as, in 1863, the Matica Slovenská, a national cultural organization that even received a donation from Emperor Franz Josef. However, after the Compromise of 1867 and the establishment of the dual kingdom, they were again vulnerable. The Matica Slovenská was dissolved in 1875 and its property confiscated. Beginning a year earlier, the three Slovak gymnazia were closed one after another, and the Slovaks were to remain without secondary schools until the formation of Czechoslovakia in 1918.[5]

Collection and Publication of Slovak Tales

That the collection of folktales should begin with Slovak Lutherans is not at all surprising. The spirit of German Romanticism, with its emphasis on native language and traditions, clearly filtered back into Slovakia through those leaders who had been educated in Germany. Ján Kollár, for example, a 1815 graduate of the lyceum in Bratislava, became acquainted with no less a figure than Goethe during his university studies in Jena. And like the leader of German Romanticism, Herder, he collected folk songs and published over 2,000 of them in his *Folk Songs* (Národnie spievanky) in 1834–35.[6] What is surprising is that the impulse that led to the first major collections of Slovak folk prose apparently *did not* come from the direct influence of the Grimm brothers. The Grimms had first published their *Kinder- und Hausmärchen* in 1812, and Jacob began his *Circular-Brief* in 1815, thereby influencing many collectors in other nations. In spite of some similarity in methods, though, it appears that the early Slovak collectors and publishers were probably ignorant of the work of these influential leaders.

The impulse for the collecting of prose folktales in Slovakia came from the Lutheran pastor in Revúca, *Samuel Reuss*. Educated in Jena, which he left in 1806 due to the Napoleonic wars, Reuss was an enlightenment intellectual, with interests that varied from ornithology and mineralogy to history and archeology, and a member of the Learned Society of Malohont, one of a few such societies—small groups of intellectuals modeled on the enlightenment's scientific academies—that appeared in Slovakia around the turn of the nineteenth century. Members of this society had worked on Slovak folk songs, particularly historical songs, in the first half of the nineteenth century, and it was Reuss's interest in history that led him to begin collecting folktales, which he considered to be ancient in origin. Between 1839 and 1844, with his three sons and Samuel Ormis, he collected and put together the material for the manuscripts known as the Revúca Codexes A, B, and C.[7]

Augustín Horislav Škultéty (b. 7 August 1819, d. 22 January 1892) was serving as deputy professor of Czechoslovak language and literature at the Lutheran lyceum in Bratislava in 1840 and was finishing his theological studies there. In June of that year, students at the lyceum began to discuss the necessity of collecting Slovak prose folklore, and Škultéty probably initiated the students' activities. However, Škultéty himself later credited Samuel Reuss with providing the spiritual impulse for the students' collecting activities. This may be true, since the collecting did not really begin in earnest until the students' leader, *Ján Francisci*, visited the home of his fellow students Ľudovít and Adolf Reuss in 1842. In his autobiography he recalled his fascination with the tales his friends' father, Samuel Reuss, showed him from his collection. In that same year, the first volume of the students' manuscripts called "Folk Almanac" (Prostonárodní zabavník) appeared under Francisci's direction. The second volume was completed the following year. Together, these two volumes make up nearly 800 manuscript pages and include folk songs, folktales, riddles, proverbs, and descriptions of games and customs, and represent just the beginning of the students' collections.[8]

However, in December 1843 the Department of Czechoslovak Language and Literature in Bratislava was effectively shut down by a church commission, which removed its leader, Ľudovít Štúr, from his position as deputy professor (Škultéty had been filling in for Štúr while he was studying in Halle) and forbade him to continue lecturing on folk poetry and prose. Still, the collection of tales continued as the majority of the students and members of the Institute moved to the lyceum in Levoča. Ľudovit Reuss led the collecting activities of the students in Levoča, and in the 1844–45 school year, two more volumes of the "Folk Almanac" appeared, this time with the first contributions from the young *Pavol Dobšinský* (b. 16 March 1828, d. 22 October 1885), who had begun study in Levoča in 1840. These two volumes make up over 1,000 pages in manuscript. The fifth extant volume of the "Folk Almanac," an 88-page fragment from 1846, is largely the work of Dobšinský. Francisci managed to have himself installed as deputy professor of Czechoslovak language and literature, with recommendations from Samuel Reuss and Škultéty, in the fall of 1844. However, by Christmas break his lectures were prohibited and he had to continue his folklore collection activities privately.[9]

Students from other lycea in Banská Štiavnica and Kežmarok were also collecting tales in volumes of "Folk Almanacs," some of which are accessible along with the already mentioned manuscripts in the archives of the

Matica Slovenská in Martin, Slovakia, today. Another series of manuscripts, the Tisovec Codexes A, B, and C, were compiled in the same period by three lyceum graduates: Škultéty (who was chaplain in Tisovec from 1841–48), Štefan Marko Daxner, and Jonatán Dobroslav Čipka.[10] Together with the students' "Folk Almanacs," the Revúca Codexes, and several other manuscript collections of tales,[11] these manuscripts were the source of the majority of the tales for later publication efforts. Slovakia is almost unique among European nations in possessing such an extensive and early collection of folk tales in manuscript form.

Where the students collected their tales and from whom remains somewhat in the dark, for they only occasionally noted the location and rarely named the narrator when recording their tales. Thus we have to rely on the later recollections of the collectors and other witnesses. In his last year at the lyceum, Dobšinský recalled that many tales and songs came from servant girls from the Spiš region, who sang and told their tales to the students in homes and inns in Levoča.[12] Jozef Škultéty (no immediate relation to Augustín) noted that the collecting efforts covered a relatively small region in central Slovakia, and recalled that the Reuss family collected most of its tales from the teacher in Revúca, Mrs. Jochmann, whom he knew as a child in 1868–69, when she was a ninety-one-year-old widow. He wrote, "Those were the last years of her life, but even then, at such an age, her dearest joy was to tell tales. She told them to her two girls, themselves not young, all evening long. If she had someone to tell tales to, she could have gone from morning to night. Her daughters (one was a childless widow, the other an old maid) were also fertile sources of tales."[13]

Francisci succeeded, in 1845, in publishing the first collection of Slovak folk tales, *Slovak Tales* (Slovenskje povesti), under the pseudonym Janko Rimavský. This collection of ten tales included tales prepared for publication by Samuel Reuss with his sons Gustáv and Adolf, by Škultéty, by Daxner, and by Čipka.[14] Francisci promised that it would be followed by others, and he clearly meant to publish much of the material from the rich collections that were quickly being accumulated by students at that time. However, for a number of reasons, no further publications followed. Francisci himself did not have the financial means and his smallish first volume, of which only 500 copies were published, did not go over well with the public. While much interest was being generated among students in the collection and preservation of folk tales, apparently the small reading public was uninterested in purchasing publications of tales from an oral tradition it knew and generally still looked down upon. Moreover, Francisci, along with many other intellectuals in the years leading up to 1848, became involved in other aspects of the national struggle. His involvement in the collection and publication of folk tales ended when he left for Prešov to study law.[15]

Under the Bach government's administration during the ten years following the revolution of 1848 it was difficult to maintain the communal collecting efforts that had begun in the early forties and impossible to publish anything as nationally oriented as fairy tales. A few collectors remained active though, among them Dobšinský, who returned from serving in the Emperor's army in 1848 to a position as secretary to Samuel Reuss in Revúca,[16] and Škultéty, who served as chaplain in Dolná Ves from 1847–50 and minister in Rozložná from 1850–62.[17] However, it was Ľudovit Reuss who remained most active and who continued preparations for publication of another collection. Reuss tried, without success, to re-interest Francisci, but ultimately found help from Škultéty and Čipka. With them he prepared a volume for publication and sent it to Pest in 1852, but the volume never found a publisher.[18] In fact, the next collection of Slovak folk tales to be published was that of Božena Němcová, the Czech romantic novelist. Němcová herself had collected some tales on her various trips to Slovakia in the early 1850s, where she had also met Francisci. She hoped to be a facilitator for the publication of the tales of these collectors in Prague and requested tales from Ľudovit Reuss as well. In the end, Němcová was unable to find a publisher who would publish the tales in the Slovak original. What she published in Prague in 1857–58 under the title *Slovak Fairy and Folk Tales* (Slovenské pohádky a povĕsti) were essentially translations, into a Czech that contained many Slovakisms, of the material she had received from Ľudovit Reuss, tales from Francisci's 1845 publication, and tales she herself had collected.[19]

In the meantime, Ľudovit Reuss had given up his plans for publishing folk tales, but his work was continued by Dobšinský and Škultéty, who began to work together in 1855 when Dobšinský went to Rožňavské Bystré to become minister. Škultéty sent Dobšinský the codexes and manuscripts he had, so that Dobšinský could begin to prepare tales for publication.[20] The two worked well together and found that they agreed on decisions about the preparation of tales for publication more than they disagreed. Thanks to a donation by Daxner, in 1858 the first volume of *Slovak Tales* (Slovenské povesti), which would ultimately contain sixty-four titles in six small volumes, was published.[21] That same year, Dobšinský went to Banská Štiavnica to become professor at the Lutheran lyceum and to pursue his desire to edit a popular literary magazine.[22] There he found a new publisher with whom they continued to publish tales whenever enough money from the sale of the previous volume had been accumulated. Dobšinský and Škultéty were not the only ones to prepare tales for publication; Daxner, Čipka, and Francisci also contributed. However, in 1861 Dobšinský left for Drienčany to take the minister's position left by Čipka on his death. As he was unable to maintain contact with a publisher in that isolated village and unable to raise enough money for a new volume, publication stopped with the sixth volume that year.[23] For twenty years there were no new volumes published.

In addition to establishing himself as a beloved and active minister in Drienčany, and in spite of the lack of access to the outside world and a decent library, Dobšinský completed a remarkable amount of valuable work on Slovak folklore in the remainder of his life there. He continued to stay in contact with Škultéty, then principal of the gymnazium in Revúca, through the early 1870s in hopes of again publishing more folktales. But his collecting and publishing activities also broadened. In the late 1860s, the cultural organization Matica Slovenská asked Dobšinský to lead its collection and publication efforts. Dobšinský called on his countrymen to collect a variety of materials, including folktales, songs, proverbs and sayings, riddles, games, dances, customs, folk dress, folk beliefs, and tales about old castles, rock formations, glens, and wells.[24] When the Matica Slovenská published two volumes titled *A Collection of Slovak National Songs, Tales, Proverbs, Sayings, Riddles, Games, Customs, and Beliefs* (1871, 1874), not only did Dobšinský edit the second volume, he also contributed items from his own collections in all categories. And in 1880 he published his own volume, *Slovak Folk Customs, Beliefs, and Games* (Prostonárodné obyčaje, povery a hry slovenské), which was the first full (if simplified) picture of the Slovak people and a groundbreaking work in Slovak ethnography.[25] He also published, in 1871, a theoretical work on wondertales (*Märchen*), the first major work of its kind in Slovakia and the only one by the group of collectors and publishers to which he belonged. We will deal more fully with this volume, *Reflections on Slovak Folktales* (Úvahy o slovenských povestiach), below.

By the time Dobšinský was able to publish another collection of folktales, this time with resources out of his own pocket, he decided that it was worth republishing a number of tales that were already familiar, as well as bringing out previously unpublished and lesser known tales. His *Slovak Folk Tales* (Prostonárodnie slovenské povesti), published in eight volumes from 1881–83, contained ninety titles. Many had been prepared from the same manuscript versions that had been used for the previous publications of Francisci and Němcová. Others were new tales from the manuscript collections that had not yet been published and tales that had been published in various magazines. This final collection, which represents Dobšinský's culminating work, is quite different in character from his previous collaboration with Škultéty. Where the previous collection included primarily wondertales, to this later collection Dobšinský added many more legendary, novelistic, humorous, and animal tales.[26] Perhaps his work with the collection and publication of other folk materials made him more aware of the value of other types of folktales.

For whatever reason, Dobšinský succeeded in putting together a collection that more truly represented the variety of prose folk material in circulation in the nineteenth century in Slovakia.

While Dobšinský is primarily remembered for his folktales, his activities were not limited to folklore collection and publication, nor were such activities his source of income. As a lyceum student, Dobšinský wrote and published some patriotic and allegorical poems based on folk themes. He translated from a number of languages, but mostly from English, including Shakespeare's "Hamlet," Byron's "Mazeppa," and the heroic songs of Ossian, though he also translated some of Rousseau and Lermontov.[27] While in Banská Štiavnica he served as editor of the national literary magazine *Falcon* (Sokol) and thus published the work of important contemporaries like Ján Botto, Janko Kráľ, Samo Chalupa, and Andrej Sládkovič. And of course, Dobšinský's primary occupation for much of his life was his work as a Lutheran minister.

Methods and Theories of the Collectors

The opinions expressed by Samuel Reuss in his article, "On J.M. [sic] Musäus's Edition of German Folk Tales," are of particular interest if we are to understand the methodology of the Slovak tale collectors and publishers. This article was included in 1844 in the third "Folk Almanac" volume at the lyceum in Levoča by his son Ľudovít, for the benefit of the students there (including Dobšinský). This article, along with another article in German, titled "Agreement for Understanding" (Einverständigung [!]), copied, also by Ľudovít, from the Revúca Codex B into the first volume of the "Folk Almanac," gives us a good picture of the opinions of Reuss on the folktale and its importance. These two articles, coupled with Reuss's personal example, gave direction to this entire generation of collectors and publishers.[28]

An edition of Johann Karl Musäus' *Folktales of the Germans* (Volksmärchen der Deutschen) fell into Samuel Reuss's hands while he was collecting Slovak tales during the summer vacation, and he was moved upon reading it to write about the necessity of preserving and writing down Slovak tales as relics of ancient Slovak times. Before we explore Reuss's reaction, we should observe that Musäus's tales are not really folktales in the strict sense, but creative literature. As Ulrich Scheck writes in the introduction to a recent edition,

> Many of [Musäus's tales] can be regarded as early predecessors of those narrative texts that became known in the nineteenth century as "novellas." It is important to note that they were not folk tales based on popular oral or written tradition. Several are Musäus' own creations; others are adapta-

tions of Perrault's seventeenth-century fairy tales. Among those that have their roots in national legends are the "Legenden von Rübezahl," . . . "Libussa," and "Melechsala."[29]

Reuss, following a typical Romantic national prejudice, takes for granted the Slovak origin of tales that are familiar to him, and thus leaps to the conclusion that Musäus included two Slovak tales in his collection, one being the "Legenden von Rübezahl," which combines several legends into one tale (in fact, the legends of Rübezahl were shared by the Germans, Czechs, Slovaks, and Poles around the area of Silesia). He objects to what has been done to this tale. He admits that the tale has been made beautiful, that it is practically a poem, but this is not sufficient for him. The plot of the tale lacks coherence and motivation, and "Ribrcol" becomes a clown who learns nothing from his adventures and can teach the reader nothing. Musäus has played to the tastes and mores of the contemporary German civilization. To Reuss this is a distasteful mixing of old and new, and reading these tales in such a form would be like learning Homer and Virgil through parodies.[30]

Reuss therefore makes two recommendations for the work on Slovak tales. First, he would prefer "that our folktales be preserved in exactly that simple state in which we receive them from the hands of the folk."[31] This in order that the ancient history and customs of the Slovak nation be known and available for study (we should recall that it was his interest in history that led Reuss to collect folktales). He observes that the Slovaks are related to the Greeks and Romans both linguistically and culturally (the cultural significance of Indo-European ties was exaggerated whenever it could be of use), and suggests that conserving the original form of the tales would bring the Slovaks closer to Homer and the Greeks than the English, French, or Germans could come. Second, he would prefer that the tale material not be used for stories, poems, and plays for some time. Such use of the material would only risk diluting the national character of the material (which is never in doubt for Reuss) and would be premature. The tales have obviously been changed over time, and these changes need to be corrected, in order to return to the original form of the tales. Thus, he recommends that, for the moment at least, the Slovaks limit their activities to *collection* and *correction*: they must record the tales as accurately as possible, but they must also restore to the tales their ancient form when that has been lost in the recorded versions.[32]

With these suggestions, and with his own example, Reuss initiated a practice for collection and publication of tales that was to remain basically unchanged for an entire generation. The collectors were to be faithful and accurate, to record the tales as they received them "from the hands of the folk." Dobšinský, who obviously shared Reuss's concern for faithful transcription of the tales, later noted certain deficiencies in the work of these early collectors, but felt they were as faithful as they could be, given the conditions of their collection. He expressed regret that the students were not trained in stenography but *were* studying German and Latin, with an obvious effect on the language in the transcriptions.[33] Jiří (Georg) Polívka, who examined the available manuscripts from these early collectors for his monumental study in the 1920s, found the collectors' practice uneven at best, according to more modern fieldwork standards. The manuscripts occasionally record the tales in the dialect in which they were told, sometimes provide the name of the collector, occasionally give the date of the tale's collection, and only rarely provide the name of the narrator.[34]

If the transcriptions were lacking and the tales incomplete, perhaps they could be fixed—corrected, as Reuss recommended. As they prepared tales for publication, Reuss and Francisci, and later Škultéty and Dobšinský, often worked from the briefest of outlines of the tales, which they then expanded into a full tale in a folk style, as they understood it. Moreover, they often compared different variants of a tale and created their versions for print from these materials.[35] Their most frequent method was to take a particular version of the tale as the model and then to flesh this out with motifs and language from other versions.[36] Dobšinský even footnotes his manuscript sources in a way, listing the recorders' names or the manuscript sources as well as the present "narrator"—the name of the original compiler, whose work Dobšinský himself often later revised (see the notes for each tale). While Dobšinský often corrected the dialects to the written standard, he and others also occasionally completely rewrote the tale in a different dialect from the one the tale had been collected in. Polívka bemoaned these practices, noting that, in this way, the publishers moved away even from reasonably recorded oral versions in a "misguided effort to reconstruct a more original ring."[37]

Polívka responds to the methods and practices of the early Slovak collectors from the point of view of a later standard of fieldwork, influenced by positivism, that was concerned with the folktale as such, without any embellishments. This included an interest in tale narrators and a growing interest in the contexts in which tales were told, subjects of almost no concern to the early collectors. Today, as ethnographic methodologies have continued to develop and new recording technologies have become available, the recording efforts of Polívka's day have also come to seem less satisfying as they fail to answer newer questions asked by researchers about gestures, audience response, and so forth. The Romantic methods of the earliest collectors and their attempts to reconstruct the ideal tale version are now obstacles that the folktale researcher must overcome in order to make use of the collections accumulated by them.

However, it is exactly this sort of Romantic methodology that has produced some of the world's most beloved collections of tales (better field-work may produce a more authentic tale, but the more authentic tale is not necessarily more esthetically pleasing). If we compare the methods of these Slovak collectors to the work of the Grimm brothers and their students, such as Afanas'ev in Russia and Erben in Bohemia, we find numerous similarities. While the Grimms are considered the first to have introduced modern fieldwork methods to collecting tales, and the *Circular-Brief* sent out by Jacob Grimm gives good advice on the proper recording of tales and where to find good tellers, the truth is that their own methods often deviated from this standard. They recorded exact wordings only in regard to certain formula, stock phrases, rhymes, and archaic language. Otherwise they recorded brief summaries and were less than meticulous in noting their oral sources. In preparing tales for publication, they took pains to reconstruct an oral style.[38] All of this is very similar to the methods of the Slovak collectors.

If the methods of Dobšinský and his generation shared much with the Grimm's, so did their theories, though here, too, direct influence seemingly has to be ruled out.[39] In fact, when these Slovak collectors explain the tales in terms of mythology and Indo-European roots, ideas so important to the Grimms' conception of the tales, they come to entirely different conclusions. To the Grimms, the similarities between tales from all over Europe was not to be explained by the spontaneous generation of similar stories in different places (polygenesis) nor by the borrowing of tales between nations (migration), both of which hypotheses they considered, but rejected as exceptional rather than normative. Instead, they drew upon the ancient relations between European nations for explanation. What is similar in these stories, the motifs and plots, represented to them fragments of myths, like "small pieces of a shattered jewel which are lying strewn on the ground all overgrown with grass and flowers, and can only be discovered by the most far-seeing eye."[40] They considered that the boundaries of the deepest commonality extend as far as the Indo-European nations, and noted the decisive commonality of German and Slavic tales. Wilhelm Grimm draws the conclusion: "It is my belief that our German stories do not belong to the Northern and Southern parts of our fatherland alone, but that they are the absolute common property of the nearly related Dutch, English, and Scandinavians."[41]

In comparison, we can look at the introduction, from 1849, by Čipka, Ľudovit Reuss, and Škultéty to the volume of tales they prepared, but which never found a publisher. Like Samuel Reuss, they point to the similarities between Homer and their folktales as proof of the relatedness of the Slovaks to the Greeks. They explain that this is because these tales have their origin in a period when the Indo-European tribes were still in close contact. Thus, too, the obvious relatedness of the mythologies (Greek and Indian get mentioned), which are nowhere better preserved than in these tales. They add that they hope the further collection and publication of these tales will open the door to this mythology. In the next paragraph they note that these tales are the Slovaks' inheritance from their forefathers, that they "contain or describe the past, the religion, the morals, the prejudices, the customs, the economic life, and the art, in short, the entire life of the nation."[42]

Two items are worthy of note here. First is the idea that myths are well preserved in the tales. The Grimms hoped to find mere fragments of myths, but these authors find myths well preserved in folktales. In fact, they frequently asserted that Slovak folktales were better preserved than those of other nations—this is implied by Samuel Reuss when he contends that the Slovaks will better understand the Greeks than the Germans or English do. This idea developed to the point that, in his *Reflections on Slovak Tales* (1871), Dobšinský asserted something opposite to the position of the reigning mythological school, built on the Grimms' theories. Rather than folktales being built out of the fragments of myths, he writes that folktales precede myths.[43]

The second item worthy of note is the use to which the Indo-European idea and mythology are put. The authors assert the ancientness of the tales and the relation of the Slovaks to culturally influential nations, like the Greeks, Romans, and Hindus. However, they do not assert the Indo-European *origin* of the tales. The origin is always national (they state, quite precisely, that the origin of these tales dates to an era when these nations were still in close contact, if already divided). These folktales, then, are *a priori* theirs, Slovak, national. Thus, when they compare the folktales of the Germans and French and find a familiar tale, they do not point to their relatedness as Indo-European tribes, but assert that these tales are actually Slovak tales (as does Samuel Reuss concerning Musäus's collection).

Comparative mythology and comparative linguistics with its Indo-European idea were certainly "in the air" at the time, and it is not surprising that the Grimm brothers' ideas filtered into Slovakia, nor that these ideas took on new valence in the context of the Slovak national awakening. Even direct knowledge of the Grimms' work would not have necessarily prevented such changes. For example, Karel Jaromír Erben, a Czech collector and publisher of tales from the same period and a student of the writings of the Grimms, also asserted that Slavic tales were better preserved than German tales and considered that the Grimms probably collected some tales from the Slavs along the Elbe, given the similarity of those tales to Czech tales.[44] In his *Reflections on Slovak Tales*, Dobšinský says the same, probably following Erben, but leaves out the Grimm brothers, whose name apparently meant nothing to him.

Dobšinský's *Reflections on Slovak Tales* (Úvahy o slovenských povestiach) (1871) represents the most advanced theoretical statement from this group of collectors on the wondertale. He names his teachers: Štúr, Reuss, and the Czechs Hanuš and Erben. Though he apparently did not know the work of the Grimm brothers directly, he learned much from Erben, and apparently also came into contact with Vuk Karadžić's collection of Serb epics while in the Emperor's army in 1849.[45] And yet it is clear, even in this late monograph, that the opinions of Reuss and Štúr left the largest imprint on Dobšinský's imagination. Reuss was primarily interested in information on the ancient customs, beliefs, and history of the Slovak nation that could be found in the tales. He thus preferred tales with magical elements and superhuman figures, wondertales, for he counted these as older and reflective of the most ancient beliefs (see his commentary on "Lomidrevo or Valibuk," added to the notes to the tale by Dobšinský). However, by the time of his monograph *Reflections*, Dobšinský had become much more careful than Reuss in extracting historical realities from tales, and distinguished between historical legends and wondertales. Like Štúr, Dobšinský accounted for the esthetic qualities of the folktale, allowing that the tales spoke "colorfully and figuratively" about the reality of the ancient Slavs.[46] However, also like Štúr in his book *On the Folk Songs and Tales of the Slavic Peoples* (O národních písních a pověstech plemen slovanských) (Prague, 1853), Dobšinský is determined to define the nature of the society of the ancient Slovaks and their beliefs, based (more or less) on the evidence of the tales. Štúr's book is divided into two parts, which treat first the relation of Man to Nature and then Man's social relations.[47] The central part of Dobšinský's book considers "The Relations of Man According to the Tales," including "The Relations of Man to the Godhead," "The Relations of Man to Humanity," and "The Relations of Man to Nature," thus expanding on Štúr's scheme. In fact, the shape and scope of Dobšinský's entire project seem to be based on Štúr's suggestions, as we shall see.

In the first section of *Reflections*, Dobšinský considers the "Mythic Qualities of Tales." These tales originate in the nation's childhood, he argues, and thus represent metaphoric thought, rather than abstractions or representations of historical realities. The tales are clearly related to myths, which probably follow tales. The tales are not actually about human relations, but are about nature, and villains such as witches represent winter, bad weather, and similar phenomena. Dobšinský ends this section with an analysis of three tales ("The Enchanted Forest," "Lomidrevo or Valibuk," and "Dalajláma") in terms of solar mythology. The obvious model and influence here is Erben, who represented the solar mythology school in Bohemia.

The transition to the next three sections is worth noting. While Dobšinský has just told us that the figures in the tales actually represent natural phenomena, he also wants to say the opposite, that Dalajláma is not just a symbol of the sun, but the sun is also a symbol of Dalajláma as a god. Dobšinský proceeds to outline the theology, cosmology, and anthropology of the tales. These three sections can be traced to a comment of Štúr's in his review of the first collection of Slovak tales by Francisci: "If we had all of these ancient tales and nothing had perished, we would see the entire science of our forebears about the gods, the creation and the order of the earth (theology and cosmology) . . ."[48] The main influence on Dobšinský here is no longer the mythological school, but rather his education as a Lutheran minister, and he draws conclusions that will surprise any modern student of folktales with an eye for their pagan elements. Dobšinský concludes that the ancient Slovaks practiced a strangely familiar monotheism, with the omniscient, omnipresent, eternal, omnipotent God represented by the King of Time in the tale of that name. He draws upon a Russian earthdiver tale for the Slav creation story (which he probably knew through Erben's collection of Slavic tales for his planned mythological study), and yet concludes that the personal God was the creator of matter, since matter already exists in that tale. Finally, he draws upon a Slovenian tale in which humans are created from a drop of sweat that falls from God's brow onto the earth, and invokes a convoluted etymological argument to show that the ancient Slovaks must have had the same belief.

The next section, to which we have already referred, outlines "The Relations of Man According to the Tales." Unfortunately, while Dobšinský took his structure from Štúr, he did not follow Štúr's exemplary method of argumentation based on numerous concrete examples. Leafing through Štúr's book, one feels that one is looking at an anthology of Slavic folk songs with interspersed commentary, so many and so extensive are the examples. But with Dobšinský it is clear that his commentary comes from his religious training, and the references to the tales always illustrate that commentary, rather than producing it. If the conflict between the unreconciled and opposing ethical views of paganism and Christianity "is one of the most serious defects" of Štúr's book,[49] Dobšinský's book is disturbing for the lack of any such conflict.

However, the final section on "The Ancientness and Well-Preserved Nature of the Tales" remains of interest even today, for, in order to argue the ancientness and well-preserved nature of the tales, Dobšinský provides what is essentially a description of the poetics of the wondertale. This section develops the thoughts of Reuss, who, in his "Agreement for Understanding" article, argued that the tales' completeness, simplicity, and orderedness demonstrated their ancientness.[50] Dobšinský develops this into five points that show the tales' ancientness. First and foremost is the fantastic nature of the tales, which shows that the tales proceed from the nation's childhood. The tales do not take place in a specified time and place, and the characters represent types rather than specific figures. Second is the spirit in which the tales are told. The tales are serious, reverent, and not joking. The fantastic is narrated like reality and is not placed in doubt. The third sign is the expressive means of the tales, which use short, pithy sentences and occasionally even poetic rhythm. Next is the simplicity of description characteristic of the tales, which often use formulaic descriptions (commonplaces) and rely more on the listener's imagination. Finally, the wholeness and completeness of the tales show how well preserved they are.

Much in Dobšinský's description of the wondertale coincides with present-day descriptions (see the Introduction to this volume) and shows how familiar Dobšinský was with the oral tradition. His own recognition of the particular qualities of the tales enabled him to preserve those qualities in the tales he prepared for publication. Thus, in spite of the datedness and peculiarity of many of Dobšinský's theories about the tales, the tales themselves remain fresh and lively, and well reflect the best of what was in circulation at the time. Dobšinský monumentalized the Slovak oral tradition and returned it to the nation as a lasting gift.

In Slovakia today, the name Pavol Dobšinský is nearly synonymous with folktales. For reasons that are unclear, the name of Augustín Horislav Škultéty has frequently been dropped from editions of tales that clearly benefited from his contributions. Although the title of this volume reflects that practice, care has been taken both here and in the Introduction to note the contributions of Škultéty and others to "Dobšinský's tales." These tales have been republished more frequently and in a greater variety of editions, both scholarly and popular, than those of any other Slovak collector, so that nearly every home in Slovakia has a volume that includes tales "by Dobšinský." The tales are a national monument, but also clearly belong to the grand tradition of the world folktale, a tradition that has never heeded national borders.

Notes

1. Robert William Seton-Watson, "The Slovaks Under Hungarian Rule," pp. 252–59. Seton-Watson incorrectly gives the date of Bernolák's grammar as 1787, which is the date of an earlier work on Slavic/Slovak orthography.

2. Ibid., pp. 259–60.

3. Ibid., p. 261.

4. Ibid., pp. 261–64.

5. Ibid., pp. 265–70.

6. Jana Spiessová, "Ján Kollár," pp. 206–7.

7. Andrej Melicherčík, *Pavol Dobšinský*, pp. 39–41.

8. Ibid., pp. 42–43.

9. Ibid., pp. 26, 43–4. Also, Jiří (Georg) Polívka, *Súpis slovenských rozprávok*, vol. 1, pp. 25–26.

10. Melicherčík, *Pavol Dobšinský*, p. 41.

11. See Polívka, *Súpis slovenských rozprávok*, vol. 1, for a full listing.

12. Melicherčík, *Pavol Dobšinský*, p. 44.
13. Jozef Škultéty, "Sbierajme piesne a povesti!" p. 799.
14. Melicherčík, *Pavol Dobšinský*, p. 48.
15. Polívka, *Súpis slovenských rozprávok*, vol. 1, pp. 46, 26.
16. "Dobšinský, Pavol," *Encyklopédia slovenských spisovateľov*, vol. 1, p. 111.
17. Viera Gašparíková, "Škultéty, Augustín Horislav," p. 235.
18. Polívka, *Súpis slovenských rozprávok*, vol. 1, pp. 46–49, 68–70.
19. Ibid., pp. 112–29.
20. Ibid., p. 72.
21. Melicherčík, *Pavol Dobšinský*, p. 83.
22. Ibid., pp. 116, 123.
23. Ibid., pp. 83, 96–98. See also Polívka, *Súpis slovenských rozprávok*, vol. 1, pp. 72–73, 111–12.
24. Melicherčík, *Pavol Dobšinský*, pp. 134–35, 138.
25. Ibid., pp. 139, 145–46.
26. Polívka, *Súpis slovenských rozprávok*, vol. 1, pp. 149–54.
27. Melicherčík, *Pavol Dobšinský*, pp. 106–8.
28. Polívka, *Súpis slovenských rozprávok*, vol. 1, pp. 8, 16.
29. *Stories by Musäus and Fouqué, Translated by Thomas Carlyle; with an introduction by Ulrich Scheck*, p. x.
30. Polívka, *Súpis slovenských rozprávok*, vol. 1, pp. 16–18.
31. Ibid., p. 18.
32. Ibid., pp. 17–20.
33. Pavol Dobšinský, *Úvahy o slovenských povestiach*, p. 154.
34. Polívka, *Súpis slovenských rozprávok*, vol. 1, pp. 6–39.
35. See the numerous examples in ibid., pp. 39ff.
36. Ibid., p. 75.
37. Ibid., p. 68.
38. Christa Kamenetsky, *The Brothers Grimm and Their Critics*, pp. 151–67.
39. See Polívka, *Súpis slovenských rozprávok*, vol. 1, p. 69. For a full analysis of the problem, see Viera Gašparíková, "Folklórna próza na Slovensku v druhej tretine 19. storočia (pod zorným uhlom diela bratov Grimmovcov)," pp. 107–19.
40. Stith Thompson, *The Folktale*, p. 369.
41. Ibid., p. 370.
42. Polívka, *Súpis slovenských rozprávok*, vol. 1, p. 52.
43. Dobšinský, *Úvahy*, p. 17.
44. Antonín Grund, *Karel Jaromír Erben*, pp. 51, 165.
45. Melicherčík, *Pavol Dobšinský*, p. 69.
46. Dobšinský, *Úvahy*, pp. 9, 11.
47. See William Harkins, *The Russian Folk Epos in Czech Literature 1800–1900*, pp. 131–137, for an overview of Štúr's views and a concise summary of the contents of the book. See Ľudovít Štúr, *Slovanská ľudová slovesnosť*, (Bratislava: Slovenské vydavateľstvo krasnej literatúry, 1955) for the text of both the book and Štúr's review of Francisci's publication.
48. Štúr, *Slovanská ľudová slovesnosť*, p. 232.
49. Harkins, *The Russian Folk Epos*, p. 134.
50. Polívka, *Súpis slovenských rozprávok*, vol. 1, p. 14.

Bibliography

Aarne, Antti, and Stith Thompson. *The Types of the Folktale.* Helsinki: Suomalainen Tiedeakatemia, 1964.

Botík, Ján, and Peter Slavkovský, eds. *Encyklopédia ľudovej kultúry slovenska.* Bratislava: VEDA, 1995.

Dégh, Linda. *Folktales and Society: Storytelling in a Hungarian Peasant Community.* Trans. Emily M. Schossberger. Bloomington, IN: Indiana University Press, 1969.

Dobšinský, Pavol. *Prostonárodné slovenské povesti,* ed. Eugen Pauliny. 3 vols. Bratislava, Slovakia: Tatran, 1966.

———. *Úvahy o slovenských povestiach.* Turčiansky sv. Martin, Slovakia: Matica Slovenská, 1871.

"Dobšinský, Pavol." In *Encyklopédia slovenských spisovateľov*, vol. 1, pp. 111–12. Bratislava: Obzor, 1984.

Fillmore, Parker. *The Shoemaker's Apron: Czechoslovak Folk and Fairy Tales.* New York: Harcourt, 1920.

Filová, Božena, and Viera Gašparíková, eds. *Slovenské ľudové rozprávky,* vol. 1. Bratislava: VEDA, 1993.

Gašparíková, Viera. *Catalogue of Slovak Folk Prose*, 2 vols. Bratislava: SAV, 1991–92.

———. "Folklórna próza na Slovensku v druhej tretine 19. storočia (pod zorným uhlom diela bratov Grimmovcov)." In *Bracia Grimm i folklor narodów słowiańskich: materiały z międzynarodowej konferencji (Warszawa, 18–19 listopada 1985),* eds. Jerzy Ślinziński and Maria Czurak, pp. 107–19. Wrocłow: Zakład Narodowy imienia Ossolińskich, 1989.

———. "Pohádka." In *Československá Vlastivěda Díl III: Lidová Kultura,* ed. Josef Macek, pp. 594–615. Prague: Orbis, 1968.

———. "Škultéty, Augustín Horislav." In *Encyklopédia ľudovej kultúry slovenska,* ed. Ján Botík and Peter Slavkovský, pp. 235–36.

Grund, Antonín. *Karel Jaromir Erben.* Prague: Melantrich, 1935.

Harkins, William. *The Russian Folk Epos in Czech Literature 1800–1900.* New York: King's Crown Press, 1951.

Kamenetsky, Christa. *The Brothers Grimm and Their Critics.* Athens, OH: Ohio University Press, 1992.

Kosová, Mária. "Rozprávkar Jozef Rusnák-Bronda." In *Horehronie: Folklórne prejavy v živote ľudu,* pp. 13–19. Bratislava: VEDA, 1988.

Krčmery, Štefan. "O poesii našich povestí." *Slovenské Pohľady,* 1928, 44: 803–13.

Krzyżanowski, Julian. *Polske bajka ludowa w układzie systematycznym* I-II. Wrocław–Warszawa–Kraków: n.p., 1963.

Lüthi, Max, *The European Folktale: Form and Nature*, Bloomington: Indiana University Press, 1982.

Máchal, Hanuš (Ján). *Nákres slovanského bájesloví*. Prague: F. Simáček, 1891.

Melicherčík, Andrej. *Pavol Dobšinský: Portrét života a diela*. Bratislava: Slovenské Vydavateľstvo Krásnej Literatury, 1959.

———. "Prostonárodné slovenské povesti Pavla Dobšinského." In Pavol Dobšinský, *Prostonárodné slovenské povesti*, vol. 1, pp. 9–29.

Polívka, Jiří (Georg). *Súpis slovenských rozprávok*. 3 vols. Turčiansky sv. Martin, Slovakia: Matica Slovenská, 1923–31.

Seton-Watson, Robert William. "The Slovaks Under Hungarian Rule." Ch. 14 of *A History of the Czechs and Slovaks*, pp. 252–83. Hamden, CT: Archon Books, 1965.

Škultéty, Jozef. "Sbierajme piesne a povesti!" *Slovenské Pohľady*, 1928, 44: 794–803.

Spiessová, Jana. "Ján Kollár." In *Kdo byl kdo v našich dejinách do roku 1918*, ed. František Honzák, pp. 206–7. Praha: Nakladatelství Libri, 1996.

Stefánik, Ján. *Bibliografia vydaní slovenských ľudových rozprávok slovenských zberateľov a Slovenských pohádek a povesti B. Němcovej (1845–1974)*. Martin, Slovakia: Matica Slovenská, 1975.

Stories by Musäus and Fouqué, Translated by Thomas Carlyle; with an introduction by Ulrich Scheck. Studies in German Literature, Linguistics, and Culture, vol. 61. Columbia, SC: Camden House, 1991.

Štúr, Ľudovít. *Slovanská ľudová slovesnosť*. Bratislava: Slovenské vydavateľstvo krasnej literatúry, 1955.

Thompson, Stith. *Motif-Index of Folk Literature*. 6 vols. Bloomington, IN: Indiana University Press, 1955–58.

———. *The Folktale*. New York: Holt, Rinehart and Winston, 1946.

About the Author

David L. Cooper first went to Slovakia as a Peace Corps volunteer in the early 1990s. While in Slovakia, he taught English. When he returned to the United States he did the reverse and taught Slovak language and culture at Pennsylvania State University. He is currently completing doctoral studies in Czech and Russian literature at Columbia University.